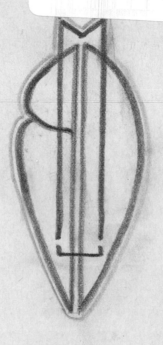

Henry D. Thoreau.

The Riverside Literature Series

WALDEN

OR

LIFE IN THE WOODS

BY

HENRY D. THOREAU

WITH AN INTRODUCTION AND NOTES

BY

FRANCIS H. ALLEN

ASSOCIATE EDITOR OF THOREAU'S JOURNAL, AUTHOR
OF A BIBLIOGRAPHY OF HENRY DAVID THOREAU

AND WITH

SUGGESTIVE QUESTIONS AND COMMENTS

BOSTON   NEW YORK   CHICAGO   SAN FRANCISCO
HOUGHTON MIFFLIN COMPANY
The Riverside Press Cambridge

The Riverside Press
CAMBRIDGE · MASSACHUSETTS
PRINTED IN THE U.S.A

PREFACE

In the preparation of this school edition of Thoreau's *Walden* it has seemed best to lay the emphasis on the literary and human qualities of the book rather than on the philosophy contained in it. Much of the latter is beyond the full comprehension of youthful readers, and anything like a thorough discussion of it would be out of place here. The text used is that of the "Walden Edition," which is as yet sold only by subscription to the entire set of Thoreau's writings. This text was revised with some care at the time of the printing of the Walden Edition in 1906, and has now again been subjected to the most careful scrutiny in the course of the annotation for the present edition. It is therefore believed to be very nearly free from errors, except such as the author alone is responsible for. No attempt has been made, of course, to correct the slight misstatements of fact which are likely to be found in the works of any author, but such slips, so far as they have been observed, are pointed out in the notes.

In annotation an effort has been made to cite the originals of Thoreau's many quotations and allusions; but a diligent search has left a few of them undiscovered, while it is more than possible that some veiled allusions may have entirely escaped the editor's apprehension. Among those which are not accounted for are a number of quotations from Oriental literature. An attempt to locate these would seem almost hopeless to an editor who is not an Orientalist, and even in the case of success, the value of the results would be out of proportion to the labor involved.

For assistance in locating quotations and explaining allusions, the editor is indebted to a number of persons, among whom he must make especial mention of Miss Jane Hosmer of Concord, Miss C. M. Hewins of the Hartford Public Library, Dr. William C. Collar, Mr. Walter Deane, Dr. W. C. Kendall of the United States Bureau of Fisheries, Dr. Arthur H. Nichols, Prof. Francis G. Allinson, Dr. E. W. Emerson, Prof. Felix E. Schelling, and Prof. R. M. Johnston.

The "Suggestive Questions and Comments" have been prepared by Mr. Charles Swain Thomas, Head of the English Department in the Newton (Mass.) High School.

Boston, January, 1910.

CONTENTS

ILLUSTRATIONS

THOREAU AND HIS BOOK "WALDEN"

WITH perhaps a single exception, the relative greatness of Thoreau [1] as a man and as a writer has been disputed more warmly than has that of any other American man of letters of the first rank. But his fame has grown astonishingly in the half-century since his death, and his importance is more and more recognized even by those who do not like him. An enjoyment of Thoreau's books and an admiration for the man is, indeed, very largely a question of personal likes and dislikes. He was so independent, so scornful of conventionalities, that no thoroughly conventional person can read him with any degree of pleasure. No writer has been more misunderstood than he, but the misunderstanding, as usually in such cases, is on the part of those who have not read his books thoroughly, who take their knowledge of him at second hand and make no effort to put themselves *en rapport* with him.

To understand and appreciate Thoreau, then, we must read him; and *Walden*, his most popular and most characteristic book, is the best of his volumes to begin on. *A Week on the Concord and Merrimack Rivers*, *Cape Cod*, *The Maine Woods*, *Excursions*, each makes its own special appeal, and one or another of them may be preferred by individual readers, but to get the full flavor of Thoreau's thought and style, we must go to *Walden*. Before beginning the book, let us learn something of the life and aims of the man who wrote it.

Henry D. Thoreau was born in Concord, Massachusetts, July 12, 1817. His grandfather, John Thoreau, had come to America from the island of Jersey, where his collateral descendants are still living, though the name is now extinct

[1] The name is pronounced Thō′rō.

there, as it is in this country. The son of this first John, also named John, was born in Boston, but was brought as a boy to Concord, where he grew up and married Cynthia, daughter of the Rev. Asa Dunbar of that town. Of their four children, Henry, the subject of this sketch, was the third. Though he was christened David Henry and signed that name to his college exercises, he was always called Henry by his family and friends, and about the time he left college he definitely adopted the reverse order of the two names, signing himself Henry D., or H. D., Thoreau.

He was a rather unusual boy, even though on one occasion he went to bed with his new boots on as many another child has done, and again, after having received the medal for geography at school, he asked his mother if Boston was in Concord. (Since in later life he found the whole world in Concord, the question is perhaps not to be wondered at!) But, as Mr. Ellery Channing has told us, he was "a thoughtful, serious boy, in advance of his years, — wishing to have and do things his own way, and ever fond of wood and field; honest, pure, and good." On one occasion, says Mr. Channing, he was accused of taking a knife belonging to another boy. "Henry said, 'I did not take it,' and was believed. In a few days the culprit was found, and Henry then said, 'I knew all the time who it was, and the day it was taken I went to Newton with father.' 'Well, then,' of course, was the question, 'why did you not say so at the time?' 'I did not take it,' was his reply."

Henry Thoreau was brought up in simple circumstances, his father never being a rich, or even what is called a well-to-do, man. After a few years in Chelmsford, Mass., and in Boston, the family returned to Concord in 1823, and there and at Harvard College the boy got his education. After taking his degree in 1837, he taught school for a while; lived in the family of his fellow townsman Ralph Waldo Emerson for two years, making himself generally useful there, and, as Mr. Sanborn puts it, "performing the office of a younger brother or a grown-up son"; was a tutor in the family of Mr. William Emerson, on Staten Island, N. Y., for six months in 1843; and in 1844 devoted himself to making lead-pencils for his father, who was engaged in that business. Then came the two years' life at Walden Pond which forms the subject of this book. Thoreau remained at Walden from July, 1845, to September, 1847, after which he lived at Emerson's house again for a year, while Emerson himself was abroad. As a member of the Emerson household, he was much loved and depended upon by Mrs. Emerson and the children. After that, Thoreau lived at his father's house for the rest of his life, making his living by surveying land for his Concord neighbors, lecturing, writing, and, in the earlier years, as he tells in *Walden*, doing odd jobs of manual labor of various kinds. After his father's death in 1859, he carried on the business of lead-pencil manufacturing and dealing in plumbago.

But whatever Thoreau did in the way of merely earning a living, his real occupation in life was literature. It is evident to every reader of his *Journal* that the business of writing was always in his mind. He was constantly on the outlook for material for his lectures, essays, and books. He early found that he had a message for the world, and he devoted his energies to getting ready the vehicle to carry it. As is frequently the case with authors, he found his expression at first largely in the form of verse. As an outlet for this *The Dial* appeared, a quarterly journal edited by Emerson and Margaret Fuller, and Thoreau's first published piece, the poem "Sympathy," was printed in the first number, in July, 1840, when he was twenty-three years old. This was followed by other poems and prose essays. In 1839 Thoreau and his brother John took a memorable excursion in a boat of their own making down the Concord River to the Merrimac and up that stream to the head of

easy navigation, whence they proceeded on foot to the White
Mountains. After a week of pedestrian travel, they returned to
their boat and rowed back to Concord again, having spent just
a week in the nautical part of the excursion. This first journey
into the world outside of Concord, though Thoreau was sufficiently well read to perceive the relative unimportance of it
from the ordinary point of view, yet served as an admirable
text for a book. He had begun to keep a journal two years before, and the record therein for this week forms the framework
of his *A Week on the Concord and Merrimack Rivers*, but the
book was not actually written until 1845 to 1847, and Thoreau
drew extensively upon his *Journal* for the ten years from 1837
to fill it out. The book is far from being a mere record of daily
experiences on the river voyage, therefore, but contains many
of its author's thoughts, experiences, and observations during
ten years or more of his life. The *Week*, as the title is commonly abbreviated, was published in 1849.

While Thoreau was engaged in writing the *Week* he was
also accumulating the material for another book. Indeed,
much of *Walden* was written in the Journal form contempo-
raneously with the earlier book, though the bulk of it, as its
author assures us, was written during his residence at Walden
Pond, where he had gone partly for the purpose of writing the
Week. Just what and where Walden Pond is, and how Thoreau built his cabin on its shore and lived there alone for a
little more than two years, the book itself tells us. Thoreau's
purpose in going there we also learn from the book. It was
twofold, — to "transact some private business," by which he
is understood to mean the writing of his book, and to learn by
experience with a simpler style of living, by reducing life to its
lowest terms, just what life is. The common belief that Thoreau was making an ineffectual attempt to realize the life of a
hermit is wholly wrong. He never pretended to give up human
companionship during his stay in the woods, nor is there any

PUR-
POSE

reason to think that he ever contemplated spending his entire life in such retirement as he found there. The Walden "experiment" was a complete success, — from Thoreau's point of view in that it enabled him to accomplish what he had in mind in going there, and from the world's point of view in that it resulted in the book *Walden*.

Walden was issued in August, 1854. At this time Thoreau had published — besides the *Week* and many poems and essays in *The Dial* and other periodicals — "Ktaadn and the Maine Woods" as a five-months serial in the *Union Magazine*, and three chapters of a Canadian narrative under the title of "Excursion to Canada" in *Putnam's Magazine*. These two narratives, like the *Week*, owe their origin to excursions away from Concord, and they confine themselves much more strictly to the subject in hand than does the first of Thoreau's books. The only journey that Thoreau made outside of the United States was his trip to Montreal and Quebec in the autumn of 1850. The complete story of this excursion appeared after his death under the title of "A Yankee in Canada" in a volume together with some "Anti-Slavery and Reform Papers."

The "Ktaadn" paper was the result of the first of three excursions into the forests of northern Maine. The second of them was described under the title of "Chesuncook," and the third under the title of "The Allegash and East Branch." All three papers finally appeared in a volume entitled *The Maine Woods*. Thoreau also made three walking-trips on Cape Cod, which resulted eventually in a book. *Cape Cod*, like *The Maine Woods*, did not appear in book form till after Thoreau's death, but a part of it was published by him in *Putnam's Magazine* in 1855.

Not only did these larger works of Thoreau's owe their origin to somewhat extended excursions, but all his writing was very closely connected with his walks. Every walk was chronicled in his Journal, and the Journal was the source of lectures, essays, and books. Walking was necessary to Thoreau. He could not write without walking daily, — and that not merely in the way of "taking exercise," but because walking in the woods and fields promoted the flow of his thoughts. "I think I cannot preserve my health and spirits," he says, "unless I spend four hours a day at least — and it is commonly more than that — sauntering through the woods and over the hills and fields, absolutely free from all worldly engagements." And he could not walk without writing, since writing was his vocation and it was imperative with him that he put upon paper the thoughts and observations of the day's excursion.

These walks of Thoreau's took the place of foreign travel, for to him Concord represented the world. He could see and feel all that was best worth seeing and feeling without leaving his native town. Of course this implies internal resources which not every man possesses. Not every one can see the beauty and interest in plain things, in simple landscapes. And Concord's was, and is, a simple landscape. Thoreau knew that very well; he had no illusions on that score. "The scenery of Walden is on a humble scale," he says, " . . . nor can it much concern one who has not long frequented it or lived by its shore." If one, after reading the book, visits the pond itself and is disappointed, he need not blame Thoreau for his disappointment. He does not see it through Thoreau's eyes. Perhaps he has not yet learned that every landscape unspoiled by human hands is beautiful. To Thoreau the Concord woods and fields as he saw them morning and evening, by sunshine and by moonlight, at every season of the year, had all the elements of beauty that more pretentious landscapes possess, and summer and winter he traversed them daily in all weathers.

It was during one of his winter walks, in December, 1860, that Thoreau, never very robust in spite of his outdoor life, exposed himself unduly, and caught a severe cold. His illness developed into a form of tuberculosis, and though he was able to write pretty regularly in his Journal for a time, his long walks and active outdoor life were practically over. In May of the following year he set out for Minnesota, with the hope that the dry climate there would help him, but he returned in July without having made any substantial improvement in health. He wrote last in his Journal November 3, 1861, and he wrote his last letter (by the hand of his sister) March 21, 1862. On May 6, 1862, he died, after a long period of help-lessness borne patiently and even cheerfully.

As we have seen, the *Week* and *Walden* were the only books that Thoreau himself saw through the press. After his death, a succession of volumes appeared, beginning with *Excursions* (1863), a collection of essays on subjects connected with na-ture, edited by his sister Sophia. Then, in 1864, came *The Maine Woods* and *Cape Cod*, both edited jointly by his sister and his friend Ellery Channing. *Letters to Various Persons*, collected and edited by Ralph Waldo Emerson, followed in 1865, and *A Yankee in Canada, with Anti-Slavery and Reform Papers*, in 1866. On the death of Sophia Thoreau, the last of the family, Thoreau's journals and manuscripts were left to his old friend Harrison G. O. Blake of Worcester, who, from 1881 to 1892, brought out four volumes of extracts from the Journal arranged according to season, under the titles of *Early Spring in Massachusetts*, *Summer*, *Winter*, and *Autumn*. In 1894 a new and enlarged collection of Thoreau's letters appeared, edited by Mr. F. B. Sanborn, with a connective tissue of biographical and explanatory matter which makes it virtually a narrative biography. The last important addition to the list of Thoreau's books is the complete *Journal* itself, which was published in 1906, in fourteen volumes, under the editorship of Mr. Bradford Torrey.

Thoreau was a philosopher, a student of nature, and a man

of letters, and these three activities were very closely inter-woven in him. His eyes were always open as he walked, and his mind was ever ready to perceive the spiritual relations of things, while back of it all, the literary expression of his thought was never quite out of his consciousness. He was a staunch individualist, believing in his own personal responsi-bility to his Maker and impatient of the fetters of convention. His plea for individuality and simplicity is nowhere more strongly put than in *Walden*, and a reading of this book has revealed new possibilities in life to many earnest and thought-ful souls. To get help from Thoreau's teachings, it is not necessary to go to extremes. Many of us feel more strongly than he did the advantage of certain things that make for ease and comfort in modern life among one's kind, and we may have different views of our duty to our neighbors. Each must live his own life, not another's; each must follow his own genius. Thoreau himself says in the book we have before us that he does not want people to live his way, but he wishes that every man would be sure to find out his own way of life, not his father's, or his mother's, or his neighbor's, and live that. Of course we cannot all be Thoreaus, and we must not at-tempt to follow the Walden philosopher blindly through thick and thin. Nevertheless, the reader, to get the best from Tho-reau, as from any other author worth studying, must approach him with an open mind, ready to sympathize rather than to criticise, and willing to learn.

As a student of nature, an observer, Thoreau has been over-rated by some of his friends and perhaps underrated by others. The truth seems to be that he *saw* things clearly, but was sometimes hasty in drawing conclusions. It is to be remem-bered that he was without the multitude of more or less trust-worthy books at the hands of the present-day students of natural history, that when it came to ornithology he lacked the handy opera-glass which is now thought indispensable to field-students of birds, and that there were no scientific men with whom he had intimate association. Then, too, we must consider the breadth of his outdoor interests. He tried to make all nature his field, and could not, therefore, attain to the specialist's knowledge of any one branch. Another reason why he failed to make many important contributions to the world's knowledge in the field of science was the fact that he was not looking for scientific discoveries. He was intent chiefly on tracing some analogy between nature and the spiritual life. When the Secretary of the American Association for the Advancement of Science sent him a circular asking what particular branch he was especially interested in, he felt that he could not describe his studies properly in terms of the science of the day, though he thought that the secretary of a society of which Plato was president might understand him.

But however Thoreau may have failed occasionally as an observer, he was probably unexcelled, in America at least, as a *describer* of outdoor things. Who but he could so happily have suggested the quality of the first notes of the bobolink's song? "He is just touching the strings of his theorbo, his glassichord, his water organ, and one or two notes globe themselves, and fall in liquid bubbles from his teeming throat. It is as if he touched his harp within a vase of liquid melody, and when he lifted it out, the notes fell like bubbles from the trembling strings. Methinks they are the most *liquidly* sweet and melodious sounds I ever heard. . . . Oh, never advance farther in your art; never let us hear your full strain, sir. But away he launches, and the meadow is all bespattered with melody." (This, it will be seen, is a poet's description; it would perhaps be inappropriate in an ornithological treatise.) The following bit from *Walden* illustrates Thoreau's attitude of mind towards what he saw in nature: "Or sometimes I watched a pair of hen-hawks circling high in the sky, alternately soaring and descending, approaching and leaving one another, as if they

were the embodiment of my own thoughts." The reader of
this book will have many opportunities to study Thoreau's
powers of description.

Thoreau was a sincere, straightforward, uncompromising
soul, rather combative in temperament, saying "no" more
easily than "yes." He had something of the Stoic in his per-
sonality as well as in his philosophy. This quality impressed
Emerson so strongly that in compiling the volume of *Letters to
Various Persons* it was his endeavor, as he afterwards avowed,
to present as complete a piece of stoicism as possible, and he
made his selections from Thoreau's correspondence with that
in mind. This, as Thoreau's sister thought, did not "seem
quite fair to Henry," and Mr. Sanborn rectified the matter in
producing his *Familiar Letters of Thoreau;* but this has been
the view of him to be accepted by many who have not found
themselves drawn to make a sympathetic study of the man.
In reality Thoreau was a man not without the tenderest feelings for his family and friends. His ideals of friendship were
high and certain kinds of intimacy were repugnant to him,
but few men have had more devoted friends than he had in
Emerson, William Ellery Channing (the younger of the name,
the Concord poet), Harrison Blake, Daniel Ricketson, and
Thomas Cholmondeley. He loved a chat with the farmer
folk, too, and all persons of the simpler walks of life, but he
demanded sincerity in his companion, and had no patience
with mere forms of etiquette. He was particularly fond of children, as we have seen in the case of the Emerson family, and
he conducted many a blueberry party and birds'-nesting
excursion with his young friends.

But though children enjoyed their walks with him and back-
woodsmen liked his conversation, he was understood by very
few of his townspeople, and he came but slowly into his own
among lovers of literature. His attitude towards life was so
independent, so foreign to the thoughts of the average man,

that except by persons of keen perceptions and independent judgment he was long regarded as eccentric rather than great. His fame has been steadily growing, however, both here and abroad, and to-day he is admitted to be one of the few original thinkers and writers in American literature.

In studying *Walden* as a piece of literature, we must first recognize the fact that, regarded as a whole, it is not an artistic composition. It lacks form. It cannot be taken as a model for the building of a book. It disregards the rules of essay construction. This is perhaps due to the nature of its origin. It was written piecemeal in Thoreau's Journal during a period of fifteen years, and in a great part, perhaps for the most part, the descriptions, reflections, and arguments of which it is composed were written without any definite plan as to just how they were to be used, as to just what sort of book they were to be used in. Thoreau's problem in writing *Walden*, or rather in putting it together, was to make the best use possible of as much of his Journal as had not already been worked into the *Week* and as could properly be put into such a book as he had now planned. This method of making a book has its advantages as well as its disadvantages. The latter are obvious. One advantage, in the case of *Walden*, is that the book is really Thoreau himself, — his own thoughts and feelings and opinions from the time he began to express himself in writing up to the time when *Walden* was published.

Yet, in spite of the fact that *Walden* is not a model of orderliness, there is a certain amount of order in its make-up. It has a beginning and an end, and the succession of the seasons governs to some extent the arrangement of the intervening chapters. The first chapter considers the general conditions of modern life, shows the slavery under which most men are living, and points out a way to independence and happiness. It also introduces the subject of the so-called Walden experiment and gives a detailed account of the expenses involved in it. The second chapter tells of the location of the house by the pond and of Thoreau's manner of life there. As reading and writing were perhaps the chief objects of this life, it is natural that the subject of reading should be taken up in the next chapter. The next nine chapters are concerned chiefly with the summer activities. From the character of their subjects they form no natural series, but almost every one of them is introduced by an appropriate connecting link with the one that precedes, so that the transitions are easy and natural. Chapter XIII has to do with the autumn and the preparations for winter, Chapters XIV, XV, and XVI with the winter itself, and Chapter XVII with spring, bringing the year round to summer again and completing the story of the author's life in the woods. Then follows the Conclusion with its summing-up of the book's teachings.

We have seen that *Walden* is not without form. And it is certainly not void. Thoreau has a crisp and sharp way of saying things that makes every paragraph full of meaning. The book is rich in thoughts, and the thoughts are expressed in a manner that commands attention. The style is dignified and at the same time pungent. Its slightly antiquated form adds to its impressiveness without being pronounced enough to savor of affectation. It is, perhaps, best expressed by the word epigrammatic, and this quality makes Thoreau one of the most quotable of prose writers. Even when he makes a seemingly matter-of-fact statement about some material thing, he couches it in dignified language, and on almost every page of *Walden* we may find a sentence that would bear transplanting.

Thoreau himself was a free quoter, as we shall see in *Walden*, and his range of sources is wide, — the Hindoo and Chinese scriptures, the Greek and Latin authors, the English poets; histories, books of travel, scientific books; — for he was a wide reader, and he had a habit of transcribing into his commonplace-books and journals. The number of more or less veiled allusions to be found in *Walden* is, perhaps, still more striking. Many of these are very obscure and probably fall outside of the knowledge of many well-read persons. Thoreau seemed to delight in this game of allusion, and sometimes one cannot resist the suspicion that he overdid the thing a little, and used a puzzling expression when a more familiar one would have been just as forcible.

An abundance of allusions in a book is generally agreeable to a reader in proportion to the extent of his acquaintance with literature and to the amount of "general information" he has at call. Allusion is a favorite device with many authors. With some — those of a sophisticated, or perhaps pedantic, sort — it plays so important a part that the unlearned reader can get no pleasure whatever out of them. This is not the case with Thoreau, however, and many of his most devoted readers have been men of little learning.

Another device of Thoreau's — for to some extent this, too, is a device, though an innocent one — is the localization of *Walden*, the playful restriction of the attention to Concord, as if the book were addressed exclusively to the citizens of that small town. This appears in the very name of the book, and again and again, as in the latter part of the chapter on "Reading," we find the author devoting himself especially to Concord and its interests. To be sure, to him Concord represented the world, so that in addressing its citizens he addresses all mankind, as it were, but the principal advantage of this method is that it enables Thoreau to say what he has to say with the more directness and simplicity. It provides him with a text to preach from. Concord is the handle by which he takes hold of the reading world. It is not provincialism, then, this localization of the book. It is the deliberate plan by which a skilful writer seeks to make his most forcible appeal to his readers.

To most readers Thoreau is best known as a student of nature. As a philosopher he studied men also, partly by self-examination, but not a little by a keen observation of persons with whom he came in contact. This habit of observing men, together with that sympathy for the simple and sincere in the lower walks of life which has been referred to, is responsible for some delightful glimpses of human nature to be found in *Walden*, — the description of the French-Canadian wood-chopper, for instance, the sad story of ignorant John Field and his poverty-stricken family, the still sadder one of the drunken soldier of Waterloo.

Underneath his contempt for the mere conventions of society Thoreau had a genuine love for his fellow men, and we shall miss the best part of *Walden* if we overlook these bits of real humanity, and if we fail to perceive the deep interest in mankind and the earnest desire to serve them which animates the whole book.

LIST OF THOREAU'S BOOKS AS NOW PUBLISHED

RIVERSIDE EDITION

With four portraits.

A Week on the Concord and Merrimack Rivers.

Walden; or, Life in the Woods.

The Maine Woods.

Cape Cod.

Early Spring in Massachusetts: From the Journal of Thoreau.

Summer: From the Journal of Thoreau.

Autumn: From the Journal of Thoreau.

Winter: From the Journal of Thoreau.

Excursions (including A Yankee in Canada).

Miscellanies (including Poems, the Biographical Sketch by Emerson, and General Index to the ten volumes).

Familiar Letters of Henry David Thoreau. Edited by F. B. Sanborn.

WALDEN EDITION

With three portraits and 101 illustrations from photographs by Herbert W. Gleason. Sold only by subscription for the entire set.

Volume I. A Week on the Concord and Merrimack Rivers.

Volume II. Walden.

Volume III. The Maine Woods.

Volume IV. Cape Cod, and Miscellanies.

Volume V. Excursions, and Poems.

Volume VI. Familiar Letters. Revised Edition.

Volumes VII–XX. Journal. Edited by Bradford Torrey, with an Introductory Essay.

WALDEN. *Holiday Edition*. With an Introduction by Bradford Torrey and photogravures of Concord scenes and persons.

CAPE COD. *Holiday Edition*. Illustrated in water-colors by Miss Amelia M. Watson. 2 vols.

THE SUCCESSION OF FOREST TREES, WILD APPLES, AND SOUNDS. *Riverside Literature Series*, No. 27.

KATAHDIN AND CHESUNCOOK. From "The Maine Woods." Abridged and edited by Clifton Johnson. *Riverside Literature Series*, No. 186.

THOREAU'S THOUGHTS. Selections from Thoreau's Writing, Edited by H. G. O. Blake.

WALDEN. 2 vols. Printed for the Bibliophile Society, Boston, 1909. This edition, which was limited to 483 copies and is unobtainable by the general public, was printed from a preliminary draft of the book found among manuscripts left by Thoreau. The manuscript was in a somewhat inchoate state, and was arranged and edited with Introduction and notes by Mr. F. B. Sanborn.

BIOGRAPHIES OF THOREAU

William Ellery Channing.
  Thoreau, the Poet-Naturalist. New Edition, enlarged. Edited by F. B. Sanborn, Boston, 1902.

H. A. Page, pseud. (A. H. Japp).
  Thoreau: His Life and Aims. Boston, 1877.

Annie Russell Marble.
  Thoreau: His Home, Friends, and Books. New York, 1902.

Henry S. Salt.
  The Life of Henry David Thoreau. Revised Edition, London, 1896.

F. B. Sanborn.
   Henry D. Thoreau. Revised Edition. Boston, 1909.
   Familiar Letters of Henry David Thoreau. Boston, 1894.

A BIBLIOGRAPHY OF HENRY DAVID THOREAU. Compiled
   by Francis H. Allen. Boston, 1908.

WALDEN

OR

LIFE IN THE WOODS

"

I do not propose to write an ode to dejection, but to brag as lustily as chanticleer in the morning, standing on his roost, *if* only to wake my neighbors up.

"

ECONOMY

W<small>HEN</small> I wrote the following pages, or rather the bulk of them, I lived alone, in the woods, a mile from any neighbor, in a house which I had built myself, on the shore of Walden Pond, in Concord, Massachusetts, and earned my living by the labor of my hands only. I lived there two years and two months. At present I am a sojourner in civilized life again.

I should not obtrude my affairs so much on the notice of my readers if very particular inquiries had not been made by my townsmen concerning my mode of life, which some would call impertinent, though they do not appear to me at all impertinent, but, considering the circumstances, very natural and pertinent. Some have asked what I got to eat; if I did not feel lonesome; if I was not afraid; and the like. Others have been curious to learn what portion of my income I devoted to charitable purposes; and some, who have large families, how many poor children I maintained. I will therefore ask those of my readers who feel no particular interest in me to pardon me if I undertake to answer some of these questions in this book. In most books, the *I*, or first person, is omitted; in this it will be retained; that, in respect to egotism, is the main difference. We commonly do not remember that it is, after all, always the first person that is speaking. I should not talk so much about myself if there were anybody else whom I knew as well. Unfortunately, I am confined to this theme by the narrowness of my experience. Moreover, I, on my side, require of every writer, first or last, a simple and sincere account of his own life, and not merely what he has heard of other men's lives; some such account as he would send to his kindred from a distant land; for if he has lived sincerely, it must have been in a distant land to me. Perhaps these pages are more particularly addressed to poor students. As for the rest of my readers, they will accept such portions as apply to them. I trust that none will stretch the seams in putting on the coat, for it may do good service to him whom it fits.

I would fain say something, not so much concerning the Chinese and Sandwich Islanders as you who read these pages, who are said to live in New England; something about your condition, especially your outward condition or circumstances in this world, in this town, what it is, whether it is necessary that it be as bad as it is, whether it cannot be improved as well as not. I have travelled a good deal in Concord; and everywhere, in shops, and offices, and fields, the inhabitants have appeared to me to be doing penance in a thousand remarkable ways. What I have heard of Bramins sitting exposed to four fires and looking in the face of the sun; or hanging suspended, with their heads downward, over flames; or looking at the heavens over their shoulders "until it becomes impossible for them to resume their natural position, while from the twist of the neck nothing but liquids can pass into the stomach;" or dwelling, chained for life, at the foot of a tree; or measuring with their bodies, like caterpillars, the breadth of vast empires; or standing on one leg on the tops of pillars, — even these forms of conscious penance are hardly more incredible and astonishing than the scenes which I daily witness. The twelve labors of Hercules were trifling in comparison with those which my neighbors have undertaken; for they were only twelve, and had an end; but I could never see that these men slew or captured any monster or finished any labor. They have no friend Iolaus to burn with a hot iron the root of the hydra's head, but as soon as one head is crushed, two spring up.

I see young men, my townsmen, whose misfortune it is to have inherited farms, houses, barns, cattle, and farming tools: for these are more easily acquired than got rid of. Better if they had been born in the open pasture and suckled by a wolf, that they might have seen with clearer eyes what field they were called to labor in. Who made them serfs of the soil? Why should they eat their sixty acres, when man is condemned to eat only his peck of dirt? Why should they begin digging their graves as soon as they are born? They have got to live a man's life, pushing all these things before them, and get on as well as they can. How many a poor immortal soul have I met well-nigh crushed and smothered under its load, creeping down the road of life, pushing before it a barn seventy-five feet by forty, its Augean stables never cleansed, and one hundred acres of land, tillage, mowing, pasture, and wood-lot! The portionless, who struggle with no such unnecessary inherited encumbrances,

find it labor enough to subdue and cultivate a few cubic
feet of flesh.

But men labor under a mistake. The better part of the
man is soon plowed into the soil for compost. By a
seeming fate, commonly called necessity, they are employed, as it says in an old book, laying up treasures
which moth and rust will corrupt and thieves break
through and steal. It is a fool's life, as they will find
when they get to the end of it, if not before. It is said
that Deucalion and Pyrrha created men by throwing
stones over their heads behind them: —

> Inde genus durum sumus, experiensque laborum,
> Et documenta damus quâ simus origine nati.

Or, as Raleigh rhymes it in his sonorous way, —

> "From thence our kind hard-hearted is, enduring pain and care,
> Approving that our bodies of a stony nature are."

So much for a blind obedience to a blundering oracle,
throwing the stones over their heads behind them, and
not seeing where they fell.

Most men, even in this comparatively free country,
through mere ignorance and mistake, are so occupied
with the factitious cares and superfluously coarse labors
of life that its finer fruits cannot be plucked by them.
Their fingers, from excessive toil, are too clumsy and
tremble too much for that. Actually, the laboring man
has not leisure for a true integrity day by day; he cannot afford to sustain the manliest relations to men; his
labor would be depreciated in the market. He has no
time to be anything but a machine. How can he remember well his ignorance — which his growth requires —

who has so often to use his knowledge? We should feed and clothe him gratuitously sometimes, and recruit him with our cordials, before we judge of him. The finest qualities of our nature, like the bloom on fruits, can be preserved only by the most delicate handling. Yet we do not treat ourselves nor one another thus tenderly.

Some of you, we all know, are poor, find it hard to live, are sometimes, as it were, gasping for breath. I have no doubt that some of you who read this book are unable to pay for all the dinners which you have actually eaten, or for the coats and shoes which are fast wearing or are already worn out, and have come to this page to spend borrowed or stolen time, robbing your creditors of an hour. It is very evident what mean and sneaking lives many of you live, for my sight has been whetted by experience; always on the limits, trying to get into business and trying to get out of debt, a very ancient slough, called by the Latins *aes alienum*, another's brass, for some of their coins were made of brass; still living, and dying, and buried by this other's brass; always promising to pay, promising to pay, to-morrow, and dying to-day, insolvent; seeking to curry favor, to get custom, by how many modes, only not state-prison offences; lying, flattering, voting, contracting yourselves into a nutshell of civility, or dilating into an atmosphere of thin and vaporous generosity, that you may persuade your neighbor to let you make his shoes, or his hat, or his coat, or his carriage, or import his groceries for him; making yourselves sick, that you may lay up something against a sick day, something to be tucked away in an old chest, or in a stocking behind the plas-

tering, or, more safely, in the brick bank; no matter
where, no matter how much or how little.

I sometimes wonder that we can be so frivolous, I
may almost say, as to attend to the gross but somewhat
foreign form of servitude called Negro Slavery, there are
so many keen and subtle masters that enslave both North
and South. It is hard to have a Southern overseer; it is
worse to have a Northern one; but worst of all when you
are the slave-driver of yourself. Talk of a divinity in
man! Look at the teamster on the highway, wending to
market by day or night; does any divinity stir within
him? His highest duty to fodder and water his horses!
What is his destiny to him compared with the shipping
interests? Does not he drive for Squire Make-a-stir?
How godlike, how immortal, is he? See how he cowers
and sneaks, how vaguely all the day he fears, not being
immortal nor divine, but the slave and prisoner of his
own opinion of himself, a fame won by his own deeds.
Public opinion is a weak tyrant compared with our own
private opinion. What a man thinks of himself, that it is
which determines, or rather indicates, his fate. Self-
emancipation even in the West Indian provinces of the
fancy and imagination, — what Wilberforce is there to
bring that about? Think, also, of the ladies of the land
weaving toilet cushions against the last day, not to betray too green an interest in their fates! As if you could
kill time without injuring eternity.

The mass of men lead lives of quiet desperation. What
is called resignation is confirmed desperation. From
the desperate city you go into the desperate country, and
have to console yourself with the bravery of minks and

muskrats. A stereotyped but unconscious despair is concealed even under what are called the games and amusements of mankind. There is no play in them, for this comes after work. But it is a characteristic of wisdom not to do desperate things.

When we consider what, to use the words of the catechism, is the chief end of man, and what are the true necessaries and means of life, it appears as if men had deliberately chosen the common mode of living because they preferred it to any other. Yet they honestly think there is no choice left. But alert and healthy natures remember that the sun rose clear. It is never too late to give up our prejudices. No way of thinking or doing, however ancient, can be trusted without proof. What everybody echoes or in silence passes by as true to-day may turn out to be falsehood to-morrow, mere smoke of opinion, which some had trusted for a cloud that would sprinkle fertilizing rain on their fields. What old people say you cannot do, you try and find that you can. Old deeds for old people, and new deeds for new. Old people did not know enough once, perchance, to fetch fresh fuel to keep the fire a-going; new people put a little dry wood under a pot, and are whirled round the globe with the speed of birds, in a way to kill old people, as the phrase is. Age is no better, hardly so well, qualified for an instructor as youth, for it has not profited so much as it has lost. One may almost doubt if the wisest man has learned anything of absolute value by living. Practically, the old have no very important advice to give the young, their own experience has been so partial, and their lives have been such miserable failures, for private reasons,

as they must believe; and it may be that they have some
faith left which belies that experience, and they are only
less young than they were. I have lived some thirty years
on this planet, and I have yet to hear the first syllable of
valuable or even earnest advice from my seniors. They
have told me nothing, and probably cannot tell me anything to the purpose. Here is life, an experiment to a
great extent untried by me; but it does not avail me that
they have tried it. If I have any experience which I
think valuable, I am sure to reflect that this my Mentors
said nothing about.

One farmer says to me, "You cannot live on vegetable
food solely, for it furnishes nothing to make bones with;"
and so he religiously devotes a part of his day to supplying his system with the raw material of bones; walking
all the while he talks behind his oxen, which, with vege-
table-made bones, jerk him and his lumbering plow
along in spite of every obstacle. Some things are really
necessaries of life in some circles, the most helpless and
diseased, which in others are luxuries merely, and in
others still are entirely unknown.

The whole ground of human life seems to some to
have been gone over by their predecessors, both the
heights and the valleys, and all things to have been cared
for. According to Evelyn, "the wise Solomon prescribed
ordinances for the very distances of trees; and the Roman prætors have decided how often you may go into
your neighbor's land to gather the acorns which fall on
it without trespass, and what share belongs to that neighbor." Hippocrates has even left directions how we should
cut our nails; that is, even with the ends of the fingers,

neither shorter nor longer. Undoubtedly the very tedium and ennui which presume to have exhausted the variety and the joys of life are as old as Adam. But man's capacities have never been measured; nor are we to judge of what he can do by any precedents, so little has been tried. Whatever have been thy failures hitherto, "be not afflicted, my child, for who shall assign to thee what thou hast left undone?"

We might try our lives by a thousand simple tests; as, for instance, that the same sun which ripens my beans illumines at once a system of earths like ours. If I had remembered this it would have prevented some mistakes. This was not the light in which I hoed them. The stars are the apexes of what wonderful triangles! What distant and different beings in the various mansions of the universe are contemplating the same one at the same moment! Nature and human life are as various as our several constitutions. Who shall say what prospect life offers to another? Could a greater miracle take place than for us to look through each other's eyes for an instant? We should live in all the ages of the world in an hour; ay, in all the worlds of the ages. History, Poetry, Mythology! — I know of no reading of another's experience so startling and informing as this would be.

The greater part of what my neighbors call good I believe in my soul to be bad, and if I repent of anything, it is very likely to be my good behavior. What demon possessed me that I behaved so well? You may say the wisest thing you can, old man, — you who have lived seventy years, not without honor of a kind, — I hear an irresistible voice which invites me away from all that.

One generation abandons the enterprises of another like stranded vessels.

I think that we may safely trust a good deal more than we do. We may waive just so much care of ourselves as we honestly bestow elsewhere. Nature is as well adapted to our weakness as to our strength. The incessant anxiety and strain of some is a well-nigh incurable form of disease. We are made to exaggerate the importance of what work we do; and yet how much is not done by us! or, what if we had been taken sick? How vigilant we are! determined not to live by faith if we can avoid it; all the day long on the alert, at night we unwillingly say our prayers and commit ourselves to uncertainties. So thoroughly and sincerely are we compelled to live, reverencing our life, and denying the possibility of change. This is the only way, we say; but there are as many ways as there can be drawn radii from one centre. All change is a miracle to contemplate; but it is a miracle which is taking place every instant. Confucius said, "To know that we know what we know, and that we do not know what we do not know, that is true knowledge." When one man has reduced a fact of the imagination to be a fact to his understanding, I foresee that all men will at length establish their lives on that basis.

Let us consider for a moment what most of the trouble and anxiety which I have referred to is about, and how much it is necessary that we be troubled, or at least careful. It would be some advantage to live a primitive and frontier life, though in the midst of an outward civilization, if only to learn what are the gross necessaries of life and what methods have been taken to obtain them;

or even to look over the old day-books of the merchants, to see what it was that men most commonly bought at the stores, what they stored, that is, what are the grossest groceries. For the improvements of ages have had but little influence on the essential laws of man's existence: as our skeletons, probably, are not to be distinguished from those of our ancestors.

By the words, *necessary of life*, I mean whatever, of all that man obtains by his own exertions, has been from the first, or from long use has become, so important to human life that few, if any, whether from savageness, or poverty, or philosophy, ever attempt to do without it. To many creatures there is in this sense but one necessary of life, Food. To the bison of the prairie it is a few inches of palatable grass, with water to drink; unless he seeks the Shelter of the forest or the mountain's shadow. None of the brute creation requires more than Food and Shelter. The necessaries of life for man in this climate may, accurately enough, be distributed under the several heads of Food, Shelter, Clothing, and Fuel; for not till we have secured these are we prepared to entertain the true problems of life with freedom and a prospect of success. Man has invented, not only houses, but clothes and cooked food; and possibly from the accidental discovery of the warmth of fire, and the consequent use of it, at first a luxury, arose the present necessity to sit by it. We observe cats and dogs acquiring the same second nature. By proper Shelter and Clothing we legitimately retain our own internal heat; but with an excess of these, or of Fuel, that is, with an external heat greater than our own internal, may not cookery properly be said to begin ? Darwin, the naturalist, says of the inhabitants of Tierra del Fuego, that while his own party, who were well clothed and sitting close to a fire, were far from too warm, these naked savages, who were farther off, were observed, to his great surprise, "to be streaming with perspiration at undergoing such a roasting." So, we are told, the New Hollander goes naked with impunity, while the European shivers in his clothes. Is it impossible to combine the hardiness of these savages with the intellectualness of the civilized man ? According to Liebig, man's body is a stove, and food the fuel which keeps up the internal combustion in the lungs. In cold weather we eat more, in warm less. The animal heat is the result of a slow combustion, and disease and death take place when this is too rapid; or for want of fuel, or from some defect in the draught, the fire goes out. Of course the vital heat is not to be confounded with fire; but so much for analogy. It appears, therefore, from the above list, that the expression, *animal life*, is nearly synonymous with the expression, *animal heat;* for while Food may be regarded as the Fuel which keeps up the fire within us, — and Fuel serves only to prepare that Food or to increase the warmth of our bodies by addition from without, — Shelter and Clothing also serve only to retain the *heat* thus generated and absorbed.

The grand necessity, then, for our bodies, is to keep warm, to keep the vital heat in us. What pains we accordingly take, not only with our Food, and Clothing, and Shelter, but with our beds, which are our night-clothes, robbing the nests and breasts of birds to prepare this shelter within a shelter, as the mole has its bed of grass and leaves at the end of its burrow! The poor man is wont to complain that this is a cold world; and to cold, no less physical than social, we refer directly a great part of our ails. The summer, in some climates, makes possible to man a sort of Elysian life. Fuel, except to cook his Food, is then unnecessary; the sun is his fire, and many of the fruits are sufficiently cooked by its rays; while Food generally is more various, and more easily obtained, and Clothing and Shelter are wholly or half unnecessary. At the present day, and in this country, as I find by my own experience, a few implements, a knife, an axe, a spade, a wheelbarrow, etc., and for the studious, lamplight, stationery, and access to a few books, rank next to necessaries, and can all be obtained at a trifling cost. Yet some, not wise, go to the other side of the globe, to barbarous and unhealthy regions, and devote themselves to trade for ten or twenty years, in order that they may live, — that is, keep comfortably warm, — and die in New England at last. The luxuriously rich are not simply kept comfortably warm, but unnaturally hot; as I implied before, they are cooked, of course à la mode.

Most of the luxuries, and many of the so-called comforts of life, are not only not indispensable, but positive hindrances to the elevation of mankind. With respect to luxuries and comforts, the wisest have ever lived a more simple and meagre life than the poor. The ancient philosophers, Chinese, Hindoo, Persian, and Greek, were a class than which none has been poorer in outward riches, none so rich in inward. We know not much about them. It is remarkable that *we* know so much of them as we do. The same is true of the more modern reformers and benefactors of their race. None can be an impartial or wise observer of human life but from the vantage ground of what *we* should call voluntary poverty. Of a life of luxury the fruit is luxury, whether in agriculture, or commerce, or literature, or art. There are nowadays professors of philosophy, but not philosophers. Yet it is admirable to profess because it was once admirable to live. To be a philosopher is not merely to have subtle thoughts, nor even to found a school, but so to love wisdom as to live according to its dictates, a life of simplicity, independence, magnanimity, and trust. It is to solve some of the problems of life, not only theoretically, but practically. The success of great scholars and thinkers is commonly a courtier-like success, not kingly, not manly. They make shift to live merely by conformity, practically as their fathers did, and are in no sense the progenitors of a nobler race of men. But why do men degenerate ever? What makes families run out? What is the nature of the luxury which enervates and destroys nations? Are we sure that there is none of it in our own lives? The philosopher is in advance of his age even in the outward form of his life. He is not fed, sheltered, clothed, warmed, like his contemporaries. How can a man be a philosopher and not maintain his vital heat by better methods than other men?

When a man is warmed by the several modes which I have described, what does he want next? Surely not more warmth of the same kind, as more and richer food, larger and more splendid houses, finer and more abundant clothing, more numerous, incessant, and hotter fires, and the like. When he has obtained those things which are necessary to life, there is another alternative than to obtain the superfluities; and that is, to adventure on life now, his vacation from humbler toil having commenced. The soil, it appears, is suited to the seed, for it has sent its radicle downward, and it may now send its shoot upward also with confidence. Why has man rooted himself thus firmly in the earth, but that he may rise in the same proportion into the heavens above? — for the nobler plants are valued for the fruit they bear at last in the air and light, far from the ground, and are not treated like the humbler esculents, which, though they may be biennials, are cultivated only till they have perfected their root, and often cut down at top for this purpose, so that most would not know them in their flowering season.

I do not mean to prescribe rules to strong and valiant natures, who will mind their own affairs whether in heaven or hell, and perchance build more magnificently and spend more lavishly than the richest, without ever impoverishing themselves, not knowing how they live, — if, indeed, there are any such, as has been dreamed; nor to those who find their encouragement and inspiration in precisely the present condition of things, and cherish it with the fondness and enthusiasm of lovers, — and, to some extent, I reckon myself in this number; I do not speak to those who are well employed, in whatever circumstances, and they know whether they are well employed or not; — but mainly to the mass of men who are discontented, and idly complaining of the hardness of their lot or of the times, when they might improve them. There are some who complain most energetically and inconsolably of any, because they are, as they say, doing their duty. I also have in my mind that seemingly wealthy, but most terribly impoverished class of all, who have accumulated dross, but know not how to use it, or get rid of it, and thus have forged their own golden or silver fetters.

If I should attempt to tell how I have desired to spend my life in years past, it would probably surprise those of my readers who are somewhat acquainted with its actual history; it would certainly astonish those who know nothing about it. I will only hint at some of the enterprises which I have cherished.

In any weather, at any hour of the day or night, I have been anxious to improve the nick of time, and notch it on my stick too; to stand on the meeting of two eternities, the past and future, which is precisely the present moment; to toe that line. You will pardon some obscurities, for there are more secrets in my trade than in most men's, and yet not voluntarily kept, but inseparable from its very nature. I would gladly tell all that I know about it, and never paint "No Admittance" on my gate.

I long ago lost a hound, a bay horse, and a turtledove, and am still on their trail. Many are the travellers I have spoken concerning them, describing their tracks and what calls they answered to. I have met one or two who had heard the hound, and the tramp of the horse, and even seen the dove disappear behind a cloud, and they seemed as anxious to recover them as if they had lost them themselves.

To anticipate, not the sunrise and the dawn merely, but, if possible, Nature herself! How many mornings, summer and winter, before yet any neighbor was stirring about his business, have I been about mine! No doubt, many of my townsmen have met me returning from this enterprise, farmers starting for Boston in the twilight, or woodchoppers going to their work. It is true, I never assisted the sun materially in his rising, but, doubt not, it was of the last importance only to be present at it.

So many autumn, ay, and winter days, spent outside the town, trying to hear what was in the wind, to hear and carry it express! I well-nigh sunk all my capital in it, and lost my own breath into the bargain, running in the face of it. If it had concerned either of the political parties, depend upon it, it would have appeared in the Gazette with the earliest intelligence. At other times watching from the observatory of some cliff or tree, to telegraph any new arrival; or waiting at evening on the hill-tops for the sky to fall, that I might catch something, though I never caught much, and that, manna-wise, would dissolve again in the sun.

For a long time I was reporter to a journal, of no very wide circulation, whose editor has never yet seen fit to print the bulk of my contributions, and, as is too common with writers, I got only my labor for my pains. However, in this case my pains were their own reward.

For many years I was self-appointed inspector of snow-storms and rain-storms, and did my duty faith-

This is excellent and shows
Thoreau at his best.

fully; surveyor, if not of highways, then of forest paths and all across-lot routes, keeping them open, and ravines bridged and passable at all seasons, where the public heel had testified to their utility.

I have looked after the wild stock of the town, which give a faithful herdsman a good deal of trouble by leaping fences; and I have had an eye to the unfrequented nooks and corners of the farm; though I did not always know whether Jonas or Solomon worked in a particular field to-day; that was none of my business. I have watered the red huckleberry, the sand cherry and the nettle-tree, the red pine and the black ash, the white grape and the yellow violet, which might have withered else in dry seasons.

In short, I went on thus for a long time (I may say it without boasting), faithfully minding my business, till it became more and more evident that my townsmen would not after all admit me into the list of town officers, nor make my place a sinecure with a moderate allowance. My accounts, which I can swear to have kept faithfully, I have, indeed, never got audited, still less accepted, still less paid and settled. However, I have not set my heart on that.

Not long since, a strolling Indian went to sell baskets at the house of a well-known lawyer in my neighborhood. "Do you wish to buy any baskets?" he asked. "No, we do not want any," was the reply. "What!" exclaimed the Indian as he went out the gate, "do you mean to starve us?" Having seen his industrious white neighbors so well off, — that the lawyer had only to weave arguments, and, by some magic, wealth and standing followed, — he had said to himself: I will go into business; I will weave baskets; it is a thing which I can do. Thinking that when he had made the baskets he would have done his part, and then it would be the white man's to buy them. He had not discovered that it was necessary for him to make it worth the other's while to buy them, or at least make him think that it was so, or to make something else which it would be worth his while to buy. I too had woven a kind of basket of a delicate texture, but I had not made it worth any one's while to buy them. Yet not the less, in my case, did I think it worth my while to weave them, and instead of studying how to make it worth men's while to buy my baskets, I studied rather how to avoid the necessity of selling them. The life which men praise and regard as successful is but one kind. Why should we exaggerate any one kind at the expense of the others?

Finding that my fellow-citizens were not likely to offer me any room in the court house, or any curacy or living anywhere else, but I must shift for myself, I turned my face more exclusively than ever to the woods, where I was better known. I determined to go into business at once, and not wait to acquire the usual capital, using such slender means as I had already got. My purpose in going to Walden Pond was not to live cheaply nor to live dearly there, but to transact some private business with the fewest obstacles; to be hindered from accomplishing which for want of a little common sense, a little enterprise and business talent, appeared not so sad as foolish.

I have always endeavored to acquire strict business

habits; they are indispensable to every man. If your trade is with the Celestial Empire, then some small counting house on the coast, in some Salem harbor, will be fixture enough. You will export such articles as the country affords, purely native products, much ice and pine timber and a little granite, always in native bottoms. These will be good ventures. To oversee all the details yourself in person; to be at once pilot and captain, and owner and underwriter; to buy and sell and keep the accounts; to read every letter received, and write or read every letter sent; to superintend the discharge of imports night and day; to be upon many parts of the coast almost at the same time, — often the richest freight will be discharged upon a Jersey shore; — to be your own telegraph, unweariedly sweeping the horizon, speaking all passing vessels bound coastwise; to keep up a steady despatch of commodities, for the supply of such a distant and exorbitant market; to keep yourself informed of the state of the markets, prospects of war and peace everywhere, and anticipate the tendencies of trade and civilization, — taking advantage of the results of all exploring expeditions, using new passages and all improvements in navigation; — charts to be studied, the position of reefs and new lights and buoys to be ascertained, and ever, and ever, the logarithmic tables to be corrected, for by the error of some calculator the vessel often splits upon a rock that should have reached a friendly pier, — there is the untold fate of La Pérouse; — universal science to be kept pace with, studying the lives of all great discoverers and navigators, great adventurers and merchants, from

Hanno and the Phœnicians down to our day; in fine, account of stock to be taken from time to time, to know how you stand. It is a labor to task the faculties of a man, — such problems of profit and loss, of interest, of tare and tret, and gauging of all kinds in it, as demand a universal knowledge.

I have thought that Walden Pond would be a good place for business, not solely on account of the railroad and the ice trade; it offers advantages which it may not be good policy to divulge; it is a good port and a good foundation. No Neva marshes to be filled; though you must everywhere build on piles of your own driving. It is said that a flood-tide, with a westerly wind, and ice in the Neva, would sweep St. Petersburg from the face of the earth.

As this business was to be entered into without the usual capital, it may not be easy to conjecture where those means, that will still be indispensable to every such undertaking, were to be obtained. As for Clothing, to come at once to the practical part of the question, perhaps we are led oftener by the love of novelty and a regard for the opinions of men, in procuring it, than by a true utility. Let him who has work to do recollect that the object of clothing is, first, to retain the vital heat, and secondly, in this state of society, to cover nakedness, and he may judge how much of any necessary or important work may be accomplished without adding to his wardrobe. Kings and queens who wear a suit but once, though made by some tailor or dressmaker to their majesties, cannot know the comfort of wearing a suit that fits. They are no better than wooden horses to hang the clean clothes on. Every day our garments become more assimilated to ourselves, receiving the impress of the wearer's character, until we hesitate to lay them aside without such delay and medical appliances and some such solemnity even as our bodies. No man ever stood the lower in my estimation for having a patch in his clothes; yet I am sure that there is greater anxiety, commonly, to have fashionable, or at least clean and unpatched clothes, than to have a sound conscience. But even if the rent is not mended, perhaps the worst vice betrayed is improvidence. I sometimes try my acquaintances by such tests as this, — Who could wear a patch, or two extra seams only, over the knee? Most behave as if they believed that their prospects for life would be ruined if they should do it. It would be easier for them to hobble to town with a broken leg than with a broken pantaloon. Often if an accident happens to a gentleman's legs, they can be mended; but if a similar accident happens to the legs of his pantaloons, there is no help for it; for he considers, not what is truly respectable, but what is respected. We know but few men, a great many coats and breeches. Dress a scarecrow in your last shift, you standing shiftless by, who would not soonest salute the scarecrow? Passing a cornfield the other day, close by a hat and coat on a stake, I recognized the owner of the farm. He was only a little more weather-beaten than when I saw him last. I have heard of a dog that barked at every stranger who approached his master's premises with clothes on, but was easily quieted by a naked thief. It is an interesting question how far men would retain their relative rank if they were divested of their clothes. Could you, in such a case, tell surely of any company of civilized men which belonged to the most respected class? When Madam Pfeiffer, in her adventurous travels round the world, from east to west, had got so near home as Asiatic Russia, she says that she felt the necessity of wearing other than a travelling dress, when she went to meet the authorities, for she "was now in a civilized country, where . . . people are judged of by their clothes." Even in our democratic New England towns the accidental possession of wealth, and its manifestation in dress and equipage alone, obtain for the possessor almost universal respect. But they who yield such respect, numerous as they are, are so far heathen, and need to have a missionary sent to them. Beside, clothes introduced sewing, a kind of work which you may call endless; a woman's dress, at least, is never done.

A man who has at length found something to do will not need to get a new suit to do it in; for him the old will do, that has lain dusty in the garret for an indeterminate period. Old shoes will serve a hero longer than they have served his valet, — if a hero ever has a valet, — bare feet are older than shoes, and he can make them do. Only they who go to soirées and legislative halls must have new coats, coats to change as often as the man changes in them. But if my jacket and trousers, my hat and shoes, are fit to worship God in, they will do; will they not? Who ever saw his old clothes, — his old coat, actually worn out, resolved into its primitive elements, so that it was not a deed of charity to bestow it on some poor boy, by him perchance to be bestowed on some poorer still, or shall we say richer, who could do with less? I say, beware of all enterprises that require new clothes, and not rather a new wearer of clothes. If there is not a new man, how can the new clothes be made to fit? If you have any enterprise before you, try it in your old clothes. All men want, not something to *do with*, but something to *do*, or rather something to *be.* Perhaps we should never procure a new suit, however ragged or dirty the old, until we have so conducted, so enterprised or sailed in some way, that we feel like new men in the old, and that to retain it would be like keeping new wine in old bottles. Our moulting season, like that of the fowls, must be a crisis in our lives. The loon retires to solitary ponds to spend it. Thus also the snake casts its slough, and the caterpillar its wormy coat, by an internal industry and expansion; for clothes are but our outmost cuticle and mortal coil. Otherwise we shall be found sailing under false colors, and be inevitably cashiered at last by our own opinion, as well as that of mankind.

We don garment after garment, as if we grew like exogenous plants by addition without. Our outside and often thin and fanciful clothes are our epidermis, or false skin, which partakes not of our life, and may be stripped off here and there without fatal injury; our thicker garments, constantly worn, are our cellular integument, or cortex; but our shirts are our liber, or true bark, which cannot be removed without girdling and so destroying the man. I believe that all races at some seasons wear something equivalent to the shirt. It is desirable that a man be clad so simply that he can lay his hands on himself in the dark, and that he live in all respects so compactly and preparedly that, if an enemy take the town, he can, like the old philosopher, walk out the gate empty-handed without anxiety. While one thick garment is, for most purposes, as good as three thin ones, and cheap clothing can be obtained at prices really to suit customers; while a thick coat can be bought for five dollars, which will last as many years, thick pantaloons for two dollars, cowhide boots for a dollar and a half a pair, a summer hat for a quarter of a dollar, and a winter cap for sixty-two and a half cents, or a better be made at home at a nominal cost, where is he so poor that, clad in such a suit, *of his own earning*, there will not be found wise men to do him reverence?

When I ask for a garment of a particular form, my tailoress tells me gravely, "They do not make them so now," not emphasizing the "They" at all, as if she quoted an authority as impersonal as the Fates, and I find it difficult to get made what I want, simply because she cannot believe that I mean what I say, that I am so rash. When I hear this oracular sentence, I am for a moment absorbed in thought, emphasizing to myself each word separately that I may come at the meaning of it, that I may find out by what degree of consanguinity *They* are related to *me*, and what authority they may have in an affair which affects me so nearly; and, finally, I am inclined to answer her with equal mystery, and without any more emphasis of the "they," — "It is true, they did not make them so recently, but they do now." Of what use this measuring of me if she does not measure my character, but only the breadth of my

shoulders, as it were a peg to hang the coat on ? We worship not the Graces, nor the Parcæ, but Fashion. She
spins and weaves and cuts with full authority. The head
monkey at Paris puts on a traveller's cap, and all the
monkeys in America do the same. I sometimes despair
of getting anything quite simple and honest done in this
world by the help of men. They would have to be passed
through a powerful press first, to squeeze their old notions out of them, so that they would not soon get upon
their legs again; and then there would be some one in
the company with a maggot in his head, hatched from
an egg deposited there nobody knows when, for not
even fire kills these things, and you would have lost
your labor. Nevertheless, we will not forget that some
Egyptian wheat was handed down to us by a mummy.

On the whole, I think that it cannot be maintained
that dressing has in this or any country risen to the
dignity of an art. At present men make shift to wear
what they can get. Like shipwrecked sailors, they put
on what they can find on the beach, and at a little distance, whether of space or time, laugh at each other's
masquerade. Every generation laughs at the old fashions, but follows religiously the new. We are amused
at beholding the costume of Henry VIII., or Queen
Elizabeth, as much as if it was that of the King and
Queen of the Cannibal Islands. All costume off a man
is pitiful or grotesque. It is only the serious eye peering
from and the sincere life passed within it which restrain
laughter and consecrate the costume of any people. Let
Harlequin be taken with a fit of the colic and his trap-
pings will have to serve that mood too. When the

soldier is hit by a cannon-ball, rags are as becoming as purple.

The childish and savage taste of men and women for new patterns keeps how many shaking and squinting through kaleidoscopes that they may discover the particular figure which this generation requires to-day. The manufacturers have learned that this taste is merely whimsical. Of two patterns which differ only by a few threads more or less of a particular color, the one will be sold readily, the other lie on the shelf, though it frequently happens that after the lapse of a season the latter becomes the most fashionable. Comparatively, tattooing is not the hideous custom which it is called. It is not barbarous merely because the printing is skin-deep and unalterable.

I cannot believe that our factory system is the best mode by which men may get clothing. The condition of the operatives is becoming every day more like that of the English; and it cannot be wondered at, since, as far as I have heard or observed, the principal object is, not that mankind may be well and honestly clad, but, unquestionably, that the corporations may be enriched. In the long run men hit only what they aim at. Therefore, though they should fail immediately, they had better aim at something high.

As for a Shelter, I will not deny that this is now a necessary of life, though there are instances of men having done without it for long periods in colder countries than this. Samuel Laing says that "the Laplander in his skin dress, and in a skin bag which he puts over his head and shoulders, will sleep night after night on the snow . . . in a degree of cold which would extinguish the life of one exposed to it in any woollen clothing." He had seen them asleep thus. Yet he adds, "They are not hardier than other people." But, probably, man did not live long on the earth without discovering the convenience which there is in a house, the domestic comforts, which phrase may have originally signified the satisfactions of the house more than of the family; though these must be extremely partial and occasional in those climates where the house is associated in our thoughts with winter or the rainy season chiefly, and two thirds of the year, except for a parasol, is unnecessary. In our climate, in the summer, it was formerly almost solely a covering at night. In the Indian gazettes a wigwam was the symbol of a day's march, and a row of them cut or painted on the bark of a tree signified that so many times they had camped. Man was not made so large limbed and robust but that he must seek to narrow his world, and wall in a space such as fitted him. He was at first bare and out of doors; but though this was pleasant enough in serene and warm weather, by daylight, the rainy season and the winter, to say nothing of the torrid sun, would perhaps have nipped his race in the bud if he had not made haste to clothe himself with the shelter of a house. Adam and Eve, according to the fable, wore the bower before other clothes. Man wanted a home, a place of warmth, or comfort, first of physical warmth, then the warmth of the affections.

We may imagine a time when, in the infancy of the human race, some enterprising mortal crept into a hollow in a rock for shelter. Every child begins the world

again, to some extent, and loves to stay outdoors, even
in wet and cold. It plays house, as well as horse, having
an instinct for it. Who does not remember the interest
with which, when young, he looked at shelving rocks,
or any approach to a cave? It was the natural yearning
of that portion of our most primitive ancestor which
still survived in us. From the cave we have advanced
to roofs of palm leaves, of bark and boughs, of linen
woven and stretched, of grass and straw, of boards and
shingles, of stones and tiles. At last, we know not what
it is to live in the open air, and our lives are domestic
in more senses than we think. From the hearth the
field is a great distance. It would be well, perhaps, if
we were to spend more of our days and nights without
any obstruction between us and the celestial bodies, if
the poet did not speak so much from under a roof, or
the saint dwell there so long. Birds do not sing in caves,
nor do doves cherish their innocence in dovecots.

However, if one designs to construct a dwelling-house,
it behooves him to exercise a little Yankee shrewdness,
lest after all he find himself in a workhouse, a labyrinth
without a clue, a museum, an almshouse, a prison, or a
splendid mausoleum instead. Consider first how slight
a shelter is absolutely necessary. I have seen Penobscot
Indians, in this town, living in tents of thin cotton cloth,
while the snow was nearly a foot deep around them, and
I thought that they would be glad to have it deeper to
keep out the wind. Formerly, when how to get my living honestly, with freedom left for my proper pursuits,
was a question which vexed me even more than it does
now, for unfortunately I am become somewhat callous,

I used to see a large box by the railroad, six feet long
by three wide, in which the laborers locked up their
tools at night; and it suggested to me that every man
who was hard pushed might get such a one for a dollar,
and, having bored a few auger holes in it, to admit the
air at least, get into it when it rained and at night, and
hook down the lid, and so have freedom in his love, and
in his soul be free. This did not appear the worst, nor
by any means a despicable alternative. You could sit
up as late as you pleased, and, whenever you got up, go
abroad without any landlord or house-lord dogging you
for rent. Many a man is harassed to death to pay the
rent of a larger and more luxurious box who would not
have frozen to death in such a box as this. I am far
from jesting. Economy is a subject which admits of
being treated with levity, but it cannot so be disposed
of. A comfortable house for a rude and hardy race, tha·
lived mostly out of doors, was once made here almos·
entirely of such materials as Nature furnished ready to
their hands. Gookin, who was superintendent of the
Indians subject to the Massachusetts Colony, writing
in 1674, says, "The best of their houses are covered
very neatly, tight and warm, with barks of trees, slipped
from their bodies at those seasons when the sap is up,
and made into great flakes, with pressure of weighty
timber, when they are green. . . . The meaner sort
are covered with mats which they make of a kind of bulrush, and are also indifferently tight and warm, but
not so good as the former. . . . Some I have seen,
sixty or a hundred feet long and thirty feet broad. . . .
I have often lodged in their wigwams, and found them

as warm as the best English houses." He adds that they were commonly carpeted and lined within with well-wrought embroidered mats, and were furnished with various utensils. The Indians had advanced so far as to regulate the effect of the wind by a mat suspended over the hole in the roof and moved by a string. Such a lodge was in the first instance constructed in a day or two at most, and taken down and put up in a few hours; and every family owned one, or its apartment in one.

In the savage state every family owns a shelter as good as the best, and sufficient for its coarser and simpler wants; but I think that I speak within bounds when I say that, though the birds of the air have their nests, and the foxes their holes, and the savages their wigwams, in modern civilized society not more than one half the families own a shelter. In the large towns and cities, where civilization especially prevails, the number of those who own a shelter is a very small fraction of the whole. The rest pay an annual tax for this outside garment of all, become indispensable summer and winter, which would buy a village of Indian wigwams, but now helps to keep them poor as long as they live. I do not mean to insist here on the disadvantage of hiring compared with owning, but it is evident that the savage owns his shelter because it costs so little, while the civilized man hires his commonly because he cannot afford to own it; nor can he, in the long run, any better afford to hire. But, answers one, by merely paying this tax the poor civilized man secures an abode which is a palace compared with the savage's. An annual rent of from twenty-five to a hundred dollars (these are the country rates) entitles him to the benefit of the improvements of centuries, spacious apartments, clean paint and paper, Rumford fireplace, back plastering, Venetian blinds, copper pump, spring lock, a commodious cellar, and many other things. But how happens it that he who is said to enjoy these things is so commonly a *poor* civilized man, while the savage, who has them not, is rich as a savage? If it is asserted that civilization is a real advance in the condition of man, — and I think that it is, though only the wise improve their advantages, — it must be shown that it has produced better dwellings without making them more costly; and the cost of a thing is the amount of what I will call life which is required to be exchanged for it, immediately or in the long run. An average house in this neighborhood costs perhaps eight hundred dollars, and to lay up this sum will take from ten to fifteen years of the laborer's life, even if he is not encumbered with a family, — estimating the pecuniary value of every man's labor at one dollar a day, for if some receive more, others receive less; — so that he must have spent more than half his life commonly before *his* wigwam will be earned. If we suppose him to pay a rent instead, this is but a doubtful choice of evils. Would the savage have been wise to exchange his wigwam for a palace on these terms?

It may be guessed that I reduce almost the whole advantage of holding this superfluous property as a fund in store against the future, so far as the individual is concerned, mainly to the defraying of funeral expenses. But perhaps a man is not required to bury himself. Nevertheless this points to an important distinction between the civilized man and the savage; and, no doubt, they have designs on us for our benefit, in making the life of a civilized people an *institution*, in which the life of the individual is to a great extent absorbed, in order to preserve and perfect that of the race. But I wish to show at what a sacrifice this advantage is at present obtained, and to suggest that we may possibly so live as to secure all the advantage without suffering any of the disadvantage. What mean ye by saying that the poor ye have always with you, or that the fathers have eaten sour grapes, and the children's teeth are set on edge?

"As I live, saith the Lord God, ye shall not have occasion any more to use this proverb in Israel.

"Behold all souls are mine; as the soul of the father, so also the soul of the son is mine: the soul that sinneth, it shall die."

When I consider my neighbors, the farmers of Concord, who are at least as well off as the other classes, I find that for the most part they have been toiling twenty, thirty, or forty years, that they may become the real owners of their farms, which commonly they have inherited with encumbrances, or else bought with hired money, — and we may regard one third of that toil as the cost of their houses, — but commonly they have not paid for them yet. It is true, the encumbrances sometimes outweigh the value of the farm, so that the farm itself becomes one great encumbrance, and still a man is found to inherit it, being well acquainted with it, as he says. On applying to the assessors, I am surprised to learn that they cannot at once name a dozen in the town who own their farms free and clear. If you would know the history of these homesteads, inquire at the bank where they are mortgaged. The man who has actually paid for his farm with labor on it is so rare that every neighbor can point to him. I doubt if there are three such men in Concord. What has been said of the merchants, that a very large majority, even ninety-seven in a hundred, are sure to fail, is equally true of the farmers. With regard to the merchants, however, one of them says pertinently that a great part of their failures are not genuine pecuniary failures, but merely failures to fulfil their engagements, because it is inconvenient; that is, it is the moral character that breaks down. But this puts an infinitely worse face on the matter, and suggests, beside, that probably not even the other three succeed in saving their souls, but are perchance bankrupt in a worse sense than they who fail honestly. Bankruptcy and repudiation are the spring-boards from which much of our civilization vaults and turns its somersets, but the savage stands on the unelastic plank of famine. Yet the Middlesex Cattle Show goes off here with *éclat* annually, as if all the joints of the agricultural machine were suent.

The farmer is endeavoring to solve the problem of a livelihood by a formula more complicated than the problem itself. To get his shoestrings he speculates in herds of cattle. With consummate skill he has set his trap with a hair springe to catch comfort and independence, and then, as he turned away, got his own leg into it. This is the reason he is poor; and for a similar reason we are all poor in respect to a thousand savage

comforts, though surrounded by luxuries. As Chapman
sings, —

> " The false society of men —
> — for earthly greatness
> All heavenly comforts rarefies to air."

And when the farmer has got his house, he may not
be the richer but the poorer for it, and it be the house
that has got him. As I understand it, that was a valid
objection urged by Momus against the house which
Minerva made, that she "had not made it movable, by
which means a bad neighborhood might be avoided;"
and it may still be urged, for our houses are such unwieldy property that we are often imprisoned rather
than housed in them; and the bad neighborhood to be
avoided is our own scurvy selves. I know one or two
families, at least, in this town, who, for nearly a generation, have been wishing to sell their houses in the
outskirts and move into the village, but have not been
able to accomplish it, and only death will set them free.

Granted that the *majority* are able at last either to
own or hire the modern house with all its improvements.
While civilization has been improving our houses, it has
not equally improved the men who are to inhabit them.
It has created palaces, but it was not so easy to create
noblemen and kings. And *if the civilized man's pursuits
are no worthier than the savage's, if he is employed the
greater part of his life in obtaining gross necessaries and
comforts merely, why should he have a better dwelling
than the former?*

But how do the poor *minority* fare? Perhaps it will
be found that just in proportion as some have been

placed in outward circumstances above the savage, others have been degraded below him. The luxury of one class is counterbalanced by the indigence of another. On the one side is the palace, on the other are the almshouse and "silent poor." The myriads who built the pyramids to be the tombs of the Pharaohs were fed on garlic, and it may be were not decently buried themselves. The mason who finishes the cornice of the palace returns at night perchance to a hut not so good as a wigwam. It is a mistake to suppose that, in a country where the usual evidences of civilization exist, the condition of a very large body of the inhabitants may not be as degraded as that of savages. I refer to the degraded poor, not now to the degraded rich. To know this I should not need to look farther than to the shanties which everywhere border our railroads, that last improvement in civilization; where I see in my daily walks human beings living in sties, and all winter with an open door, for the sake of light, without any visible, often imaginable, wood-pile, and the forms of both old and young are permanently contracted by the long habit of shrinking from cold and misery, and the development of all their limbs and faculties is checked. It certainly is fair to look at that class by whose labor the works which distinguish this generation are accomplished. Such too, to a greater or less extent, is the condition of the operatives of every denomination in England, which is the great workhouse of the world. Or I could refer you to Ireland, which is marked as one of the white or enlightened spots on the map. Contrast the physical condition of the Irish with that of the North

American Indian, or the South Sea Islander, or any other savage race before it was degraded by contact with the civilized man. Yet I have no doubt that that people's rulers are as wise as the average of civilized rulers. Their condition only proves what squalidness may consist with civilization. I hardly need refer now to the laborers in our Southern States who produce the staple exports of this country, and are themselves a staple production of the South. But to confine myself to those who are said to be in *moderate* circumstances.

Most men appear never to have considered what a house is, and are actually though needlessly poor all their lives because they think that they must have such a one as their neighbors have. As if one were to wear any sort of coat which the tailor might cut out for him, or, gradually leaving off palm-leaf hat or cap of wood-chuck skin, complain of hard times because he could not afford to buy him a crown! It is possible to invent a house still more convenient and luxurious than we have, which yet all would admit that man could not afford to pay for. Shall we always study to obtain more of these things, and not sometimes to be content with less? Shall the respectable citizen thus gravely teach, by precept and example, the necessity of the young man's providing a certain number of superfluous glow-shoes, and umbrellas, and empty guest chambers for empty guests, before he dies? Why should not our furniture be as simple as the Arab's or the Indian's? When I think of the benefactors of the race, whom we have apotheosized as messengers from heaven, bearers of divine gifts to man, I do not see in my mind any retinue at their heels, any carload of fashionable furniture. Or what if I were to allow — would it not be a singular allowance? — that our furniture should be more complex than the Arab's, in proportion as we are morally and intellectually his superiors! At present our houses are cluttered and defiled with it, and a good housewife would sweep out the greater part into the dust hole, and not leave her morning's work undone. Morning work! By the blushes of Aurora and the music of Memnon, what should be man's *morning work* in this world? I had three pieces of limestone on my desk, but I was terrified to find that they required to be dusted daily, when the furniture of my mind was all undusted still, and I threw them out the window in disgust. How, then, could I have a furnished house? I would rather sit in the open air, for no dust gathers on the grass, unless where man has broken ground.

It is the luxurious and dissipated who set the fashions which the herd so diligently follow. The traveller who stops at the best houses, so called, soon discovers this, for the publicans presume him to be a Sardanapalus, and if he resigned himself to their tender mercies he would soon be completely emasculated. I think that in the railroad car we are inclined to spend more on luxury than on safety and convenience, and it threatens with out attaining these to become no better than a modern drawing-room, with its divans, and ottomans, and sunshades, and a hundred other oriental things, which we are taking west with us, invented for the ladies of the harem and the effeminate natives of the Celestial Empire, which Jonathan should be ashamed to know the names of. I would rather sit on a pumpkin and have it all to myself than be crowded on a velvet cushion. I would rather ride on earth in an ox cart, with a free circulation, than go to heaven in the fancy car of an excursion train and breathe a *malaria* all the way.

The very simplicity and nakedness of man's life in the primitive ages imply this advantage, at least, that they left him still but a sojourner in nature. When he was refreshed with food and sleep, he contemplated his journey again. He dwelt, as it were, in a tent in this world, and was either threading the valleys, or crossing the plains, or climbing the mountain-tops. But lo! men have become the tools of their tools. The man who independently plucked the fruits when he was hungry is become a farmer; and he who stood under a tree for shelter, a housekeeper. We now no longer camp as for a night, but have settled down on earth and forgotten heaven. We have adopted Christianity merely as an improved method of *agri*-culture. We have built for this world a family mansion, and for the next a family tomb. The best works of art are the expression of man's struggle to free himself from this condition, but the effect of our art is merely to make this low state comfortable and that higher state to be forgotten. There is actually no place in this village for a work of *fine* art, if any had come down to us, to stand, for our lives, our houses and streets, furnish no proper pedestal for it. There is not a nail to hang a picture on, nor a shelf to receive the bust of a hero or a saint. When I consider how our houses are built and paid for, or not paid for, and their internal economy managed and sustained, I wonder that the floor does not give way under the visitor while he is admiring the gewgaws upon the mantel-piece, and let him through into the cellar, to some solid and honest though earthy foundation. I cannot but perceive that this so-called rich and refined life is a thing jumped at, and I do not get on in the enjoy-ment of the *fine* arts which adorn it, my attention being wholly occupied with the jump; for I remember that the greatest genuine leap, due to human muscles alone, on record, is that of certain wandering Arabs, who are said to have cleared twenty-five feet on level ground. Without factitious support, man is sure to come to earth again beyond that distance. The first question which I am tempted to put to the proprietor of such great impropriety is, Who bolsters you? Are you one of the ninety-seven who fail, or the three who succeed? An-swer me these questions, and then perhaps I may look at your bawbles and find them ornamental. The cart before the horse is neither beautiful nor useful. Before we can adorn our houses with beautiful objects the walls must be stripped, and our lives must be stripped, and beautiful housekeeping and beautiful living be laid for a foundation: now, a taste for the beautiful is most cultivated out of doors, where there is no house and no housekeeper.

Old Johnson, in his "Wonder-Working Providence," speaking of the first settlers of this town, with whom he was contemporary, tells us that "they burrow them-selves in the earth for their first shelter under some hill-side, and, casting the soil aloft upon timber, they make a smoky fire against the earth, at the highest side." They did not "provide them houses," says he, "till the earth, by the Lord's blessing, brought forth bread to feed them," and the first year's crop was so light that "they were forced to cut their bread very thin for a long season." The secretary of the Province of New Netherland, writing in Dutch, in 1650, for the information of those who wished to take up land there, states more particularly that "those in New Netherland, and especially in New England, who have no means to build farmhouses at first according to their wishes, dig a square pit in the ground, cellar fashion, six or seven feet deep, as long and as broad as they think proper, case the earth inside with wood all round the wall, and line the wood with the bark of trees or something else to prevent the caving in of the earth; floor this cellar with plank, and wainscot it overhead for a ceiling, raise a roof of spars clear up, and cover the spars with bark or green sods, so that they can live dry and warm in these houses with their entire families for two, three, and four years, it being understood that partitions are run through those cellars which are adapted to the size of the family. The wealthy and principal men in New England, in the beginning of the colonies, commenced their first dwelling-houses in this fashion for two reasons: firstly, in order not to waste time in building, and not to want food the next season; secondly, in order not to discourage poor laboring people whom they brought over in numbers from Fatherland. In the course of three or four years, when the country became adapted to agriculture, they built themselves handsome houses, spending on them several thousands."

In this course which our ancestors took there was a show of prudence at least, as if their principle were to satisfy the more pressing wants first. But are the more pressing wants satisfied now? When I think of acquiring for myself one of our luxurious dwellings, I am deterred, for, so to speak, the country is not yet adapted to *human* culture, and we are still forced to cut our *spiritual* bread far thinner than our forefathers did their wheaten. Not that all architectural ornament is to be neglected even in the rudest periods; but let our houses first be lined with beauty, where they come in contact with our lives, like the tenement of the shell-fish, and not overlaid with it. But, alas! I have been inside one or two of them, and know what they are lined with.

Though we are not so degenerate but that we might possibly live in a cave or a wigwam or wear skins to-day, it certainly is better to accept the advantages, though so dearly bought, which the invention and industry of mankind offer. In such a neighborhood as this, boards and shingles, lime and bricks, are cheaper and more easily obtained than suitable caves, or whole logs, or bark in sufficient quantities, or even well-tempered clay or flat stones. I speak understandingly on this subject, for I have made myself acquainted with it both theoretically and practically. With a little more wit we might use these materials so as to become richer than the richest now are, and make our civilization a blessing. The civilized man is a more experienced and wiser savage. But to make haste to my own experiment.

WALDEN POND

Near the end of March, 1845, I borrowed an axe and went down to the woods by Walden Pond, nearest to where I intended to build my house, and began to cut down some tall, arrowy white pines, still in their youth, for timber. It is difficult to begin without borrowing, but perhaps it is the most generous course thus to permit your fellow-men to have an interest in your enterprise. The owner of the axe, as he released his hold on it, said that it was the apple of his eye; but I returned it sharper than I received it. It was a pleasant hillside where I worked, covered with pine woods, through which I looked out on the pond, and a small open field in the woods where pines and hickories were springing up. The ice in the pond was not yet dissolved, though there were some open spaces, and it was all dark-colored and saturated with water. There were some slight flurries of snow during the days that I worked there; but for the most part when I came out on to the railroad, on my way home, its yellow sand-heap stretched away gleaming in the hazy atmosphere, and the rails shone in the spring sun, and I heard the lark and pewee and other birds already come to commence another year with us. They were pleasant spring days, in which the winter of man's discontent was thawing as well as the earth, and the life that had lain torpid began to stretch itself. One day, when my axe had come off and I had cut a green hickory for a wedge, driving it with a stone, and had placed the whole to soak in a pond-hole in order to swell the wood, I saw a striped snake run into the water, and he lay on the bottom, apparently without inconvenience, as long as I stayed there, or more than

This description of the house-building stands Thoreau at his best.

a quarter of an hour; perhaps because he had not yet fairly come out of the torpid state. It appeared to me that for a like reason men remain in their present low and primitive condition; but if they should feel the influence of the spring of springs arousing them, they would of necessity rise to a higher and more ethereal life. I had previously seen the snakes in frosty mornings in my path with portions of their bodies still numb and inflexible, waiting for the sun to thaw them. On the 1st of April it rained and melted the ice, and in the early part of the day, which was very foggy, I heard a stray goose groping about over the pond and cackling as if lost, or like the spirit of the fog.

So I went on for some days cutting and hewing timber, and also studs and rafters, all with my narrow axe, not having many communicable or scholar-like thoughts singing to myself, —

> Men say they know many things;
> But lo! they have taken wings, —
> The arts and sciences,
> And a thousand appliances:
> The wind that blows
> Is all that anybody knows.

I hewed the main timbers six inches square, most of the studs on two sides only, and the rafters and floor timbers on one side, leaving the rest of the bark on, so that they were just as straight and much stronger than sawed ones. Each stick was carefully mortised or tenoned by its stump, for I had borrowed other tools by this time. My days in the woods were not very long ones; yet I usually carried my dinner of bread and butter, and read the newspaper in which it was wrapped, at noon, sitting amid the green pine boughs which I had cut off, and to my bread was imparted some of their fragrance, for my hands were covered with a thick coat of pitch. Before I had done I was more the friend than the foe of the pine tree, though I had cut down some of them, having become better acquainted with it. Sometimes a rambler in the wood was attracted by the sound of my axe, and we chatted pleasantly over the chips which I had made.

By the middle of April, for I made no haste in my work, but rather made the most of it, my house was framed and ready for the raising. I had already bought the shanty of James Collins, an Irishman who worked on the Fitchburg Railroad, for boards. James Collins' shanty was considered an uncommonly fine one. When I called to see it he was not at home. I walked about the outside, at first unobserved from within, the window was so deep and high. It was of small dimensions, with a peaked cottage roof, and not much else to be seen, the dirt being raised five feet all around as if it were a compost heap. The roof was the soundest part, though a good deal warped and made brittle by the sun. Door-sill there was none, but a perennial passage for the hens under the door-board. Mrs. C. came to the door and asked me to view it from the inside. The hens were driven in by my approach. It was dark, and had a dirt floor for the most part, dank, clammy, and aguish, only here a board and there a board which would not bear removal. She lighted a lamp to show me the inside of the roof and the walls, and also that the board floor extended under the bed, warning me not to step into the cellar, a sort of dust hole two feet deep. In her own words, they were "good boards overhead, good boards all around, and a good window," — of two whole squares originally, only the cat had passed out that way lately. There was a stove, a bed, and a place to sit, an infant in the house where it was born, a silk parasol, gilt-framed looking-glass, and a patent new coffee-mill nailed to an oak sapling, all told. The bargain was soon concluded, for James had in the meanwhile returned. I to pay four dollars and twenty-five cents to-night, he to vacate at five to-morrow morning, selling to nobody else meanwhile: I to take possession at six. It were well, he said, to be there early, and anticipate certain indistinct but wholly unjust claims on the score of ground rent and fuel. This he assured me was the only encumbrance. At six I passed him and his family on the road. One large bundle held their all, — bed, coffee-mill, looking-glass, hens, — all but the cat; she took to the woods and became a wild cat, and, as I learned afterward, trod in a trap set for woodchucks, and so became a dead cat at last.

I took down this dwelling the same morning, drawing the nails, and removed it to the pond-side by small cartloads, spreading the boards on the grass there to bleach and warp back again in the sun. One early thrush gave me a note or two as I drove along the woodland path. I was informed treacherously by a young Patrick that neighbor Seeley, an Irishman, in the intervals of the carting, transferred the still tolerable, straight, and drivable nails, staples, and spikes to his pocket, and then stood when I came back to pass the time of day, and look freshly up, unconcerned, with spring thoughts, at the devastation; there being a dearth of work, as he said. He was there to represent spectatordom, and help make this seemingly insignificant event one with the removal of the gods of Troy.

I dug my cellar in the side of a hill sloping to the south, where a woodchuck had formerly dug his burrow, down through sumach and blackberry roots, and the lowest stain of vegetation, six feet square by seven deep, to a fine sand where potatoes would not freeze in any winter. The sides were left shelving, and not stoned; but the sun having never shone on them, the sand still keeps its place. It was but two hours' work. I took particular pleasure in this breaking of ground, for in almost all latitudes men dig into the earth for an equable temperature. Under the most splendid house in the city is still to be found the cellar where they store their roots as of old, and long after the superstructure has disappeared posterity remark its dent in the earth. The house is still but a sort of porch at the entrance of a burrow.

At length, in the beginning of May, with the help of some of my acquaintances, rather to improve so good an occasion for neighborliness than from any necessity, I set up the frame of my house. No man was ever more honored in the character of his raisers than I. They are destined, I trust, to assist at the raising of loftier structures one day. I began to occupy my house on the 4th of July, as soon as it was boarded and roofed, for the boards were carefully feather-edged and lapped, so that it was perfectly impervious to rain, but before boarding I laid the foundation of a chimney at one end, bringing two cartloads of stones up the hill from the pond in my arms. I built the chimney after my hoeing in the fall, before a fire became necessary for warmth, doing my cooking in the meanwhile out of doors on the ground, early in the morning: which mode I still think is in some respects more convenient and agreeable than the usual one. When it stormed before my bread was baked, I fixed a few boards over the fire, and sat under them to watch my loaf, and passed some pleasant hours in that way. In those days, when my hands were much employed, I read but little, but the least scraps of paper which lay on the ground, my holder, or tablecloth, afforded me as much entertainment, in fact answered the same purpose as the Iliad.

It would be worth the while to build still more deliberately than I did, considering, for instance, what foundation a door, a window, a cellar, a garret, have in the nature of man, and perchance never raising any superstructure until we found a better reason for it than our temporal necessities even. There is some of the same fitness in a man's building his own house that there is in a bird's building its own nest. Who knows but if men constructed their dwellings with their own hands, and provided food for themselves and families simply and honestly enough, the poetic faculty would be universally developed, as birds universally sing when they are so engaged? But alas! we do like cowbirds and cuckoos, which lay their eggs in nests which other birds have built, and cheer no traveller with their chattering and unmusical notes. Shall we forever resign the pleasure of construction to the carpenter? What does architecture amount to in the experience of the mass of men? I never in all my walks came across a man engaged in so simple and natural an occupation as building his house. We belong to the community. It is not the tailor alone who is the ninth part of a man; it is as much the preacher, and the merchant, and the farmer. Where is this division of labor to end? and what object does it finally serve? No doubt another *may* also think for me; but it is not therefore desirable that he should do so to the exclusion of my thinking for myself.

True, there are architects so called in this country, and I have heard of one at least possessed with the idea of making architectural ornaments have a core of truth, a necessity, and hence a beauty, as if it were a revelation to him. All very well perhaps from his point of view, but only a little better than the common dilettantism. A sentimental reformer in architecture, he began at the cornice, not at the foundation. It was only how to put a core of truth within the ornaments, that every sugar-plum, in fact, might have an almond or caraway seed in it, — though I hold that almonds are most wholesome without the sugar, — and not how the inhabitant, the indweller, might build truly within and without, and let the ornaments take care of themselves. What reasonable man ever supposed that ornaments were something outward and in the skin merely, — that the tortoise got his spotted shell, or the shell-fish its mother-o'-pearl tints, by such a contract as the inhabitants of Broad-

way their Trinity Church ? But a man has no more to do
with the style of architecture of his house than a tortoise
with that of its shell: nor need the soldier be so idle as
to try to paint the precise *color* of his virtue on his standard. The enemy will find it out. He may turn pale
when the trial comes. This man seemed to me to lean
over the cornice, and timidly whisper his half truth to
the rude occupants who really knew it better than he.
What of architectural beauty I now see, I know has
gradually grown from within outward, out of the necessities and character of the indweller, who is the only
builder, — out of some unconscious truthfulness, and
nobleness, without ever a thought for the appearance
and whatever additional beauty of this kind is destined
to be produced will be preceded by a like unconscious
beauty of life. The most interesting dwellings in this
country, as the painter knows, are the most unpretend-
ing, humble log huts and cottages of the poor commonly; it is the life of the inhabitants whose shells they
are, and not any peculiarity in their surfaces merely,
which makes them *picturesque;* and equally interesting
will be the citizen's suburban box, when his life shall be
as simple and as agreeable to the imagination, and there
is as little straining after effect in the style of his dwelling. A great proportion of architectural ornaments are
literally hollow, and a September gale would strip them
off, like borrowed plumes, without injury to the sub-
stantials. They can do without *architecture* who have
no olives nor wines in the cellar. What if an equal ado
were made about the ornaments of style in literature,
and the architects of our bibles spent as much time

about their cornices as the architects of our churches do? So are made the *belles-lettres* and the *beaux-arts* and their professors. Much it concerns a man, forsooth, how a few sticks are slanted over him or under him, and what colors are daubed upon his box. It would signify somewhat, if, in any earnest sense, *he* slanted them and daubed it; but the spirit having departed out of the tenant, it is of a piece with constructing his own coffin, — the architecture of the grave, — and "carpenter" is but another name for "coffin-maker." One man says, in his despair or indifference to life, take up a handful of the earth at your feet, and paint your house that color. Is he thinking of his last and narrow house? Toss up a copper for it as well. What an abundance of leisure he must have! Why do you take up a handful of dirt? Better paint your house your own complexion; let it turn pale or blush for you. An enterprise to improve the style of cottage architecture! When you have got my ornaments ready, I will wear them.

Before winter I built a chimney, and shingled the sides of my house, which were already impervious to rain, with imperfect and sappy shingles made of the first slice of the log, whose edges I was obliged to straighten with a plane.

I have thus a tight shingled and plastered house, ten feet wide by fifteen long, and eight-feet posts, with a garret and a closet, a large window on each side, two trap-doors, one door at the end, and a brick fireplace opposite. The exact cost of my house, paying the usual price for such materials as I used, but not counting the work, all of which was done by myself, was as follows:

and I give the details because very few are able to tell exactly what their houses cost, and fewer still, if any, the separate cost of the various materials which compose them: —

Boards	$8 03½,	mostly shanty boards.
Refuse shingles for roof and sides	4 00	
Laths	1 25	
Two second-hand windows with glass	2 43	
One thousand old brick .	4 00	
Two casks of lime . . .	2 40	That was high.
Hair	0 31	More than I needed.
Mantle-tree iron	0 15	
Nails	3 90	
Hinges and screws . . .	0 14	
Latch	0 10	
Chalk	0 01	
Transportation	1 40	{ I carried a good part on my back.
In all	$28 12½	

These are all the materials, excepting the timber, stones, and sand, which I claimed by squatter's right. I have also a small woodshed adjoining, made chiefly of the stuff which was left after building the house.

I intend to build me a house which will surpass any on the main street in Concord in grandeur and luxury, as soon as it pleases me as much and will cost me no more than my present one.

I thus found that the student who wishes for a shelter can obtain one for a lifetime at an expense not greater than the rent which he now pays annually. If I seem to boast more than is becoming, my excuse is that I brag for humanity rather than for myself; and my short-comings and inconsistencies do not affect the truth of my statement. Notwithstanding much cant and hypoc-risy, — chaff which I find it difficult to separate from my wheat, but for which I am as sorry as any man, — I will breathe freely and stretch myself in this respect, it is such a relief to both the moral and physical sys-tem; and I am resolved that I will not through humility become the devil's attorney. I will endeavor to speak a good word for the truth. At Cambridge College the mere rent of a student's room, which is only a little larger than my own, is thirty dollars each year, though the corporation had the advantage of building thirty-two side by side and under one roof, and the occupant suffers the inconvenience of many and noisy neighbors, and perhaps a residence in the fourth story. I cannot but think that if we had more true wisdom in these respects, not only less education would be needed, be-cause, forsooth, more would already have been acquired, but the pecuniary expense of getting an education would in a great measure vanish. Those conveniences which the student requires at Cambridge or elsewhere cost him or somebody else ten times as great a sacrifice of life as they would with proper management on both sides. Those things for which the most money is de-manded are never the things which the student most wants. Tuition, for instance, is an important item in the term bill, while for the far more valuable education which he gets by associating with the most cultivated of his contemporaries no charge is made. The mode of founding a college is, commonly, to get up a subscription of dollars and cents, and then, following blindly the principles of a division of labor to its extreme, — a principle which should never be followed but with circumspection, — to call in a contractor who makes this a subject of speculation, and he employs Irishmen or other operatives actually to lay the foundations, while the students that are to be are said to be fitting themselves for it; and for these oversights successive generations have to pay. I think that it would be *better than this*, for the students, or those who desire to be benefited by it, even to lay the foundation themselves. The student who secures his coveted leisure and retirement by systematically shirking any labor necessary to man obtains but an ignoble and unprofitable leisure, defrauding himself of the experience which alone can make leisure fruitful. "But," says one, "you do not mean that the students should go to work with their hands instead of their heads?" I do not mean that exactly, but I mean something which he might think a good deal like that; I mean that they should not *play* life, or *study* it merely, while the community supports them at this expensive game, but earnestly *live* it from beginning to end. How could youths better learn to live than by at once trying the experiment of living? Methinks this would exercise their minds as much as mathematics. If I wished a boy to know something about the arts and sciences, for instance, I would not pursue the common course, which is merely to send him into the neighborhood of some professor, where anything is professed and practised

but the art of life; — to survey the world through a
telescope or a microscope, and never with his natural
eye; to study chemistry, and not learn how his bread is
made, or mechanics, and not learn how it is earned; to
discover new satellites to Neptune, and not detect the
motes in his eyes, or to what vagabond he is a satellite
himself; or to be devoured by the monsters that swarm
all around him, while contemplating the monsters in a
drop of vinegar. Which would have advanced the most
at the end of a month, — the boy who had made his
own jackknife from the ore which he had dug and
smelted, reading as much as would be necessary for
this — or the boy who had attended the lectures on
metallurgy at the Institute in the meanwhile, and had
received a Rodgers penknife from his father? Which
would be most likely to cut his fingers? . . . To my
astonishment I was informed on leaving college that I
had studied navigation! — why, if I had taken one turn
down the harbor I should have known more about it.
Even the *poor* student studies and is taught only *political*
economy, while that economy of living which is synonymous with philosophy is not even sincerely professed
in our colleges. The consequence is, that while he is
reading Adam Smith, Ricardo, and Say, he runs his
father in debt irretrievably.

As with our colleges, so with a hundred "modern
improvements;" there is an illusion about them; there
is not always a positive advance. The devil goes on
exacting compound interest to the last for his early share
and numerous succeeding investments in them. Our
inventions are wont to be pretty toys, which distract

our attention from serious things.] They are but improved means to an unimproved end, an end which it was already but too easy to arrive at; as railroads lead to Boston or New York. We are in great haste to construct a magnetic telegraph from Maine to Texas; but Maine and Texas, it may be, have nothing important to communicate. Either is in such a predicament as the man who was earnest to be introduced to a distinguished deaf woman, but when he was presented, and one end of her ear trumpet was put into his hand, had nothing to say. As if the main object were to talk fast and not to talk sensibly. We are eager to tunnel under the Atlantic and bring the Old World some weeks nearer to the New; but perchance the first news that will leak through into the broad, flapping American ear will be that the Princess Adelaide has the whooping cough. After all, the man whose horse trots a mile in a minute does not carry the most important messages; he is not an evangelist, nor does he come round eating locusts and wild honey. I doubt if Flying Childers ever carried a peck of corn to mill. [HUMOR AGAIN]

One says to me, "I wonder that you do not lay up money; you love to travel; you might take the cars and go to Fitchburg to-day and see the country." But I am wiser than that. I have learned that the swiftest traveller is he that goes afoot. I say to my friend, Suppose we try who will get there first. The distance is thirty miles; the fare ninety cents. That is almost a day's wages. I remember when wages were sixty cents a day for laborers on this very road. Well, I start now on foot, and get there before night; I have travelled at that rate by the week together. You will in the meanwhile have earned your fare, and arrive there some time to-morrow, or possibly this evening, if you are lucky enough to get a job in season. Instead of going to Fitchburg, you will be working here the greater part of the day. And so, if the railroad reached round the world, I think that I should keep ahead of you; and as for seeing the country and getting experience of that kind, I should have to cut your acquaintance altogether.

Such is the universal law, which no man can ever out-wit, and with regard to the railroad even we may say it is as broad as it is long. To make a railroad round the world available to all mankind is equivalent to grading the whole surface of the planet. Men have an indistinct notion that if they keep up this activity of joint stocks and spades long enough all will at length ride some-where, in next to no time, and for nothing; but though a crowd rushes to the depot, and the conductor shouts "All aboard!" when the smoke is blown away and the vapor condensed, it will be perceived that a few are riding, but the rest are run over, — and it will be called, and will be, "A melancholy accident." No doubt they can ride at last who shall have earned their fare, that is, if they survive so long, but they will probably have lost their elasticity and desire to travel by that time. This spending of the best part of one's life earning money in order to enjoy a questionable liberty during the least valuable part of it reminds me of the English-man who went to India to make a fortune first, in order that he might return to England and live the life of a poet. He should have gone up garret at once. "What!"

exclaim a million Irishmen starting up from all the shanties in the land,"is not this railroad which we have built a good thing?" Yes, I answer, *comparatively* good, that is, you might have done worse; but I wish, as you are brothers of mine, that you could have spent your time better than digging in this dirt.

Before I finished my house, wishing to earn ten or twelve dollars by some honest and agreeable method, in order to meet my unusual expenses, I planted about two acres and a half of light and sandy soil near it chiefly with beans, but also a small part with potatoes, corn, peas, and turnips. The whole lot contains eleven acres, mostly growing up to pines and hickories, and was sold the preceding season for eight dollars and eight cents an acre. One farmer said that it was "good for nothing but to raise cheeping squirrels on." I put no manure whatever on this land, not being the owner, but merely a squatter, and not expecting to cultivate so much again, and I did not quite hoe it all once. I got out several cords of stumps in plowing, which supplied me with fuel for a long time, and left small circles of virgin mould, easily distinguishable through the summer by the greater luxuriance of the beans there. The dead and for the most part unmerchantable wood behind my house, and the driftwood from the pond, have supplied the remainder of my fuel. I was obliged to hire a team and a man for the plowing, though I held the plow myself. My farm outgoes for the first season were, for implements, seed, work, etc., \$14.72½. The seed corn was given me. This never costs anything to speak of, unless you plant more than enough. I got twelve bushels of beans, and eighteen bushels of potatoes, beside some peas and sweet corn. The yellow corn and turnips were too late to come to anything. My whole income from the farm was

$$\text{\$23 \ 44}$$

Deducting the outgoes 14 72½

There are left $8 71½,

beside produce consumed and on hand at the time this estimate was made of the value of $4.50, — the amount on hand much more than balancing a little grass which I did not raise. All things considered, that is, considering the importance of a man's soul and of to-day, notwithstanding the short time occupied by my experiment, nay, partly even because of its transient character, I believe that that was doing better than any farmer in Concord did that year.

The next year I did better still, for I spaded up all the land which I required, about a third of an acre, and I learned from the experience of both years, not being in the least awed by many celebrated works on husbandry, Arthur Young among the rest, that if one would live simply and eat only the crop which he raised, and raise no more than he ate, and not exchange it for an insufficient quantity of more luxurious and expensive things, he would need to cultivate only a few rods of ground, and that it would be cheaper to spade up that than to use oxen to plow it, and to select a fresh spot from time to time than to manure the old, and he could do all his necessary farm work as it were with his left hand at odd hours in the summer; and thus he would not be tied to an ox, or horse, or cow, or pig, as at present. I desire to speak impartially on this point, and as one not interested in the success or failure of the present economical and social arrangements. I was more independent than any farmer in Concord, for I was not anchored to a house or farm, but could follow the bent of my genius, which is a very crooked one, every moment. Beside being better off than they already, if my house had been burned or my crops had failed, I should have been nearly as well off as before.

I am wont to think that men are not so much the keepers of herds as herds are the keepers of men, the former are so much the freer. Men and oxen exchange work; but if we consider necessary work only, the oxen will be seen to have greatly the advantage, their farm is so much the larger. Man does some of his part of the exchange work in his six weeks of haying, and it is no boy's play. Certainly no nation that lived simply in all respects, that is, no nation of philosophers, would commit so great a blunder as to use the labor of animals. True, there never was and is not likely soon to be a nation of philosophers, nor am I certain it is desirable that there should be. However, *I* should never have broken a horse or bull and taken him to board for any work he might do for me, for fear I should become a horseman or a herds-man merely; and if society seems to be the gainer by so doing, are we certain that what is one man's gain is not another's loss, and that the stable-boy has equal cause with his master to be satisfied? Granted that some public works would not have been constructed

without this aid, and let man share the glory of such with
the ox and horse; does it follow that he could not have
accomplished works yet more worthy of himself in that
case? When men begin to do, not merely unnecessary
or artistic, but luxurious and idle work, with their assistance, it is inevitable that a few do all the exchange
work with the oxen, or, in other words, become the
slaves of the strongest. Man thus not only works for
the animal within him, but, for a symbol of this, he
works for the animal without him. Though we have
many substantial houses of brick or stone, the prosperity
of the farmer is still measured by the degree to which
the barn overshadows the house. This town is said to
have the largest houses for oxen, cows, and horses hereabouts, and it is not behindhand in its public buildings;
but there are very few halls for free worship or free speech
in this county. It should not be by their architecture,
but why not even by their power of abstract thought,
that nations should seek to commemorate themselves?
How much more admirable the Bhagvat-Geeta than
all the ruins of the East! Towers and temples are the
luxury of princes. A simple and independent mind
does not toil at the bidding of any prince. Genius
is not a retainer to any emperor, nor is its material
silver, or gold, or marble, except to a trifling extent.
To what end, pray, is so much stone hammered? In
Arcadia, when I was there, I did not see any hammering stone. Nations are possessed with an insane ambition to perpetuate the memory of themselves by the
amount of hammered stone they leave. What if equal
pains were taken to smooth and polish their manners?

One piece of good sense would be more memorable than a monument as high as the moon. I love better to see stones in place. The grandeur of Thebes was a vulgar grandeur. More sensible is a rod of stone wall that bounds an honest man's field than a hundred-gated Thebes that has wandered farther from the true end of life. The religion and civilization which are barbaric and heathenish build splendid temples; but what you might call Christianity does not. Most of the stone a nation hammers goes toward its tomb only. It buries itself alive. As for the Pyramids, there is nothing to wonder at in them so much as the fact that so many men could be found degraded enough to spend their lives constructing a tomb for some ambitious booby, whom it would have been wiser and manlier to have drowned in the Nile, and then given his body to the dogs. I might possibly invent some excuse for them and him, but I have no time for it. As for the religion and love of art of the builders, it is much the same all the world over, whether the building be an Egyptian temple or the United States Bank. It costs more than it comes to. The mainspring is vanity, assisted by the love of garlic and bread and butter. Mr. Balcom, a promising young architect, designs it on the back of his Vitruvius, with hard pencil and ruler, and the job is let out to Dobson & Sons, stonecutters. When the thirty centuries begin to look down on it, mankind begin to look up at it. As for your high towers and monuments, there was a crazy fellow once in this town who undertook to dig through to China, and he got so far that, as he said, he heard the Chinese pots and kettles rattle; but I think

that I shall not go out of my way to admire the hole
which he made. Many are concerned about the monuments of the West and the East, — to know who built
them. For my part, I should like to know who in those
days did not build them, — who were above such trifling.
But to proceed with my statistics.

By surveying, carpentry, and day-labor of various
other kinds in the village in the meanwhile, for I have
as many trades as fingers, I had earned $13.34. The
expense of food for eight months, namely, from July 4th
to March 1st, the time when these estimates were made,
though I lived there more than two years, — not counting potatoes, a little green corn, and some peas, which
I had raised, nor considering the value of what was on
hand at the last date, — was

Rice	$1 73½	
Molasses	1 73	Cheapest form of the saccharine.
Rye meal	1 04¾	
Indian meal . . .	0 99¾	Cheaper than rye.
Pork	0 22	
Flour	0 88	Costs more than Indian meal, both money and trouble.
Sugar	0 80	
Lard	0 65	
Apples	0 25	
Dried apple . . .	0 22	
Sweet potatoes . .	0 10	
One pumpkin . . .	0 6	
One watermelon . .	0 2	
Salt	0 3	

All experiments which failed.

Yes, I did eat $8.74, all told; but I should not thus
unblushingly publish my guilt, if I did not know that
most of my readers were equally guilty with myself, and
that their deeds would look no better in print. The next
year I sometimes caught a mess of fish for my dinner,
and once I went so far as to slaughter a woodchuck
which ravaged my bean-field, — effect his transmigra-
tion, as a Tartar would say, — and devour him, partly
for experiment's sake; but though it afforded me a
momentary enjoyment, notwithstanding a musky flavor,
I saw that the longest use would not make that a good
practice, however it might seem to have your woodchucks ready dressed by the village butcher.

Clothing and some incidental expenses within the
same dates, though little can be inferred from this item,
amounted to

$$\$8 \ 40\tfrac{3}{4}$$

Oil and some household utensils . .   2 00

So that all the pecuniary outgoes, excepting for washing
and mending, which for the most part were done out
of the house, and their bills have not yet been received,
— and these are all and more than all the ways by
which money necessarily goes out in this part of the
world, — were

House	$28 12½
Farm one year	14 72½
Food eight months	8 74
Clothing, etc., eight months . . .	8 40¾
Oil, etc., eight months	2 00
In all	$61 99¾

I address myself now to those of my readers who have a living to get. And to meet this I have for farm produce sold

$23 44

Earned by day-labor 13 34

In all $36 78,

which subtracted from the sum of the outgoes leaves a balance of $25.21¾ on the one side, — this being very nearly the means with which I started, and the measure of expenses to be incurred, — and on the other, beside the leisure and independence and health thus secured, a comfortable house for me as long as I choose to occupy it.

These statistics, however accidental and therefore uninstructive they may appear, as they have a certain completeness, have a certain value also. Nothing was given me of which I have not rendered some account. It appears from the above estimate, that my food alone cost me in money about twenty-seven cents a week. It was, for nearly two years after this, rye and Indian meal without yeast, potatoes, rice, a very little salt pork, molasses, and salt; and my drink, water. It was fit that I should live on rice, mainly, who loved so well the philosophy of India. To meet the objections of some inveterate cavillers, I may as well state, that if I dined out occasionally, as I always had done, and I trust shall have opportunities to do again, it was frequently to the detriment of my domestic arrangements. But the dining out, being, as I have stated, a constant element, does not in the least affect a comparative statement like this.

I learned from my two years' experience that it would cost incredibly little trouble to obtain one's necessary food, even in this latitude; that a man may use as simple a diet as the animals, and yet retain health and strength. I have made a satisfactory dinner, satisfactory on several accounts, simply off a dish of purslane (*Portulaca oleracea*) which I gathered in my cornfield, boiled and salted. I give the Latin on account of the savoriness of the trivial name. And pray what more can a reasonable man desire, in peaceful times, in ordinary noons, than a sufficient number of ears of green sweet corn boiled, with the addition of salt? Even the little variety which I used was a yielding to the demands of appetite, and not of health. Yet men have come to such a pass that they frequently starve, not for want of necessaries, but for want of luxuries; and I know a good woman who thinks that her son lost his life because he took to drinking water only.

The reader will perceive that I am treating the subject rather from an economic than a dietetic point of view, and he will not venture to put my abstemiousness to the test unless he has a well-stocked larder.

Bread I at first made of pure Indian meal and salt, genuine hoe-cakes, which I baked before my fire out of doors on a shingle or the end of a stick of timber sawed off in building my house; but it was wont to get smoked and to have a piny flavor. I tried flour also; but have at last found a mixture of rye and Indian meal most convenient and agreeable. In cold weather it was no little amusement to bake several small loaves of this in succession, tending and turning them as carefully as a

Egyptian his hatching eggs. They were a real cereal fruit which I ripened, and they had to my senses a fragrance like that of other noble fruits, which I kept in as long as possible by wrapping them in cloths. I made a study of the ancient and indispensable art of bread-making, consulting such authorities as offered, going back to the primitive days and first invention of the unleavened kind, when from the wildness of nuts and meats men first reached the mildness and refinement of this diet, and travelling gradually down in my studies through that accidental souring of the dough which, it is supposed, taught the leavening process, and through the various fermentations thereafter, till I came to "good, sweet, wholesome bread," the staff of life. Leaven, which some deem the soul of bread, the *spiritus* which fills its cellular tissue, which is religiously preserved like the vestal fire, — some precious bottleful, I suppose, first brought over in the Mayflower, did the business for America, and its influence is still rising, swelling, spreading, in cerealian billows over the land, — this seed I regularly and faithfully procured from the village, till at length one morning I forgot the rules, and scalded my yeast; by which accident I discovered that even this was not indispensable, — for my discoveries were not by the synthetic but analytic process, — and I have gladly omitted it since, though most housewives earnestly assured me that safe and wholesome bread without yeast might not be, and elderly people prophesied a speedy decay of the vital forces. Yet I find it not to be an essential ingredient, and after going without it for a year am still in the land of the living; and I

Long centuna.

am glad to escape the trivialness of carrying a bottleful in my pocket, which would sometimes pop and discharge its contents to my discomfiture. It is simpler and
more respectable to omit it. Man is an animal who
more than any other can adapt himself to all climates
and circumstances. Neither did I put any sal-soda, or
other acid or alkali, into my bread. It would seem that I
made it according to the recipe which Marcus Porcius
Cato gave about two centuries before Christ. "Panem
depsticium sic facito. Manus mortariumque bene lavato.
Farinam in mortarium indito, aquae paulatim addito,
subigitoque pulchre. Ubi bene subegeris, defingito, co-
quitoque sub testu." Which I take to mean, "Make
kneaded bread thus. Wash your hands and trough well.
Put the meal into the trough, add water gradually, and
knead it thoroughly. When you have kneaded it
well, mould it, and bake it under a cover," that is, in a
baking-kettle. Not a word about leaven. But I did not
always use this staff of life. At one time, owing to the
emptiness of my purse, I saw none of it for more than a
month.

Every New Englander might easily raise all his own
breadstuffs in this land of rye and Indian corn, and not
depend on distant and fluctuating markets for them.
Yet so far are we from simplicity and independence
that, in Concord, fresh and sweet meal is rarely sold in
the shops, and hominy and corn in a still coarser form are
hardly used by any. For the most part the farmer gives
to his cattle and hogs the grain of his own producing,
and buys flour, which is at least no more wholesome, at
a greater cost, at the store. I saw that I could easily

raise my bushel or two of rye and Indian corn, for the former will grow on the poorest land, and the latter does not require the best, and grind them in a hand-mill, and so do without rice and pork; and if I must have some concentrated sweet, I found by experiment that I could make a very good molasses either of pumpkins or beets, and I knew that I needed only to set out a few maples to obtain it more easily still, and while these were growing I could use various substitutes beside those which I have named. "For," as the Forefathers sang, —

> "we can make liquor to sweeten our lips
> Of pumpkins and parsnips and walnut-tree chips."

Finally, as for salt, that grossest of groceries, to obtain this might be a fit occasion for a visit to the seashore, or, if I did without it altogether, I should probably drink the less water. I do not learn that the Indians ever troubled themselves to go after it.

Thus I could avoid all trade and barter, so far as my food was concerned, and having a shelter already, it would only remain to get clothing and fuel. The pantaloons which I now wear were woven in a farmer's family, — thank Heaven there is so much virtue still in man; for I think the fall from the farmer to the operative as great and memorable as that from the man to the farmer; — and in a new country, fuel is an encumbrance. As for a habitat, if I were not permitted still to squat, I might purchase one acre at the same price for which the land I cultivated was sold — namely, eight dollars and eight cents. But as it was, I considered that I enhanced the value of the land by squatting on it.

There is a certain class of unbelievers who sometimes ask me such questions as, if I think that I can live on vegetable food alone; and to strike at the root of the matter at once, — for the root is faith, — I am accustomed to answer such, that I can live on board nails. If they cannot understand that, they cannot understand much that I have to say. For my part, I am glad to hear of experiments of this kind being tried; as that a young man tried for a fortnight to live on hard, raw corn on the ear, using his teeth for all mortar. The squirrel tribe tried the same and succeeded. The human race is interested in these experiments, though a few old women who are incapacitated for them, or who own their thirds in mills, may be alarmed.

My furniture, part of which I made myself, — and the rest cost me nothing of which I have not rendered an account, — consisted of a bed, a table, a desk, three chairs, a looking-glass three inches in diameter, a pair of tongs and andirons, a kettle, a skillet, and a frying-pan, a dipper, a wash-bowl, two knives and forks, three plates, one cup, one spoon, a jug for oil, a jug for molasses, and a japanned lamp. None is so poor that he need sit on a pumpkin. That is shiftlessness. There is a plenty of such chairs as I like best in the village garrets to be had for taking them away. Furniture! Thank God, I can sit and I can stand without the aid of a furniture warehouse. What man but a philosopher would not be ashamed to see his furniture packed in a cart and going up country exposed to the light of heaven and the yes of men, a beggarly account of empty boxes? Tha is Spaulding's furniture. I could never tell from inspecting such a load whether it belonged to a so-called rich man or a poor one; the owner always seemed poverty-stricken. Indeed, the more you have of such things the poorer you are. Each load looks as if it contained the contents of a dozen shanties; and if one shanty is poor, this is a dozen times as poor. Pray, for what do we *move* ever but to get rid of our furniture, our *exuviæ;* at last to go from this world to another newly furnished, and leave this to be burned? It is the same as if all these traps were buckled to a man's belt, and he could not move over the rough country where our lines are cast without dragging them, — dragging his trap. He was a lucky fox that left his tail in the trap. The muskrat will gnaw his third leg off to be free. No wonder man has lost his elasticity. How often he is at a dead set! "Sir, if I may be so bold, what do you mean by a dead set?" If you are a seer, whenever you meet a man you will see all that he owns, ay, and much that he pretends to disown, behind him, even to his kitchen furniture and all the trumpery which he saves and will not burn, and he will appear to be harnessed to it and making what headway he can. I think that the man is at a dead set who has got through a knot-hole or gateway where his sledge load of furniture cannot follow him. I cannot but feel compassion when I hear some trig, compact-looking man, seemingly free, all girded and ready, speak of his "furniture," as whether it is insured or not. "But what shall I do with my furniture?" My gay butterfly is entangled in a spider's web then. Even those who seem for a long while not to have any, if you inquire more narrowly you will find have some stored in somebody's barn. I look upon England to-day as an old gentleman who is travelling with a great deal of baggage, trumpery which has accumulated from long housekeeping, which he has not the courage to burn; great trunk, little trunk, bandbox, and bundle. Throw away the first three at least. It would surpass the powers of a well man nowadays to take up his bed and walk, and I should certainly advise a sick one to lay down his bed and run. When I have met an immi-grant tottering under a bundle which contained his all, — looking like an enormous wen which had grown out of the nape of his neck, — I have pitied him, not because that was his all, but because he had all *that* to carry. If I have got to drag my trap, I will take care that it be a light one and do not nip me in a vital part. But perchance it would be wisest never to put one's paw into it.

I would observe, by the way, that it costs me nothing for curtains, for I have no gazers to shut out but the sun and moon, and I am willing that they should look in. The moon will not sour milk nor taint meat of mine, nor will the sun injure my furniture or fade my carpet; and if he is sometimes too warm a friend, I find it still better economy to retreat behind some curtain which nature has provided, than to add a single item to the details of housekeeping. A lady once offered me a mat, but as I had no room to spare within the house, nor time to spare within or without to shake it, I declined it, preferring to wipe my feet on the sod before my door. It is best to avoid the beginnings of evil.

Not long since I was present at the auction of a deacon's effects, for his life had not been ineffectual: —

"The evil that men do lives after them."

As usual, a great proportion was trumpery which had begun to accumulate in his father's day. Among the rest was a dried tapeworm. And now, after lying half a century in his garret and other dust holes, these things were not burned; instead of a *bonfire*, or purifying destruction of them, there was an *auction*, or increasing of them. The neighbors eagerly collected to view them, bought them all, and carefully transported them to their garrets and dust holes, to lie there till their estates are settled, when they will start again. When a man dies he kicks the dust.

The customs of some savage nations might, perchance, be profitably imitated by us, for they at least go through the semblance of casting their slough annually; they have the idea of the thing, whether they have the reality or not. Would it not be well if we were to celebrate such a "busk," or "feast of first fruits," as Bartram describes to have been the custom of the Mucclasse Indians? "When a town celebrates the busk," says he, "having previously provided themselves with new clothes, new pots, pans, and other household utensils and furniture, they collect all their worn out clothes and other despicable things, sweep and cleanse their houses, squares, and the whole town of their filth, which with all the remaining grain and other old provisions they cast together into one common heap, and consume it with fire. After having taken medicine, and fasted for three days, all the fire in the town is extinguished. During this fast they abstain from the gratification of every appetite and passion whatever. A general amnesty is proclaimed; all malefactors may return to their town."

"On the fourth morning, the high priest, by rubbing dry wood together, produces new fire in the public square, from whence every habitation in the town is supplied with the new and pure flame."

They then feast on the new corn and fruits, and dance and sing for three days, "and the four following days they receive visits and rejoice with their friends from neighboring towns who have in like manner purified and prepared themselves."

The Mexicans also practised a similar purification at the end of every fifty-two years, in the belief that it was time for the world to come to an end.

I have scarcely heard of a truer sacrament, that is, as the dictionary defines it, "outward and visible sign of an inward and spiritual grace," than this, and I have no doubt that they were originally inspired directly from Heaven to do thus, though they have no Biblical record of the revelation.

For more than five years I maintained myself thus solely by the labor of my hands, and I found that, by working about six weeks in a year, I could meet all the expenses of living. The whole of my winters, as well as most of my summers, I had free and clear for study. I have thoroughly tried school-keeping, and found that my expenses were in proportion, or rather out of proportion, to my income, for I was obliged to dress and train, not to say think and believe, accordingly, and I lost my time into the bargain. As I did not teach for the good of my fellow-men, but simply for a livelihood, this was a failure. I have tried trade; but I found that it would take ten years to get under way in that, and that then I should probably be on my way to the devil. I was actually afraid that I might by that time be doing what is called a good business. When formerly I was looking about to see what I could do for a living, some sad experience in conforming to the wishes of friends being fresh in my mind to tax my ingenuity, I thought often and seriously of picking huckleberries; that surely I could do, and its small profits might suffice, — for my greatest skill has been to want but little, — so little capital it required, so little distraction from my wonted moods, I foolishly thought. While my acquaintances went unhesitatingly into trade or the professions, I contemplated this occupation as most like theirs; ranging the hills all summer to pick the berries which came in my way, and thereafter carelessly dispose of them; so, to keep the flocks of Admetus. I also dreamed that I might gather the wild herbs, or carry evergreens to such villagers as loved to be reminded of the woods, even to the city, by hay-cart loads. But I have since learned that trade curses everything it handles; and though you trade in messages from heaven, the whole curse of trade attaches to the business.

As I preferred some things to others, and especially valued my freedom, as I could fare hard and yet succeed well, I did not wish to spend my time in earning rich carpets or other fine furniture, or delicate cookery, or a house in the Grecian or the Gothic style just yet. If there are any to whom it is no interruption to acquire these things, and who know how to use them when acquired, I relinquish to them the pursuit. Some are "industrious," and appear to love labor for its own sake, or perhaps because it keeps them out of worse mischief; to such I have at present nothing to say. Those who would not know what to do with more leisure than they now enjoy, I might advise to work twice as hard as they do, — work till they pay for themselves, and get their free papers. For myself I found that the occupation of a day-laborer was the most independent of any, especially as it required only thirty or forty days in a year to support one. The laborer's day ends with the going down of the sun, and he is then free to devote himself to his chosen pursuit, independent of his labor; but his employer, who speculates from month to month, has no respite from one end of the year to the other.

In short, I am convinced, both by faith and experience, that to maintain one's self on this earth is not a hardship but a pastime, if we will live simply and wisely; as the pursuits of the simpler nations are still the sports of the more artificial. It is not necessary that a man should earn his living by the sweat of his brow, unless he sweats easier than I do.

One young man of my acquaintance, who has inherited some acres, told me that he thought he should live as I did, *if he had the means.* I would not have any one adopt *my* mode of living on any account; for, beside that before he has fairly learned it I may have found out another for myself, I desire that there may be as many different persons in the world as possible; but I would have each one be very careful to find out and pursue *his own* way, and not his father's or his mother's or his neighbor's instead. The youth may build or plant or sail, only let him not be hindered from doing that which he tells me he would like to do. It is by a mathematical point only that we are wise, as the sailor or the fugitive slave keeps the polestar in his eye; but that is sufficient guidance for all our life. We may not arrive at our port within a calculable period, but we would preserve the true course.

Undoubtedly, in this case, what is true for one is truer still for a thousand, as a large house is not proportionally more expensive than a small one, since one roof may cover, one cellar underlie, and one wall separate several apartments. But for my part, I preferred the solitary dwelling. Moreover, it will commonly be cheaper to build the whole yourself than to convince another of the advantage of the common wall; and when you have done this, the common partition, to be much cheaper, must be a thin one, and that other may prove a bad neighbor, and also not keep his side in repair. The only coöperation which is commonly possible is exceedingly partial and superficial; and what little true coöperation there is, is as if it were not, being a harmony inaudible to men. If a man has faith, he will coöperate with equal faith everywhere; if he has not faith, he will continue to live like the rest of the world, whatever company he is joined to. To coöperate in the highest as well as the lowest sense, means *to get our living together*. I heard it

proposed lately that two young men should travel together over the world, the one without money, earning his means as he went, before the mast and behind
the plow, the other carrying a bill of exchange in his
pocket. It was easy to see that they could not long be
companions or coöperate, since one would not *operate*
at all. They would part at the first interesting crisis in
their adventures. Above all, as I have implied, the man
who goes alone can start to-day; but he who travels
with another must wait till that other is ready, and it
may be a long time before they get off.

But all this is very selfish, I have heard some of my
townsmen say. I confess that I have hitherto indulged
very little in philanthropic enterprises. I have made
some sacrifices to a sense of duty, and among others have
sacrificed this pleasure also. There are those who have
used all their arts to persuade me to undertake the support of some poor family in the town; and if I had nothing to do — for the devil finds employment for the idle
— I might try my hand at some such pastime as that.
However, when I have thought to indulge myself in this
respect, and lay their Heaven under an obligation by
maintaining certain poor persons in all respects as comfortably as I maintain myself, and have even ventured
so far as to make them the offer, they have one and all
unhesitatingly preferred to remain poor. While my
townsmen and women are devoted in so many ways to
the good of their fellows, I trust that one at least may be
spared to other and less humane pursuits. You must
have a genius for charity as well as for anything else. As

for Doing-good, that is one of the professions which are full. Moreover, I have tried it fairly, and, strange as it may seem, am satisfied that it does not agree with my constitution. Probably I should not consciously and deliberately forsake my particular calling to do the good which society demands of me, to save the universe from annihilation; and I believe that a like but infinitely greater steadfastness elsewhere is all that now preserves it. But I would not stand between any man and his genius; and to him who does this work, which I decline, with his whole heart and soul and life, I would say, Persevere, even if the world call it doing evil, as it is most likely they will.

I am far from supposing that my case is a peculiar one; no doubt many of my readers would make a similar defence. At doing something, — I will not engage that my neighbors shall pronounce it good, — I do not hesitate to say that I should be a capital fellow to hire; but what that is, it is for my employer to find out. What *good* I do, in the common sense of that word, must be aside from my main path, and for the most part wholly unintended. Men say, practically, Begin where you are and such as you are, without aiming mainly to become of more worth, and with kindness aforethought go about doing good. If I were to preach at all in this strain, I should say rather, Set about being good. As if the sun should stop when he had kindled his fires up to the splendor of a moon or a star of the sixth magnitude, and go about like a Robin Goodfellow, peeping in at every cottage window, inspiring lunatics, and tainting meats, and making darkness visible, instead of steadily increasing his genial heat and beneficence till he is of such brightness that no mortal can look him in the face, and then, and in the meanwhile too, going about the world in his own orbit, doing it good, or rather, as a truer philosophy has discovered, the world going about him getting good. When Phaëton, wishing to prove his heavenly birth by his beneficence, had the sun's chariot but one day, and drove out of the beaten track, he burned several blocks of houses in the lower streets of heaven, and scorched the surface of the earth, and dried up every spring, and made the great desert of Sahara, till at length Jupiter hurled him headlong to the earth with a thunderbolt, and the sun, through grief at his death, did not shine for a year.

There is no odor so bad as that which arises from goodness tainted. It is human, it is divine, carrion. If I knew for a certainty that a man was coming to my house with the conscious design of doing me good, I should run for my life, as from that dry and parching wind of the African deserts called the simoom, which fills the mouth and nose and ears and eyes with dust till you are suffocated, for fear that I should get some of his good done to me, — some of its virus mingled with my blood. No, — in this case I would rather suffer evil the natural way. A man is not a good *man* to me because he will feed me if I should be starving, or warm me if I should be freezing, or pull me out of a ditch if I should ever fall into one. I can find you a Newfoundland dog that will do as much. Philanthropy is not love for one's fellow-man in the broadest sense. Howard was no doubt an exceedingly kind and worthy man in his way, and has his reward; but, comparatively speaking, what are a hundred How-

ards to *us*, if their philanthropy do not help *us* in our
best estate, when we are most worthy to be helped? I
never heard of a philanthropic meeting in which it was
sincerely proposed to do any good to me, or the like
of me.

The Jesuits were quite balked by those Indians who,
being burned at the stake, suggested new modes of tor-
ture to their tormentors. Being superior to physical suffering, it sometimes chanced that they were superior to
any consolation which the missionaries could offer; and
the law to do as you would be done by fell with less per-
suasiveness on the ears of those who, for their part, did
not care how they were done by, who loved their enemies after a new fashion, and came very near freely
forgiving them all they did.

Be sure that you give the poor the aid they most need,
though it be your example which leaves them far behind.
If you give money, spend yourself with it, and do not
merely abandon it to them. We make curious mistakes
sometimes. Often the poor man is not so cold and hungry as he is dirty and ragged and gross. It is partly his
taste, and not merely his misfortune. If you give him
money, he will perhaps buy more rags with it. I was
wont to pity the clumsy Irish laborers who cut ice on the
pond, in such mean and ragged clothes, while I shivered
in my more tidy and somewhat more fashionable garments, till, one bitter cold day, one who had slipped into
the water came to my house to warm him, and I saw
him strip off three pairs of pants and two pairs of stock-
ings ere he got down to the skin, though they were dirty
and ragged enough, it is true, and that he could afford

to refuse the *extra* garments which I offered him, he had so many *intra* ones. This ducking was the very thing he needed. Then I began to pity myself, and I saw that it would be a greater charity to bestow on me a flannel shirt than a whole slop-shop on him. There are a thousand hacking at the branches of evil to one who is striking at the root, and it may be that he who bestows the largest amount of time and money on the needy is doing the most by his mode of life to produce that misery which he strives in vain to relieve. It is the pious slave-breeder devoting the proceeds of every tenth slave to buy a Sunday's liberty for the rest. Some show their kindness to the poor by employing them in their kitchens. Would they not be kinder if they employed themselves there? You boast of spending a tenth part of your income in charity; maybe you should spend the nine tenths so, and done with it. Society recovers only a tenth part of the property then. Is this owing to the generosity of him in whose possession it is found, or to the remissness of the officers of justice?

Philanthropy is almost the only virtue which is sufficiently appreciated by mankind. Nay, it is greatly overrated; and it is our selfishness which overrates it. A robust poor man, one sunny day here in Concord, praised a fellow-townsman to me, because, as he said, he was kind to the poor; meaning himself. The kind uncles and aunts of the race are more esteemed than its true spiritual fathers and mothers. I once heard a reverend lecturer on England, a man of learning and intelligence, after enumerating her scientific, literary, and political worthies, Shakespeare, Bacon, Crom-

well, Milton, Newton, and others, speak next of her
Christian heroes, whom, as if his profession required it
of him, he elevated to a place far above all the rest, as
the greatest of the great. They were Penn, Howard,
and Mrs. Fry. Every one must feel the falsehood and
cant of this. The last were not England's best men and
women; only, perhaps, her best philanthropists.

I would not subtract anything from the praise that
is due to philanthropy, but merely demand justice for
all who by their lives and works are a blessing to mankind. I do not value chiefly a man's uprightness and
benevolence, which are, as it were, his stem and leaves.
Those plants of whose greenness withered we make
herb tea for the sick serve but a humble use, and are
most employed by quacks. I want the flower and fruit
of a man; that some fragrance be wafted over from him
to me, and some ripeness flavor our intercourse. His
goodness must not be a partial and transitory act, but
a constant superfluity, which costs him nothing and of
which he is unconscious. This is a charity that hides a
multitude of sins. The philanthropist too often surrounds mankind with the remembrance of his own cast-
off griefs as an atmosphere, and calls it sympathy. We
should impart our courage, and not our despair, our
health and ease, and not our disease, and take care that
this does not spread by contagion. From what southern
plains comes up the voice of wailing? Under what latitudes reside the heathen to whom we would send light?
Who is that intemperate and brutal man whom we would
redeem? If anything ail a man, so that he does not per-
form his functions, if he have a pain in his bowels even,

— for that is the seat of sympathy, — he forthwith sets
about reforming — the world. Being a microcosm himself, he discovers — and it is a true discovery, and he
is the man to make it — that the world has been eating green apples; to his eyes, in fact, the globe itself is
a great green apple, which there is danger awful to think
of that the children of men will nibble before it is ripe;
and straightway his drastic philanthropy seeks out the
Esquimau and the Patagonian, and embraces the populous Indian and Chinese villages; and thus, by a few
years of philanthropic activity, the powers in the meanwhile using him for their own ends, no doubt, he cures
himself of his dyspepsia, the globe acquires a faint blush
on one or both of its cheeks, as if it were beginning to
be ripe, and life loses its crudity and is once more sweet
and wholesome to live. I never dreamed of any enor-
mity greater than I have committed. I never knew, and
never shall know, a worse man than myself.

I believe that what so saddens the reformer is not his
sympathy with his fellows in distress, but, though he be
the holiest son of God, is his private ail. Let this be
righted, let the spring come to him, the morning rise
over his couch, and he will forsake his generous companions without apology. My excuse for not lecturing
against the use of tobacco is, that I never chewed it,
that is a penalty which reformed tobacco-chewers have
to pay; though there are things enough I have chewed
which I could lecture against. If you should ever be
betrayed into any of these philanthropies, do not let your
left hand know what your right hand does, for it is not
worth knowing. Rescue the drowning and tie your shoe-

strings. Take your time, and set about some free labor.

Our manners have been corrupted by communication with the saints. Our hymn-books resound with a melodious cursing of God and enduring Him forever. One would say that even the prophets and redeemers had rather consoled the fears than confirmed the hopes of man. There is nowhere recorded a simple and irrepressible satisfaction with the gift of life, any memorable praise of God. All health and success does me good, however far off and withdrawn it may appear; all disease and failure helps to make me sad and does me evil, however much sympathy it may have with me or I with it. If, then, we would indeed restore mankind by truly Indian, botanic, magnetic, or natural means, let us first be as simple and well as Nature ourselves, dispel the clouds which hang over our own brows, and take up a little life into our pores. Do not stay to be an overseer of the poor, but endeavor to become one of the worthies of the world.

I read in the Gulistan, or Flower Garden, of Sheik Sadi of Shiraz, that "they asked a wise man, saying: Of the many celebrated trees which the Most High God has created lofty and umbrageous, they call none azad, or free, excepting the cypress, which bears no fruit; what mystery is there in this? He replied: Each has its appropriate produce, and appointed season, during the continuance of which it is fresh and blooming, and during their absence dry and withered; to neither of which states is the cypress exposed, being always flourishing; and of this nature are the azads, or religious independents. — Fix not thy heart on that which is transitory; for the Dijlah, or Tigris, will continue to flow through Bagdad after the race of caliphs is extinct: if thy hand has plenty, be liberal as the date tree; but if it affords nothing to give away, be an azad, or free man, like the cypress."

COMPLEMENTAL VERSES

THE PRETENSIONS OF POVERTY

Thou dost presume too much, poor needy wretch,
To claim a station in the firmament
Because thy humble cottage, or thy tub,
Nurses some lazy or pedantic virtue
In the cheap sunshine or by shady springs,
With roots and pot-herbs; where thy right hand,
Tearing those humane passions from the mind,
Upon whose stocks fair blooming virtues flourish,
Degradeth nature, and benumbeth sense,
And, Gorgon-like, turns active men to stone.
We not require the dull society
Of your necessitated temperance,
Or that unnatural stupidity
That knows nor joy nor sorrow; nor your forc'd
Falsely exalted passive fortitude
Above the active. This low abject brood,
That fix their seats in mediocrity,
Become your servile minds; but we advance
Such virtues only as admit excess,
Brave, bounteous acts, regal magnificence,
All-seeing prudence, magnanimity
That knows no bound, and that heroic virtue
For which antiquity hath left no name,
But patterns only, such as Hercules,
Achilles, Theseus. Back to thy loath'd cell;
And when thou seest the new enlightened sphere,
Study to know but what those worthies were.

T. CAREW

WHERE I LIVED, AND WHAT I LIVED FOR

At a certain season of our life we are accustomed to consider every spot as the possible site of a house. I have thus surveyed the country on every side within a dozen miles of where I live. In imagination I have bought all the farms in succession, for all were to be bought, and I knew their price. I walked over each farmer's premises, tasted his wild apples, discoursed on husbandry with him, took his farm at his price, at any price, mortgaging it to him in my mind; even put a higher price on it, — took everything but a deed of it, — took his word for his deed, for I dearly love to talk, — cultivated it, and him too to some extent, I trust, and withdrew when I had enjoyed it long enough, leaving him to carry it on. This experience entitled me to be regarded as a sort of real-estate broker by my friends. Wherever I sat, there I might live, and the landscape radiated from me accordingly. What is a house but a *sedes*, a seat? — better if a country seat. I discovered many a site for a house not likely to be soon improved, which some might have thought too far from the village, but to my eyes the village was too far from it. Well, there I might live, I said; and there I did live, for an hour, a summer and a winter life; saw how I could let the years run off, buffet the

winter through, and see the spring come in. The future
inhabitants of this region, wherever they may place
their houses, may be sure that they have been anticipated.
An afternoon sufficed to lay out the land into orchard,
wood-lot, and pasture, and to decide what fine oaks or
pines should be left to stand before the door, and whence
each blasted tree could be seen to the best advantage;
and then I let it lie, fallow perchance, for a man is
rich in proportion to the number of things which he can
afford to let alone.

My imagination carried me so far that I even had the
refusal of several farms, — the refusal was all I wanted,
— but I never got my fingers burned by actual possession. The nearest that I came to actual possession was
when I bought the Hollowell place, and had begun to
sort my seeds, and collected materials with which to
make a wheelbarrow to carry it on or off with; but before the owner gave me a deed of it, his wife — every
man has such a wife — changed her mind and wished
to keep it, and he offered me ten dollars to release him.
Now, to speak the truth, I had but ten cents in the world,
and it surpassed my arithmetic to tell, if I was that man
who had ten cents, or who had a farm, or ten dollars, or
all together. However, I let him keep the ten dollars and
the farm too, for I had carried it far enough; or rather,
to be generous, I sold him the farm for just what I gave
for it, and, as he was not a rich man, made him a present of ten dollars, and still had my ten cents, and seeds,
and materials for a wheelbarrow left. I found thus that
I had been a rich man without any damage to my poverty. But I retained the landscape, and I have since

HUMOR YAYA
LOOY.

annually carried off what it yielded without a wheelbarrow. With respect to landscapes, —

> "I am monarch of all I *survey*,
> My right there is none to dispute."

I have frequently seen a poet withdraw, having enjoyed the most valuable part of a farm, while the crusty
farmer supposed that he had got a few wild apples only.
Why, the owner does not know it for many years when a
poet has put his farm in rhyme, the most admirable kind
of invisible fence, has fairly impounded it, milked it,
skimmed it, and got all the cream, and left the farmer
only the skimmed milk.

The real attractions of the Hollowell farm, to me,
were: its complete retirement, being about two miles
from the village, half a mile from the nearest neighbor,
and separated from the highway by a broad field; its
bounding on the river, which the owner said protected
it by its fogs from frosts in the spring, though that was
nothing to me; the gray color and ruinous state of the
house and barn, and the dilapidated fences, which put
such an interval between me and the last occupant; the
hollow and lichen-covered apple trees, gnawed by rabbits, showing what kind of neighbors I should have; but
above all, the recollection I had of it from my earliest
voyages up the river, when the house was concealed behind a dense grove of red maples, through which I heard
the house-dog bark. I was in haste to buy it, before the
proprietor finished getting out some rocks, cutting down
the hollow apple trees, and grubbing up some young
birches which had sprung up in the pasture, or, in short,
had made any more of his improvements. To enjoy

these advantages I was ready to carry it on; like Atlas, to take the world on my shoulders, — I never heard what compensation he received for that, — and do all those things which had no other motive or excuse but that I might pay for it and be unmolested in my possession of it; for I knew all the while that it would yield the most abundant crop of the kind I wanted, if I could only afford to let it alone. But it turned out as I have said.

All that I could say, then, with respect to farming on a large scale — I have always cultivated a garden — was, that I had had my seeds ready. Many think that seeds improve with age. I have no doubt that time discriminates between the good and the bad; and when at last I shall plant, I shall be less likely to be disappointed. But I would say to my fellows, once for all, As long as possible live free and uncommitted. It makes but little difference whether you are committed to a farm or the county jail.

Old Cato, whose "De Re Rusticâ" is my "Cultivator," says, — and the only translation I have seen makes sheer nonsense of the passage, — "When you think of getting a farm turn it thus in your mind, not to buy greedily; nor spare your pains to look at it, and do not think it enough to go round it once. The oftener you go there the more it will please you, if it is good." I think I shall not buy greedily, but go round and round it as long as I live, and be buried in it first, that it may please me the more at last.

The present was my next experiment of this kind, which I purpose to describe more at length, for con-

venience putting the experience of two years into one
As I have said, I do not propose to write an ode to
dejection, but to brag as lustily as chanticleer in the
morning, standing on his roost, if only to wake my
neighbors up.

When first I took up my abode in the woods, that is,
began to spend my nights as well as days there, which,
by accident, was on Independence Day, or the Fourth
of July, 1845, my house was not finished for winter, but
was merely a defence against the rain, without plastering
or chimney, the walls being of rough, weather-stained
boards, with wide chinks, which made it cool at night.
The upright white hewn studs and freshly planed door
and window casings gave it a clean and airy look, especially in the morning, when its timbers were saturated
with dew, so that I fancied that by noon some sweet gum
would exude from them. To my imagination it retained
throughout the day more or less of this auroral character, reminding me of a certain house on a mountain
which I had visited a year before. This was an airy and
unplastered cabin, fit to entertain a travelling god, and
where a goddess might trail her garments. The winds
which passed over my dwelling were such as sweep over
the ridges of mountains, bearing the broken strains, or
celestial parts only, of terrestrial music. The morning
wind forever blows, the poem of creation is uninterrupted; but few are the ears that hear it. Olympus is
but the outside of the earth everywhere.

The only house I had been the owner of before, if I
except a boat, was a tent, which I used occasionally
when making excursions in the summer, and this is still

rolled up in my garret; but the boat, after passing from hand to hand, has gone down the stream of time. With this more substantial shelter about me, I had made some progress toward settling in the world. This frame, so slightly clad, was a sort of crystallization around me, and reacted on the builder. It was suggestive somewhat as a picture in outlines. I did not need to go outdoors to take the air, for the atmosphere within had lost none of its freshness. It was not so much within-doors as behind a door where I sat, even in the rainiest weather. The Harivansa says, "An abode without birds is like a meat without seasoning." Such was not my abode, for I found myself suddenly neighbor to the birds; not by having imprisoned one, but having caged myself near them. I was not only nearer to some of those which commonly frequent the garden and the orchard, but to those wilder and more thrilling songsters of the forest which never, or rarely, serenade a villager, — the wood thrush, the veery, the scarlet tanager, the field sparrow, the whip-poor-will, and many others.

I was seated by the shore of a small pond, about a mile and a half south of the village of Concord and somewhat higher than it, in the midst of an extensive wood between that town and Lincoln, and about two miles south of that our only field known to fame, Concord Battle Ground; but I was so low in the woods that the opposite shore, half a mile off, like the rest, covered with wood, was my most distant horizon. For the first week, whenever I looked out on the pond it impressed me like a tarn high up on the side of a mountain, its bottom far above the surface of other lakes, and, as the

sun arose, I saw it throwing off its nightly clothing of
mist, and here and there, by degrees, its soft ripples or
its smooth reflecting surface was revealed, while the
mists, like ghosts, were stealthily withdrawing in every
direction into the woods, as at the breaking up of some
nocturnal conventicle. The very dew seemed to hang
upon the trees later into the day than usual, as on the
sides of mountains.

This small lake was of most value as a neighbor in
the intervals of a gentle rain-storm in August, when,
both air and water being perfectly still, but the sky overcast, mid-afternoon had all the serenity of evening, and
the wood thrush sang around, and was heard from shore
to shore. A lake like this is never smoother than at such
a time; and the clear portion of the air above it being
shallow and darkened by clouds, the water, full of light
and reflections, becomes a lower heaven itself so much
the more important. From a hill-top near by, where the
wood had been recently cut off, there was a pleasing
vista southward across the pond, through a wide inden-
tation in the hills which form the shore there, where
their opposite sides sloping toward each other suggested
a stream flowing out in that direction through a wooded
valley, but stream there was none. That way I looked
between and over the near green hills to some distant
and higher ones in the horizon, tinged with blue. Indeed, by standing on tiptoe I could catch a glimpse
of some of the peaks of the still bluer and more distant mountain ranges in the northwest, those true-blue
coins from heaven's own mint, and also of some portion
of the village. But in other directions, even from this

point, I could not see over or beyond the woods which surrounded me. It is well to have some water in your neighborhood, to give buoyancy to and float the earth. One value even of the smallest well is, that when you look into it you see that earth is not continent but insular. This is as important as that it keeps butter cool. When I looked across the pond from this peak toward the Sudbury meadows, which in time of flood I distinguished elevated perhaps by a mirage in their seething valley, like a coin in a basin, all the earth beyond the pond appeared like a thin crust insulated and floated even by this small sheet of intervening water, and I was reminded that this on which I dwelt was but *dry land*.

Though the view from my door was still more contracted, I did not feel crowded or confined in the least. There was pasture enough for my imagination. The low shrub oak plateau to which the opposite shore arose stretched away toward the prairies of the West and the steppes of Tartary, affording ample room for all the roving families of men. "There are none happy in the world but beings who enjoy freely a vast horizon," — said Damodara, when his herds required new and larger pastures.

Both place and time were changed, and I dwelt nearer to those parts of the universe and to those eras in history which had most attracted me. Where I lived was as far off as many a region viewed nightly by astronomers. We are wont to imagine rare and delectable places in some remote and more celestial corner of the system, behind the constellation of Cassiopeia's Chair, far from noise and disturbance. I discovered that my

house actually had its site in such a withdrawn, but forever new and unprofaned, part of the universe. If it
were worth the while to settle in those parts near to the
Pleiades or the Hyades, to Aldebaran or Altair, then
I was really there, or at an equal remoteness from the
life which I had left behind, dwindled and twinkling with
as fine a ray to my nearest neighbor, and to be seen only
in moonless nights by him. Such was that part of creation where I had squatted; —

> "There was a shepherd that did live,
>   And held his thoughts as high
> As were the mounts whereon his flocks
>   Did hourly feed him by."

What should we think of the shepherd's life if his flocks
always wandered to higher pastures than his thoughts?

Every morning was a cheerful invitation to make
my life of equal simplicity, and I may say innocence,
with Nature herself. I have been as sincere a worshipper
of Aurora as the Greeks. I got up early and bathed in
the pond; that was a religious exercise, and one of the
best things which I did. They say that characters were
engraven on the bathing tub of King Tching-thang to
this effect: "Renew thyself completely each day; do
it again, and again, and forever again." I can understand that. Morning brings back the heroic ages. I was
as much affected by the faint hum of a mosquito making its invisible and unimaginable tour through my
apartment at earliest dawn, when I was sitting with door
and windows open, as I could be by any trumpet that
ever sang of fame. It was Homer's requiem; itself an
Iliad and Odyssey in the air, singing its own wrath and

wanderings. There was something cosmical about it; a standing advertisement, till forbidden, of the everlasting vigor and fertility of the world. [The morning, which is the most memorable season of the day, is the awakening hour.] Then there is least somnolence in us; and for an hour, at least, some part of us awakes which slumbers all the rest of the day and night. Little is to be expected of that day, if it can be called a day, to which we are not awakened by our Genius, but by the mechanical nudgings of some servitor, are not awakened by our own newly acquired force and aspirations from within, accompanied by the undulations of celestial music, instead of factory bells, and a fragrance filling the air — to a higher life than we fell asleep from; and thus the darkness bear its fruit, and prove itself to be good, no less than the light. That man who does not believe that each day contains an earlier, more sacred, and auroral hour than he has yet profaned, has despaired of life, and is pursuing a descending and darkening way. After a partial cessation of his sensuous life, the soul of man, or its organs rather, are reinvigorated each day, and his Genius tries again what noble life it can make. All memorable events, I should say, transpire in morning time and in a morning atmosphere. The Vedas say, " All intelligences awake with the morning." Poetry and art, and the fairest and most memorable of the actions of men, date from such an hour. All poets and heroes, like Memnon, are the children of Aurora, and emit their music at sunrise. To him whose elastic and vigorous thought keeps pace with the sun, the day is a perpetual morning. It matters not what the clocks say or the attitudes and labors of men. Morning is when I am awake and there is a dawn in me. Moral reform is the effort to throw off sleep. Why is it that men give so poor an account of their day if they have not been slumbering? They are not such poor calculators. If they had not been overcome with drowsiness, they would have performed something. The millions are awake enough for physical labor; but only one in a million is awake enough for effective intellectual exertion, only one in a hundred millions to a poetic or divine life. To be awake is to be alive. I have never yet met a man who was quite awake. How could I have looked him in the face?

We must learn to reawaken and keep ourselves awake, not by mechanical aids, but by an infinite expectation of the dawn, which does not forsake us in our soundest sleep. I know of no more encouraging fact than the unquestionable ability of man to elevate his life by a conscious endeavor. It is something to be able to paint a particular picture, or to carve a statue, and so to make a few objects beautiful; but it is far more glorious to carve and paint the very atmosphere and medium through which we look, which morally we can do. To affect the quality of the day, that is the highest of arts. Every man is tasked to make his life, even in its details, worthy of the contemplation of his most elevated and critical hour. If we refused, or rather used up, such paltry information as we get, the oracles would distinctly inform us how this might be done.

I went to the woods because I wished to live deliberately, to front only the essential facts of life, and see

His Purpose.

if I could not learn what it had to teach, and not, when I came to die, discover that I had not lived. I did not wish to live what was not life, living is so dear; nor did I wish to practise resignation, unless it was quite necessary. I wanted to live deep and suck out all the marrow of life, to live so sturdily and Spartan-like as to put to rout all that was not life, to cut a broad swath and shave close, to drive life into a corner, and reduce it to its lowest terms, and, if it proved to be mean, why then to get the whole and genuine meanness of it, and publish its meanness to the world; or if it were sublime, to know it by experience, and be able to give a true account of it in my next excursion. For most men, it appears to me, are in a strange uncertainty about it, whether it is of the devil or of God, and have *somewhat hastily* concluded that it is the chief end of man here to "glorify God and enjoy him forever."

Still we live meanly, like ants; though the fable tells us that we were long ago changed into men; like pygmies we fight with cranes; it is error upon error, and clout upon clout, and our best virtue has for its occasion a superfluous and evitable wretchedness. Our life is frittered away by detail. An honest man has hardly need to count more than his ten fingers, or in extreme cases he may add his ten toes, and lump the rest. Simplicity, simplicity, simplicity! I say, let your affairs be as two or three, and not a hundred or a thousand; instead of a million count half a dozen, and keep your accounts on your thumb-nail. In the midst of this chopping sea of civilized life, such are the clouds and storms and quicksands and thousand-and-one items to be allowed for, that a man has to live, if he would not founder and go to the bottom and not make his port at all, by dead reckoning, and he must be a great calculator indeed who succeeds. Simplify, simplify. Instead of three meals a day, if it be necessary eat but one; instead of a hundred dishes, five; and reduce other things in proportion. Our life is like a German Confederacy, made up of petty states, with its boundary forever fluctuating, so that even a German cannot tell you how it is bounded at any moment. The nation itself, with all its so-called internal improvements, which, by the way are all external and superficial, is just such an unwieldy and overgrown establishment, cluttered with furniture and tripped up by its own traps, ruined by luxury and heedless expense, by want of calculation and a worthy aim, as the million households in the land; and the only cure for it, as for them, is in a rigid economy, a stern and more than Spartan simplicity of life and elevation of purpose. It lives too fast. Men think that it is essential that the *Nation* have commerce, and export ice, and talk through a telegraph, and ride thirty miles an hour, without a doubt, whether *they* do or not; but whether we should live like baboons or like men, is a little uncertain. If we do not get out sleepers, and forge rails, and devote days and nights to the work, but go to tinkering upon our *lives* to improve *them*, who will build railroads? And if railroads are not built, how shall we get to heaven in season? But if we stay at home and mind our business, who will want railroads? We do not ride on the railroad; it rides upon us. Did you ever think what those sleepers are that underlie the railroad? Each one is a man, an

Irishman, or a Yankee man. The rails are laid on them,
and they are covered with sand, and the cars run
smoothly over them. They are sound sleepers, I assure
you. And every few years a new lot is laid down and
run over; so that, if some have the pleasure of riding
on a rail, others have the misfortune to be ridden upon.
And when they run over a man that is walking in his
sleep, a supernumerary sleeper in the wrong position,
and wake him up, they suddenly stop the cars, and
make a hue and cry about it, as if this were an exception. I am glad to know that it takes a gang of men for
every five miles to keep the sleepers down and level in
their beds as it is, for this is a sign that they may some-
time get up again.

Why should we live with such hurry and waste of life?
We are determined to be starved before we are hungry.
Men say that a stitch in time saves nine, and so they
take a thousand stitches to-day to save nine to-morrow.
As for *work*, we have n't any of any consequence. We
have the Saint Vitus' dance, and cannot possibly keep
our heads still. If I should only give a few pulls at the
parish bell-rope, as for a fire, that is, without setting the
bell, there is hardly a man on his farm in the outskirts
of Concord, notwithstanding that press of engagements
which was his excuse so many times this morning, nor
a boy, nor a woman, I might almost say, but would forsake all and follow that sound, not mainly to save property from the flames, but, if we will confess the truth,
much more to see it burn, since burn it must, and we,
be it known, did not set it on fire, — or to see it put out,
and have a hand in it, if that is done as handsomely;

yes, even if it were the parish church itself. Hardly a man takes a half-hour's nap after dinner, but when he wakes he holds up his head and asks, "What's the news?" as if the rest of mankind had stood his sentinels. Some give directions to be waked every half-hour, doubtless for no other purpose; and then, to pay for it, they tell what they have dreamed. After a night's sleep the news is as indispensable as the breakfast. "Pray tell me anything new that has happened to a man anywhere on this globe," — and he reads it over his coffee and rolls, that a man has had his eyes gouged out this morning on the Wachito River; never dreaming the while that he lives in the dark unfathomed mammoth cave of this world, and has but the rudiment of an eye himself.

Could He? For my part, I could easily do without the post-office. I think that there are very few important communications made through it. To speak critically, I never received more than one or two letters in my life — I wrote this some years ago — that were worth the postage. The penny-post is, commonly, an institution through which you seriously offer a man that penny for his thoughts which is so often safely offered in jest. And I am sure that I never read any memorable news in a newspaper. *True?* If we read of one man robbed, or murdered, or killed by accident, or one house burned, or one vessel wrecked, or one steamboat blown up, or one cow run over on the Western Railroad, or one mad dog killed, or one lot of grasshoppers in the winter, — we never need read of another. One is enough. If you are acquainted with the principle, what do you care for a myriad instances and applications? To a philosopher all *news*, as it is called, is gossip, and they who edit and read it are old women over their tea. Yet not a few are greedy after this gossip. There was such a rush, as I hear, the other day at one of the offices to learn the foreign news by the last arrival, that several large squares of plate glass belonging to the establishment were broken by the pressure, — news which I seriously think a ready wit might write a twelvemonth, or twelve years, beforehand with sufficient accuracy. As for Spain, for instance, if you know how to throw in Don Carlos and the Infanta, and Don Pedro and Seville and Granada, from time to time in the right proportions, — they may have changed the names a little since I saw the papers, — and serve up a bull-fight when other entertainments fail, it will be true to the letter, and give us as good an idea of the exact state or ruin of things in Spain as the most succinct and lucid reports under this head in the newspapers: and as for England, almost the last significant scrap of news from that quarter was the revolution of 1649; and if you have learned the history of her crops for an average year, you never need attend to that thing again, unless your speculations are of a merely pecuniary character. If one may judge who rarely looks into the newspapers, nothing new does ever happen in foreign parts, a French revolution not excepted.

What news! how much more important to know what that is which was never old! " Kieou-he-yu (great dignitary of the state of Wei) sent a man to Khoung-tseu to know his news. Khoung-tseu caused the messenger to be seated near him, and questioned him in these terms:

What is your master doing? The messenger answered with respect: My master desires to diminish the number of his faults, but he cannot come to the end of them. The messenger being gone, the philosopher remarked: What a worthy messenger! What a worthy messenger!" The preacher, instead of vexing the ears of drowsy farmers on their day of rest at the end of the week, — for Sunday is the fit conclusion of an ill-spent week, and not the fresh and brave beginning of a new one, — with this one other draggle-tail of a sermon, should shout with thundering voice, " Pause! Avast! Why so seeming fast, but deadly slow?"

Shams and delusions are esteemed for soundest truths, while reality is fabulous. If men would steadily observe realities only, and not allow themselves to be deluded, life, to compare it with such things as we know, would be like a fairy tale and the Arabian Nights' Entertainments. If we respected only what is inevitable and has a right to be, music and poetry would resound along the streets. When we are unhurried and wise, we perceive that only great and worthy things have any permanent and absolute existence, that petty fears and petty pleasures are but the shadow of the reality. This is always exhilarating and sublime. By closing the eyes and slumbering, and consenting to be deceived by shows, men establish and confirm their daily life of routine and habit everywhere, which still is built on purely illusory foundations. Children, who play life, discern its true law and relations more clearly than men, who fail to live it worthily, but who think that they are wiser by experience, that is, by failure. I have read in a Hindoo book, that "there was a king's son, who, being expelled in infancy from his native city, was brought up by a forester, and, growing up to maturity in that state, imagined himself to belong to the barbarous race with which he lived. One of his father's ministers having discovered him, revealed to him what he was, and the misconception of his character was removed, and he knew himself to be a prince. So soul," continues the Hindoo philosopher, "from the circumstances in which it is placed, mistakes its own character, until the truth is revealed to it by some holy teacher, and then it knows itself to be *Brahme*." I perceive that we inhabitants of New England live this mean life that we do because our vision does not penetrate the surface of things. We think that that *is* which *appears* to be. If a man should walk through this town and see only the reality, where, think you, would the "Mill-dam" go to? If he should give us an account of the realities he beheld there, we should not recognize the place in his description. Look at a meeting-house, or a court-house, or a jail, or a shop, or a dwelling-house, and say what that thing really is before a true gaze, and they would all go to pieces in your account of them. Men esteem truth remote, in the outskirts of the system, behind the farthest star, before Adam and after the last man. In eternity there is indeed something true and sublime. But all these times and places and occasions are now and here. God himself culminates in the present moment, and will never be more divine in the lapse of all the ages. And we are enabled to apprehend at all what is sublime and noble only by the perpetual instilling and drenching of the reality that surrounds us. The universe constantly and obediently answers to our conceptions; whether we travel fast or slow, the track is laid for us. Let us spend our lives in conceiving then. The poet or the artist never yet had so fair and noble a design but some of his posterity at least could accomplish it.

Let us spend one day as deliberately as Nature, and not be thrown off the track by every nutshell and mosquito's wing that falls on the rails. Let us rise early and fast, or break fast, gently and without perturbation; let company come and let company go, let the bells ring and the children cry, — determined to make a day of it. Why should we knock under and go with the stream? Let us not be upset and overwhelmed in that terrible rapid and whirlpool called a dinner, situated in the meridian shallows. Weather this danger and you are safe, for the rest of the way is down hill. With unrelaxed nerves, with morning vigor, sail by it, looking another way, tied to the mast like Ulysses. If the engine whistles, let it whistle till it is hoarse for its pains. If the bell rings, why should we run? We will consider what kind of music they are like. Let us settle ourselves, and work and wedge our feet downward through the mud and slush of opinion, and prejudice, and tradition, and delusion, and appearance, that alluvion which covers the globe, through Paris and London, through New York and Boston and Concord, through Church and State, through poetry and philosophy and religion, till we come to a hard bottom and rocks in place, which we can call *reality*, and say, This is, and no mistake; and then begin, having a *point d'appui*, below freshet and frost and fire, a place where you might found a wall or a state, or set a lamp-post safely, or perhaps a gauge, not a Nilometer, but a Realometer, that future ages might know how deep a freshet of shams and appearances had gathered from time to time. If you stand right fronting and face to face to a fact, you will see the sun glimmer on both its surfaces, as if it were a cimeter, and feel its sweet edge dividing you through the heart and marrow, and so you will happily conclude your mortal career. Be it life or death, we crave only reality. If we are really dying, let us hear the rattle in our throats and feel cold in the extremities; if we are alive, let us go about our business.

Time is but the stream I go a-fishing in. I drink at it; but while I drink I see the sandy bottom and detect how shallow it is. Its thin current slides away, but eternity remains. I would drink deeper; fish in the sky, whose bottom is pebbly with stars. I cannot count one. I know not the first letter of the alphabet. I have always been regretting that I was not as wise as the day I was born. The intellect is a cleaver; it discerns and rifts its way into the secret of things. I do not wish to be any more busy with my hands than is necessary. My head is hands and feet. I feel all my best faculties concentrated in it. My instinct tells me that my head is an organ for burrowing, as some creatures use their snout and fore paws, and with it I would mine and burrow my way through these hills. I think that the richest vein is somewhere hereabouts; so by the divining-rod and thin rising vapors I judge; and here I will begin to mine.

III

READING

WITH a little more deliberation in the choice of their pursuits, all men would perhaps become essentially students and observers, for certainly their nature and destiny are interesting to all alike. In accumulating property for ourselves or our posterity, in founding a family or a state, or acquiring fame even, we are mortal; but in dealing with truth we are immortal, and need fear no change nor accident. The oldest Egyptian or Hindoo philosopher raised a corner of the veil from the statue of the divinity; and still the trembling robe remains raised, and I gaze upon as fresh a glory as he did, since it was I in him that was then so bold, and it is he in me that now reviews the vision. No dust has settled on that robe; no time has elapsed since that divinity was revealed. That time which we really improve, or which is improvable, is neither past, present, nor future.

My residence was more favorable, not only to thought, but to serious reading, than a university; and though I was beyond the range of the ordinary circulating library, I had more than ever come within the influence of those books which circulate round the world, whose sentences were first written on bark, and are now merely copied from time to time on to linen paper. Says the poet Mîr

Camar Uddin Mast, "Being seated, to run through the region of the spiritual world; I have had this advantage in books. To be intoxicated by a single glass of wine; I have experienced this pleasure when I have drunk the liquor of the esoteric doctrines." I kept Homer's Iliad on my table through the summer, though I looked at his page only now and then. Incessant labor with my hands, at first, for I had my house to finish and my beans to hoe at the same time, made more study impossible. Yet I sustained myself by the prospect of such reading in future. I read one or two shallow books of travel in the intervals of my work, till that employment made me ashamed of myself, and I asked where it was then that *I* lived.

The student may read Homer or Æschylus in the Greek without danger of dissipation or luxuriousness, for it implies that he in some measure emulate their heroes, and consecrate morning hours to their pages. The heroic books, even if printed in the character of our mother tongue, will always be in a language dead to degenerate times; and we must laboriously seek the meaning of each word and line, conjecturing a larger sense than common use permits out of what wisdom and valor and generosity we have. The modern cheap and fertile press, with all its translations, has done little to bring us nearer to the heroic writers of antiquity. They seem as solitary, and the letter in which they are printed as rare and curious, as ever. It is worth the expense of youthful days and costly hours, if you learn only some words of an ancient language, which are raised out of the trivialness of the street, to be perpetual suggestions and provocations. It is not in vain that the farmer remembers and repeats the few Latin words which he has heard. Men sometimes speak as if the study of the classics would at length make way for more modern and practical studies; but the adventurous student will always study classics, in whatever language they may be written and however ancient they may be. For what are the classics but the noblest recorded thoughts of man? They are the only oracles which are not decayed, and there are such answers to the most modern inquiry in them as Delphi and Dodona never gave. We might as well omit to study Nature because she is old. To read well, that is, to read true books in a true spirit, is a noble exercise, and one that will task the reader more than any exercise which the customs of the day esteem. It requires a training such as the athletes underwent, the steady intention almost of the whole life to this object. Books must be read as deliberately and reservedly as they were written. It is not enough even to be able to speak the language of that nation by which they are written, for there is a memorable interval between the spoken and the written language, the language heard and the language read. The one is commonly transitory, a sound, a tongue, a dialect merely, almost brutish, and we learn it unconsciously, like the brutes, of our mothers. The other is the maturity and experience of that; if that is our mother tongue, this is our father tongue, a reserved and select expression, too significant to be heard by the ear, which we must be born again in order to speak. The crowds of men who merely *spoke* the Greek and Latin tongues in the Mid-

dle Ages were not entitled by the accident of birth to
read the works of genius written in those languages;
for these were not written in that Greek or Latin which
they knew, but in the select language of literature. They
had not learned the nobler dialects of Greece and Rome,
but the very materials on which they were written were
waste paper to them, and they prized instead a cheap
contemporary literature. But when the several nations
of Europe had acquired distinct though rude written
languages of their own, sufficient for the purposes of
their rising literatures, then first learning revived, and
scholars were enabled to discern from that remoteness
the treasures of antiquity. What the Roman and Grecian
multitude could not *hear*, after the lapse of ages a few
scholars *read*, and a few scholars only are still reading it.

However much we may admire the orator's occasional
bursts of eloquence, the noblest written words are commonly as far behind or above the fleeting spoken language as the firmament with its stars is behind the
clouds. *There* are the stars, and they who can may read
them. The astronomers forever comment on and observe them. They are not exhalations like our daily
colloquies and vaporous breath. What is called eloquence in the forum is commonly found to be rhetoric
in the study. The orator yields to the inspiration of a
transient occasion, and speaks to the mob before him,
to those who can *hear* him; but the writer, whose more
equable life is his occasion, and who would be distracted
by the event and the crowd which inspire the orator,
speaks to the intellect and heart of mankind, to all in
any age who can *understand* him.

No wonder that Alexander carried the Iliad with him on his expeditions in a precious casket. A written word is the choicest of relics. It is something at once more intimate with us and more universal than any other work of art. It is the work of art nearest to life itself. It may be translated into every language, and not only be read but actually breathed from all human lips; — not be represented on canvas or in marble only, but be carved out of the breath of life itself. The symbol of an ancient man's thought becomes a modern man's speech. Two thousand summers have imparted to the monuments of Grecian literature, as to her marbles, only a maturer golden and autumnal tint, for they have carried their own serene and celestial atmosphere into all lands to protect them against the corrosion of time. Books are the treasured wealth of the world and the fit inheritance of generations and nations. Books, the oldest and the best, stand naturally and rightfully on the shelves of every cottage. They have no cause of their own to plead, but while they enlighten and sustain the reader his common sense will not refuse them. Their authors are a natural and irresistible aristocracy in every society, and, more than kings or emperors, exert an influence on mankind. When the illiterate and perhaps scornful trader has earned by enterprise and industry his coveted leisure and independence, and is admitted to the circles of wealth and fashion, he turns inevitably at last to those still higher but yet inaccessible circles of intellect and genius, and is sensible only of the imperfection of his culture and the vanity and insufficiency of all his riches, and further proves his good

sense by the pains which he takes to secure for his children that intellectual culture whose want he so keenly
feels; and thus it is that he becomes the founder of a
family.

Those who have not learned to read the ancient
classics in the language in which they were written must
have a very imperfect knowledge of the history of the
human race; for it is remarkable that no transcript of
them has ever been made into any modern tongue,
unless our civilization itself may be regarded as such a
transcript. Homer has never yet been printed in English, nor Æschylus, nor Virgil even, — works as refined,
as solidly done, and as beautiful almost as the morning
itself; for later writers, say what we will of their genius,
have rarely, if ever, equalled the elaborate beauty and
finish and the lifelong and heroic literary labors of the
ancients. They only talk of forgetting them who never
knew them. It will be soon enough to forget them when
we have the learning and the genius which will enable
us to attend to and appreciate them. That age will be
rich indeed when those relics which we call Classics,
and the still older and more than classic but even less
known Scriptures of the nations, shall have still further
accumulated, when the Vaticans shall be filled with
Vedas and Zendavestas and Bibles, with Homers and
Dantes and Shakespeares, and all the centuries to come
shall have successively deposited their trophies in the
forum of the world. By such a pile we may hope to
scale heaven at last.

The works of the great poets have never yet been
read by mankind, for only great poets can read them.

They have only been read as the multitude read the stars, at most astrologically, not astronomically. Most men have learned to read to serve a paltry convenience, as they have learned to cipher in order to keep accounts and not be cheated in trade; but of reading as a noble intellectual exercise they know little or nothing; yet this only is reading, in a high sense, not that which lulls us as a luxury and suffers the nobler faculties to sleep the while, but what we have to stand on tip-toe to read and devote our most alert and wakeful hours to.

I think that having learned our letters we should read the best that is in literature, and not be forever repeating our a-b-abs, and words of one syllable, in the fourth or fifth classes, sitting on the lowest and foremost form all our lives. Most men are satisfied if they read or hear read, and perchance have been convicted by the wisdom of one good book, the Bible, and for the rest of their lives vegetate and dissipate their faculties in what is called easy reading. There is a work in several volumes in our Circulating Library entitled " Little Reading," which I thought referred to a town of that name which I had not been to. There are those who, like cormorants and ostriches, can digest all sorts of this, even after the fullest dinner of meats and vegetables, for they suffer nothing to be wasted. If others are the machines to provide this provender, they are the machines to read it. They read the nine thousandth tale about Zebulon and Sophronia, and how they loved as none had ever loved before, and neither did the course of their true love run smooth,— at any rate, how it did run and stumble, and get up again and go on! how some poor unfortunate got up on to a steeple, who had better never have gone up as far as the belfry; and then, having needlessly got him up there, the happy novelist rings the bell for all the world to come together and hear, O dear! how he did get down again! For my part, I think that they had better metamorphose all such aspiring heroes of universal noveldom into man weather-cocks, as they used to put heroes among the constellations, and let them swing round there till they are rusty, and not come down at all to bother honest men with their pranks. The next time the novelist rings the bell I will not stir though the meeting-house burn down. "The Skip of the Tip-Toe-Hop, a Romance of the Middle Ages, by the celebrated author of 'Tittle-Tol-Tan,' to appear in monthly parts; a great rush; don't all come together." All this they read with saucer eyes, and erect and primitive curiosity, and with unwearied gizzard, whose corrugations even yet need no sharpening, just as some little four-year-old bencher his two-cent gilt-covered edition of Cinderella, — without any improvement, that I can see, in the pronunciation, or accent, or emphasis, or any more skill in extracting or inserting the moral. The result is dulness of sight, a stagnation of the vital circulations, and a general deliquium and sloughing off of all the intellectual faculties. This sort of gingerbread is baked daily and more sedulously than pure wheat or rye-and-Indian in almost every oven, and finds a surer market.

The best books are not read even by those who are called good readers. What does our Concord culture amount to? There is in this town, with a very few exceptions, no taste for the best or for very good books even in English literature, whose words all can read and spell. Even the college-bred and so-called liberally educated men here and elsewhere have really little or no acquaintance with the English classics; and as for the recorded wisdom of mankind, the ancient classics and Bibles, which are accessible to all who will know of them, there are the feeblest efforts anywhere made to become acquainted with them. I know a woodchopper, of middle age, who takes a French paper, not for news as he says, for he is above that, but to "keep himself in practice," he being a Canadian by birth; and when I ask him what he considers the best thing he can do in this world, he says, beside this, to keep up and add to his English. This is about as much as the college-bred generally do or aspire to do, and they take an English paper for the purpose. One who has just come from reading perhaps one of the best English books will find how many with whom he can converse about it? Or suppose he comes from reading a Greek or Latin classic in the original, whose praises are familiar even to the so-called illiterate; he will find nobody at all to speak to, but must keep silence about it. Indeed, there is hardly the professor in our colleges, who, if he has mastered the difficulties of the language, has proportionally mastered the difficulties of the wit and poetry of a Greek poet, and has any sympathy to impart to the alert and heroic reader; and as for the sacred Scriptures, or Bibles of mankind, who in this town can tell me even their titles? Most men do not know that any nation but the Hebrews have had a scripture. A man, any man, will go considerably out of his way to pick up a silver dollar; but here are golden words, which the wisest men of antiquity have uttered, and whose worth the wise of every succeeding age have assured us of; — and yet we learn to read only as far as Easy Reading, the primers and class-books, and when we leave school, the "Little Reading," and story-books, which are for boys and beginners; and our reading, our conversation and thinking, are all on a very low level, worthy only of pygmies and manikins.

I aspire to be acquainted with wiser men than this our Concord soil has produced, whose names are hardly known here. Or shall I hear the name of Plato and never read his book? As if Plato were my townsman and I never saw him, — my next neighbor and I never heard him speak or attended to the wisdom of his words. But how actually is it? His Dialogues, which contain what was immortal in him, lie on the next shelf, and yet I never read them. We are underbred and low-lived and illiterate; and in this respect I confess I do not make any very broad distinction between the illiterateness of my townsman who cannot read at all and the illiterateness of him who has learned to read only what is for children and feeble intellects. We should be as good as the worthies of antiquity, but partly by first knowing how good they were. We are a race of tit-men, and soar but little higher in our intellectual flights than the columns of the daily paper.

It is not all books that are as dull as their readers. There are probably words addressed to our condition exactly, which, if we could really hear and understand, would be more salutary than the morning or the spring

to our lives, and possibly put a new aspect on the face
of things for us. How many a man has dated a new
era in his life from the reading of a book! The book
exists for us, perchance, which will explain our miracles
and reveal new ones. The at present unutterable things
we may find somewhere uttered. These same questions
that disturb and puzzle and confound us have in their
turn occurred to all the wise men; not one has been
omitted; and each has answered them, according to his
ability, by his words and his life. Moreover, with wisdom we shall learn liberality. The solitary hired man
on a farm in the outskirts of Concord, who has had his
second birth and peculiar religious experience, and is
driven as he believes into silent gravity and exclusive-
ness by his faith, may think it is not true; but Zoroaster,
thousands of years ago, travelled the same road and
had the same experience; but he, being wise, knew it
to be universal, and treated his neighbors accordingly,
and is even said to have invented and established worship among men. Let him humbly commune with
Zoroaster then, and through the liberalizing influence
of all the worthies, with Jesus Christ himself, and let
"our church" go by the board.

We boast that we belong to the Nineteenth Century
and are making the most rapid strides of any nation.
But consider how little this village does for its own culture. I do not wish to flatter my townsmen, nor to be
flattered by them, for that will not advance either of
us. We need to be provoked, — goaded like oxen, as
we are, into a trot. We have a comparatively decent
system of common schools, schools for infants only; but

excepting the half-starved Lyceum in the winter, and latterly the puny beginning of a library suggested by the State, no school for ourselves. We spend more on almost any article of bodily aliment or ailment than on our mental aliment. It is time that we had uncommon schools, that we did not leave off our education when we begin to be men and women. It is time that villages were universities, and their elder inhabitants the fellows of universities, with leisure — if they are, indeed, so well off — to pursue liberal studies the rest of their lives. Shall the world be confined to one Paris or one Oxford forever? Cannot students be boarded here and get a liberal education under the skies of Concord? Can we not hire some Abélard to lecture to us? Alas! what with foddering the cattle and tending the store, we are kept from school too long, and our education is sadly neglected. In this country, the village should in some respects take the place of the nobleman of Europe. It should be the patron of the fine arts. It is rich enough. It wants only the magnanimity and refinement. It can spend money enough on such things as farmers and traders value, but it is thought Utopian to propose spending money for things which more intelligent men know to be of far more worth. This town has spent seventeen thousand dollars on a town-house, thank fortune or politics, but probably it will not spend so much on living wit, the true meat to put into that shell, in a hundred years. The one hundred and twenty-five dollars annually subscribed for a Lyceum in the winter is better spent than any other equal sum raised in the town. If we live in the Nineteenth Century, why should we not enjoy

the advantages which the Nineteenth Century offers?
Why should our life be in any respect provincial? If we
will read newspapers, why not skip the gossip of Boston
and take the best newspaper in the world at once? — not
be sucking the pap of "neutral family" papers, or brows-
ing "Olive-Branches" here in New England. Let the
reports of all the learned societies come to us, and we
will see if they know anything. Why should we leave
it to Harper & Brothers and Redding & Co. to select
our reading? As the nobleman of cultivated taste surrounds himself with whatever conduces to his culture,
— genius — learning — wit — books — paintings — stat-
uary — music — philosophical instruments, and the like;
so let the village do, — not stop short at a pedagogue,
a parson, a sexton, a parish library, and three select-
men, because our Pilgrim forefathers got through a cold
winter once on a bleak rock with these. To act col-
lectively is according to the spirit of our institutions;
and I am confident that, as our circumstances are more
flourishing, our means are greater than the nobleman's.
New England can hire all the wise men in the world to
come and teach her, and board them round the while,
and not be provincial at all. That is the *uncommon*
school we want. Instead of noblemen, let us have noble
villages of men. If it is necessary, omit one bridge over
the river, go round a little there, and throw one arch
at least over the darker gulf of ignorance which surrounds us.

SOUNDS

POETIC.

BUT while we are confined to books, though the most
select and classic, and read only particular written languages, which are themselves but dialects and provincial,
we are in danger of forgetting the language which all
things and events speak without metaphor, which alone
is copious and standard. Much is published, but little
printed. The rays which stream through the shutter
will be no longer remembered when the shutter is wholly
removed. No method nor discipline can supersede the
necessity of being forever on the alert. What is a course
of history or philosophy, or poetry, no matter how well
selected, or the best society, or the most admirable
routine of life, compared with the discipline of looking
always at what is to be seen? Will you be a reader,
a student merely, or a seer? Read your fate, see what is
before you, and walk on into futurity.

I did not read books the first summer; I hoed beans.
Nay, I often did better than this. There were times
when I could not afford to sacrifice the bloom of the
present moment to any work, whether of the head or
hands. I love a broad margin to my life. Sometimes,
in a summer morning, having taken my accustomed
bath, I sat in my sunny doorway from sunrise till noon,
rapt in a revery, amidst the pines and hickories and

sumachs, in undisturbed solitude and stillness, while the birds sang around or flitted noiseless through the house, until by the sun falling in at my west window, or the noise of some traveller's wagon on the distant highway, I was reminded of the lapse of time. I grew in those seasons like corn in the night, and they were far better than any work of the hands would have been. They were not time subtracted from my life, but so much over and above my usual allowance. I realized what the Orientals mean by contemplation and the forsaking of works. For the most part, I minded not how the hours went. The day advanced as if to light some work of mine; it was morning, and lo, now it is evening, and nothing memorable is accomplished. Instead of singing like the birds, I silently smiled at my incessant good fortune. As the sparrow had its trill, sitting on the hickory before my door, so had I my chuckle or suppressed warble which he might hear out of my nest. My days were not days of the week, bearing the stamp of any heathen deity, nor were they minced into hours and fretted by the ticking of a clock; for I lived like the Puri Indians, of whom it is said that "for yesterday, to-day, and to-morrow they have only one word, and they express the variety of meaning by pointing backward for yesterday, forward for to-morrow, and overhead for the passing day." This was sheer idleness to my fellow-townsmen, no doubt; but if the birds and flowers had tried me by their standard, I should not have been found wanting. A man must find his occasions in himself, it is true. The natural day is very calm, and will hardly reprove his indolence.

I had this advantage, at least, in my mode of life,
over those who were obliged to look abroad for amusement, to society and the theatre, that my life itself was
become my amusement and never ceased to be novel.
It was a drama of many scenes and without an end. If
we were always, indeed, getting our living, and regulat-
ing our lives according to the last and best mode we
had learned, we should never be troubled with ennui.
Follow your genius closely enough, and it will not fail
to show you a fresh prospect every hour. Housework
was a pleasant pastime. When my floor was dirty, I rose
early, and, setting all my furniture out of doors on the
grass, bed and bedstead making but one budget, dashed
water on the floor, and sprinkled white sand from the
pond on it, and then with a broom scrubbed it clean
and white; and by the time the villagers had broken
their fast the morning sun had dried my house sufficiently to allow me to move in again, and my meditations were almost uninterrupted. It was pleasant to see
my whole household effects out on the grass, making a
little pile like a gypsy's pack, and my three-legged table,
from which I did not remove the books and pen and
ink, standing amid the pines and hickories. They
seemed glad to get out themselves, and as if unwilling
to be brought in. I was sometimes tempted to stretch
an awning over them and take my seat there. It was
worth the while to see the sun shine on these things, and
hear the free wind blow on them; so much more interesting most familiar objects look out of doors than in
the house. A bird sits on the next bough, life-everlasting
grows under the table, and blackberry vines run round

its legs; pine cones, chestnut burs, and strawberry leaves are strewn about. It looked as if this was the way these forms came to be transferred to our furniture, to tables, chairs, and bedsteads, — because they once stood in their midst.

My house was on the side of a hill, immediately on the edge of the larger wood, in the midst of a young forest of pitch pines and hickories, and half a dozen rods from the pond, to which a narrow footpath led down the hill. In my front yard grew the strawberry, blackberry, and life-everlasting, johnswort and golden-rod, shrub oaks and sand cherry, blueberry and ground-nut. Near the end of May, the sand cherry (*Cerasus pumila*) adorned the sides of the path with its delicate flowers arranged in umbels cylindrically about its short stems, which last, in the fall, weighed down with good-sized and handsome cherries, fell over in wreaths like rays on every side. I tasted them out of compliment to Nature, though they were scarcely palatable. The sumach (*Rhus glabra*) grew luxuriantly about the house, pushing up through the embankment which I had made, and growing five or six feet the first season. Its broad pinnate tropical leaf was pleasant though strange to look on. The large buds, suddenly pushing out late in the spring from dry sticks which had seemed to be dead, developed themselves as by magic into graceful green and tender boughs, an inch in diameter; and sometimes, as I sat at my window, so heedlessly did they grow and tax their weak joints, I heard a fresh and tender bough suddenly fall like a fan to the ground, when there was not a breath of air stirring, broken off by its own weight. In August, the large masses of berries, which, when in flower, had attracted many wild bees, gradually assumed their bright velvety crimson hue, and by their weight again bent down and broke the tender limbs.

As I sit at my window this summer afternoon, hawks are circling about my clearing; the tantivy of wild pigeons, flying by twos and threes athwart my view, or perching restless on the white pine boughs behind my house, gives a voice to the air; a fish hawk dimples the glassy surface of the pond and brings up a fish; a mink steals out of the marsh before my door and seizes a frog by the shore; the sedge is bending under the weight of the reed-birds flitting hither and thither; and for the last half-hour I have heard the rattle of railroad cars, now dying away and then reviving like the beat of a partridge, conveying travellers from Boston to the country. For I did not live so out of the world as that boy who, as I hear, was put out to a farmer in the east part of the town, but ere long ran away and came home again, quite down at the heel and homesick. He had never seen such a dull and out-of-the-way place; the folks were all gone off; why, you could n't even hear the whistle! I doubt if there is such a place in Massachusetts now: —

> "In truth, our village has become a butt
> For one of those fleet railroad shafts, and o'er
> Our peaceful plain its soothing sound is — Concord."

The Fitchburg Railroad touches the pond about a hundred rods south of where I dwell. I usually go to the village along its causeway, and am, as it were, related to society by this link. The men on the freight trains, who go over the whole length of the road, bow to me as to an old acquaintance, they pass me so often, and apparently they take me for an employee; and so I am. I too would fain be a track-repairer somewhere in the orbit of the earth.

The whistle of the locomotive penetrates my woods summer and winter, sounding like the scream of a hawk sailing over some farmer's yard, informing me that many restless city merchants are arriving within the circle of the town, or adventurous country traders from the other side. As they come under one horizon, they shout their warning to get off the track to the other, heard sometimes through the circles of two towns. Here come your groceries, country; your rations, countrymen! Nor is there any man so independent on his farm that he can say them nay. And here's your pay for them! screams the countryman's whistle; timber like long battering-rams going twenty miles an hour against the city's walls, and chairs enough to seat all the weary and heavy-laden that dwell within them. With such huge and lumbering civility the country hands a chair to the city. All the Indian huckleberry hills are stripped, all the cranberry meadows are raked into the city. Up comes the cotton, down goes the woven cloth; up comes the silk, down goes the woollen; up come the books, but down goes the wit that writes them.

When I meet the engine with its train of cars moving off with planetary motion, — or, rather, like a comet, for the beholder knows not if with that velocity and with that

direction it will ever revisit this system, since its orbit
does not look like a returning curve, — with its steam
cloud like a banner streaming behind in golden and
silver wreaths, like many a downy cloud which I have
seen, high in the heavens, unfolding its masses to the
light, — as if this travelling demigod, this cloud-compeller, would ere long take the sunset sky for the livery
of his train; when I hear the iron horse make the hills
echo with his snort like thunder, shaking the earth with
his feet, and breathing fire and smoke from his nostrils
(what kind of winged horse or fiery dragon they will put
into the new Mythology I don't know), it seems as if
the earth had got a race now worthy to inhabit it. If all
were as it seems, and men made the elements their
servants for noble ends! If the cloud that hangs over
the engine were the perspiration of heroic deeds, or as
beneficent as that which floats over the farmer's fields,
then the elements and Nature herself would cheerfully
accompany men on their errands and be their escort.

I watch the passage of the morning cars with the same
feeling that I do the rising of the sun, which is hardly
more regular. Their train of clouds stretching far behind and rising higher and higher, going to heaven while
the cars are going to Boston, conceals the sun for a
minute and casts my distant field into the shade, a celestial train beside which the petty train of cars which
hugs the earth is but the barb of the spear. The stabler
of the iron horse was up early this winter morning by the
light of the stars amid the mountains, to fodder and har-
ness his steed. Fire, too, was awakened thus early to
put the vital heat in him and get him off. If the enter-

prise were as innocent as it is early! If the snow lies deep, they strap on his snowshoes, and, with the giant plow, plow a furrow from the mountains to the seaboard, in which the cars, like a following drill-barrow, sprinkle all the restless men and floating merchandise in the country for seed. All day the fire-steed flies over the country, stopping only that his master may rest, and I am awakened by his tramp and defiant snort at midnight, when in some remote glen in the woods he fronts the elements incased in ice and snow; and he will reach his stall only with the morning star, to start once more on his travels without rest or slumber. Or perchance, at evening, I hear him in his stable blowing off the superfluous energy of the day, that he may calm his nerves and cool his liver and brain for a few hours of iron slumber. If the enterprise were as heroic and commanding as it is protracted and unwearied!

Far through unfrequented woods on the confines of towns, where once only the hunter penetrated by day, in the darkest night dart these bright saloons without the knowledge of their inhabitants; this moment stopping at some brilliant station-house in town or city, where a social crowd is gathered, the next in the Dismal Swamp, scaring the owl and fox. The startings and arrivals of the cars are now the epochs in the village day. They go and come with such regularity and precision, and their whistle can be heard so far, that the farmers set their clocks by them, and thus one well-conducted institution regulates a whole country. Have not men improved somewhat in punctuality since the railroad was invented? Do they not talk and think faster in the depot than they did in the stage-office? There is something electrifying in the atmosphere of the former place. I have been astonished at the miracles it has wrought; that some of my neighbors, who, I should have prophesied, once for all, would never get to Boston by so prompt a conveyance, are on hand when the bell rings. To do things "railroad fashion" is now the byword; and it is worth the while to be warned so often and so sincerely by any power to get off its track. There is no stopping to read the riot act, no firing over the heads of the mob, in this case. We have constructed a fate, an *Atropos*, that never turns aside. (Let that be the name of your engine.) Men are advertised that at a certain hour and minute these bolts will be shot toward particular points of the compass; yet it interferes with no man's business, and the children go to school on the other track. We live the steadier for it. We are all educated thus to be sons of Tell. The air is full of invisible bolts. Every path but your own is the path of fate. Keep on your own track, then.

What recommends commerce to me is its enterprise and bravery. It does not clasp its hands and pray to Jupiter. I see these men every day go about their business with more or less courage and content, doing more even than they suspect, and perchance better employed than they could have consciously devised. I am less affected by their heroism who stood up for half an hour in the front line at Buena Vista, than by the steady and cheerful valor of the men who inhabit the snow-plow for their winter quarters; who have not merely the three-o'-clock-in-the-morning courage, which Bonaparte

THOREAUESQUE!

thought was the rarest, but whose courage does not go to rest so early, who go to sleep only when the storm sleeps or the sinews of their iron steed are frozen. On this morning of the Great Snow, perchance, which is still raging and chilling men's blood, I hear the muffled tone of their engine bell from out the fog bank of their chilled breath, which announces that the cars *are coming*, without long delay, notwithstanding the veto of a New England northeast snow-storm, and I behold the plowmen covered with snow and rime, their heads peering above the mould-board which is turning down other than daisies and the nests of field mice, like bowlders of the Sierra Nevada, that occupy an outside place in the universe.

Commerce is unexpectedly confident and serene, alert, adventurous, and unwearied. It is very natural in its methods withal, far more so than many fantastic enterprises and sentimental experiments, and hence its singular success. I am refreshed and expanded when the freight train rattles past me, and I smell the stores which go dispensing their odors all the way from Long Wharf to Lake Champlain, reminding me of foreign parts, of coral reefs, and Indian oceans, and tropical climes, and the extent of the globe. I feel more like a citizen of the world at the sight of the palm-leaf which will cover so many flaxen New England heads the next summer, the Manilla hemp and cocoanut husks, the old junk, gunny bags, scrap iron, and rusty nails. This carload of torn sails is more legible and interesting now than if they should be wrought into paper and printed books. Who can write so graphically the history of the storms they have weathered as these rents have done? They are proof-sheets which need no correction. Here goes lumber from the Maine woods, which did not go out to sea in the last freshet, risen four dollars on the thousand because of what did go out or was split up; pine, spruce, cedar, — first, second, third, and fourth qualities, so lately all of one quality, to wave over the bear, and moose, and caribou. Next rolls Thomaston lime, a prime lot, which will get far among the hills before it gets slacked. These rags in bales, of all hues and qualities, the lowest condition to which cotton and linen descend, the final result of dress, — of patterns which are now no longer cried up, unless it be in Milwaukee, as those splendid articles, English, French, or American prints, ginghams, muslins, etc., gathered from all quarters both of fashion and poverty, going to become paper of one color or a few shades only, on which, forsooth, will be written tales of real life, high and low, and founded on fact! This closed car smells of salt fish, the strong New England and commercial scent, reminding me of the Grand Banks and the fisheries. Who has not seen a salt fish, thoroughly cured for this world, so that nothing can spoil it, and putting the perseverance of the saints to the blush? with which you may sweep or pave the streets, and split your kindlings, and the teamster shelter himself and his lading against sun, wind, and rain behind it, — and the trader, as a Concord trader once did, hang it up by his door for a sign when he commences business, until at last his oldest customer cannot tell surely whether it be animal, vegetable, or mineral, and yet it shall be as pure as a snowflake, and if it be

put into a pot and boiled, will come out an excellent dun-
fish for a Saturday's dinner. Next Spanish hides, with
the tails still preserving their twist and the angle of elevation they had when the oxen that wore them were
careering over the pampas of the Spanish Main, — a type
of all obstinacy, and evincing how almost hopeless and
incurable are all constitutional vices. I confess, that
practically speaking, when I have learned a man's real
disposition, I have no hopes of changing it for the better
or worse in this state of existence. As the Orientals say,
"A cur's tail may be warmed, and pressed, and bound
round with ligatures, and after a twelve years' labor bestowed upon it, still it will retain its natural form." The
only effectual cure for such inveteracies as these tails
exhibit is to make glue of them, which I believe is what is
usually done with them, and then they will stay put and
stick. Here is a hogshead of molasses or of brandy directed to John Smith, Cuttingsville, Vermont, some trader
among the Green Mountains, who imports for the farmers
near his clearing, and now perchance stands over his
bulkhead and thinks of the last arrivals on the coast, how
they may affect the price for him, telling his customers
this moment, as he has told them twenty times before
this morning, that he expects some by the next train of
prime quality. It is advertised in the Cuttingsville
Times.

While these things go up other things come down.
Warned by the whizzing sound, I look up from my book
and see some tall pine, hewn on far northern hills, which
has winged its way over the Green Mountains and the
Connecticut, shot like an arrow through the township

within ten minutes, and scarce another eye beholds it;
going

> "to be the mast
> Of some great ammiral."

And hark! here comes the cattle-train bearing the cattle
of a thousand hills, sheepcots, stables, and cow-yards in
the air, drovers with their sticks, and shepherd boys in
the midst of their flocks, all but the mountain pastures,
whirled along like leaves blown from the mountains by
the September gales. The air is filled with the bleating
of calves and sheep, and the hustling of oxen, as if a pastoral valley were going by. When the old bell-wether at
the head rattles his bell, the mountains do indeed skip
like rams and the little hills like lambs. A carload of
drovers, too, in the midst, on a level with their droves
now, their vocation gone, but still clinging to their useless sticks as their badge of office. But their dogs, where
are they? It is a stampede to them; they are quite
thrown out; they have lost the scent. Methinks I hear
them barking behind the Peterboro' Hills, or panting up
the western slope of the Green Mountains. They will not
be in at the death. Their vocation, too, is gone. Their
fidelity and sagacity are below par now. They will slink
back to their kennels in disgrace, or perchance run wild
and strike a league with the wolf and the fox. So is
your pastoral life whirled past and away. But the bell
rings, and I must get off the track and let the cars go
by; —

> What's the railroad to me?
> I never go to see
> Where it ends.

It fills a few hollows,
And makes banks for the swallows,
It sets the sand a-blowing,
And the blackberries a-growing,

but I cross it like a cart-path in the woods. I will not have my eyes put out and my ears spoiled by its smoke and steam and hissing.

Now that the cars are gone by and all the restless world with them, and the fishes in the pond no longer feel their rumbling, I am more alone than ever. For the rest of the long afternoon, perhaps, my meditations are interrupted only by the faint rattle of a carriage or team along the distant highway.

Sometimes, on Sundays, I heard the bells, the Lincoln, Acton, Bedford, or Concord bell, when the wind was favorable, a faint, sweet, and, as it were, natural melody, worth importing into the wilderness. At a sufficient distance over the woods this sound acquires a certain vibratory hum, as if the pine needles in the horizon were the strings of a harp which it swept. All sound heard at the greatest possible distance produces one and the same effect, a vibration of the universal lyre, just as the intervening atmosphere makes a distant ridge of earth interesting to our eyes by the azure tint it imparts to it. There came to me in this case a melody which the air had strained, and which had conversed with every leaf and needle of the wood, that portion of the sound which the elements had taken up and modulated and echoed from vale to vale. The echo is, to some extent, an original sound, and therein is the magic and charm of it. It is not merely a repetition of what was worth repeating in the bell, but partly the voice of the wood; the same trivial words and notes sung by a wood-nymph.

At evening, the distant lowing of some cow in the horizon beyond the woods sounded sweet and melodious, and at first I would mistake it for the voices of certain minstrels by whom I was sometimes serenaded, who might be straying over hill and dale; but soon I was not unpleasantly disappointed when it was prolonged into the cheap and natural music of the cow. I do not mean to be satirical, but to express my appreciation of those youths' singing, when I state that I perceived clearly that it was akin to the music of the cow, and they were at length one articulation of Nature.

Regularly at half-past seven, in one part of the summer, after the evening train had gone by, the whip-poor-wills chanted their vespers for half an hour, sitting on a stump by my door, or upon the ridge-pole of the house. They would begin to sing almost with as much precision as a clock, within five minutes of a particular time, referred to the setting of the sun, every evening. I had a rare opportunity to become acquainted with their habits. Sometimes I heard four or five at once in different parts of the wood, by accident one a bar behind another, and so near me that I distinguished not only the cluck after each note, but often that singular buzzing sound like a fly in a spider's web, only proportionally louder. Sometimes one would circle round and round me in the woods a few feet distant as if tethered by a string, when probably I was near its eggs. They sang at intervals throughout the

night, and were again as musical as ever just before and
about dawn.

When other birds are still, the screech owls take up
the strain, like mourning women their ancient u-lu-lu.
Their dismal scream is truly Ben Jonsonian. Wise midnight hags! It is no honest and blunt tu-whit tu-who of
the poets, but, without jesting, a most solemn graveyard
ditty, the mutual consolations of suicide lovers remembering the pangs and the delights of supernal love in the infernal groves. Yet I love to hear their wailing, their dole-
ful responses, trilled along the woodside; reminding me
sometimes of music and singing birds; as if it were the
dark and tearful side of music, the regrets and sighs that
would fain be sung. They are the spirits, the low spirits
and melancholy forebodings, of fallen souls that once in
human shape night-walked the earth and did the deeds
of darkness, now expiating their sins with their wailing
hymns or threnodies in the scenery of their transgressions.
They give me a new sense of the variety and capacity of
that nature which is our common dwelling. *Oh-o-o-o-o
that I never had been bor-r-r-r-n!* sighs one on this side
of the pond, and circles with the restlessness of despair
to some new perch on the gray oaks. Then — *that I
never had been bor-r-r-r-n!* echoes another on the farther
side with tremulous sincerity, and — *bor-r-r-r-n!* comes
faintly from far in the Lincoln woods.

I was also serenaded by a hooting owl. Near at hand
you could fancy it the most melancholy sound in Nature,
as if she meant by this to stereotype and make permanent in her choir the dying moans of a human being, —
some poor weak relic of mortality who has left hope be-

hind, and howls like an animal, yet with human sobs, on entering the dark valley, made more awful by a certain gurgling melodiousness, — I find myself beginning with the letters *gl* when I try to imitate it, — expressive of a mind which has reached the gelatinous, mildewy stage in the mortification of all healthy and courageous thought. It reminded me of ghouls and idiots and insane howlings. But now one answers from far woods in a strain made really melodious by distance, — *Hoo hoo hoo, hoorer hoo;* and indeed for the most part it suggested only pleasing associations, whether heard by day or night, summer or winter.

I rejoice that there are owls. Let them do the idiotic and maniacal hooting for men. It is a sound admirably suited to swamps and twilight woods which no day illustrates, suggesting a vast and undeveloped nature which men have not recognized. They represent the stark twilight and unsatisfied thoughts which all have. All day the sun has shone on the surface of some savage swamp, where the single spruce stands hung with usnea lichens, and small hawks circulate above, and the chickadee lisps amid the evergreens, and the partridge and rabbit skulk beneath; but now a more dismal and fitting day dawns, and a different race of creatures awakes to express the meaning of Nature there.

Late in the evening I heard the distant rumbling of wagons over bridges, — a sound heard farther than almost any other at night, — the baying of dogs, and sometimes again the lowing of some disconsolate cow in a distant barn-yard. In the meanwhile all the shore rang with the trump of bullfrogs, the sturdy spirits of

ancient wine-bibbers and wassailers, still unrepentant,
trying to sing a catch in their Stygian lake, — if the
Walden nymphs will pardon the comparison, for
though there are almost no weeds, there are frogs there,
— who would fain keep up the hilarious rules of their
old festal tables, though their voices have waxed hoarse
and solemnly grave, mocking at mirth, and the wine
has lost its flavor, and become only liquor to distend
their paunches, and sweet intoxication never comes to
drown the memory of the past, but mere saturation and
waterloggedness and distention. The most aldermanic,
with his chin upon a heart-leaf, which serves for a nap-
kin to his drooling chaps, under this northern shore
quaffs a deep draught of the once scorned water, and
passes round the cup with the ejaculation *tr-r-r-oonk*,
tr-r-r-oonk, *tr-r-r-oonk !* and straightway comes over the
water from some distant cove the same password repeated, where the next in seniority and girth has gulped
down to his mark; and when this observance has made
the circuit of the shores, then ejaculates the master of
ceremonies, with satisfaction, *tr-r-r-oonk !* and each in
his turn repeats the same down to the least distended,
leakiest, and flabbiest paunched, that there be no mistake; and then the bowl goes round again and again,
until the sun disperses the morning mist, and only the
patriarch is not under the pond, but vainly bellowing
troonk from time to time, and pausing for a reply.

I am not sure that I ever heard the sound of cock-
crowing from my clearing, and I thought that it might be
worth the while to keep a cockerel for his music merely,
as a singing bird. The note of this once wild Indian

pheasant is certainly the most remarkable of any bird's, and if they could be naturalized without being domesticated, it would soon become the most famous sound in our woods, surpassing the clangor of the goose and the hooting of the owl; and then imagine the cackling of the hens to fill the pauses when their lords' clarions rested! No wonder that man added this bird to his tame stock, — to say nothing of the eggs and drumsticks. To walk in a winter morning in a wood where these birds abounded, their native woods, and hear the wild cockerels crow on the trees, clear and shrill for miles over the resounding earth, drowning the feebler notes of other birds, — think of it! It would put nations on the alert. Who would not be early to rise, and rise earlier and earlier every successive day of his life, till he became unspeakably healthy, wealthy, and wise? This foreign bird's note is celebrated by the poets of all countries along with the notes of their native songsters. All climates agree with brave Chanticleer. He is more indigenous even than the natives. His health is ever good, his lungs are sound, his spirits never flag. Even the sailor on the Atlantic and Pacific is awakened by his voice; but its shrill sound never roused me from my slumbers. I kept neither dog, cat, cow, pig, nor hens, so that you would have said there was a deficiency of domestic sounds; neither the churn, nor the spinning-wheel, nor even the singing of the kettle, nor the hissing of the urn, nor children crying, to comfort one. An old-fashioned man would have lost his senses or died of ennui before this. Not even rats in the wall, for they were starved out, or rather were never baited in, — only squirrels on the roof and under the floor, a whip-poor-will on the ridge-pole, a blue jay screaming beneath the window, a hare or woodchuck under the house, a screech owl or a cat owl behind it, a flock of wild geese or a laughing loon on the pond, and a fox to bark in the night. Not even a lark or an oriole, those mild plantation birds, ever visited my clearing. No cockerels to crow nor hens to cackle in the yard. No yard! but unfenced nature reaching up to your very sills. A young forest growing up under your windows, and wild sumachs and blackberry vines breaking through into your cellar; sturdy pitch pines rubbing and creaking against the shingles for want of room, their roots reaching quite under the house. Instead of a scuttle or a blind blown off in the gale, — a pine tree snapped off or torn up by the roots behind your house for fuel. Instead of no path to the front-yard gate in the Great Snow, — no gate — no front-yard, — and no path to the civilized world.

WHAT MORE COULD ONE WISH ?

V

SOLITUDE

THIS is a delicious evening, when the whole body is one sense, and imbibes delight through every pore. I go and come with a strange liberty in Nature, a part of herself. As I walk along the stony shore of the pond in my shirt-sleeves, though it is cool as well as cloudy and windy, and I see nothing special to attract me, all the elements are unusually congenial to me. The bullfrogs trump to usher in the night, and the note of the whip-poor-will is borne on the rippling wind from over the water. Sympathy with the fluttering alder and poplar leaves almost takes away my breath; yet, like the lake, my serenity is rippled but not ruffled. These small waves raised by the evening wind are as remote from storm as the smooth reflecting surface. Though it is now dark, the wind still blows and roars in the wood, the waves still dash, and some creatures lull the rest with their notes. The repose is never complete. The wildest animals do not repose, but seek their prey now; the fox, and skunk, and rabbit, now roam the fields and woods without fear. They are Nature's watchmen, — links which connect the days of animated life.

When I return to my house I find that visitors have been there and left their cards, either a bunch of flowers, or a wreath of evergreen, or a name in pencil on a yellow walnut leaf or a chip. They who come rarely to the woods take some little piece of the forest into their hands to play with by the way, which they leave, either intentionally or accidentally. One has peeled a willow wand, woven it into a ring, and dropped it on my table. I could always tell if visitors had called in my absence, either by the bended twigs or grass, or the print of their shoes, and generally of what sex or age or quality they were by some slight trace left, as a flower dropped, or a bunch of grass plucked and thrown away, even as far off as the railroad, half a mile distant, or by the lingering odor of a cigar or pipe. Nay, I was frequently notified of the passage of a traveller along the highway sixty rods off by the scent of his pipe.

There is commonly sufficient space about us. Our horizon is never quite at our elbows. The thick wood is not just at our door, nor the pond, but somewhat is always clearing, familiar and worn by us, appropriated and fenced in some way, and reclaimed from Nature. For what reason have I this vast range and circuit, some square miles of unfrequented forest, for my privacy, abandoned to me by men? My nearest neighbor is a mile distant, and no house is visible from any place but the hill-tops within half a mile of my own. I have my horizon bounded by woods all to myself; a distant view of the railroad where it touches the pond on the one hand, and of the fence which skirts the woodland road on the other. But for the most part it is as solitary where I live as on the prairies. It is as much Asia or Africa as New England. I have, as it were, my own sun and moon and stars, and a little world all to myself. At night there

was never a traveller passed my house, or knocked at
my door, more than if I were the first or last man; unless it were in the spring, when at long intervals some
came from the village to fish for pouts, — they plainly
fished much more in the Walden Pond of their own
natures, and baited their hooks with darkness, — but
they soon retreated, usually with light baskets, and left
"the world to darkness and to me," and the black kernel of the night was never profaned by any human
neighborhood. I believe that men are generally still a
little afraid of the dark, though the witches are all hung,
and Christianity and candles have been introduced.

Yet I experienced sometimes that the most sweet and
tender, the most innocent and encouraging society may
be found in any natural object, even for the poor mis-
anthrope and most melancholy man. There can be no
very black melancholy to him who lives in the midst of
nature and has his senses still. There was never yet
such a storm but it was Æolian music to a healthy and
innocent ear. Nothing can rightly compel a simple
and brave man to a vulgar sadness. While I enjoy the
friendship of the seasons I trust that nothing can make
life a burden to me. The gentle rain which waters my
beans and keeps me in the house to-day is not drear and
melancholy, but good for me too. Though it prevents
my hoeing them, it is of far more worth than my hoeing.
If it should continue so long as to cause the seeds to rot
in the ground and destroy the potatoes in the low lands,
it would still be good for the grass on the uplands, and,
being good for the grass, it would be good for me. Sometimes, when I compare myself with other men, it seems

as if I were more favored by the gods than they, beyond any deserts that I am conscious of; as if I had a warrant and surety at their hands which my fellows have not, and were especially guided and guarded. I do not flatter myself, but if it be possible they flatter me. I have never felt lonesome, or in the least oppressed by a sense of solitude, but once, and that was a few weeks after I came to the woods, when, for an hour, I doubted if the near neighborhood of man was not essential to a serene and healthy life. To be alone was something unpleasant. But I was at the same time conscious of a slight insanity in my mood, and seemed to foresee my recovery. In the midst of a gentle rain while these thoughts prevailed, I was suddenly sensible of such sweet and beneficent society in Nature, in the very pattering of the drops, and in every sound and sight around my house, an infinite and unaccountable friendliness all at once like an atmosphere sustaining me, as made the fancied advantages of human neighborhood insignificant, and I have never thought of them since. Every little pine needle expanded and swelled with sympathy and befriended me. I was so distinctly made aware of the presence of something kindred to me, even in scenes which we are accustomed to call wild and dreary, and also that the nearest of blood to me and humanest was not a person nor a villager, that I thought no place could ever be strange to me again. —

> "Mourning untimely consumes the sad;
> Few are their days in the land of the living,
> Beautiful daughter of Toscar."

Some of my pleasantest hours were during the long

rain-storms in the spring or fall, which confined me to the house for the afternoon as well as the forenoon, soothed by their ceaseless roar and pelting; when an early twilight ushered in a long evening in which many thoughts had time to take root and unfold themselves. In those driving northeast rains which tried the village houses so, when the maids stood ready with mop and pail in front entries to keep the deluge out, I sat behind my door in my little house, which was all entry, and thoroughly enjoyed its protection. In one heavy thunder-shower the lightning struck a large pitch pine across the pond, making a very conspicuous and perfectly regular spiral groove from top to bottom, an inch or more deep, and four or five inches wide, as you would groove a walking-stick. I passed it again the other day, and was struck with awe on looking up and beholding that mark, now more distinct than ever, where a terrific and resist-less bolt came down out of the harmless sky eight years ago. Men frequently say to me, "I should think you would feel lonesome down there, and want to be nearer to folks, rainy and snowy days and nights especially." I am tempted to reply to such, — This whole earth which we inhabit is but a point in space. How far apart, think you, dwell the two most distant inhabitants of yonder star, the breadth of whose disk cannot be appreciated by our instruments? Why should I feel lonely? is not our planet in the Milky Way? This which you put seems to me not to be the most important question. What sort of space is that which separates a man from his fellows and makes him solitary? I have found that no exertion of the legs can bring two minds much nearer

to one another. What do we want most to dwell near
to? Not to many men surely, the depot, the post-office,
the bar-room, the meeting-house, the school-house, the
grocery, Beacon Hill, or the Five Points, where men
most congregate, but to the perennial source of our life,
whence in all our experience we have found that to issue,
as the willow stands near the water and sends out its
roots in that direction. This will vary with different
natures, but this is the place where a wise man will dig
his cellar. . . . I one evening overtook one of my townsmen, who has accumulated what is called "a handsome
property," — though I never got a *fair* view of it, — on
the Walden road, driving a pair of cattle to market, who
inquired of me how I could bring my mind to give up
so many of the comforts of life. I answered that I was
very sure I liked it passably well; I was not joking.
And so I went home to my bed, and left him to pick his
way through the darkness and the mud to Brighton, —
or Bright-town, — which place he would reach some
time in the morning.

Any prospect of awakening or coming to life to a
dead man makes indifferent all times and places. The
place where that may occur is always the same, and in-
describably pleasant to all our senses. For the most
part we allow only outlying and transient circumstances
to make our occasions. They are, in fact, the cause
of our distraction. Nearest to all things is that power
which fashions their being. *Next* to us the grandest
laws are continually being executed. *Next* to us is not
the workman whom we have hired, with whom we love
so well to talk, but the workman whose work we are.

" How vast and profound is the influence of the subtile powers of Heaven and of Earth!"

" We seek to perceive them, and we do not see them; we seek to hear them, and we do not hear them; identified with the substance of things, they cannot be separated from them."

"They cause that in all the universe men purify and sanctify their hearts, and clothe themselves in their holiday garments to offer sacrifices and oblations to their ancestors. It is an ocean of subtile intelligences. They are everywhere, above us, on our left, on our right; they environ us on all sides."

We are the subjects of an experiment which is not a little interesting to me. Can we not do without the society of our gossips a little while under these circumstances, — have our own thoughts to cheer us? Confucius says truly, " Virtue does not remain as an abandoned orphan; it must of necessity have neighbors."

With thinking we may be beside ourselves in a sane sense. By a conscious effort of the mind we can stand aloof from actions and their consequences; and all things, good and bad, go by us like a torrent. We are not wholly involved in Nature. I may be either the driftwood in the stream, or Indra in the sky looking down on it. I *may* be affected by a theatrical exhibition; on the other hand, I *may not* be affected by an actual event which appears to concern me much more. I only know myself as a human entity; the scene, so to speak, of thoughts and affections; and am sensible of a certain doubleness by which I can stand as remote from myself as from another. However intense my experience, I am conscious of the presence and criticism of a part of me, which, as it were, is not a part of me, but spectator, sharing no experience, but taking note of it, and that is no more I than it is you. When the play, it may be the tragedy, of life is over, the spectator goes his way. It was a kind of fiction, a work of the imagination only, so far as he was concerned. This doubleness may easily make us poor neighbors and friends sometimes.

I find it wholesome to be alone the greater part of the time. To be in company, even with the best, is soon wearisome and dissipating. I love to be alone. I never found the companion that was so companionable as solitude. We are for the most part more lonely when we go abroad among men than when we stay in our chambers. A man thinking or working is always alone, let him be where he will. Solitude is not measured by the miles of space that intervene between a man and his fellows. The really diligent student in one of the crowded hives of Cambridge College is as solitary as a dervis in the desert. The farmer can work alone in the field or the woods all day, hoeing or chopping, and not feel lonesome, because he is employed; but when he comes home at night he cannot sit down in a room alone, at the mercy of his thoughts, but must be where he can "see the folks," and recreate, and, as he thinks, remunerate himself for his day's solitude; and hence he wonders how the student can sit alone in the house all night and most of the day without ennui and "the blues;" but he does not realize that the student, though in the house, is still at work in *his* field, and chopping in *his* woods, as the farmer in his, and in turn seeks the same

recreation and society that the latter does, though it
may be a more condensed form of it.

Society is commonly too cheap. We meet at very
short intervals, not having had time to acquire any new
value for each other. We meet at meals three times a
day, and give each other a new taste of that old musty
cheese that we are. We have had to agree on a certain set
of rules, called etiquette and politeness, to make this
frequent meeting tolerable and that we need not come
to open war. We meet at the post-office, and at the
sociable, and about the fireside every night; we live
thick and are in each other's way, and stumble over one
another, and I think that we thus lose some respect for
one another. Certainly less frequency would suffice for
all important and hearty communications. Consider
the girls in a factory, — never alone, hardly in their
dreams. It would be better if there were but one inhabitant to a square mile, as where I live. The value of
a man is not in his skin, that we should touch him.

I have heard of a man lost in the woods and dying of
famine and exhaustion at the foot of a tree, whose lone-
liness was relieved by the grotesque visions with which,
owing to bodily weakness, his diseased imagination
surrounded him, and which he believed to be real. So
also, owing to bodily and mental health and strength,
we may be continually cheered by a like but more normal and natural society, and come to know that we are
never alone.

I have a great deal of company in my house; especially in the morning, when nobody calls. Let me suggest
a few comparisons, that some one may convey an idea

of my situation. I am no more lonely than the loon in
the pond that laughs so loud, or than Walden Pond
itself. What company has that lonely lake, I pray?
And yet it has not the blue devils, but the blue angels
in it, in the azure tint of its waters. The sun is alone,
except in thick weather, when there sometimes appear
to be two, but one is a mock sun. God is alone, — but
the devil, he is far from being alone; he sees a great
deal of company; he is legion. I am no more lonely
than a single mullein or dandelion in a pasture, or a bean
leaf, or sorrel, or a horse-fly, or a humblebee. I am no
more lonely than the Mill Brook, or a weathercock,
or the north star, or the south wind, or an April shower,
or a January thaw, or the first spider in a new house.
I have occasional visits in the long winter evenings,
when the snow falls fast and the wind howls in the
wood, from an old settler and original proprietor, who
is reported to have dug Walden Pond, and stoned it,
and fringed it with pine woods; who tells me stories of
old time and of new eternity; and between us we man-
age to pass a cheerful evening with social mirth and
pleasant views of things, even without apples or cider, —
a most wise and humorous friend, whom I love much,
who keeps himself more secret than ever did Goffe or
Whalley; and though he is thought to be dead, none
can show where he is buried. An elderly dame, too,
dwells in my neighborhood, invisible to most persons,
in whose odorous herb garden I love to stroll sometimes, gathering simples and listening to her fables;
for she has a genius of unequalled fertility, and her
memory runs back farther than mythology, and she can

tell me the original of every fable, and on what fact every one is founded, for the incidents occurred when she was young. A ruddy and lusty old dame, who delights in all weathers and seasons, and is likely to outlive all her children yet.

The indescribable innocence and beneficence of Nature, — of sun and wind and rain, of summer and winter, — such health, such cheer, they afford forever! and such sympathy have they ever with our race, that all Nature would be affected, and the sun's brightness fade, and the winds would sigh humanely, and the clouds rain tears, and the woods shed their leaves and put on mourning in midsummer, if any man should ever for a just cause grieve. Shall I not have intelligence with the earth? Am I not partly leaves and vegetable mould myself?

What is the pill which will keep us well, serene, contented? Not my or thy great-grandfather's, but our great-grandmother Nature's universal, vegetable, botanic medicines, by which she has kept herself young always, outlived so many old Parrs in her day, and fed her health with their decaying fatness. For my panacea, instead of one of those quack vials of a mixture dipped from Acheron and the Dead Sea, which come out of those long shallow black-schooner looking wagons which we sometimes see made to carry bottles, let me have a draught of undiluted morning air. Morning air! If men will not drink of this at the fountain-head of the day, why, then, we must even bottle up some and sell it in the shops, for the benefit of those who have lost their subscription ticket to morning time in this world. But remember, it will not keep quite till noonday even in the coolest cellar, but drive out the stopples long ere that and follow westward the steps of Aurora. I am no worshipper of Hygeia, who was the daughter of that old herb-doctor Æsculapius, and who is represented on monuments holding a serpent in one hand, and in the other a cup out of which the serpent sometimes drinks; but rather of Hebe, cup-bearer to Jupiter, who was the daughter of Juno and wild lettuce, and who had the power of restoring gods and men to the vigor of youth. She was probably the only thoroughly sound-conditioned, healthy, and robust young lady that ever walked the globe, and wherever she came it was spring.

VI

VISITORS

I THINK that I love society as much as most, and am ready enough to fasten myself like a bloodsucker for the time to any full-blooded man that comes in my way. I am naturally no hermit, but might possibly sit out the sturdiest frequenter of the bar-room, if my business called me thither.

I had three chairs in my house; one for solitude, two for friendship, three for society. When visitors came in larger and unexpected numbers there was but the third chair for them all, but they generally economized the room by standing up. It is surprising how many great men and women a small house will contain. I have had twenty-five or thirty souls, with their bodies, at once under my roof, and yet we often parted without being aware that we had come very near to one another. Many of our houses, both public and private, with their almost innumerable apartments, their huge halls and their cellars for the storage of wines and other munitions of peace, appear to me extravagantly large for their inhabitants. They are so vast and magnificent that the latter seem to be only vermin which infest them. I am surprised when the herald blows his summons before some Tremont or Astor or Middlesex House, to see come creeping out over the piazza for all inhabitants a ridiculous mouse, which soon again slinks into some hole in the pavement.

One inconvenience I sometimes experienced in so small a house, the difficulty of getting to a sufficient distance from my guest when we began to utter the big thoughts in big words. You want room for your thoughts to get into sailing trim and run a course or two before they make their port. The bullet of your thought must have overcome its lateral and ricochet motion and fallen into its last and steady course before it reaches the ear of the hearer, else it may plow out again through the side of his head. Also, our sentences wanted room to unfold and form their columns in the interval. Individuals, like nations, must have suitable broad and natural boundaries, even a considerable neutral ground, between them. I have found it a singular luxury to talk across the pond to a companion on the opposite side. In my house we were so near that we could not begin to hear, — we could not speak low enough to be heard; as when you throw two stones into calm water so near that they break each other's undulations. If we are merely loquacious and loud talkers, then we can afford to stand very near together, cheek by jowl, and feel each other's breath; but if we speak reservedly and thoughtfully, we want to be farther apart, that all animal heat and moisture may have a chance to evaporate. If we would enjoy the most intimate society with that in each of us which is without, or above, being spoken to, we must not only be silent, but commonly so far apart bodily that we cannot possibly hear each other's voice in any case. Referred to this standard, speech is for the convenience of those who are hard of hearing; but there are many fine things which we cannot say if we have to shout. As the conversation began to assume a loftier and grander tone, we gradually shoved our chairs farther apart till they touched the wall in opposite corners, and then commonly there was not room enough.

My "best" room, however, my withdrawing room, always ready for company, on whose carpet the sun rarely fell, was the pine wood behind my house. Thither in summer days, when distinguished guests came, I took them, and a priceless domestic swept the floor and dusted the furniture and kept the things in order.

If one guest came he sometimes partook of my frugal meal, and it was no interruption to conversation to be stirring a hasty-pudding, or watching the rising and maturing of a loaf of bread in the ashes, in the meanwhile. But if twenty came and sat in my house there was nothing said about dinner, though there might be bread enough for two, more than if eating were a forsaken habit; but we naturally practised abstinence; and this was never felt to be an offence against hospitality, but the most proper and considerate course. The waste and decay of physical life, which so often needs repair, seemed miraculously retarded in such a case, and the vital vigor stood its ground. I could entertain thus a thousand as well as twenty; and if any ever went away disappointed or hungry from my house when they found me at home, they may depend upon it that I sympathized with them at least. So easy is it, though many housekeepers doubt it, to establish new and better customs in the place of the old. You need not rest your reputation on the dinners you give. For my own part, I was never so effectually deterred from frequenting a man's house, by any kind of Cerberus whatever, as by the parade one made about dining me, which I took to be a very polite and roundabout hint never to trouble him so again. I think I shall never revisit those scenes. I should be proud to have for the motto of my cabin those lines of Spenser which one of my visitors inscribed on a yellow walnut leaf for a card: —

> "Arrivèd there, the little house they fill,
>   Ne looke for entertainment where none was;
>   Rest is their feast, and all things at their will:
>   The noblest mind the best contentment has."

When Winslow, afterward governor of the Plymouth Colony, went with a companion on a visit of ceremony to Massasoit on foot through the woods, and arrived tired and hungry at his lodge, they were well received by the king, but nothing was said about eating that day. When the night arrived, to quote their own words,— "He laid us on the bed with himself and his wife, they at the one end and we at the other, it being only planks laid a foot from the ground and a thin mat upon them. Two more of his chief men, for want of room, pressed by and upon us; so that we were worse weary of our lodging than of our journey." At one o'clock the next day Massasoit "brought two fishes that he had shot," about thrice as big as a bream. "These being boiled, there were at least forty looked for a share in them; the most eat of them. This meal only we had in two nights and a day; and had not one of us bought a partridge, we had taken our journey fasting." Fearing that they

would be light-headed for want of food and also sleep,
owing to "the savages' barbarous singing, (for they
use to sing themselves asleep,)" and that they might
get home while they had strength to travel, they departed.
As for lodging, it is true they were but poorly entertained,
though what they found an inconvenience was no doubt
intended for an honor; but as far as eating was concerned, I do not see how the Indians could have done
better. They had nothing to eat themselves, and they
were wiser than to think that apologies could supply the
place of food to their guests; so they drew their belts
tighter and said nothing about it. Another time when
Winslow visited them, it being a season of plenty with
them, there was no deficiency in this respect.

As for men, they will hardly fail one anywhere. I had
more visitors while I lived in the woods than at any other
period of my life; I mean that I had some. I met several
there under more favorable circumstances than I could
anywhere else. But fewer came to see me on trivial business. In this respect, my company was winnowed by my
mere distance from town. I had withdrawn so far within
the great ocean of solitude, into which the rivers of society empty, that for the most part, so far as my needs
were concerned, only the finest sediment was deposited
around me. Beside, there were wafted to me evidences
of unexplored and uncultivated continents on the other
side.

Who should come to my lodge this morning but a true
Homeric or Paphlagonian man, — he had so suitable
and poetic a name that I am sorry I cannot print it here,
— a Canadian, a woodchopper and post-maker, who

can hole fifty posts in a day, who made his last supper
on a woodchuck which his dog caught. He, too, has
heard of Homer, and, "if it were not for books," would
"not know what to do rainy days," though perhaps he
has not read one wholly through for many rainy seasons.
Some priest who could pronounce the Greek itself taught
him to read his verse in the Testament in his native parish far away; and now I must translate to him, while
he holds the book, Achilles' reproof to Patroclus for his
sad countenance. — "Why are you in tears, Patroclus,
like a young girl?" —

> "Or have you alone heard some news from Phthia?
> They say that Menœtius lives yet, son of Actor,
> And Peleus lives, son of Æacus, among the Myrmidons,
> Either of whom having died, we should greatly grieve."

He says, "That's good." He has a great bundle of white
oak bark under his arm for a sick man, gathered this
Sunday morning. "I suppose there's no harm in going
after such a thing to-day," says he. To him Homer was
a great writer, though what his writing was about he did
not know. A more simple and natural man it would be
hard to find. Vice and disease, which cast such a sombre moral hue over the world, seemed to have hardly
any existence for him. He was about twenty-eight years
old, and had left Canada and his father's house a dozen
years before to work in the States, and earn money to
buy a farm with at last, perhaps in his native country.
He was cast in the coarsest mould; a stout but sluggish
body, yet gracefully carried, with a thick sunburnt neck,
dark bushy hair, and dull sleepy blue eyes, which were
occasionally lit up with expression. He wore a flat gray

cloth cap, a dingy wool-colored greatcoat, and cow-hide boots. He was a great consumer of meat, usually carrying his dinner to his work a couple of miles past my house, — for he chopped all summer, — in a tin pail; cold meats, often cold woodchucks, and coffee in a stone bottle which dangled by a string from his belt; and sometimes he offered me a drink. He came along early, crossing my bean-field, though without anxiety or haste to get to his work, such as Yankees exhibit. He was n't a-going to hurt himself. He did n't care if he only earned his board. Frequently he would leave his dinner in the bushes, when his dog had caught a wood-chuck by the way, and go back a mile and a half to dress it and leave it in the cellar of the house where he boarded, after deliberating first for half an hour whether he could not sink it in the pond safely till nightfall, — loving to dwell long upon these themes. He would say, as he went by in the morning, "How thick the pigeons are! If work-ing every day were not my trade, I could get all the meat I should want by hunting, — pigeons, woodchucks, rab-bits, partridges, — by gosh! I could get all I should want for a week in one day."

He was a skilful chopper, and indulged in some flour-ishes and ornaments in his art. He cut his trees level and close to the ground, that the sprouts which came up afterward might be more vigorous and a sled might slide over the stumps; and instead of leaving a whole tree to support his corded wood, he would pare it away to a slender stake or splinter which you could break off with your hand at last.

He interested me because he was so quiet and solitary

and so happy withal; a well of good humor and contentment which overflowed at his eyes. His mirth was without alloy. Sometimes I saw him at his work in the woods, felling trees, and he would greet me with a laugh of inexpressible satisfaction, and a salutation in Canadian French, though he spoke English as well. When I approached him he would suspend his work, and with half-suppressed mirth lie along the trunk of a pine which he had felled, and, peeling off the inner bark, roll it up into a ball and chew it while he laughed and talked. Such an exuberance of animal spirits had he that he sometimes tumbled down and rolled on the ground with laughter at anything which made him think and tickled him. Looking round upon the trees he would exclaim, — "By George! I can enjoy myself well enough here chopping; I want no better sport." Sometimes, when at leisure, he amused himself all day in the woods with a pocket pistol, firing salutes to himself at regular intervals as he walked. In the winter he had a fire by which at noon he warmed his coffee in a kettle; and as he sat on a log to eat his dinner the chickadees would sometimes come round and alight on his arm and peck at the potato in his fingers; and he said that he "liked to have the little *fellers* about him."

In him the animal man chiefly was developed. In physical endurance and contentment he was cousin to the pine and the rock. I asked him once if he was not sometimes tired at night, after working all day; and he answered, with a sincere and serious look, "Gorrappit, I never was tired in my life." But the intellectual and what is called spiritual man in him were slumbering as in an infant. He had been instructed only in that innocent and ineffectual way in which the Catholic priests teach the aborigines, by which the pupil is never educated to the degree of consciousness, but only to the degree of trust and reverence, and a child is not made a man, but kept a child. When Nature made him, she gave him a strong body and contentment for his portion, and propped him on every side with reverence and reliance, that he might live out his threescore years and ten a child. He was so genuine and unsophisticated that no introduction would serve to introduce him, more than if you introduced a woodchuck to your neighbor. He had got to find him out as you did. He would not play any part. Men paid him wages for work, and so helped to feed and clothe him; but he never exchanged opinions with them. He was so simply and naturally humble — if he can be called humble who never aspires — that humility was no distinct quality in him, nor could he conceive of it. Wiser men were demigods to him. If you told him that such a one was coming, he did as if he thought that anything so grand would expect nothing of himself, but take all the responsibility on itself, and let him be forgotten still. He never heard the sound of praise. He particularly reverenced the writer and the preacher. Their performances were miracles. When I told him that I wrote considerably, he thought for a long time that it was merely the handwriting which I meant, for he could write a remarkably good hand himself. I sometimes found the name of his native parish handsomely written in the snow by the highway, with the proper French accent, and knew that he had passed. I asked him if he ever wished to write his thoughts. He said that he had read and written letters for those who could not, but he never tried to write thoughts, — no, he could not, he could not tell what to put first, it would kill him, and then there was spelling to be attended to at the same time!

I heard that a distinguished wise man and reformer asked him if he did not want the world to be changed; but he answered with a chuckle of surprise in his Canadian accent, not knowing that the question had ever been entertained before, "No, I like it well enough." It would have suggested many things to a philosopher to have dealings with him. To a stranger he appeared to know nothing of things in general; yet I sometimes saw in him a man whom I had not seen before, and I did not know whether he was as wise as Shakespeare or as simply ignorant as a child, whether to suspect him of a fine poetic consciousness or of stupidity. A townsman told me that when he met him sauntering through the village in his small close-fitting cap, and whistling to himself, he reminded him of a prince in disguise.

His only books were an almanac and an arithmetic, in which last he was considerably expert. The former was a sort of cyclopædia to him, which he supposed to contain an abstract of human knowledge, as indeed it does to a considerable extent. I loved to sound him on the various reforms of the day, and he never failed to look at them in the most simple and practical light. He had never heard of such things before. Could he do without factories? I asked. He had worn the home-made Vermont gray, he said, and that was good. Could

he dispense with tea and coffee? Did this country afford
any beverage beside water? He had soaked hemlock
leaves in water and drank it, and thought that was better than water in warm weather. When I asked him if
he could do without money, he showed the convenience
of money in such a way as to suggest and coincide with
the most philosophical accounts of the origin of this
institution, and the very derivation of the word *pecunia*.
If an ox were his property, and he wished to get needles
and thread at the store, he thought it would be inconvenient and impossible soon to go on mortgaging some
portion of the creature each time to that amount. He
could defend many institutions better than any philosopher, because, in describing them as they concerned
him, he gave the true reason for their prevalence, and
speculation had not suggested to him any other. At
another time, hearing Plato's definition of a man, — a
biped without feathers, — and that one exhibited a cock
plucked and called it Plato's man, he thought it an important difference that the *knees* bent the wrong way.
He would sometimes exclaim, "How I love to talk! By
George, I could talk all day!" I asked him once, when I
had not seen him for many months, if he had got a new
idea this summer. "Good Lord," said he, "a man that
has to work as I do, if he does not forget the ideas he has
had, he will do well. May be the man you hoe with is
inclined to race; then, by gorry, your mind must be
there; you think of weeds." He would sometimes ask me
first on such occasions, if I had made any improvement.
One winter day I asked him if he was always satisfied
with himself, wishing to suggest a substitute within him

for the priest without, and some higher motive for living. "Satisfied!" said he; "some men are satisfied with one thing, and some with another. One man, perhaps, if he has got enough, will be satisfied to sit all day with his back to the fire and his belly to the table, by George!" Yet I never, by any manœuvring, could get him to take the spiritual view of things; the highest that he appeared to conceive of was a simple expediency, such as you might expect an animal to appreciate; and this, practically, is true of most men. If I suggested any improvement in his mode of life, he merely answered, without expressing any regret, that it was too late. Yet he thoroughly believed in honesty and the like virtues.

There was a certain positive originality, however slight, to be detected in him, and I occasionally observed that he was thinking for himself and expressing his own opinion, a phenomenon so rare that I would any day walk ten miles to observe it, and it amounted to the re-origination of many of the institutions of society. Though he hesitated, and perhaps failed to express himself distinctly, he always had a presentable thought behind. Yet his thinking was so primitive and immersed in his animal life, that, though more promising than a merely learned man's, it rarely ripened to anything which can be reported. He suggested that there might be men of genius in the lowest grades of life, however permanently humble and illiterate, who take their own view always, or do not pretend to see at all; who are as bottomless even as Walden Pond was thought to be, though they may be dark and muddy.

Many a traveller came out of his way to see me and the inside of my house, and, as an excuse for calling, asked for a glass of water. I told them that I drank at the pond, and pointed thither, offering to lend them a dipper. Far off as I lived, I was not exempted from that annual visitation which occurs, methinks, about the first of April, when everybody is on the move; and I had my share of good luck, though there were some curious specimens among my visitors. Half-witted men from the almshouse and elsewhere came to see me; but I endeavored to make them exercise all the wit they had, and make their confessions to me; in such cases making wit the theme of our conversation; and so was compensated. Indeed, I found some of them to be wiser than the so-called *overseers* of the poor and select-men of the town, and thought it was time that the tables were turned. With respect to wit, I learned that there was not much difference between the half and the whole. One day, in particular, an inoffensive, simple-minded pauper, whom with others I had often seen used as fencing stuff, standing or sitting on a bushel in the fields to keep cattle and himself from straying, visited me, and expressed a wish to live as I did. He told me, with the utmost simplicity and truth, quite superior, or rather *inferior*, to anything that is called humility, that he was "deficient in intellect." These were his words. The Lord had made him so, yet he supposed the Lord cared as much for him as for another. "I have always been so," said he, "from my child-hood; I never had much mind; I was not like other children; I am weak in the head. It was the Lord's will, I suppose." And there he was to prove the truth of his words. He was a metaphysical puzzle to me. I have rarely met a fellow-man on such promising ground, — it was so simple and sincere and so true all that he said. And, true enough, in proportion as he appeared to humble himself was he exalted. I did not know at first but it was the result of a wise policy. It seemed that from such a basis of truth and frankness as the poor weak-headed pauper had laid, our intercourse might go forward to something better than the intercourse of sages.

I had some guests from those not reckoned commonly among the town's poor, but who should be; who are among the world's poor, at any rate; guests who appeal, not to your hospitality, but to your *hospitalality;* who earnestly wish to be helped, and preface their appeal with the information that they are resolved, for one thing, never to help themselves. I require of a visitor that he be not actually starving, though he may have the very best appetite in the world, however he got it. Objects of charity are not guests. Men who did not know when their visit had terminated, though I went about my business again, answering them from greater and greater remoteness. Men of almost every degree of wit called on me in the migrating season. Some who had more wits than they knew what to do with; runaway slaves with plantation manners, who listened from time to time, like the fox in the fable, as if they heard the hounds a-baying on their track, and looked at me beseechingly, as much as to say, —

"O Christian, will you send me back?"

One real runaway slave, among the rest, whom I helped to forward toward the north star. Men of one idea, like a hen with one chicken, and that a duckling; men of a thousand ideas, and unkempt heads, like those hens which are made to take charge of a hundred chickens, all in pursuit of one bug, a score of them lost in every morning's dew, — and become frizzled and mangy in consequence; men of ideas instead of legs, a sort of intellectual centipede that made you crawl all over. One man proposed a book in which visitors should write their names, as at the White Mountains; but, alas! I have too good a memory to make that necessary.

I could not but notice some of the peculiarities of my visitors. Girls and boys and young women generally seemed glad to be in the woods. They looked in the pond and at the flowers, and improved their time. Men of business, even farmers, thought only of solitude and employment, and of the great distance at which I dwelt from something or other; and though they said that they loved a ramble in the woods occasionally, it was obvious that they did not. Restless committed men, whose time was all taken up in getting a living or keeping it; ministers who spoke of God as if they enjoyed a monopoly of the subject, who could not bear all kinds of opinions; doctors, lawyers, uneasy housekeepers who pried into my cupboard and bed when I was out, — how came Mrs. —— to know that my sheets were not as clean as hers? — young men who had ceased to be young, and had concluded that it was safest to follow the beaten track of the professions, — all these generally said that it was not possible to do so much good in my position. Ay! there was the rub. The old and infirm and the timid, of whatever age or sex, thought most of sickness, and sudden accident and death; to them life seemed full of danger, — what danger is there if you don't think of any? — and they thought that a prudent man would carefully select the safest position, where Dr. B. might be on hand at a moment's warning. To them the village was literally a *com-munity*, a league for mutual defence, and you would suppose that they would not go a-huckleberrying without a medicine chest. The amount of it is, if a man is alive, there is always *danger* that he may die, though the danger must be allowed to be less in proportion as he is dead-and-alive to begin with. A man sits as many risks as he runs. Finally, there were the self-styled reformers, the greatest bores of all, who thought that I was forever singing, —

> This is the house that I built;
> This is the man that lives in the house that I built;

but they did not know that the third line was, —

> These are the folks that worry the man
> That lives in the house that I built.

I did not fear the hen-harriers, for I kept no chickens; but I feared the men-harriers rather.

I had more cheering visitors than the last. Children come a-berrying, railroad men taking a Sunday morning walk in clean shirts, fishermen and hunters, poets and philosophers; in short, all honest pilgrims, who came out to the woods for freedom's sake, and really left the village behind, I was ready to greet with, — "Welcome, Englishmen! welcome, Englishmen!" for I had had communication with that race.

VII

THE BEAN–FIELD

MEANWHILE my beans, the length of whose rows, added together, was seven miles already planted, were impatient to be hoed, for the earliest had grown considerably before the latest were in the ground; indeed they were not easily to be put off. What was the meaning of this so steady and self-respecting, this small Herculean labor, I knew not. I came to love my rows, my beans, though so many more than I wanted. They attached me to the earth, and so I got strength like Antæus. But why should I raise them? Only Heaven knows. This was my curious labor all summer, — to make this portion of the earth's surface, which had yielded only cinquefoil, blackberries, johnswort, and the like, before, sweet wild fruits and pleasant flowers, produce instead this pulse. What shall I learn of beans or beans of me? I cherish them, I hoe them, early and late I have an eye to them; and this is my day's work. It is a fine broad leaf to look on. My auxiliaries are the dews and rains which water this dry soil, and what fertility is in the soil itself, which for the most part is lean and effete. My enemies are worms, cool days, and most of all woodchucks. The last have nibbled for me a quarter of an acre clean. But what right had I to oust johnswort and the rest, and break up their ancient herb garden? Soon, however, the remaining beans will be too tough for them, and go forward to meet new foes.

When I was four years old, as I well remember, I was brought from Boston to this my native town, through these very woods and this field, to the pond. It is one of the oldest scenes stamped on my memory. And now to-night my flute has waked the echoes over that very water. The pines still stand here older than I; or, if some have fallen, I have cooked my supper with their stumps, and a new growth is rising all around, preparing another aspect for new infant eyes. Almost the same johnswort springs from the same perennial root in this pasture, and even I have at length helped to clothe that fabulous landscape of my infant dreams, and one of the results of my presence and influence is seen in these bean leaves, corn blades, and potato vines.

I planted about two acres and a half of upland; and as it was only about fifteen years since the land was cleared, and I myself had got out two or three cords of stumps, I did not give it any manure; but in the course of the summer it appeared by the arrowheads which I turned up in hoeing, that an extinct nation had anciently dwelt here and planted corn and beans ere white men came to clear the land, and so, to some extent, had exhausted the soil for this very crop.

Before yet any woodchuck or squirrel had run across the road, or the sun had got above the shrub oaks, while all the dew was on, though the farmers warned me against it, — I would advise you to do all your work if possible while the dew is on, — I began to level the ranks of haughty weeds in my bean-field and throw

a sound from fairy land.

dust upon their heads. Early in the morning I worked barefooted, dabbling like a plastic artist in the dewy and crumbling sand, but later in the day the sun blistered my feet. There the sun lighted me to hoe beans, pacing slowly backward and forward over that yellow gravelly upland, between the long green rows, fifteen rods, the one end terminating in a shrub oak copse where I could rest in the shade, the other in a blackberry field where the green berries deepened their tints by the time I had made another bout. Removing the weeds, putting fresh soil about the bean stems, and encouraging this weed which I had sown, making the yellow soil express its summer thought in bean leaves and blossoms rather than in wormwood and piper and millet grass, making the earth say beans instead of grass, — this was my daily work. As I had little aid from horses or cattle, or hired men or boys, or improved implements of husbandry, I was much slower, and became much more intimate with my beans than usual. But labor of the hands, even when pursued to the verge of drudgery, is perhaps never the worst form of idleness. It has a constant and imperishable moral, and to the scholar it yields a classic result. A very *agricola laboriosus* was I to travellers bound westward through Lincoln and Wayland to nobody knows where; they sitting at their ease in gigs, with elbows on knees, and reins loosely hanging in festoons; I the home-staying, laborious native of the soil. But soon my homestead was out of their sight and thought. It was the only open and cultivated field for a great distance on either side of the road, so they made the most of it; and sometimes the man in the field heard more of travellers' gossip and comment than was meant for his ear: "Beans so late! peas so late!" — for I continued to plant when others had begun to hoe, — the ministerial husbandman had not suspected it. "Corn, my boy, for fodder; corn for fodder." "Does he *live* there?" asks the black bonnet of the gray coat; and the hard-featured farmer reins up his grateful dobbin to inquire what you are doing where he sees no manure in the furrow, and recommends a little chip dirt, or any little waste stuff, or it may be ashes or plaster. But here were two acres and a half of furrows, and only a hoe for cart and two hands to draw it, — there being an aversion to other carts and horses, — and chip dirt far away. Fellow-travellers as they rattled by compared it aloud with the fields which they had passed, so that I came to know how I stood in the agricultural world. This was one field not in Mr. Colman's report. And, by the way, who estimates the value of the crop which nature yields in the still wilder fields unimproved by man? The crop of *English* hay is carefully weighed, the moisture calculated, the silicates and the potash; but in all dells and pond-holes in the woods and pastures and swamps grows a rich and various crop only unreaped by man. Mine was, as it were, the connecting link between wild and cultivated fields; as some states are civilized, and others half-civilized, and others savage or barbarous, so my field was, though not in a bad sense, a half-cultivated field. They were beans cheerfully returning to their wild and primitive state that I cultivated, and my hoe played the *Ranz des Vaches* for them.

Near at hand, upon the topmost spray of a birch, sings the brown thrasher — or red mavis, as some love to call him — all the morning, glad of your society, that would find out another farmer's field if yours were not here. While you are planting the seed, he cries, — "Drop it, drop it, — cover it up, cover it up, — pull it up, pull it up, pull it up." But this was not corn, and so it was safe from such enemies as he. You may wonder what his rigmarole, his amateur Paganini performances on one string or on twenty, have to do with your planting, and yet prefer it to leached ashes or plaster. It was a cheap sort of top dressing in which I had entire faith.

As I drew a still fresher soil about the rows with my hoe, I disturbed the ashes of unchronicled nations who in primeval years lived under these heavens, and their small implements of war and hunting were brought to the light of this modern day. They lay mingled with other natural stones, some of which bore the marks of having been burned by Indian fires, and some by the sun, and also bits of pottery and glass brought hither by the recent cultivators of the soil. When my hoe tinkled against the stones, that music echoed to the woods and the sky, and was an accompaniment to my labor which yielded an instant and immeasurable crop. It was no longer beans that I hoed, nor I that hoed beans; and I remembered with as much pity as pride, if I remembered at all, my acquaintances who had gone to the city to attend the oratorios. The nighthawk circled overhead in the sunny afternoons — for I sometimes made a day of it — like a mote in the eye, or in heaven's eye, falling from time to time with a swoop and a sound as if the heavens were rent, torn at last to very rags and tatters, and yet a seamless cope remained; small imps that fill the air and lay their eggs on the ground on bare sand or rocks on the tops of hills, where few have found them; graceful and slender like ripples caught up from the pond, as leaves are raised by the wind to float in the heavens; such kindredship is in nature. The hawk is aerial brother of the wave which he sails over and surveys, those his perfect air-inflated wings answering to the elemental unfledged pinions of the sea. (Or sometimes I watched a pair of hen-hawks circling high in the sky, alternately soaring and descending, approaching and leaving one another, as if they were the embodiment of my own thoughts) Or I was attracted by the passage of wild pigeons from this wood to that, with a slight quivering winnowing sound and carrier haste; or from under a rotten stump my hoe turned up a sluggish portentous and outlandish spotted salamander, a trace of Egypt and the Nile, yet our contemporary. When I paused to lean on my hoe, these sounds and sights I heard and saw anywhere in the row, a part of the inexhaustible entertainment which the country offers.)

On gala days the town fires its great guns, which echo like popguns to these woods, and some waifs of martial music occasionally penetrate thus far. To me, away there in my bean-field at the other end of the town, the big guns sounded as if a puffball had burst; and when there was a military turnout of which I was ignorant, I have sometimes had a vague sense all the day of some sort of itching and disease in the horizon, as if some eruption would break out there soon, either scarlatina or canker-rash, until at length some more favorable puff of wind, making haste over the fields and up the Wayland road, brought me information of the "trainers." It seemed by the distant hum as if somebody's bees had swarmed, and that the neighbors, according to Virgil's advice, by a faint *tintinnabulum* upon the most sonorous of their domestic utensils, were endeavoring to call them down into the hive again. And when the sound died quite away, and the hum had ceased, and the most favorable breezes told no tale, I knew that they had got the last drone of them all safely into the Middlesex hive, and that now their minds were bent on the honey with which it was smeared.

I felt proud to know that the liberties of Massachusetts and of our fatherland were in such safe keeping; and as I turned to my hoeing again I was filled with an inexpressible confidence, and pursued my labor cheerfully with a calm trust in the future.

When there were several bands of musicians, it sounded as if all the village was a vast bellows, and all the buildings expanded and collapsed alternately with a din. But sometimes it was a really noble and inspiring strain that reached these woods, and the trumpet that sings of fame, and I felt as if I could spit a Mexican with a good relish, — for why should we always stand for trifles ? — and looked round for a woodchuck or a skunk to exercise my chivalry upon. These martial strains seemed as far away as Palestine, and reminded me of a march of crusaders in the horizon, with a slight tantivy and tremulous motion of the elm tree tops which overhang the village. This was one of the *great* days; though the sky had from my clearing only the same everlastingly great look that it wears daily, and I saw no difference in it.

It was a singular experience that long acquaintance which I cultivated with beans, what with planting, and hoeing, and harvesting, and threshing, and picking over and selling them, — the last was the hardest of all, — I might add eating, for I did taste. I was determined to know beans. When they were growing, I used to hoe from five o'clock in the morning till noon, and commonly spent the rest of the day about other affairs. Consider the intimate and curious acquaintance one makes with various kinds of weeds, — it will bear some iteration in the account, for there was no little iteration in the labor, — disturbing their delicate organizations so ruthlessly, and making such invidious distinctions with his hoe, levelling whole ranks of one species, and sedulously cultivating another. That 's Roman wormwood, — that 's pigweed, — that 's sorrel, — that 's piper-grass, — have at him, chop him up, turn his roots upward to the sun, don't let him have a fibre in the shade, if you do he 'll turn himself t'other side up and be as green as a leek in two days. A long war, not with cranes, but with weeds, those Trojans who had sun and rain and dews on their side. Daily the beans saw me come to their rescue armed with a hoe, and thin the ranks of their enemies, filling up the trenches with weedy dead. Many a lusty crest-waving Hector, that towered a whole foot above his crowding comrades, fell before my weapon and rolled in the dust.

Those summer days which some of my contemporaries devoted to the fine arts in Boston or Rome, and others to contemplation in India, and others to trade in London or New York, I thus, with the other farmers of New England, devoted to husbandry. Not that I wanted beans to eat, for I am by nature a Pythagorean, so far as beans are concerned, whether they mean porridge or voting, and exchanged them for rice; but, perchance, as some must work in fields if only for the sake of tropes and expression, to serve a parable-maker one day. It was on the whole a rare amusement, which, continued too long, might have become a dissipation. Though I gave them no manure, and did not hoe them all once, I hoed them unusually well as far as I went, and was paid for it in the end, "there being in truth," as Evelyn says, "no compost or lætation whatsoever comparable to this continual motion, repastination, and turning of the mould with the spade." "The earth," he adds elsewhere, "especially if fresh, has a certain magnetism in it, by which it attracts the salt, power, or virtue (call it either) which gives it life, and is the logic of all the labor and stir we keep about it, to sustain us; all dungings and other sordid temperings being but the vicars succedaneous to this improvement." Moreover, this being one of those "worn-out and exhausted lay fields which enjoy their sabbath," had perchance, as Sir Kenelm Digby thinks likely, attracted "vital spirits" from the air. I harvested twelve bushels of beans.

But to be more particular, for it is complained that Mr. Colman has reported chiefly the expensive experiments of gentlemen farmers, my outgoes were, —

For a hoe	$0 54	
Plowing, harrowing, and furrowing .	7 50	Too much.
Beans for seed	3 12½	
Potatoes "	1 33	
Peas "	0 40	
Turnip seed	0 06	
White line for crow fence	0 02	
Horse cultivator and boy three hours .	1 00	
Horse and cart to get crop	0 75	

In all $14 72½

My income was (patremfamilias vendacem, non emàcem esse oportet), from

Nine bushels and twelve quarts of beans sold .	$16 94
Five " large potatoes	2 50
Nine " small	2 25
Grass	1 00
Stalks	0 75

In all $23 44

Leaving a pecuniary profit, as I have elsewhere said, of $8 71½

This is the result of my experience in raising beans: Plant the common small white bush bean about the first of June, in rows three feet by eighteen inches apart, being careful to select fresh round and unmixed seed. First look out for worms, and supply vacancies by planting anew. Then look out for woodchucks, if it is an exposed place, for they will nibble off the earliest tender leaves almost clean as they go; and again, when the young tendrils make their appearance, they have notice of it and will shear them off with both buds and young pods, sitting erect like a squirrel. But above all harvest as early as possible, if you would escape frosts and have a fair and salable crop; you may save much loss by this means.

This further experience also I gained: I said to myself, I will not plant beans and corn with so much industry another summer, but such seeds, if the seed is not lost, as sincerity, truth, simplicity, faith, innocence, and the like, and see if they will not grow in this soil, even with less toil and manurance, and sustain me, for surely it has not been exhausted for these crops. Alas! I said this to myself; but now another summer is gone, and another, and another, and I am obliged to say to you, Reader, that the seeds which I planted, if indeed they *were* the seeds of those virtues, were wormeaten or had lost their vitality, and so did not come up. Commonly men will only be brave as their fathers were brave, or timid. This generation is very sure to plant corn and beans each new year precisely as the Indians did centuries ago and taught the first settlers to do, as if there were a fate in it. I saw an old man the other day, to my astonishment, making the holes with a hoe for the seventieth time at least, and not for himself to lie down in'! But why should not the New Englander try new adventures, and not lay so much stress on his grain, his potato and grass crop, and his orchards, — raise other crops than these? Why concern ourselves so much about our beans for seed, and not be concerned at all about a new generation of men? We should really be fed and cheered if when we met a man we were sure to see that some of the qualities which I have named, which we all prize more than those other productions, but which are for the most part broadcast and floating in the air, had taken root and grown in him. Here comes such a subtile and ineffable quality, for instance, as truth or justice, though the slightest amount or new variety of it, along the road. Our ambassadors should be instructed to send home such seeds as these, and Congress help to distribute them over all the land. We should never stand upon ceremony with sincerity. We should never cheat and insult and banish one another by our meanness, if there were present the kernel of worth and friendliness. We should not meet thus in haste. Most men I do not meet at all, for they seem not to have time; they are busy about their beans. We would not deal with a man thus plodding ever, leaning on a hoe or a spade as a staff between his work, not as a mushroom, but partially risen out of the earth, something more than erect, like swallows alighted and walking on the ground: —

> "And as he spake, his wings would now and then
> Spread, as he meant to fly, then close again, —"

so that we should suspect that we might be conversing with an angel. Bread may not always nourish us; but it always does us good, it even takes stiffness out of our joints, and makes us supple and buoyant, when we knew not what ailed us, to recognize any generosity in man or Nature, to share any unmixed and heroic joy.

Ancient poetry and mythology suggest, at least, that husbandry was once a sacred art; but it is pursued with irreverent haste and heedlessness by us, our object being to have large farms and large crops merely. We have no festival, nor procession, nor ceremony, not excepting our cattle-shows and so-called Thanksgivings, by which the farmer expresses a sense of the sacredness of his calling, or is reminded of its sacred origin. It is the premium and the feast which tempt him. He sacrifices not to Ceres and the Terrestrial Jove, but to the infernal Plutus rather. By avarice and selfishness, and a grovelling habit, from which none of us is free, of regarding the soil as property, or the means of acquiring property chiefly, the landscape is deformed, husbandry is degraded with us, and the farmer leads the meanest of lives. He knows Nature but as a robber. Cato says that the profits of agriculture are particularly pious or just (*maximeque pius quaestus*), and according to Varro the old Romans "called the same earth Mother and Ceres, and thought that they who cultivated it led a pious and useful life, and that they alone were left of the race of King Saturn."

We are wont to forget that the sun looks on our cultivated fields and on the prairies and forests without distinction. They all reflect and absorb his rays alike, and the former make but a small part of the glorious picture which he beholds in his daily course. In his view the earth is all equally cultivated like a garden. Therefore we should receive the benefit of his light and heat with a corresponding trust and magnanimity. What though I value the seed of these beans, and harvest that in the fall of the year? This broad field which I have looked at so long looks not to me as the principal cultivator, but away from me to influences more genial to it, which water and make it green. These beans have results which are not harvested by me. Do they not grow for wood-chucks partly? The ear of wheat (in Latin *spica*, ob-soletely *speca*, from *spe*, hope) should not be the only hope of the husbandman; its kernel or grain (*granum*, from *gerendo*, bearing) is not all that it bears. How, then, can our harvest fail? Shall I not rejoice also at the abundance of the weeds whose seeds are the granary of the birds? It matters little comparatively whether the fields fill the farmer's barns. The true husbandman will cease from anxiety, as the squirrels manifest no con-cern whether the woods will bear chestnuts this year or not, and finish his labor with every day, relinquishing all claim to the produce of his fields, and sacrificing in his mind not only his first but his last fruits also.

VIII

THE VILLAGE

AFTER hoeing, or perhaps reading and writing, in the forenoon, I usually bathed again in the pond, swimming across one of its coves for a stint, and washed the dust of labor from my person, or smoothed out the last wrinkle which study had made, and for the afternoon was absolutely free. Every day or two I strolled to the village to hear some of the gossip which is incessantly going on there, circulating either from mouth to mouth, or from newspaper to newspaper, and which, taken in homœopathic doses, was really as refreshing in its way as the rustle of leaves and the peeping of frogs. As I walked in the woods to see the birds and squirrels, so I walked in the village to see the men and boys; instead of the wind among the pines I heard the carts rattle. In one direction from my house there was a colony of muskrats in the river meadows; under the grove of elms and buttonwoods in the other horizon was a village of busy men, as curious to me as if they had been prairie-dogs, each sitting at the mouth of its burrow, or running over to a neighbor's to gossip. I went there frequently to observe their habits. The village appeared to me a great news room; and on one side, to support it, as once at Redding & Company's on State Street, they kept nuts and raisins, or salt and meal and other groceries. Some have such a vast appetite for the former commodity, that is, the news, and such sound digestive organs, that they can sit forever in public avenues without stirring, and let it simmer and whisper through them like the Etesian winds, or as if inhaling ether, it only producing numbness and insensibility to pain, — otherwise it would often be painful to hear, — without affecting the consciousness. I hardly ever failed, when I rambled through the village, to see a row of such worthies, either sitting on a ladder sunning themselves, with their bodies inclined forward and their eyes glancing along the line this way and that, from time to time, with a voluptuous expression, or else leaning against a barn with their hands in their pockets, like caryatides, as if to prop it up. They, being commonly out of doors, heard whatever was in the wind. These are the coarsest mills, in which all gossip is first rudely digested or cracked up before it is emptied into finer and more delicate hoppers within doors. I observed that the vitals of the village were the grocery, the bar-room, the post-office, and the bank; and, as a necessary part of the machinery, they kept a bell, a big gun, and a fire-engine, at convenient places; and the houses were so arranged as to make the most of mankind, in lanes and fronting one another, so that every traveller had to run the gauntlet, and every man, woman, and child might get a lick at him. Of course, those who were stationed nearest to the head of the line, where they could most see and be seen, and have the first blow at him, paid the highest prices for their places; and the few straggling inhabitants in the outskirts, where long gaps in the line began to occur, and the traveller

could get over walls or turn aside into cow-paths, and so
escape, paid a very slight ground or window tax. Signs
were hung out on all sides to allure him; some to catch
him by the appetite, as the tavern and victualling cellar;
some by the fancy, as the dry goods store and the jewel-
ler's; and others by the hair or the feet or the skirts, as
the barber, the shoemaker, or the tailor. Besides, there
was a still more terrible standing invitation to call at
every one of these houses, and company expected about
these times. For the most part I escaped wonderfully
from these dangers, either by proceeding at once boldly
and without deliberation to the goal, as is recommended
to those who run the gauntlet, or by keeping my thoughts
on high things, like Orpheus, who, "loudly singing the
praises of the gods to his lyre, drowned the voices of the
Sirens, and kept out of danger." Sometimes I bolted
suddenly, and nobody could tell my whereabouts, for I
did not stand much about gracefulness, and never hesitated at a gap in a fence. I was even accustomed to
make an irruption into some houses, where I was well
entertained, and after learning the kernels and very last
sieveful of news, — what had subsided, the prospects of
war and peace, and whether the world was likely to hold
together much longer, — I was let out through the rear
avenues, and so escaped to the woods again.

It was very pleasant, when I stayed late in town, to
launch myself into the night, especially if it was dark
and tempestuous, and set sail from some bright village
parlor or lecture room, with a bag of rye or Indian meal
upon my shoulder, for my snug harbor in the woods,
having made all tight without and withdrawn under

hatches with a merry crew of thoughts, leaving only my outer man at the helm, or even tying up the helm when it was plain sailing. I had many a genial thought by the cabin fire "as I sailed." I was never cast away nor distressed in any weather, though I encountered some severe storms. It is darker in the woods, even in common nights, than most suppose. I frequently had to look up at the opening between the trees above the path in order to learn my route, and, where there was no cartpath, to feel with my feet the faint track which I had worn, or steer by the known relation of particular trees which I felt with my hands, passing between two pines for instance, not more than eighteen inches apart, in the midst of the woods, invariably, in the darkest night. Sometimes, after coming home thus late in a dark and muggy night, when my feet felt the path which my eyes could not see, dreaming and absent-minded all the way, until I was aroused by having to raise my hand to lift the latch, I have not been able to recall a single step of my walk, and I have thought that perhaps my body would find its way home if its master should forsake it, as the hand finds its way to the mouth without assistance. Several times, when a visitor chanced to stay into evening, and it proved a dark night, I was obliged to conduct him to the cart-path in the rear of the house, and then point out to him the direction he was to pursue, and in keeping which he was to be guided rather by his feet than his eyes. One very dark night I directed thus on their way two young men who had been fishing in the pond. They lived about a mile off through the woods, and were quite used to the route. A day or two after one of them told me that they wandered about the greater part of the night, close by their own premises, and did not get home till toward morning, by which time, as there had been several heavy showers in the meanwhile, and the leaves were very wet, they were drenched to their skins. I have heard of many going astray even in the village streets, when the darkness was so thick that you could cut it with a knife, as the saying is. Some who live in the outskirts, having come to town a-shopping in their wagons, have been obliged to put up for the night; and gentlemen and ladies making a call have gone half a mile out of their way, feeling the sidewalk only with their feet, and not knowing when they turned. It is a surprising and memorable, as well as valuable experience, to be lost in the woods any time. Often in a snow-storm, even by day, one will come out upon a well-known road and yet find it impossible to tell which way leads to the village. Though he knows that he has travelled it a thousand times, he cannot recognize a feature in it, but it is as strange to him as if it were a road in Siberia. By night, of course, the perplexity is infinitely greater. In our most trivial walks, we are constantly, though unconsciously, steering like pilots by certain well-known beacons and headlands, and if we go beyond our usual course we still carry in our minds the bearing of some neighboring cape; and not till we are completely lost, or turned round, — for a man needs only to be turned round once with his eyes shut in this world to be lost, — do we appreciate the vastness and strangeness of nature. Every man has to learn the points of compass again as often as he awakes, whether from sleep or any abstraction. Not till we are lost, in other words not till we have lost the world, do we begin to find ourselves, and realize where we are and the infinite extent of our relations.

One afternoon, near the end of the first summer, when I went to the village to get a shoe from the cobbler's, I was seized and put into jail, because, as I have elsewhere related, I did not pay a tax to, or recognize the authority of, the State which buys and sells men, women, and children, like cattle, at the door of its senate-house. I had gone down to the woods for other purposes. But, wherever a man goes, men will pursue and paw him with their dirty institutions, and, if they can, constrain him to belong to their desperate odd-fellow society. It is true, I might have resisted forcibly with more or less effect, might have run "amok" against society; but I preferred that society should run "amok" against me, it being the desperate party. However, I was released the next day, obtained my mended shoe, and returned to the woods in season to get my dinner of huckleberries on Fair Haven Hill. I was never molested by any person but those who represented the State. I had no lock nor bolt but for the desk which held my papers, not even a nail to put over my latch or windows. I never fastened my door night or day, though I was to be absent several days; not even when the next fall I spent a fortnight in the woods of Maine. And yet my house was more respected than if it had been surrounded by a file of soldiers. The tired rambler could rest and warm himself by my fire, the literary amuse himself with the few books on my table, or the curious, by opening my closet door, see what was left of my dinner, and what prospect I had of a supper. Yet, though many people of every class came this way to the pond, I suffered no serious inconvenience from these sources, and I never missed anything but one small book, a volume of Homer, which perhaps was improperly gilded, and this I trust a soldier of our camp has found by this time. I am convinced, that if all men were to live as simply as I then did, thieving and robbery would be unknown. These take place only in communities where some have got more than is sufficient while others have not enough. The Pope's Homers would soon get properly distributed.

> " Nec bella fuerunt,
> Faginus astabat dum scyphus ante dapes."

> " Nor wars did men molest,
> When only beechen bowls were in request."

"You who govern public affairs, what need have you to employ punishments ? Love virtue, and the people will be virtuous. The virtues of a superior man are like the wind; the virtues of a common man are like the grass; the grass, when the wind passes over it, bends."

IX

THE PONDS

Sometimes, having had a surfeit of human society and gossip, and worn out all my village friends, I rambled still farther westward than I habitually dwell, into yet more unfrequented parts of the town, "to fresh woods and pastures new," or, while the sun was setting, made my supper of huckleberries and blueberries on Fair Haven Hill, and laid up a store for several days. The fruits do not yield their true flavor to the purchaser of them, nor to him who raises them for the market. There is but one way to obtain it, yet few take that way. If you would know the flavor of huckleberries, ask the cow-boy or the partridge. It is a vulgar error to suppose that you have tasted huckleberries who never plucked them. A huckleberry never reaches Boston; they have not been known there since they grew on her three hills. The ambrosial and essential part of the fruit is lost with the bloom which is rubbed off in the market cart, and they become mere provender. As long as Eternal Justice reigns, not one innocent huckleberry can be transported thither from the country's hills.

Occasionally, after my hoeing was done for the day, I joined some impatient companion who had been fishing on the pond since morning, as silent and motionless as a duck or a floating leaf, and, after practising various kinds of philosophy, had concluded commonly, by the time I arrived, that he belonged to the ancient sect of Cœnobites. There was one older man, an excellent fisher and skilled in all kinds of woodcraft, who was pleased to look upon my house as a building erected for the convenience of fishermen; and I was equally pleased when he sat in my doorway to arrange his lines. Once in a while we sat together on the pond, he at one end of the boat, and I at the other; but not many words passed between us, for he had grown deaf in his later years, but he occasionally hummed a psalm, which harmonized well enough with my philosophy. Our intercourse was thus altogether one of unbroken harmony, far more pleasing to remember than if it had been carried on by speech. When, as was commonly the case, I had none to commune with, I used to raise the echoes by striking with a paddle on the side of my boat, filling the surrounding woods with circling and dilating sound, stirring them up as the keeper of a menagerie his wild beasts, until I elicited a growl from every wooded vale and hillside.

In warm evenings I frequently sat in the boat playing the flute, and saw the perch, which I seem to have charmed, hovering around me, and the moon travelling over the ribbed bottom, which was strewed with the wrecks of the forest. Formerly I had come to this pond adventurously, from time to time, in dark summer nights, with a companion, and, making a fire close to the water's edge, which we thought attracted the fishes, we caught pouts with a bunch of worms strung on a thread, and when we had done, far in the night, threw the burn-

ing brands high into the air like skyrockets, which, coming down into the pond, were quenched with a loud
hissing, and we were suddenly groping in total darkness. Through this, whistling a tune, we took our way
to the haunts of men again. But now I had made my
home by the shore.

Sometimes, after staying in a village parlor till the
family had all retired, I have returned to the woods,
and, partly with a view to the next day's dinner, spent
the hours of midnight fishing from a boat by moonlight,
serenaded by owls and foxes, and hearing, from time to
time, the creaking note of some unknown bird close at
hand. These experiences were very memorable and
valuable to me, — anchored in forty feet of water, and
twenty or thirty rods from the shore, surrounded sometimes by thousands of small perch and shiners, dimpling the surface with their tails in the moonlight, and
communicating by a long flaxen line with mysterious
nocturnal fishes which had their dwelling forty feet below, or sometimes dragging sixty feet of line about the
pond as I drifted in the gentle night breeze, now and
then feeling a slight vibration along it, indicative of
some life prowling about its extremity, of dull uncertain
blundering purpose there, and slow to make up its
mind. At length you slowly raise, pulling hand over
hand, some horned pout squeaking and squirming to
the upper air. It was very queer, especially in dark
nights, when your thoughts had wandered to vast and
cosmogonal themes in other spheres, to feel this faint
jerk, which came to interrupt your dreams and link
you to Nature again. It seemed as if I might next cast

my line upward into the air, as well as downward into
this element, which was scarcely more dense. Thus I
caught two fishes as it were with one hook.

The scenery of Walden is on a humble scale, and,
though very beautiful, does not approach to grandeur,
nor can it much concern one who has not long frequented
it or lived by its shore; yet this pond is so remarkable
for its depth and purity as to merit a particular description. It is a clear and deep green well, half a mile long
and a mile and three quarters in circumference, and
contains about sixty-one and a half acres; a perennial
spring in the midst of pine and oak woods, without any
visible inlet or outlet except by the clouds and evaporation. The surrounding hills rise abruptly from the
water to the height of forty to eighty feet, though on the
southeast and east they attain to about one hundred
and one hundred and fifty feet respectively, within a
quarter and a third of a mile. They are exclusively
woodland. All our Concord waters have two colors at
least; one when viewed at a distance, and another, more
proper, close at hand. The first depends more on the
light, and follows the sky. In clear weather, in summer,
they appear blue at a little distance, especially if agitated,
and at a great distance all appear alike. In stormy
weather they are sometimes of a dark slate-color. The
sea, however, is said to be blue one day and green another without any perceptible change in the atmosphere.
I have seen our river, when, the landscape being covered
with snow, both water and ice were almost as green as
grass. Some consider blue "to be the color of pure

water, whether liquid or solid." But, looking directly down into our waters from a boat, they are seen to be of very different colors. Walden is blue at one time and green at another, even from the same point of view. Lying between the earth and the heavens, it partakes of the color of both. Viewed from a hilltop it reflects the color of the sky; but near at hand it is of a yellowish tint next the shore where you can see the sand, then a light green, which gradually deepens to a uniform dark green in the body of the pond. In some lights, viewed even from a hilltop, it is of a vivid green next the shore. Some have referred this to the reflection of the verdure; but it is equally green there against the railroad sand-bank, and in the spring, before the leaves are expanded, and it may be simply the result of the prevailing blue mixed with the yellow of the sand. Such is the color of its iris. This is that portion, also, where in the spring, the ice being warmed by the heat of the sun reflected from the bottom, and also transmitted through the earth, melts first and forms a narrow canal about the still frozen middle. Like the rest of our waters, when much agitated, in clear weather, so that the surface of the waves may reflect the sky at the right angle, or because there is more light mixed with it, it appears at a little distance of a darker blue than the sky itself; and at such a time, being on its surface, and looking with divided vision, so as to see the reflection, I have discerned a matchless and indescribable light blue, such as watered or changeable silks and sword blades suggest, more cerulean than the sky itself, alternating with the original dark green on the opposite sides of the waves, which last appeared but muddy in comparison. It is a vitreous greenish blue, as I remember it, like those patches of the winter sky seen through cloud vistas in the west before sundown. Yet a single glass of its water held up to the light is as colorless as an equal quantity of air. It is well known that a large plate of glass will have a green tint, owing, as the makers say, to its "body," but a small piece of the same will be colorless. How large a body of Walden water would be required to reflect a green tint I have never proved. The water of our river is black or a very dark brown to one looking directly down on it, and, like that of most ponds, imparts to the body of one bathing in it a yellowish tinge; but this water is of such crystalline purity that the body of the bather appears of an alabaster whiteness, still more unnatural, which, as the limbs are magnified and distorted withal, produces a monstrous effect, making fit studies for a Michael Angelo.

The water is so transparent that the bottom can easily be discerned at the depth of twenty-five or thirty feet. Paddling over it, you may see, many feet beneath the surface, the schools of perch and shiners, perhaps only an inch long, yet the former easily distinguished by their transverse bars, and you think that they must be ascetic fish that find a subsistence there. Once, in the winter, many years ago, when I had been cutting holes through the ice in order to catch pickerel, as I stepped ashore I tossed my axe back on to the ice, but, as if some evil genius had directed it, it slid four or five rods directly into one of the holes, where the water was twenty-five feet deep. Out of curiosity, I lay down on

the ice and looked through the hole, until I saw the axe
a little on one side, standing on its head, with its helve
erect and gently swaying to and fro with the pulse of the
pond; and there it might have stood erect and swaying
till in the course of time the handle rotted off, if I had
not disturbed it. Making another hole directly over it
with an ice chisel which I had, and cutting down the
longest birch which I could find in the neighborhood
with my knife, I made a slip-noose, which I attached to
its end, and, letting it down carefully, passed it over the
knob of the handle, and drew it by a line along the
birch, and so pulled the axe out again.

The shore is composed of a belt of smooth rounded
white stones like paving-stones, excepting one or two
short sand beaches, and is so steep that in many places
a single leap will carry you into water over your head;
and were it not for its remarkable transparency, that
would be the last to be seen of its bottom till it rose on
the opposite side. Some think it is bottomless. It is
nowhere muddy, and a casual observer would say that
there were no weeds at all in it; and of noticeable plants,
except in the little meadows recently overflowed, which
do not properly belong to it, a closer scrutiny does not
detect a flag nor a bulrush, nor even a lily, yellow or
white, but only a few small heart-leaves and potamo-
getons, and perhaps a water-target or two; all which
however a bather might not perceive; and these plants
are clean and bright like the element they grow in. The
stones extend a rod or two into the water, and then the
bottom is pure sand, except in the deepest parts, where
there is usually a little sediment, probably from the de-

cay of the leaves which have been wafted on to it so many successive falls, and a bright green weed is brought up on anchors even in midwinter.

We have one other pond just like this, White Pond, in Nine Acre Corner, about two and a half miles westerly ; but, though I am acquainted with most of the ponds within a dozen miles of this centre, I do not know a third of this pure and well-like character. Successive nations perchance have drank at, admired, and fathomed it, and passed away, and still its water is green and pellucid as ever. Not an intermitting spring! Perhaps on that spring morning when Adam and Eve were driven out of Eden Walden Pond was already in existence, and even then breaking up in a gentle spring rain accompanied with mist and a southerly wind, and covered with myriads of ducks and geese, which had not heard of the fall, when still such pure lakes sufficed them. Even then it had commenced to rise and fall, and had clarified its waters and colored them of the hue they now wear, and obtained a patent of Heaven to be the only Walden Pond in the world and distiller of celestial dews. Who knows in how many unremembered nations' literatures this has been the Castalian Fountain ? or what nymphs presided over it in the Golden Age ? It is a gem of the first water which Concord wears in her coronet.

Yet perchance the first who came to this well have left some trace of their footsteps. I have been surprised to detect encircling the pond, even where a thick wood has just been cut down on the shore, a narrow shelf-like path in the steep hillside, alternately rising and falling, approaching and receding from the water's edge, as old probably as the race of man here, worn by the feet of aboriginal hunters, and still from time to time unwittingly trodden by the present occupants of the land. This is particularly distinct to one standing on the middle of the pond in winter, just after a light snow has fallen, appearing as a clear undulating white line, unobscured by weeds and twigs, and very obvious a quarter of a mile off in many places where in summer it is hardly distinguishable close at hand. The snow reprints it, as it were, in clear white type alto-relievo. The ornamented grounds of villas which will one day be built here may still preserve some trace of this.

The pond rises and falls, but whether regularly or not, and within what period, nobody knows, though, as usual, many pretend to know. It is commonly higher in the winter and lower in the summer, though not corresponding to the general wet and dryness. I can remember when it was a foot or two lower, and also when it was at least five feet higher, than when I lived by it. There is a narrow sand-bar running into it, with very deep water on one side, on which I helped boil a kettle of chowder, some six rods from the main shore, about the year 1824, which it has not been possible to do for twenty-five years; and, on the other hand, my friends used to listen with incredulity when I told them, that a few years later I was accustomed to fish from a boat in a secluded cove in the woods, fifteen rods from the only shore they knew, which place was long since converted into a meadow. But the pond has risen steadily for two years, and now, in the summer of '52, is just

INDIAN PATH AROUND WALDEN

five feet higher than when I lived there, or as high as it was thirty years ago, and fishing goes on again in the meadow. This makes a difference of level, at the outside, of six or seven feet; and yet the water shed by the surrounding hills is insignificant in amount, and this overflow must be referred to causes which affect the deep springs. This same summer the pond has begun to fall again. It is remarkable that this fluctuation, whether periodical or not, appears thus to require many years for its accomplishment. I have observed one rise and a part of two falls, and I expect that a dozen or fifteen years hence the water will again be as low as I have ever known it. Flint's Pond, a mile eastward, allowing for the disturbance occasioned by its inlets and outlets, and the smaller intermediate ponds also, sympathize with Walden, and recently attained their greatest height at the same time with the latter. The same is true, as far as my observation goes, of White Pond.

This rise and fall of Walden at long intervals serves this use at least; the water standing at this great height for a year or more, though it makes it difficult to walk round it, kills the shrubs and trees which have sprung up about its edge since the last rise, — pitch pines, birches, alders, aspens, and others, — and, falling again, leaves an unobstructed shore; for, unlike many ponds and all waters which are subject to a daily tide, its shore is cleanest when the water is lowest. On the side of the pond next my house a row of pitch pines, fifteen feet high, has been killed and tipped over as if by a lever, and thus a stop put to their encroachments; and their size indicates how many years have elapsed since the last rise to this height. By this fluctuation the pond asserts its title to a shore, and thus the *shore* is *shorn*, and the trees cannot hold it by right of possession. These are the lips of the lake, on which no beard grows. It licks its chaps from time to time. When the water is at its height, the alders, willows, and maples send forth a mass of fibrous red roots several feet long from all sides of their stems in the water, and to the height of three or four feet from the ground, in the effort to maintain themselves; and I have known the high blueberry bushes about the shore, which commonly produce no fruit, bear an abundant crop under these circumstances.

Some have been puzzled to tell how the shore became so regularly paved. My townsmen have all heard the tradition — the oldest people tell me that they heard it in their youth — that anciently the Indians were holding a pow-wow upon a hill here, which rose as high into the heavens as the pond now sinks deep into the earth, and they used much profanity, as the story goes, though this vice is one of which the Indians were never guilty, and while they were thus engaged the hill shook and suddenly sank, and only one old squaw, named Walden, escaped, and from her the pond was named. It has been conjectured that when the hill shook these stones rolled down its side and became the present shore. It is very certain, at any rate, that once there was no pond here, and now there is one; and this Indian fable does not in any respect conflict with the account of that ancient settler whom I have mentioned, who remembers so well when he first came here with his divining-rod, saw a thin vapor rising from the sward, and the hazel pointed steadily downward, and he concluded to dig a well here. As for the stones, many still think that they are hardly to be accounted for by the action of the waves on these hills; but I observe that the surrounding hills are remarkably full of the same kind of stones, so that they have been obliged to pile them up in walls on both sides of the railroad cut nearest the pond; and, moreover, there are most stones where the shore is most abrupt; so that, unfortunately, it is no longer a mystery to me. I detect the paver. If the name was not derived from that of some English locality, — Saffron Walden, for instance, — one might suppose that it was called originally *Walled-in* Pond.

The pond was my well ready dug. For four months in the year its water is as cold as it is pure at all times; and I think that it is then as good as any, if not the best, in the town. In the winter, all water which is exposed to the air is colder than springs and wells which are protected from it. The temperature of the pond water which had stood in the room where I sat from five o'clock in the afternoon till noon the next day, the sixth of March, 1846, the thermometer having been up to 65° or 70° some of the time, owing partly to the sun on the roof, was 42°, or one degree colder than the water of one of the coldest wells in the village just drawn. The temperature of the Boiling Spring the same day was 45°, or the warmest of any water tried, though it is the coldest that I know of in summer, when, beside, shallow and stagnant surface water is not mingled with it. Moreover, in summer, Walden never becomes so warm as

most water which is exposed to the sun, on account of its
depth. In the warmest weather I usually placed a pailful in my cellar, where it became cool in the night, and
remained so during the day; though I also resorted to
a spring in the neighborhood. It was as good when a
week old as the day it was dipped, and had no taste of
the pump. Whoever camps for a week in summer by
the shore of a pond, needs only bury a pail of water a
few feet deep in the shade of his camp to be independent
of the luxury of ice.

There have been caught in Walden pickerel, one
weighing seven pounds, — to say nothing of another
which carried off a reel with great velocity, which the
fisherman safely set down at eight pounds because he
did not see him, — perch and pouts, some of each
weighing over two pounds, shiners, chivins or roach
(*Leuciscus pulchellus*), a very few breams, and a couple
of eels, one weighing four pounds, — I am thus particular
because the weight of a fish is commonly its only title to
fame, and these are the only eels I have heard of here;
— also, I have a faint recollection of a little fish some
five inches long, with silvery sides and a greenish back,
somewhat dace-like in its character, which I mention
here chiefly to link my facts to fable. Nevertheless,
this pond is not very fertile in fish. Its pickerel, though
not abundant, are its chief boast. I have seen at one
time lying on the ice pickerel of at least three different
kinds: a long and shallow one, steel-colored, most like
those caught in the river; a bright golden kind, with
greenish reflections and remarkably deep, which is the
most common here; and another, golden-colored, and

shaped like the last, but peppered on the sides with small dark brown or black spots, intermixed with a few faint blood-red ones, very much like a trout. The specific name *reticulatus* would not apply to this; it should be *guttatus* rather. These are all very firm fish, and weigh more than their size promises. The shiners, pouts, and perch also, and indeed all the fishes which inhabit this pond, are much cleaner, handsomer, and firmer-fleshed than those in the river and most other ponds, as the water is purer, and they can easily be distinguished from them. Probably many ichthyologists would make new varieties of some of them. There are also a clean race of frogs and tortoises, and a few mussels in it; muskrats and minks leave their traces about it, and occasionally a travelling mud-turtle visits it. Sometimes, when I pushed off my boat in the morning, I disturbed a great mud-turtle which had secreted himself under the boat in the night. Ducks and geese frequent it in the spring and fall, the white-bellied swallows (*Hirundo bicolor*) skim over it, and the peetweets (*Totanus macularius*) "teeter" along its stony shores all summer. I have sometimes disturbed a fish hawk sitting on a white pine over the water; but I doubt if it is ever profaned by the wing of a gull, like Fair Haven. At most, it tolerates one annual loon. These are all the animals of consequence which frequent it now.

You may see from a boat, in calm weather, near the sandy eastern shore, where the water is eight or ten feet deep, and also in some other parts of the pond, some circular heaps half a dozen feet in diameter by a foot in height, consisting of small stones less than a hen's egg in size, where all around is bare sand. At first you wonder if the Indians could have formed them on the ice for any purpose, and so, when the ice melted, they sank to the bottom; but they are too regular and some of them plainly too fresh for that. They are similar to those found in rivers; but as there are no suckers nor lampreys here, I know not by what fish they could be made. Perhaps they are the nests of the chivin. These lend a pleasing mystery to the bottom.

The shore is irregular enough not to be monotonous. I have in my mind's eye the western, indented with deep bays, the bolder northern, and the beautifully scalloped southern shore, where successive capes overlap each other and suggest unexplored coves between. The forest has never so good a setting, nor is so distinctly beautiful, as when seen from the middle of a small lake amid hills which rise from the water's edge; for the water in which it is reflected not only makes the best foreground in such a case, but, with its winding shore, the most natural and agreeable boundary to it. There is no rawness nor imperfection in its edge there, as where the axe has cleared a part, or a cultivated field abuts on it. The trees have ample room to expand on the water side, and each sends forth its most vigorous branch in that direction. There Nature has woven a natural selvage, and the eye rises by just gradations from the low shrubs of the shore to the highest trees. There are few traces of man's hand to be seen. The water laves the shore as it did a thousand years ago.

A lake is the landscape's most beautiful and expressive feature. It is earth's eye; looking into which the beholder measures the depth of his own nature. The fluviatile trees next the shore are the slender eyelashes which fringe it, and the wooded hills and cliffs around are its overhanging brows.

Standing on the smooth sandy beach at the east end of the pond, in a calm September afternoon, when a slight haze makes the opposite shore-line indistinct, I have seen whence came the expression, "the glassy surface of a lake." When you invert your head, it looks like a thread of finest gossamer stretched across the valley, and gleaming against the distant pine woods, separating one stratum of the atmosphere from another. You would think that you could walk dry under it to the opposite hills, and that the swallows which skim over might perch on it. Indeed, they sometimes dive below the line, as it were by mistake, and are undeceived. As you look over the pond westward you are obliged to employ both your hands to defend your eyes against the reflected as well as the true sun, for they are equally bright; and if, between the two, you survey its surface critically, it is literally as smooth as glass, except where the skater insects, at equal intervals scattered over its whole extent, by their motions in the sun produce the finest imaginable sparkle on it, or, perchance, a duck plumes itself, or, as I have said, a swallow skims so low as to touch it. It may be that in the distance a fish describes an arc of three or four feet in the air, and there is one bright flash where it emerges, and another where it strikes the water; sometimes the whole silvery arc is revealed; or here and there, perhaps, is a thistle-down floating on its surface, which the fishes dart at and so

dimple it again. It is like molten glass cooled but not
congealed, and the few motes in it are pure and beautiful
like the imperfections in glass. You may often detect a
yet smoother and darker water, separated from the rest
as if by an invisible cobweb, boom of the water nymphs,
resting on it. From a hilltop you can see a fish leap in
almost any part; for not a pickerel or shiner picks an
insect from this smooth surface but it manifestly disturbs the equilibrium of the whole lake. It is wonderful
with what elaborateness this simple fact is advertised,
— this piscine murder will out, — and from my distant
perch I distinguish the circling undulations when they
are half a dozen rods in diameter. You can even detect
a water-bug (*Gyrinus*) ceaselessly progressing over the
smooth surface a quarter of a mile off; for they furrow
the water slightly, making a conspicuous ripple bounded
by two diverging lines, but the skaters glide over it
without rippling it perceptibly. When the surface is
considerably agitated there are no skaters nor water-
bugs on it, but apparently, in calm days, they leave their
havens and adventurously glide forth from the shore by
short impulses till they completely cover it. It is a
soothing employment, on one of those fine days in the
fall when all the warmth of the sun is fully appreciated,
to sit on a stump on such a height as this, overlooking
the pond, and study the dimpling circles which are
incessantly inscribed on its otherwise invisible surface
amid the reflected skies and trees. Over this great expanse there is no disturbance but it is thus at once gently
smoothed away and assuaged, as, when a vase of water
is jarred, the trembling circles seek the shore and all is

smooth again. Not a fish can leap or an insect fall on the pond but it is thus reported in circling dimples, in lines of beauty, as it were the constant welling up of its fountain, the gentle pulsing of its life, the heaving of its breast. The thrills of joy and thrills of pain are undistinguishable. How peaceful the phenomena of the lake! Again the works of man shine as in the spring. Ay, every leaf and twig and stone and cobweb sparkles now at mid-afternoon as when covered with dew in a spring morning. Every motion of an oar or an insect produces a flash of light; and if an oar falls, how sweet the echo!

In such a day, in September or October, Walden is a perfect forest mirror, set round with stones as precious to my eye as if fewer or rarer. Nothing so fair, so pure, and at the same time so large, as a lake, perchance, lies on the surface of the earth. Sky water. It needs no fence. Nations come and go without defiling it. It is a mirror which no stone can crack, whose quicksilver will never wear off, whose gilding Nature continually repairs; no storms, no dust, can dim its surface ever fresh; — a mirror in which all impurity presented to it sinks, swept and dusted by the sun's hazy brush, — this the light dust-cloth, — which retains no breath that is breathed on it, but sends its own to float as clouds high above its surface, and be reflected in its bosom still.

A field of water betrays the spirit that is in the air. It is continually receiving new life and motion from above. It is intermediate in its nature between land and sky. On land only the grass and trees wave, but the water itself is rippled by the wind. I see where the breeze dashes across it by the streaks or flakes of light. It is remarkable that we can look down on its surface. We shall, perhaps, look down thus on the surface of air at length, and mark where a still subtler spirit sweeps over it.

The skaters and water-bugs finally disappear in the latter part of October, when the severe frosts have come; and then and in November, usually, in a calm day, there is absolutely nothing to ripple the surface. One November afternoon, in the calm at the end of a rain-storm of several days' duration, when the sky was still completely overcast and the air was full of mist, I observed that the pond was remarkably smooth, so that it was difficult to distinguish its surface; though it no longer reflected the bright tints of October, but the sombre November colors of the surrounding hills. Though I passed over it as gently as possible, the slight undulations produced by my boat extended almost as far as I could see, and gave a ribbed appearance to the reflections. But, as I was looking over the surface, I saw here and there at a distance a faint glimmer, as if some skater insects which had escaped the frosts might be collected there, or, perchance, the surface, being so smooth, betrayed where a spring welled up from the bottom. Paddling gently to one of these places, I was surprised to find myself surrounded by myriads of small perch, about five inches long, of a rich bronze color in the green water, sporting there, and constantly rising to the surface and dimpling it, sometimes leaving bubbles on it. In such transparent and seemingly bottomless water, reflecting the clouds, I seemed to be floating through the air as in a balloon, and their swimming impressed me as a kind of flight or hovering, as if they were a compact flock of birds passing just beneath my level on the right or left, their fins, like sails, set all around them. There were many such schools in the pond, apparently improving the short season before winter would draw an icy shutter over their broad sky-light, sometimes giving to the surface an appearance as if a slight breeze struck it, or a few rain-drops fell there. When I approached carelessly and alarmed them, they made a sudden plash and rippling with their tails, as if one had struck the water with a brushy bough, and instantly took refuge in the depths. At length the wind rose, the mist increased, and the waves began to run, and the perch leaped much higher than before, half out of water, a hundred black points, three inches long, at once above the surface. Even as late as the fifth of December, one year, I saw some dimples on the surface, and thinking it was going to rain hard immediately, the air being full of mist, I made haste to take my place at the oars and row homeward; already the rain seemed rapidly increasing, though I felt none on my cheek, and I anticipated a thorough soaking. But suddenly the dimples ceased, for they were produced by the perch, which the noise of my oars had scared into the depths, and I saw their schools dimly disappearing; so I spent a dry afternoon after all.

An old man who used to frequent this pond nearly sixty years ago, when it was dark with surrounding forests, tells me that in those days he sometimes saw it all alive with ducks and other water-fowl, and that there were many eagles about it. He came here a-fishing, and used an old log canoe which he found on the shore. It was made of two white pine logs dug out and pinned together, and was cut off square at the ends. It was very clumsy, but lasted a great many years before it became water-logged and perhaps sank to the bottom. He did not know whose it was; it belonged to the pond. He used to make a cable for his anchor of strips of hickory bark tied together. An old man, a potter, who lived by the pond before the Revolution, told him once that there was an iron chest at the bottom, and that he had seen it. Sometimes it would come floating up to the shore; but when you went toward it, it would go back into deep water and disappear. I was pleased to hear of the old log canoe, which took the place of an Indian one of the same material but more graceful construction, which perchance had first been a tree on the bank, and then, as it were, fell into the water, to float there for a generation, the most proper vessel for the lake. I remember that when I first looked into these depths there were many large trunks to be seen indistinctly lying on the bottom, which had either been blown over formerly, or left on the ice at the last cutting, when wood was cheaper; but now they have mostly disappeared.

When I first paddled a boat on Walden, it was completely surrounded by thick and lofty pine and oak woods, and in some of its coves grape-vines had run over the trees next the water and formed bowers under which a boat could pass. The hills which form its shores are so steep, and the woods on them were then so high, that, as you looked down from the west end, it had the appearance of an amphitheatre for some kind of sylvan spectacle. I have spent many an hour, when I was younger, floating over its surface as the zephyr willed, having paddled my boat to the middle, and lying on my back across the seats, in a summer forenoon, dreaming awake, until I was aroused by the boat touching the sand, and I arose to see what shore my fates had impelled me to; days when idleness was the most attractive and productive industry. Many a forenoon have I stolen away, preferring to spend thus the most valued part of the day; for I was rich, if not in money, in sunny hours and summer days, and spent them lavishly; nor do I regret that I did not waste more of them in the workshop or the teacher's desk. But since I left those shores the woodchoppers have still further laid them waste, and now for many a year there will be no more rambling through the aisles of the wood, with occasional vistas through which you see the water. My Muse may be excused if she is silent henceforth. How can you expect the birds to sing when their groves are cut down?

SARCASM!

Now the trunks of trees on the bottom, and the old log canoe, and the dark surrounding woods, are gone, and the villagers, who scarcely know where it lies, instead of going to the pond to bathe or drink, are thinking to bring its water, which should be as sacred as the Ganges at least, to the village in a pipe, to wash their dishes with! — to earn their Walden by the turning of a cock or drawing of a plug! That devilish Iron Horse, whose

ear-rending neigh is heard throughout the town, has
muddied the Boiling Spring with his foot, and he it is
that has browsed off all the woods on Walden shore,
that Trojan horse, with a thousand men in his belly,
introduced by mercenary Greeks! Where is the country's champion, the Moore of Moore Hall, to meet him
at the Deep Cut and thrust an avenging lance between
the ribs of the bloated pest?

Nevertheless, of all the characters I have known,
perhaps Walden wears best, and best preserves its
purity. Many men have been likened to it, but few de-
serve that honor. Though the woodchoppers have laid
bare first this shore and then that, and the Irish have
built their sties by it, and the railroad has infringed on
its border, and the ice-men have skimmed it once, it is
itself unchanged, the same water which my youthful
eyes fell on; all the change is in me. (It has not acquired
one permanent wrinkle after all its ripples.) It is peren-
nially young, and I may stand and see a swallow dip
apparently to pick an insect from its surface as of yore.
It struck me again to-night, as if I had not seen it almost
daily for more than twenty years, — Why, here is Walden, the same woodland lake that I discovered so many
years ago; where a forest was cut down last winter
another is springing up by its shore as lustily as ever;
the same thought is welling up to its surface that was
then; it is the same liquid joy and happiness to itself
and its Maker, ay, and it *may* be to me. It is the work
of a brave man surely, in whom there was no guile! He
rounded this water with his hand, deepened and clarified
it in his thought, and in his will bequeathed it to Con-

cord. I see by its face that it is visited by the same reflection; and I can almost say, Walden, is it you?

> It is no dream of mine,
> To ornament a line;
> I cannot come nearer to God and Heaven
> Than I live to Walden even.
> I am its stony shore,
> And the breeze that passes o'er;
> In the hollow of my hand
> Are its water and its sand,
> And its deepest resort
> Lies high in my thought.

The cars never pause to look at it; yet I fancy that
the engineers and firemen and brakemen, and those
passengers who have a season ticket and see it often,
are better men for the sight. The engineer does not forget at night, or his nature does not, that he has beheld
this vision of serenity and purity once at least during the
day. Though seen but once, it helps to wash out State
Street and the engine's soot. One proposes that it be
called "God's Drop."

I have said that Walden has no visible inlet nor outlet,
but it is on the one hand distantly and indirectly related
to Flint's Pond, which is more elevated, by a chain of
small ponds coming from that quarter, and on the other
directly and manifestly to Concord River, which is
lower, by a similar chain of ponds through which in
some other geological period it may have flowed, and
by a little digging, which God forbid, it can be made to
flow thither again. If by living thus reserved and austere,
like a hermit in the woods, so long, it has acquired such

wonderful purity, who would not regret that the comparatively impure waters of Flint's Pond should be mingled with it, or itself should ever go to waste its sweetness in the ocean wave?

Flint's, or Sandy Pond, in Lincoln, our greatest lake and inland sea, lies about a mile east of Walden. It is much larger, being said to contain one hundred and ninety-seven acres, and is more fertile in fish; but it is comparatively shallow, and not remarkably pure. A walk through the woods thither was often my recreation. It was worth the while, if only to feel the wind blow on your cheek freely, and see the waves run, and remember the life of mariners. I went a-chestnutting there in the fall, on windy days, when the nuts were dropping into the water and were washed to my feet; and one day, as I crept along its sedgy shore, the fresh spray blowing in my face, I came upon the mouldering wreck of a boat, the sides gone, and hardly more than the impression of its flat bottom left amid the rushes; yet its model was sharply defined, as if it were a large decayed pad, with its veins. It was as impressive a wreck as one could imagine on the seashore, and had as good a moral. It is by this time mere vegetable mould and undistinguishable pond shore, through which rushes and flags have pushed up. I used to admire the ripple marks on the sandy bottom, at the north end of this pond, made firm and hard to the feet of the wader by the pressure of the water, and the rushes which grew in Indian file, in waving lines, corresponding to these marks, rank behind rank, as if the waves had planted them. There also I have found, in considerable quantities, curious balls, composed apparently of fine grass or roots, of pipewort perhaps, from half an inch to four inches in diameter, and perfectly spherical. These wash back and forth in shallow water on a sandy bottom, and are sometimes cast on the shore. They are either solid grass, or have a little sand in the middle. At first you would say that they were formed by the action of the waves, like a pebble; yet the smallest are made of equally coarse materials, half an inch long, and they are produced only at one season of the year. Moreover, the waves, I suspect, do not so much construct as wear down a material which has already acquired consistency. They preserve their form when dry for an indefinite period.

Flint's Pond! Such is the poverty of our nomenclature. What right had the unclean and stupid farmer, whose farm abutted on this sky water, whose shores he has ruthlessly laid bare, to give his name to it? Some skin-flint, who loved better the reflecting surface of a dollar, or a bright cent, in which he could see his own brazen face; who regarded even the wild ducks which settled in it as trespassers; his fingers grown into crooked and horny talons from the long habit of grasping harpy-like; — so it is not named for me. I go not there to see him nor to hear of him; who never *saw* it, who never bathed in it, who never loved it, who never protected it, who never spoke a good word for it, nor thanked God that He had made it. Rather let it be named from the fishes that swim in it, the wild fowl or quadrupeds which frequent it, the wild flowers which grow by its shores, or some wild man or child the thread of whose history is interwoven with its own; not from him who could show no title to it but the deed which a like-minded neighbor or legislature gave him, — him who thought only of its money value; whose presence perchance cursed all the shores; who exhausted the land around it, and would fain have exhausted the waters within it; who regretted only that it was not English hay or cranberry meadow, — there was nothing to redeem it, forsooth, in his eyes, — and would have drained and sold it for the mud at its bottom. It did not turn his mill, and it was no *privilege* to him to behold it. I respect not his labors, his farm where everything has its price, who would carry the landscape, who would carry his God, to market, if he could get anything for him; who goes to market *for* his god as it is; on whose farm nothing grows free, whose fields bear no crops, whose meadows no flowers, whose trees no fruits, but dollars; who loves not the beauty of his fruits, whose fruits are not ripe for him till they are turned to dollars. Give me the poverty that enjoys true wealth. Farmers are respectable and interesting to me in proportion as they are poor, — poor farmers. A model farm! where the house stands like a fungus in a muckheap, chambers for men, horses, oxen, and swine, cleansed and uncleansed, all contiguous to one another! Stocked with men! A great grease-spot, redolent of manures and buttermilk! Under a high state of cultivation, being manured with the hearts and brains of men! As if you were to raise your potatoes in the churchyard! Such is a model farm.

No, no; if the fairest features of the landscape are to

be named after men, let them be the noblest and worthiest men alone. Let our lakes receive as true names at
least as the Icarian Sea, where " still the shore " a " brave
attempt resounds."

Goose Pond, of small extent, is on my way to Flint's;
Fair Haven, an expansion of Concord River, said to contain some seventy acres, is a mile southwest; and White
Pond, of about forty acres, is a mile and a half beyond
Fair Haven. This is my lake country. These, with Concord River, are my water privileges; and night and day,
year in year out, they grind such grist as I carry to them.
Since the wood-cutters, and the railroad, and I myself have profaned Walden, perhaps the most attractive,
if not the most beautiful, of all our lakes, the gem of the
woods, is White Pond; — a poor name from its common-
ness, whether derived from the remarkable purity of its
waters or the color of its sands. In these as in other respects, however, it is a lesser twin of Walden. They are
so much alike that you would say they must be connected
under ground. It has the same stony shore, and its
waters are of the same hue. As at Walden, in sultry dog-
day weather, looking down through the woods on some
of its bays which are not so deep but that the reflection
from the bottom tinges them, its waters are of a misty
bluish-green or glaucous color. Many years since I used
to go there to collect the sand by cartloads, to make
sandpaper with, and I have continued to visit it ever
since. One who frequents it proposes to call it Virid
Lake. Perhaps it might be called Yellow Pine Lake,
from the following circumstance. About fifteen years

ago you could see the top of a pitch pine, of the kind called yellow pine hereabouts, though it is not a distinct species, projecting above the surface in deep water, many rods from the shore. It was even supposed by some that the pond had sunk, and this was one of the primitive forest that formerly stood there. I find that even so long ago as 1792, in a "Topographical Description of the Town of Concord," by one of its citizens, in the Collections of the Massachusetts Historical Society, the author, after speaking of Walden and White Ponds, adds, "In the middle of the latter may be seen, when the water is very low, a tree which appears as if it grew in the place where it now stands, although the roots are fifty feet below the surface of the water; the top of this tree is broken off, and at that place measures fourteen inches in diameter." In the spring of '49 I talked with the man who lives nearest the pond in Sudbury, who told me that it was he who got out this tree ten or fifteen years before. As near as he could remember, it stood twelve or fifteen rods from the shore, where the water was thirty or forty feet deep. It was in the winter, and he had been getting out ice in the forenoon, and had resolved that in the afternoon, with the aid of his neighbors, he would take out the old yellow pine. He sawed a channel in the ice toward the shore, and hauled it over and along and out on to the ice with oxen; but, before he had gone far in his work, he was surprised to find that it was wrong end upward, with the stumps of the branches pointing down, and the small end firmly fastened in the sandy bottom. It was about a foot in diameter at the big end, and he had expected to get a good saw-log, but it was so rotten as to be fit only for fuel, if for that. He had some of it in his shed then. There were marks of an axe and of woodpeckers on the butt. He thought that it might have been a dead tree on the shore, but was finally blown over into the pond, and after the top had become water-logged, while the butt-end was still dry and light, had drifted out and sunk wrong end up. His father, eighty years old, could not remember when it was not there. Several pretty large logs may still be seen lying on the bottom, where, owing to the undulation of the surface, they look like huge water snakes in motion.

This pond has rarely been profaned by a boat, for there is little in it to tempt a fisherman. Instead of the white lily, which requires mud, or the common sweet flag, the blue flag (*Iris versicolor*) grows thinly in the pure water, rising from the stony bottom all around the shore, where it is visited by hummingbirds in June; and the color both of its bluish blades and its flowers and especially their reflections, is in singular harmony with the glaucous water.

White Pond and Walden are great crystals on the surface of the earth, Lakes of Light. If they were permanently congealed, and small enough to be clutched, they would, perchance, be carried off by slaves, like precious stones, to adorn the heads of emperors; but being liquid, and ample, and secured to us and our successors forever, we disregard them, and run after the diamond of Kohinoor. They are too pure to have a market value; they contain no muck. How much more beautiful than our lives, how much more transparent than our characters, are they! We never learned meanness of them. How much fairer than the pool before the farmer's door, in which his ducks swim! Hither the clean wild ducks come. Nature has no human inhabitant who appreciates her. The birds with their plumage and their notes are in harmony with the flowers, but what youth or maiden conspires with the wild luxuriant beauty of Nature? She flourishes most alone, far from the towns where they reside. Talk of heaven! ye disgrace earth.

BAKER FARM

Sometimes I rambled to pine groves, standing like temples, or like fleets at sea, full-rigged, with wavy boughs, and rippling with light, so soft and green and shady that the Druids would have forsaken their oaks to worship in them; or to the cedar wood beyond Flint's Pond, where the trees, covered with hoary blue berries, spiring higher and higher, are fit to stand before Valhalla, and the creeping juniper covers the ground with wreaths full of fruit; or to swamps where the usnea lichen hangs in festoons from the white spruce trees, and toadstools, round tables of the swamp gods, cover the ground, and more beautiful fungi adorn the stumps, like butterflies or shells, vegetable winkles; where the swamp-pink and dogwood grow, the red alder berry glows like eyes of imps, the waxwork grooves and crushes the hardest woods in its folds, and the wild holly berries make the beholder forget his home with their beauty, and he is dazzled and tempted by nameless other wild forbidden fruits, too fair for mortal taste. Instead of calling on some scholar, I paid many a visit to particular trees, of kinds which are rare in this neighborhood, standing far away in the middle of some pasture, or in the depths of a wood or swamp, or on a hilltop; such as the black birch, of which we have some handsome specimens two feet in diameter; its cousin, the yellow birch, with its loose golden vest, perfumed like the first; the beech, which has so neat a bole and beautifully lichen-painted, perfect in all its details, of which, excepting scattered specimens, I know but one small grove of sizable trees left in the township, supposed by some to have been planted by the pigeons that were once baited with beech-nuts near by; it is worth the while to see the silver grain sparkle when you split this wood; the bass; the horn-beam; the *Celtis occidentalis*, or false elm, of which we have but one well-grown; some taller mast of a pine, a shingle tree, or a more perfect hemlock than usual, stand-ing like a pagoda in the midst of the woods; and many others I could mention. These were the shrines I visited both summer and winter.

Once it chanced that I stood in the very abutment of a rainbow's arch, which filled the lower stratum of the atmosphere, tinging the grass and leaves around, and dazzling me as if I looked through colored crystal. It was a lake of rainbow light, in which, for a short while, I lived like a dolphin. If it had lasted longer it might have tinged my employments and life. As I walked on the railroad causeway, I used to wonder at the halo of light around my shadow, and would fain fancy myself one of the elect. One who visited me declared that the shadows of some Irishmen before him had no halo about them, that it was only natives that were so distinguished. Benvenuto Cellini tells us in his memoirs, that, after a certain terrible dream or vision which he had during his confinement in the castle of St. Angelo a resplendent light appeared over the shadow of his head at morning and evening, whether he was in Italy or France, and it was particularly conspicuous when the grass was moist with dew. This was probably the same phenomenon to which I have referred, which is especially observed in the morning, but also at other times, and even by moonlight. Though a constant one, it is not commonly noticed, and, in the case of an excitable imagination like Cellini's, it would be basis enough for superstition. Beside, he tells us that he showed it to very few. But are they not indeed distinguished who are conscious that they are regarded at all?

I set out one afternoon to go a-fishing to Fair Haven, through the woods, to eke out my scanty fare of vegetables. My way led through Pleasant Meadow, an adjunct of the Baker Farm, that retreat of which a poet has since sung, beginning, —

> "Thy entry is a pleasant field,
> Which some mossy fruit trees yield
> Partly to a ruddy brook,
> By gliding musquash undertook,
> And mercurial trout,
> Darting about."

I thought of living there before I went to Walden. I "hooked" the apples, leaped the brook, and scared the musquash and the trout. It was one of those afternoons which seem indefinitely long before one, in which many events may happen, a large portion of our natural life, though it was already half spent when I started. By the way there came up a shower, which compelled me to stand half an hour under a pine, piling boughs over my

head, and wearing my handkerchief for a shed; and
when at length I had made one cast over the pickerel-
weed, standing up to my middle in water, I found myself suddenly in the shadow of a cloud, and the thunder
began to rumble with such emphasis that I could do no
more than listen to it. The gods must be proud, thought
I, with such forked flashes to rout a poor unarmed fisherman. So I made haste for shelter to the nearest hut,
which stood half a mile from any road, but so much the
nearer to the pond, and had long been uninhabited: —

> "And here a poet builded,
> In the completed years,
> For behold a trivial cabin
> That to destruction steers."

So the Muse fables. But therein, as I found, dwelt now
John Field, an Irishman, and his wife, and several children, from the broad-faced boy who assisted his father
at his work, and now came running by his side from the
bog to escape the rain, to the wrinkled, sibyl-like, cone-
headed infant that sat upon its father's knee as in the
palaces of nobles, and looked out from its home in the
midst of wet and hunger inquisitively upon the stranger,
with the privilege of infancy, not knowing but it was the
last of a noble line, and the hope and cynosure of the
world, instead of John Field's poor starveling brat.
There we sat together under that part of the roof which
leaked the least, while it showered and thundered without. I had sat there many times of old before the ship
was built that floated this family to America. An honest, hard-working, but shiftless man plainly was John
Field; and his wife, she too was brave to cook so many

successive dinners in the recesses of that lofty stove;
with round greasy face and bare breast, still thinking to
improve her condition one day; with the never absent
mop in one hand, and yet no effects of it visible anywhere. The chickens, which had also taken shelter here
from the rain, stalked about the room like members of
the family, too humanized, methought, to roast well.
They stood and looked in my eye or pecked at my shoe
significantly. Meanwhile my host told me his story, how
hard he worked "bogging" for a neighboring farmer,
turning up a meadow with a spade or bog hoe at the rate
of ten dollars an acre and the use of the land with manure
for one year, and his little broad-faced son worked cheerfully at his father's side the while, not knowing how poor
a bargain the latter had made. I tried to help him with
my experience, telling him that he was one of my nearest
neighbors, and that I too, who came a-fishing here, and
looked like a loafer, was getting my living like himself;
that I lived in a tight, light, and clean house, which
hardly cost more than the annual rent of such a ruin as
his commonly amounts to; and how, if he chose, he
might in a month or two build himself a palace of his
own; that I did not use tea, nor coffee, nor butter, nor
milk, nor fresh meat, and so did not have to work to get
them; again, as I did not work hard, I did not have to
eat hard, and it cost me but a trifle for my food; but as
he began with tea, and coffee, and butter, and milk, and
beef, he had to work hard to pay for them, and when he
had worked hard he had to eat hard again to repair the
waste of his system, — and so it was as broad as it was
long, indeed it was broader than it was long, for he was

discontented and wasted his life into the bargain; and yet he had rated it as a gain in coming to America, that here you could get tea, and coffee, and meat every day. But the only true America is that country where you are at liberty to pursue such a mode of life as may enable you to do without these, and where the state does not endeavor to compel you to sustain the slavery and war and other superfluous expenses which directly or indirectly result from the use of such things. For I purposely talked to him as if he were a philosopher, or desired to be one. I should be glad if all the meadows on the earth were left in a wild state, if that were the consequence of men's beginning to redeem themselves. A man will not need to study history to find out what is best for his own culture. But alas! the culture of an Irishman is an enterprise to be undertaken with a sort of moral bog hoe. I told him, that as he worked so hard at bogging, he required thick boots and stout clothing, which yet were soon soiled and worn out, but I wore light shoes and thin clothing, which cost not half so much, though he might think that I was dressed like a gentleman (which, however, was not the case), and in an hour or two, without labor, but as a recreation, I could, if I wished, catch as many fish as I should want for two days, or earn enough money to support me a week. If he and his family would live simply, they might all go a-huckleberrying in the summer for their amusement. John heaved a sigh at this, and his wife stared with arms a-kimbo, and both appeared to be wondering if they had capital enough to begin such a course with, or arithmetic enough to carry it through. It was sailing by dead reckoning to them, and they saw not clearly how to make their port so; therefore I suppose they still take life bravely, after their fashion, face to face, giving it tooth and nail, not having skill to split its massive columns with any fine entering wedge, and rout it in detail; — thinking to deal with it roughly, as one should handle a thistle. But they fight at an overwhelming disadvantage, — living, John Field, alas! without arithmetic. and failing so.

"Do you ever fish?" I asked. "Oh yes, I catch a mess now and then when I am lying by; good perch I catch." "What's your bait?" "I catch shiners with fishworms, and bait the perch with them." "You'd better go now, John," said his wife, with glistening and hopeful face; but John demurred.

The shower was now over, and a rainbow above the eastern woods promised a fair evening; so I took my departure. When I had got without I asked for a drink, hoping to get a sight of the well bottom, to complete my survey of the premises; but there, alas! are shallows and quicksands, and rope broken withal, and bucket irrecoverable. Meanwhile the right culinary vessel was selected, water was seemingly distilled, and after consultation and long delay passed out to the thirsty one, — not yet suffered to cool, not yet to settle. Such gruel sustains life here, I thought; so, shutting my eyes, and excluding the motes by a skilfully directed undercurrent, I drank to genuine hospitality the heartiest draught I could. I am not squeamish in such cases when manners are concerned.

As I was leaving the Irishman's roof after the rain,

bending my steps again to the pond, my haste to catch pickerel, wading in retired meadows, in sloughs and bog-holes, in forlorn and savage places, appeared for an instant trivial to me who had been sent to school and college; but as I ran down the hill toward the reddening west, with the rainbow over my shoulder, and some faint tinkling sounds borne to my ear through the cleansed air, from I know not what quarter, my Good Genius seemed to say, — Go fish and hunt far and wide day by day, — farther and wider, — and rest thee by many brooks and hearth-sides without misgiving. Remember thy Creator in the days of thy youth. Rise free from care before the dawn, and seek adventures. Let the noon find thee by other lakes, and the night overtake thee every-where at home. There are no larger fields than these, no worthier games than may here be played. Grow wild according to thy nature, like these sedges and brakes, which will never become English hay. Let the thunder rumble; what if it threaten ruin to farmers' crops? that is not its errand to thee. Take shelter under the cloud, while they flee to carts and sheds. Let not to get a living be thy trade, but thy sport. Enjoy the land, but own it not. Through want of enterprise and faith men are where they are, buying and selling, and spending their lives like serfs.

O Baker Farm!

> " Landscape where the richest element
> Is a little sunshine innocent." . . .

> " No one runs to revel
> On thy rail-fenced lea." . . .

" Debate with no man hast thou,
　　With questions art never perplexed,
As tame at the first sight as now,
　　In thy plain russet gabardine dressed." . . .

" Come ye who love,
　　And ye who hate,
Children of the Holy Dove,
　　And Guy Faux of the state,
And hang conspiracies
From the tough rafters of the trees!"

Men come tamely home at night only from the next field or street, where their household echoes haunt, and their life pines because it breathes its own breath over again; their shadows, morning and evening, reach farther than their daily steps. We should come home from far, from adventures, and perils, and discoveries every day, with new experience and character.

Before I had reached the pond some fresh impulse had brought out John Field, with altered mind, letting go "bogging" ere this sunset. But he, poor man, disturbed only a couple of fins while I was catching a fair string, and he said it was his luck; but when we changed seats in the boat luck changed seats too. Poor John Field! — I trust he does not read this, unless he will improve by it, — thinking to live by some derivative old-country mode in this primitive new country, — to catch perch with shiners. It is good bait sometimes, I allow. With his horizon all his own, yet he a poor man, born to be poor, with his inherited Irish poverty or poor life, his Adam's grandmother and boggy ways, not to rise in this world, he nor his posterity, till their wading webbed bog-trotting feet get *talaria* to their heels.

XI

HIGHER LAWS

As I came home through the woods with my string of fish, trailing my pole, it being now quite dark, I caught a glimpse of a woodchuck stealing across my path, and felt a strange thrill of savage delight, and was strongly tempted to seize and devour him raw; not that I was hungry then, except for that wildness which he represented. Once or twice, however, while I lived at the pond, I found myself ranging the woods, like a half-starved hound, with a strange abandonment, seeking some kind of venison which I might devour, and no morsel could have been too savage for me. The wildest scenes had become unaccountably familiar. I found in myself, and still find, an instinct toward a higher, or, as it is named, spiritual life, as do most men, and another toward a primitive rank and savage one, and I reverence them both. I love the wild not less than the good. The wildness and adventure that are in fishing still recommended it to me. I like sometimes to take rank hold on life and spend my day more as the animals do. Perhaps I have owed to this employment and to hunting, when quite young, my closest acquaintance with Nature. They early introduce us to and detain us in scenery with which otherwise, at that age, we should have little acquaintance. Fishermen, hunters, woodchoppers, and others, spending their lives in the fields and woods, in a peculiar sense a part of Nature themselves, are often in a more favorable mood for observing her, in the intervals of their pursuits, than philosophers or poets even, who approach her with expectation. She is not afraid to exhibit herself to them. The traveller on the prairie is naturally a hunter, on the head waters of the Missouri and Columbia a trapper, and at the Falls of St. Mary a fisherman. He who is only a traveller learns things at second-hand and by the halves, and is poor authority. We are most interested when science reports what those men already know practically or instinctively, for that alone is a true *humanity*, or account of human experience.

They mistake who assert that the Yankee has few amusements, because he has not so many public holidays, and men and boys do not play so many games as they do in England, for here the more primitive but solitary amusements of hunting, fishing, and the like have not yet given place to the former. Almost every New England boy among my contemporaries shouldered a fowling-piece between the ages of ten and fourteen; and his hunting and fishing grounds were not limited, like the preserves of an English nobleman, but were more boundless even than those of a savage. No wonder, then, that he did not oftener stay to play on the common. But already a change is taking place, owing, not to an increased humanity, but to an increased scarcity of game, for perhaps the hunter is the greatest friend of the animals hunted, not excepting the Humane Society.

Moreover, when at the pond, I wished sometimes to add fish to my fare for variety. I have actually fished from the same kind of necessity that the first fishers did. Whatever humanity I might conjure up against it was all factitious, and concerned my philosophy more than my feelings. I speak of fishing only now, for I had long felt differently about fowling, and sold my gun before I went to the woods. Not that I am less humane than others, but I did not perceive that my feelings were much affected. I did not pity the fishes nor the worms. This was habit. As for fowling, during the last years that I carried a gun my excuse was that I was studying ornithology, and sought only new or rare birds. But I confess that I am now inclined to think that there is a finer way of studying ornithology than this. It requires so much closer attention to the habits of the birds, that, if for that reason only, I have been willing to omit the gun. Yet notwithstanding the objection on the score of humanity, I am compelled to doubt if equally valuable sports are ever substituted for these; and when some of my friends have asked me anxiously about their boys, whether they should let them hunt, I have answered, yes, — remembering that it was one of the best parts of my education, — *make* them hunters, though sportsmen only at first, if possible, mighty hunters at last, so that they shall not find game large enough for them in this or any vegetable wilderness, — hunters as well as fishers of men. Thus far I am of the opinion of Chaucer's nun, who

> "yave not of the text a pulled hen
> That saith that hunters ben not holy men."

There is a period in the history of the individual, as of the race, when the hunters are the "best men," as the Algonquins called them. We cannot but pity the boy who has never fired a gun; he is no more humane, while his education has been sadly neglected. This was my answer with respect to those youths who were bent on this pursuit, trusting that they would soon outgrow it. No humane being, past the thoughtless age of boyhood, will wantonly murder any creature which holds its life by the same tenure that he does. The hare in its extremity cries like a child. I warn you, mothers, that my sympathies do not always make the usual phil-*anthropic* distinctions.

Such is oftenest the young man's introduction to the forest, and the most original part of himself. He goes thither at first as a hunter and fisher, until at last, if he has the seeds of a better life in him, he distinguishes his proper objects, as a poet or naturalist it may be, and leaves the gun and fish-pole behind. The mass of men are still and always young in this respect. In some countries a hunting parson is no uncommon sight. Such a one might make a good shepherd's dog, but is far from being the Good Shepherd. I have been surprised to consider that the only obvious employment, except wood-chopping, ice-cutting, or the like business, which ever to my knowledge detained at Walden Pond for a whole half-day any of my fellow-citizens, whether fathers or children of the town, with just one exception, was fishing. Commonly they did not think that they were lucky, or well paid for their time, unless they got a long string of fish, though they had the opportunity of seeing the pond all the while. They might go there a thousand times before the sediment of fishing would sink to the bottom and leave their purpose pure; but no doubt such a clarifying process would be going on all the while. The Governor and his Council faintly re-member the pond, for they went a-fishing there when they were boys; but now they are too old and dignified to go a-fishing, and so they know it no more forever. Yet even they expect to go to heaven at last. If the legislature regards it, it is chiefly to regulate the num-ber of hooks to be used there; but they know nothing about the hook of hooks with which to angle for the pond itself, impaling the legislature for a bait. Thus, even in civilized communities, the embryo man passes through the hunter stage of development.

I have found repeatedly, of late years, that I cannot fish without falling a little in self-respect. I have tried it again and again. I have skill at it, and, like many of my fellows, a certain instinct for it, which revives from time to time, but always when I have done I feel that it would have been better if I had not fished. I think that I do not mistake. It is a faint intimation, yet so are the first streaks of morning. There is unques-tionably this instinct in me which belongs to the lower orders of creation; yet with every year I am less a fisherman, though without more humanity or even wisdom; at present I am no fisherman at all. But I see that if I were to live in a wilderness I should again be tempted to become a fisher and hunter in earnest. Beside, there is something essentially unclean about this diet and all flesh, and I began to see where housework commences, and whence the endeavor, which costs so much, to wear a tidy and respectable appearance each day, to keep the house sweet and free from all ill odors and sights. Having been my own butcher and scullion and cook, as well as the gentleman for whom the dishes were served up, I can speak from an unusually complete experience. The practical objection to animal food in my case was its uncleanness; and besides, when I had caught and cleaned and cooked and eaten my fish, they seemed not to have fed me essentially. It was insignificant and unnecessary, and cost more than it came to. A little bread or a few potatoes would have done as well, with less trouble and filth. Like many of my contemporaries, I had rarely for many years used animal food, or tea, or coffee, etc.; not so much because of any ill effects which I had traced to them, as because they were not agreeable to my imagination. The repugnance to animal food is not the effect of experience, but is an instinct. It appeared more beautiful to live low and fare hard in many respects; and though I never did so, I went far enough to please my imagination. I believe that every man who has ever been earnest to preserve his higher or poetic faculties in the best condition has been particularly inclined to abstain from animal food, and from much food of any kind. It is a significant fact, stated by entomologists, — I find it in Kirby and Spence, — that " some insects in their perfect state, though furnished with organs of feeding, make no use of them;" and they lay it down as "a general rule, that almost all insects in this state eat much less than in that of larvæ. The voracious caterpillar when transformed into a butterfly . . . and the gluttonous maggot when become a fly " content themselves with a drop or two of honey or some other sweet liquid. The abdomen under the wings of the butterfly still represents the larva. This is the tidbit which tempts his insectivorous fate. The gross feeder is a man in the larva state; and there are whole nations in that condition, nations without fancy or imagination, whose vast abdomens betray them.

It is hard to provide and cook so simple and clean a diet as will not offend the imagination; but this, I think, is to be fed when we feed the body; they should both sit down at the same table. Yet perhaps this may be done. The fruits eaten temperately need not make us ashamed of our appetites, nor interrupt the worthiest pursuits. But put an extra condiment into your dish, and it will poison you. It is not worth the while to live by rich cookery. Most men would feel shame if caught preparing with their own hands precisely such a dinner, whether of animal or vegetable food, as is every day prepared for them by others. Yet till this is otherwise we are not civilized, and, if gentlemen and ladies, are not true men and women. This certainly suggests what change is to be made. It may be vain to ask why the imagination will not be reconciled to flesh and fat. I am satisfied that it is not. Is it not a reproach that man is a carnivorous animal? True, he can and does live, in a great measure, by preying on other animals; but this is a miserable way, — as any one who will go to snaring rabbits, or slaughtering lambs, may learn, — and he will be regarded as a benefactor of his race who shall teach man to confine himself to a more innocent and wholesome diet. Whatever my own practice may be, I have no doubt that it is a part of the destiny of the human race, in its gradual improvement, to leave off eating animals, as surely as the savage tribes have left off eating each other when they came in contact with the more civilized.

If one listens to the faintest but constant suggestions of his genius, which are certainly true, he sees not to what extremes, or even insanity, it may lead him; and yet that way, as he grows more resolute and faithful, his road lies. The faintest assured objection which one healthy man feels will at length prevail over the arguments and customs of mankind. No man ever followed his genius till it misled him. Though the result were bodily weakness, yet perhaps no one can say that the consequences were to be regretted, for these were a life in conformity to higher principles. If the day and the night are such that you greet them with joy, and life emits a fragrance like flowers and sweet-scented herbs, is more elastic, more starry, more immortal, — that is your success. All nature is your congratulation, and you have cause momentarily to bless yourself. The greatest gains and values are farthest from being appreciated. We easily come to doubt if they exist. We soon forget them. They are the highest reality. Perhaps the facts most astounding and most real are never communicated by man to man. The true harvest of my daily life is somewhat as intangible and indescribable as the tints of morning or evening. It is a little star-dust caught, a segment of the rainbow which I have clutched.

Yet, for my part, I was never unusually squeamish; I could sometimes eat a fried rat with a good relish, if it were necessary. I am glad to have drunk water so long, for the same reason that I prefer the natural sky to an opium-eater's heaven. I would fain keep sober always; and there are infinite degrees of drunkenness. I believe that water is the only drink for a wise man: wine is not so noble a liquor; and think of dashing the hopes of a morning with a cup of warm coffee, or of an evening with a dish of tea! Ah, how low I fall when I am tempted by them! Even music may be intoxicating. Such apparently slight causes destroyed Greece and Rome, and will destroy England and America. Of all ebriosity, who does not prefer to be intoxicated by the air he breathes? I have found it to be the most serious objection to coarse labors long continued, that they compelled me to eat and drink coarsely also. But to tell the truth, I find myself at present somewhat less particular in these respects. I carry less religion to the table, ask no blessing; not because I am wiser than I was, but, I am obliged to confess, because, however much it is to be regretted, with years I have grown more coarse and indifferent. Perhaps these questions are entertained only in youth, as most believe of poetry. My practice is "nowhere," my opinion is here. Nevertheless I am far from regarding myself as one of those privileged ones to whom the Ved refers when it says, that "he who has true faith in the Omnipresent Supreme Being may eat all that exists," that is, is not bound to inquire what is his food, or who prepares it; and even in their case it is to be observed, as a Hindoo commentator has remarked, that the Vedant limits this privilege to "the time of distress."

Who has not sometimes derived an inexpressible satisfaction from his food in which appetite had no share? I have been thrilled to think that I owed a mental perception to the commonly gross sense of taste, that I have been inspired through the palate, that some berries which I had eaten on a hillside had fed my genius. "The soul not being mistress of herself," says Thseng-tseu, "one looks, and one does not see; one listens, and one does not hear; one eats, and one does not know the savor of food." He who distinguishes the true savor of his food can never be a glutton; he who does not cannot be otherwise. A puritan may go to his brown-bread crust with as gross an appetite as ever an alderman to his turtle. Not that food which entereth into the mouth defileth a man, but the appetite with which it is eaten. It is neither the quality nor the quantity, but the devotion to sensual savors; when that which is eaten is not a viand to sustain our animal, or inspire our spiritual life, but food for the worms that possess us. If the hunter has a taste for mud-turtles, muskrats, and other such savage tidbits, the fine lady indulges a taste for jelly made of a calf's foot, or for sardines from over the sea, and they are even. He goes to the mill-pond, she to her preserve-pot. The wonder is how they, how you and I, can live this slimy, beastly life, eating and drinking.

Our whole life is startlingly moral. There is never an instant's truce between virtue and vice. Goodness is the only investment that never fails. In the music of the harp which trembles round the world it is the insisting on this which thrills us. The harp is the travelling patterer for the Universe's Insurance Company, recommending its laws, and our little goodness is all the assessment that we pay. Though the youth at last grows indifferent, the laws of the universe are not indifferent, but are forever on the side of the most sensitive. Listen to every zephyr for some reproof, for it is surely there, and he is unfortunate who does not hear it. We cannot touch a string or move a stop but the charming moral transfixes us. Many an irksome noise, go a long way off, is heard as music, a proud, sweet satire on the meanness of our lives.

We are conscious of an animal in us, which awakens in proportion as our higher nature slumbers. It is reptile and sensual, and perhaps cannot be wholly expelled; like the worms which, even in life and health, occupy our bodies. Possibly we may withdraw from it, but never change its nature. I fear that it may enjoy a certain health of its own; that we may be well, yet not pure. The other day I picked up the lower jaw of a hog, with white and sound teeth and tusks, which suggested that there was an animal health and vigor distinct from the spiritual. This creature succeeded by other means than temperance and purity. "That in which men differ from brute beasts," says Mencius, "is a thing very inconsiderable; the common herd lose it very soon; superior men preserve it carefully." Who knows what sort of life would result if we had attained to purity? If I knew so wise a man as could teach me purity I would go to seek him forthwith. "A command over our passions, and over the external senses of the body, and good acts, are declared by the Ved to be indispensable in the mind's approximation to God." Yet the spirit can for the time pervade and control every member and function of the body, and transmute what in form is the grossest sensuality into purity and devotion. The generative energy, which, when we are loose, dissipates and makes us unclean, when we are continent invigorates and inspires us. Chastity is the flowering of man; and what are called Genius, Heroism, Holiness, and the like, are but various fruits which succeed it. Man flows at once to God when the channel of purity is open. By turns our purity inspires and our impurity casts us down. He is blessed who is assured that the animal is dying out in him day by day, and the divine being established. Perhaps there is none but has cause for shame on account of the inferior and brutish nature to which he is allied. I fear that we are such gods or demigods only as fauns and satyrs, the divine allied to beasts, the creatures of appetite, and that, to some extent, our very life is our disgrace. —

> "How happy 's he who hath due place assigned
> To his beasts and disafforested his mind!
>
> .   .   .   .
>
> Can use his horse, goat, wolf, and ev'ry beast,
> And is not ass himself to all the rest!
> Else man not only is the herd of swine,
> But he 's those devils too which did incline
> Them to a headlong rage, and made them worse."

All sensuality is one, though it takes many forms; all purity is one. It is the same whether a man eat, or drink, or cohabit, or sleep sensually. They are but one

appetite, and we only need to see a person do any one
of these things to know how great a sensualist he is.
The impure can neither stand nor sit with purity. When
the reptile is attacked at one mouth of his burrow, he
chows himself at another. If you would be chaste, you
must be temperate. What is chastity? How shall a
man know if he is chaste? He shall not know it. We
have heard of this virtue, but we know not what it is.
We speak conformably to the rumor which we have
heard. From exertion come wisdom and purity; from
sloth ignorance and sensuality. In the student sensuality
is a sluggish habit of mind. An unclean person is universally a slothful one, one who sits by a stove, whom
the sun shines on prostrate, who reposes without being
fatigued. If you would avoid uncleanness, and all the
sins, work earnestly, though it be at cleaning a stable.
Nature is hard to be overcome, but she must be overcome. What avails it that you are Christian, if you are
not purer than the heathen, if you deny yourself no
more, if you are not more religious? I know of many
systems of religion esteemed heathenish whose precepts
fill the reader with shame, and provoke him to new
endeavors, though it be to the performance of rites
merely.

I hesitate to say these things, but it is not because of
the subject, — I care not how obscene my *words* are, —
but because I cannot speak of them without betraying
my impurity. We discourse freely without shame of one
form of sensuality, and are silent about another. We
are so degraded that we cannot speak simply of the
necessary functions of human nature. In earlier ages,

in some countries, every function was reverently spoken of and regulated by law. Nothing was too trivial for the Hindoo lawgiver, however offensive it may be to modern taste. He teaches how to eat, drink, cohabit, void excrement and urine, and the like, elevating what is mean, and does not falsely excuse himself by calling these things trifles.

Every man is the builder of a temple, called his body, to the god he worships, after a style purely his own, nor can he get off by hammering marble instead. We are all sculptors and painters, and our material is our own flesh and blood and bones. Any nobleness begins at once to refine a man's features, any meanness or sensuality to imbrute them.

John Farmer sat at his door one September evening, after a hard day's work, his mind still running on his labor more or less. Having bathed, he sat down to re-create his intellectual man. It was a rather cool evening, and some of his neighbors were apprehending a frost. He had not attended to the train of his thoughts long when he heard some one playing on a flute, and that sound harmonized with his mood. Still he thought of his work; but the burden of his thought was, that though this kept running in his head, and he found himself planning and contriving it against his will, yet it concerned him very little. It was no more than the scurf of his skin, which was constantly shuffled off. But the notes of the flute came home to his ears out of a different sphere from that he worked in, and suggested work for certain faculties which slumbered in him. They gently did away with the street, and the village, and the state in which he lived. A voice said to him, — Why do you stay here and live this mean moiling life, when a glorious existence is possible for you? Those same stars twinkle over other fields than these. — But how to come out of this condition and actually migrate thither? All that he could think of was to practise some new austerity, to let his mind descend into his body and redeem it, and treat himself with ever increasing respect.

XII

BRUTE NEIGHBORS

Sometimes I had a companion in my fishing, who came through the village to my house from the other side of the town, and the catching of the dinner was as much a social exercise as the eating of it.

Hermit. I wonder what the world is doing now. I have not heard so much as a locust over the sweet-fern these three hours. The pigeons are all asleep upon their roosts, — no flutter from them. Was that a farmer's noon horn which sounded from beyond the woods just now? The hands are coming in to boiled salt beef and cider and Indian bread. Why will men worry themselves so? He that does not eat need not work. I wonder how much they have reaped. Who would live there where a body can never think for the barking of Bose? And oh, the housekeeping! to keep bright the devil's door-knobs, and scour his tubs this bright day! Better not keep a house. Say, some hollow tree; and then for morning calls and dinner-parties! Only a woodpecker tapping. Oh, they swarm; the sun is too warm there; they are born too far into life for me. I have water from the spring, and a loaf of brown bread on the shelf. — Hark! I hear a rustling of the leaves. Is it some ill-fed village hound yielding to the instinct of the chase? or the lost pig which is said to be in these woods, whose tracks I saw after the rain? It comes on apace; my sumachs and sweetbriers tremble. — Eh, Mr. Poet, is it you? How do you like the world to-day?

Poet. See those clouds; how they hang! That's the greatest thing I have seen to-day. There's nothing like it in old paintings, nothing like it in foreign lands, — unless when we were off the coast of Spain. That's a true Mediterranean sky. I thought, as I have my living to get, and have not eaten to-day, that I might go a-fishing. That's the true industry for poets. It is the only trade I have learned. Come, let's along.

Hermit. I cannot resist. My brown bread will soon be gone. I will go with you gladly soon, but I am just concluding a serious meditation. I think that I am near the end of it. Leave me alone, then, for a while. But that we may not be delayed, you shall be digging the bait meanwhile. Angleworms are rarely to be met with in these parts, where the soil was never fattened with manure; the race is nearly extinct. The sport of digging the bait is nearly equal to that of catching the fish, when one's appetite is not too keen; and this you may have all to yourself to-day. I would advise you to set in the spade down yonder among the ground-nuts, where you see the johnswort waving. I think that I may warrant you one worm to every three sods you turn up, if you look well in among the roots of the grass, as if you were weeding. Or, if you choose to go farther, it will not be unwise, for I have found the increase of fair bait to be very nearly as the squares of the distances.

Hermit alone. Let me see; where was I? Methinks I was nearly in this frame of mind; the world lay about at this angle. Shall I go to heaven or a-fishing? If I should soon bring this meditation to an end, would another so sweet occasion be likely to offer? I was as near being resolved into the essence of things as ever I was in my life. I fear my thoughts will not come back to me. If it would do any good, I would whistle for them. When they make us an offer, is it wise to say, We will think of it? My thoughts have left no track, and I cannot find the path again. What was it that I was thinking of? It was a very hazy day. I will just try these three sentences of Confut-see; they may fetch that state about again. I know not whether it was the dumps or a budding ecstasy. Mem. There never is but one opportunity of a kind.

Poet. How now, Hermit, is it too soon? I have got just thirteen whole ones, beside several which are imperfect or undersized; but they will do for the smaller fry; they do not cover up the hook so much. Those village worms are quite too large; a shiner may make a meal off one without finding the skewer.

Hermit. Well, then, let's be off. Shall we to the Concord? There's good sport there if the water be not too high.

Why do precisely these objects which we behold make a world? Why has man just these species of animals for his neighbors; as if nothing but a mouse could have filled this crevice? I suspect that Pilpay & Co. have put animals to their best use, for they are all beasts of burden, in a sense, made to carry some portion of our thoughts.

The mice which haunted my house were not the common ones, which are said to have been introduced into the country, but a wild native kind not found in the village. I sent one to a distinguished naturalist, and it interested him much. When I was building, one of these had its nest underneath the house, and before I had laid the second floor, and swept out the shavings, would come out regularly at lunch time and pick up the crumbs at my feet. It probably had never seen a man before; and it soon became quite familiar, and would run over my shoes and up my clothes. It could readily ascend the sides of the room by short impulses, like a squirrel, which it resembled in its motions. At length, as I leaned with my elbow on the bench one day, it ran up my clothes, and along my sleeve, and round and round the paper which held my dinner, while I kept the latter close, and dodged and played at bopeep with it; and when at last I held still a piece of cheese between my thumb and finger, it came and nibbled it, sitting in my hand, and afterward cleaned its face and paws, like a fly, and walked away.

A phœbe soon built in my shed, and a robin for protection in a pine which grew against the house. In June the partridge (*Tetrao umbellus*), which is so shy a bird, led her brood past my windows, from the woods in the rear to the front of my house, clucking and calling to them like a hen, and in all her behavior proving herself the hen of the woods. The young suddenly disperse on your approach, at a signal from the mother, as if a whirlwind had swept them away, and they so exactly resemble the dried leaves and twigs that many a travel-

ler has placed his foot in the midst of a brood, and heard
the whir of the old bird as she flew off, and her anxious
calls and mewing, or seen her trail her wings to attract
his attention, without suspecting their neighborhood.
The parent will sometimes roll and spin round before
you in such a dishabille, that you cannot, for a few
moments, detect what kind of creature it is. The
young squat still and flat, often running their heads
under a leaf, and mind only their mother's directions
given from a distance, nor will your approach make
them run again and betray themselves. You may even
tread on them, or have your eyes on them for a minute,
without discovering them. I have held them in my
open hand at such a time, and still their only care,
obedient to their mother and their instinct, was to squat
there without fear or trembling. So perfect is this instinct, that once, when I had laid them on the leaves
again, and one accidentally fell on its side, it was found
with the rest in exactly the same position ten minutes
afterward. They are not callow like the young of most
birds, but more perfectly developed and precocious
even than chickens. The remarkably adult yet innocent expression of their open and serene eyes is very
memorable. All intelligence seems reflected in them.
They suggest not merely the purity of infancy, but a
wisdom clarified by experience. Such an eye was not
born when the bird was, but is coeval with the sky it
reflects. The woods do not yield another such a gem.
The traveller does not often look into such a limpid
well. The ignorant or reckless sportsman often shoots
the parent at such a time, and leaves these innocents to

fall a prey to some prowling beast or bird, or gradually mingle with the decaying leaves which they so much resemble. It is said that when hatched by a hen they will directly disperse on some alarm, and so are lost, for they never hear the mother's call which gathers them again. These were my hens and chickens.

It is remarkable how many creatures live wild and free though secret in the woods, and still sustain themselves in the neighborhood of towns, suspected by hunters only. How retired the otter manages to live here! He grows to be four feet long, as big as a small boy, perhaps without any human being getting a glimpse of him. I formerly saw the raccoon in the woods behind where my house is built, and probably still heard their whinnering at night. Commonly I rested an hour or two in the shade at noon, after planting, and ate my lunch, and read a little by a spring which was the source of a swamp and of a brook, oozing from under Brister's Hill, half a mile from my field. The approach to this was through a succession of descending grassy hollows, full of young pitch pines, into a larger wood about the swamp. There, in a very secluded and shaded spot, under a spreading white pine, there was yet a clean, firm sward to sit on. I had dug out the spring and made a well of clear gray water, where I could dip up a pailful without roiling it, and thither I went for this purpose almost every day in midsummer, when the pond was warmest. Thither, too, the woodcock led her brood, to probe the mud for worms, flying but a foot above them down the bank, while they ran in a troop beneath; but at last, spying me, she would leave her young and circle round and round me, nearer and nearer till within four or five feet, pretending broken wings and legs, to attract my attention, and get off her young, who would already have taken up their march, with faint, wiry peep, single file through the swamp, as she directed. Or I heard the peep of the young when I could not see the parent bird. There too the turtle doves sat over the spring, or fluttered from bough to bough of the soft white pines over my head; or the red squirrel, coursing down the nearest bough, was particularly familiar and inquisitive. You only need sit still long enough in some attractive spot in the woods that all its inhabitants may exhibit themselves to you by turns.

I was witness to events of a less peaceful character. One day when I went out to my wood-pile, or rather my pile of stumps, I observed two large ants, the one red, the other much larger, nearly half an inch long, and black, fiercely contending with one another. Having once got hold they never let go, but struggled and wrestled and rolled on the chips incessantly. Looking farther, I was surprised to find that the chips were covered with such combatants, that it was not a *duellum*, but a *bellum*, a war between two races of ants, the red always pitted against the black, and frequently two red ones to one black. The legions of these Myrmidons covered all the hills and vales in my wood-yard, and the ground was already strewn with the dead and dying, both red and black. It was the only battle which I have ever witnessed, the only battle-field I ever trod while the battle was raging; internecine war; the red republicans on the one hand, and the black imperialists on the other. On every side they were engaged in deadly combat, yet without any noise that I could hear, and human soldiers never fought so resolutely. I watched a couple that were fast locked in each other's embraces, in a little sunny valley amid the chips, now at noonday prepared to fight till the sun went down, or life went out. The smaller red champion had fastened himself like a vice to his adversary's front, and through all the tumblings on that field never for an instant ceased to gnaw at one of his feelers near the root, having already caused the other to go by the board; while the stronger black one dashed him from side to side, and, as I saw on looking nearer, had already divested him of several of his members. They fought with more pertinacity than bulldogs. Neither manifested the least disposition to retreat. It was evident that their battle-cry was "Conquer or die." In the meanwhile there came along a single red ant on the hillside of this valley, evidently full of excitement, who either had despatched his foe, or had not yet taken part in the battle; probably the latter, for he had lost none of his limbs; whose mother had charged him to return with his shield or upon it. Or perchance he was some Achilles, who had nourished his wrath apart, and had now come to avenge or rescue his Patroclus. He saw this unequal combat from afar, — for the blacks were nearly twice the size of the red, — he drew near with rapid pace till he stood on his guard within half an inch of the combatants; then, watching his opportunity, he sprang upon the black warrior, and commenced his operations near the root of his right fore leg, leaving the foe to select among his own members; and so there were three united for life, as if a new kind of attraction had been

invented which put all other locks and cements to shame.
I should not have wondered by this time to find that they
had their respective musical bands stationed on some
eminent chip, and playing their national airs the while,
to excite the slow and cheer the dying combatants. I
was myself excited somewhat even as if they had been
men. The more you think of it, the less the difference.
And certainly there is not the fight recorded in Concord
history, at least, if in the history of America, that will
bear a moment's comparison with this, whether for the
numbers engaged in it, or for the patriotism and heroism displayed. For numbers and for carnage it was an
Austerlitz or Dresden. Concord Fight! Two killed on
the patriots' side, and Luther Blanchard wounded!
Why here every ant was a Buttrick, — " Fire! for God's
sake fire!" — and thousands shared the fate of Davis
and Hosmer. There was not one hireling there. I have
no doubt that it was a principle they fought for, as much
as our ancestors, and not to avoid a three-penny tax on
their tea; and the results of this battle will be as important and memorable to those whom it concerns as those
of the battle of Bunker Hill, at least.

I took up the chip on which the three I have particularly described were struggling, carried it into my house,
and placed it under a tumbler on my window-sill, in
order to see the issue. Holding a microscope to the first-
mentioned red ant, I saw that, though he was assidu-
ously gnawing at the near fore leg of his enemy, having
severed his remaining feeler, his own breast was all torn
away, exposing what vitals he had there to the jaws
of the black warrior, whose breastplate was apparently

too thick for him to pierce; and the dark carbuncles of the sufferer's eyes shone with ferocity such as war only could excite. They struggled half an hour longer under the tumbler, and when I looked again the black soldier had severed the heads of his foes from their bodies, and the still living heads were hanging on either side of him like ghastly trophies at his saddle-bow, still apparently as firmly fastened as ever, and he was endeavoring with feeble struggles, being without feelers and with only the remnant of a leg, and I know not how many other wounds, to divest himself of them; which at length, after half an hour more, he accomplished. I raised the glass, and he went off over the window-sill in that crippled state. Whether he finally survived that combat, and spent the remainder of his days in some Hôtel des Invalides, I do not know; but I thought that his industry would not be worth much thereafter. I never learned which party was victorious, nor the cause of the war; but I felt for the rest of that day as if I had had my feelings excited and harrowed by witnessing the struggle, the ferocity and carnage, of a human battle before my door.

Kirby and Spence tell us that the battles of ants have long been celebrated and the date of them recorded, though they say that Huber is the only modern author who appears to have witnessed them. "Æneas Sylvius," say they, "after giving a very circumstantial account of one contested with great obstinacy by a great and small species on the trunk of a pear tree," adds that "'this action was fought in the pontificate of Eugenius the Fourth, in the presence of Nicholas Pistoriensis, an eminent lawyer, who related the whole history of the

battle with the greatest fidelity.' A similar engagement
between great and small ants is recorded by Olaus
Magnus, in which the small ones, being victorious, are
said to have buried the bodies of their own soldiers, but
left those of their giant enemies a prey to the birds. This
event happened previous to the expulsion of the tyrant
Christiern the Second from Sweden." The battle which
I witnessed took place in the Presidency of Polk, five
years before the passage of Webster's Fugitive-Slave
Bill.

Many a village Bose, fit only to course a mud-turtle
in a victualling cellar, sported his heavy quarters in the
woods, without the knowledge of his master, and ineffectually smelled at old fox burrows and woodchucks'
holes; led perchance by some slight cur which nimbly
threaded the wood, and might still inspire a natural ter-
ror in its denizens; — now far behind his guide, barking
like a canine bull toward some small squirrel which had
treed itself for scrutiny, then, cantering off, bending the
bushes with his weight, imagining that he is on the track
of some stray member of the jerbilla family. Once I was
surprised to see a cat walking along the stony shore of the
pond, for they rarely wander so far from home. The surprise was mutual. Nevertheless the most domestic cat,
which has lain on a rug all her days, appears quite at
home in the woods, and, by her sly and stealthy behavior, proves herself more native there than the regular
inhabitants. Once, when berrying, I met with a cat with
young kittens in the woods, quite wild, and they all, like
their mother, had their backs up and were fiercely spit-
ting at me. A few years before I lived in the woods there

was what was called a "winged cat" in one of the farmhouses in Lincoln nearest the pond, Mr. Gilian Baker's.
When I called to see her in June, 1842, she was gone
a-hunting in the woods, as was her wont (I am not sure
whether it was a male or female, and so use the more
common pronoun), but her mistress told me that she
came into the neighborhood a little more than a year
before, in April, and was finally taken into their house;
that she was of a dark brownish-gray color, with a white
spot on her throat, and white feet, and had a large bushy
tail like a fox; that in the winter the fur grew thick and
flatted out along her sides, forming strips ten or twelve
inches long by two and a half wide, and under her chin
like a muff, the upper side loose, the under matted like
felt, and in the spring these appendages dropped off.
They gave me a pair of her "wings," which I keep still.
There is no appearance of a membrane about them.
Some thought it was part flying squirrel or some other
wild animal, which is not impossible, for, according to
naturalists, prolific hybrids have been produced by the
union of the marten and domestic cat. This would have
been the right kind of cat for me to keep, if I had kept
any; for why should not a poet's cat be winged as well
as his horse?

In the fall the loon (*Colymbus glacialis*) came, as usual,
to moult and bathe in the pond, making the woods ring
with his wild laughter before I had risen. At rumor of
his arrival all the Mill-dam sportsmen are on the alert,
in gigs and on foot, two by two and three by three, with
patent rifles and conical balls and spy-glasses. They
come rustling through the woods like autumn leaves, at

least ten men to one loon. Some station themselves on this side of the pond, some on that, for the poor bird cannot be omnipresent; if he dive here he must come up there. But now the kind October wind rises, rustling the leaves and rippling the surface of the water, so that no loon can be heard or seen, though his foes sweep the pond with spy-glasses, and make the woods resound with their discharges. The waves generously rise and dash angrily, taking sides with all water-fowl, and our sportsmen must beat a retreat to town and shop and unfinished jobs. But they were too often successful. When I went to get a pail of water early in the morning I frequently saw this stately bird sailing out of my cove within a few rods. If I endeavored to overtake him in a boat, in order to see how he would manœuvre, he would dive and be completely lost, so that I did not discover him again, sometimes, till the latter part of the day. But I was more than a match for him on the surface. He commonly went off in a rain.

As I was paddling along the north shore one very calm October afternoon, for such days especially they settle on to the lakes, like the milkweed down, having looked in vain over the pond for a loon, suddenly one, sailing out from the shore toward the middle a few rods in front of me, set up his wild laugh and betrayed himself. I pursued with a paddle and he dived, but when he came up I was nearer than before. He dived again, but I miscalculated the direction he would take, and we were fifty rods apart when he came to the surface this time, for I had helped to widen the interval; and again he laughed long and loud, and with more reason than before. He manœuvred so cunningly that I could not get within half a dozen rods of him. Each time, when he came to the surface, turning his head this way and that, he coolly surveyed the water and the land, and apparently chose his course so that he might come up where there was the widest expanse of water and at the greatest distance from the boat. It was surprising how quickly he made up his mind and put his resolve into execution. He led me at once to the widest part of the pond, and could not be driven from it. While he was thinking one thing in his brain, I was endeavoring to divine his thought in mine. It was a pretty game, played on the smooth surface of the pond, a man against a loon. Suddenly your adversary's checker disappears beneath the board, and the problem is to place yours nearest to where his will appear again. Sometimes he would come up unexpectedly on the opposite side of me, having apparently passed directly under the boat. So long-winded was he and so unweariable, that when he had swum farthest he would immediately plunge again, nevertheless; and then no wit could divine where in the deep pond, beneath the smooth surface, he might be speeding his way like a fish, for he had time and ability to visit the bottom of the pond in its deepest part. It is said that loons have been caught in the New York lakes eighty feet beneath the surface, with hooks set for trout, — though Walden is deeper than that. How surprised must the fishes be to see this ungainly visitor from another sphere speeding his way amid their schools! Yet he appeared to know his course as surely under water as on the surface, and swam much faster there. Once or twice I saw a ripple where he approached the surface, just put his head out to reconnoitre, and instantly dived again. I found that it was as well for me to rest on my oars and wait his reappearing as to endeavor to calculate where he would rise; for again and again, when I was straining my eyes over the surface one way, I would suddenly be startled by his unearthly laugh behind me. But why, after displaying so much cunning, did he invariably betray himself the moment he came up by that loud laugh? Did not his white breast enough betray him? He was indeed a silly loon, I thought. I could commonly hear the plash of the water when he came up, and so also detected him. But after an hour he seemed as fresh as ever, dived as willingly, and swam yet farther than at first. It was surprising to see how serenely he sailed off with unruffled breast when he came to the surface, doing all the work with his webbed feet beneath. His usual note was this demoniac laughter, yet somewhat like that of a water-fowl; but occasionally, when he had balked me most successfully and come up a long way off, he uttered a long-drawn unearthly howl, probably more like that of a wolf than any bird; as when a beast puts his muzzle to the ground and deliberately howls. This was his looning, — perhaps the wildest sound that is ever heard here, making the woods ring far and wide. I concluded that he laughed in derision of my efforts, confident of his own resources. Though the sky was by this time overcast, the pond was so smooth that I could see where he broke the surface when I did not hear him. His white breast, the stillness of the air, and the smoothness of the water were all against him. At length, having come up fifty rods off, he uttered one of those prolonged howls, as if calling on the god of loons to aid him, and immediately there came a wind from the east and rippled the surface, and filled the whole air with misty rain, and I was impressed as if it were the prayer of the loon answered, and his god was angry with me; and so I left him disappearing far away on the tumultuous surface.

For hours, in fall days, I watched the ducks cunningly tack and veer and hold the middle of the pond, far from the sportsman; tricks which they will have less need to practise in Louisiana bayous. When compelled to rise they would sometimes circle round and round and over the pond at a considerable height, from which they could easily see to other ponds and the river, like black motes in the sky; and, when I thought they had gone off thither long since, they would settle down by a slanting flight of a quarter of a mile on to a distant part which was left free; but what beside safety they got by sailing in the middle of Walden I do not know, unless they love its water for the same reason that I do.

XIII

HOUSE-WARMING

In October I went a-graping to the river meadows, and loaded myself with clusters more precious for their beauty and fragrance than for food. There, too, I admired, though I did not gather, the cranberries, small waxen gems, pendants of the meadow grass, pearly and red, which the farmer plucks with an ugly rake, leaving the smooth meadow in a snarl, heedlessly measuring them by the bushel and the dollar only, and sells the spoils of the meads to Boston and New York; destined to be *jammed*, to satisfy the tastes of lovers of Nature there. So butchers rake the tongues of bison out of the prairie grass, regardless of the torn and drooping plant. The barberry's brilliant fruit was likewise food for my eyes merely; but I collected a small store of wild apples for coddling, which the proprietor and travellers had overlooked. When chestnuts were ripe I laid up half a bushel for winter. It was very exciting at that season to roam the then boundless chestnut woods of Lincoln, —they now sleep their long sleep under the railroad,— with a bag on my shoulder, and a stick to open burs with in my hand, for I did not always wait for the frost, amid the rustling of leaves and the loud reproofs of the red squirrels and the jays, whose half-consumed nuts I sometimes stole, for the burs which they had selected were sure to contain sound ones. Occasionally I climbed and shook the trees. They grew also behind my house, and one large tree, which almost overshadowed it, was, when in flower, a bouquet which scented the whole neighborhood, but the squirrels and the jays got most of its fruit; the last coming in flocks early in the morning and picking the nuts out of the burs before they fell. I relinquished these trees to them and visited the more distant woods composed wholly of chestnut. These nuts, as far as they went, were a good substitute for bread. Many other substitutes might, perhaps, be found. Digging one day for fishworms, I discovered the groundnut (*Apios tuberosa*) on its string, the potato of the aborigines, a sort of fabulous fruit, which I had begun to doubt if I had ever dug and eaten in childhood, as I had told, and had not dreamed it. I had often since seen its crimpled red velvety blossom supported by the stems of other plants without knowing it to be the same. Cultivation has well-nigh exterminated it. It has a sweetish taste, much like that of a frost-bitten potato, and I found it better boiled than roasted. This tuber seemed like a faint promise of Nature to rear her own children and feed them simply here at some future period. In these days of fatted cattle and waving grain-fields this humble root, which was once the *totem* of an Indian tribe, is quite forgotten, or known only by its flowering vine; but let wild Nature reign here once more, and the tender and luxurious English grains will probably disappear before a myriad of foes, and without the care of man the crow may carry back even the last seed of corn to the great cornfield of the Indian's God in the southwest, whence he is said to have brought it; but the now almost exterminated ground-nut will perhaps revive and flourish in spite of frosts and wildness, prove itself indigenous, and resume its ancient importance and dignity as the diet of the hunter tribe. Some Indian Ceres or Minerva must have been the inventor and bestower of it; and when the reign of poetry commences here, its leaves and string of nuts may be represented on our works of art.

Already, by the first of September, I had seen two or three small maples turned scarlet across the pond, beneath where the white stems of three aspens diverged, at the point of a promontory, next the water. Ah, many a tale their color told! And gradually from week to week the character of each tree came out, and it admired itself reflected in the smooth mirror of the lake. Each morning the manager of this gallery substituted some new picture, distinguished by more brilliant or harmonious coloring, for the old upon the walls.

The wasps came by thousands to my lodge in October, as to winter quarters, and settled on my windows within and on the walls overhead, sometimes deterring visitors from entering. Each morning, when they were numbed with cold, I swept some of them out, but I did not trouble myself much to get rid of them; I even felt complimented by their regarding my house as a desirable shelter. They never molested me seriously, though they bedded with me; and they gradually disappeared, into what crevices I do not know, avoiding winter and unspeakable cold.

Like the wasps, before I finally went into winter quarters in November, I used to resort to the northeast side of Walden, which the sun, reflected from the pitch pine woods and the stony shore, made the fireside of the pond; it is so much pleasanter and wholesomer to be warmed by the sun while you can be, than by an artificial fire. I thus warmed myself by the still glowing embers which the summer, like a departed hunter, had left.

When I came to build my chimney I studied masonry. My bricks, being second-hand ones, required to be cleaned with a trowel, so that I learned more than usual of the qualities of bricks and trowels. The mortar on them was fifty years old, and was said to be still growing harder; but this is one of those sayings which men love to repeat whether they are true or not. Such sayings themselves grow harder and adhere more firmly with age, and it would take many blows with a trowel to clean an old wiseacre of them. Many of the villages of Mesopotamia are built of second-hand bricks of a very good quality, obtained from the ruins of Babylon, and the cement on them is older and probably harder still. However that may be, I was struck by the peculiar toughness of the steel which bore so many violent blows without being worn out. As my bricks had been in a chimney before, though I did not read the name of Nebuchadnezzar on them, I picked out as many fireplace bricks as I could find, to save work and waste, and I filled the spaces between the bricks about the fireplace with stones from the pond shore, and also made my mortar with the white sand from the same place. I lingered most about the fireplace, as the most vital part of the house. Indeed, I worked so deliberately, that though I commenced at the ground in the morning, a course of bricks raised a few inches above the floor served for my pillow at night; yet I did not get a stiff neck for it that I remember; my stiff neck is of older date. I took a poet to board for a fortnight about those times, which caused me to be put to it for room. He brought his own knife, though I had two, and we used to scour them by thrusting them into the earth. He shared with me the labors of cooking. I was pleased to see my work rising so square and solid by degrees, and reflected, that, if it proceeded slowly, it was calculated to endure a long time. The chimney is to some extent an independent structure, standing on the ground, and rising through the house to the heavens; even after the house is burned it still stands sometimes, and its importance and independence are apparent. This was toward the end of summer. It was now November.

The north wind had already begun to cool the pond, though it took many weeks of steady blowing to accomplish it, it is so deep. When I began to have a fire at evening, before I plastered my house, the chimney carried smoke particularly well, because of the numerous chinks between the boards. Yet I passed some cheerful evenings in that cool and airy apartment, surrounded by the rough brown boards full of knots, and rafters with the bark on high overhead. My house never pleased my eye so much after it was plastered, though I was obliged to confess that it was more comfortable. Should not every apartment in which man dwells be lofty enough to create some obscurity overhead, where flickering shadows may play at evening about the rafters? These forms are more agreeable to the fancy and imagination than fresco paintings or other the most expensive furniture. I now first began to inhabit my house, I may say, when I began to use it for warmth as well as shelter. I had got a couple of old fire-dogs to keep the wood from the hearth, and it did me good to see the soot form on the back of the chimney which I had built, and I poked the fire with more right and more satisfaction than usual. My dwelling was small, and I could hardly entertain an echo in it; but it seemed larger for being a single apartment and remote from neighbors. All the attractions of a house were concentrated in one room; it was kitchen, chamber, parlor, and keeping-room; and whatever satisfaction parent or child, master or servant, derive from living in a house, I enjoyed it all. Cato says, the master of a family (*patremfamilias*) must have in his rustic villa "cellam oleariam, vinariam, dolia multa, uti lubeat caritatem expectare, et rei, et virtuti, et gloriae erit," that is, "an oil and wine cellar, many casks, so that it may be pleasant to expect hard times; it will be for his advantage, and virtue, and glory." I had in my cellar a firkin of potatoes, about two quarts of peas with the weevil in them, and on my shelf a little rice, a jug of molasses, and of rye and Indian meal a peck each.

I sometimes dream of a larger and more populous house, standing in a golden age, of enduring materials, and without gingerbread work, which shall still consist of only one room, a vast, rude, substantial, primitive

hall, without ceiling or plastering, with bare rafters and
purlins supporting a sort of lower heaven over one's
head, — useful to keep off rain and snow, where the
king and queen posts stand out to receive your homage,
when you have done reverence to the prostrate Saturn
of an older dynasty on stepping over the sill; a cavernous house, wherein you must reach up a torch upon a
pole to see the roof; where some may live in the fireplace, some in the recess of a window, and some on set-
tles, some at one end of the hall, some at another, and
some aloft on rafters with the spiders, if they choose;
a house which you have got into when you have opened
the outside door, and the ceremony is over; where the
weary traveller may wash, and eat, and converse, and
sleep, without further journey; such a shelter as you
would be glad to reach in a tempestuous night, containing all the essentials of a house, and nothing for
house-keeping; where you can see all the treasures of
the house at one view, and everything hangs upon its
peg that a man should use; at once kitchen, pantry,
parlor, chamber, storehouse, and garret; where you
can see so necessary a thing as a barrel or a ladder, so
convenient a thing as a cupboard, and hear the pot
boil, and pay your respects to the fire that cooks your
dinner, and the oven that bakes your bread, and the
necessary furniture and utensils are the chief ornaments;
where the washing is not put out, nor the fire, nor the
mistress, and perhaps you are sometimes requested
to move from off the trap-door, when the cook would
descend into the cellar, and so learn whether the ground
is solid or hollow beneath you without stamping. A

house whose inside is as open and manifest as a bird's nest, and you cannot go in at the front door and out at the back without seeing some of its inhabitants; where to be a guest is to be presented with the freedom of the house, and not to be carefully excluded from seven eighths of it, shut up in a particular cell, and told to make yourself at home there, — in solitary confinement. Nowadays the host does not admit you to *his* hearth, but has got the mason to build one for yourself somewhere in his alley, and hospitality is the art of *keeping* you at the greatest distance. There is as much secrecy about the cooking as if he had a design to poison you. I am aware that I have been on many a man's premises, and might have been legally ordered off, but I am not aware that I have been in many men's houses. I might visit in my old clothes a king and queen who lived simply in such a house as I have described, if I were going their way; but backing out of a modern palace will be all that I shall desire to learn, if ever I am caught in one.

It would seem as if the very language of our parlors would lose all its nerve and degenerate into *palaver* wholly, our lives pass at such remoteness from its symbols, and its metaphors and tropes are necessarily so far fetched, through slides and dumb-waiters, as it were; in other words, the parlor is so far from the kitchen and workshop. The dinner even is only the parable of a dinner, commonly. As if only the savage dwelt near enough to Nature and Truth to borrow a trope from them. How can the scholar, who dwells away in the North West Territory or the Isle of Man, tell what is parliamentary in the kitchen?

However, only one or two of my guests were ever bold enough to stay and eat a hasty-pudding with me; but when they saw that crisis approaching they beat a hasty retreat rather, as if it would shake the house to its foundations. Nevertheless, it stood through a great many hasty-puddings.

I did not plaster till it was freezing weather. I brought over some whiter and cleaner sand for this purpose from the opposite shore of the pond in a boat, a sort of conveyance which would have tempted me to go much farther if necessary. My house had in the meanwhile been shingled down to the ground on every side. In lathing I was pleased to be able to send home each nail with a single blow of the hammer, and it was my ambition to transfer the plaster from the board to the wall neatly and rapidly. I remembered the story of a conceited fellow, who, in fine clothes, was wont to lounge about the village once, giving advice to workmen. Venturing one day to substitute deeds for words, he turned up his cuffs, seized a plasterer's board, and having loaded his trowel without mishap, with a complacent look toward the lathing overhead, made a bold gesture thitherward; and straightway, to his complete discomfiture, received the whole contents in his ruffled bosom. I admired anew the economy and convenience of plastering, which so effectually shuts out the cold and takes a handsome finish, and I learned the various casualties to which the plasterer is liable. I was surprised to see how thirsty the bricks were which drank up all the moisture in my plaster before I had smoothed it, and how many pailfuls of water it takes to christen a new hearth. I had the previous winter made a small quantity of lime by burning the shells of the *Unio fluviatilis*, which our river affords, for the sake of the experiment; so that I knew where my materials came from. I might have got good limestone within a mile or two and burned it myself, if I had cared to do so.

The pond had in the meanwhile skimmed over in the shadiest and shallowest coves, some days or even weeks before the general freezing. The first ice is especially interesting and perfect, being hard, dark, and transparent, and affords the best opportunity that ever offers for examining the bottom where it is shallow; for you can lie at your length on ice only an inch thick, like a skater insect on the surface of the water, and study the bottom at your leisure, only two or three inches distant, like a picture behind a glass, and the water is necessarily always smooth then. There are many furrows in the sand where some creature has travelled about and doubled on its tracks; and, for wrecks, it is strewn with the cases of caddis-worms made of minute grains of white quartz. Perhaps these have creased it, for you find some of their cases in the furrows, though they are deep and broad for them to make. But the ice itself is the object of most interest, though you must improve the earliest opportunity to study it. If you examine it closely the morning after it freezes, you find that the greater part of the bubbles, which at first appeared to be within it, are against its under surface, and that more are continually rising from the bottom; while the ice is as yet comparatively solid and dark, that is, you see the water through it. These bubbles are from an eightieth to an eighth of an inch in diameter, very clear and beautiful, and you see your face reflected in them through the ice. There may be thirty or forty of them to a square inch. There are also already within the ice narrow oblong perpendicular bubbles about half an inch long, sharp cones with the apex upward; or oftener, if the ice is quite fresh, minute spherical bubbles one directly above another, like a string of beads. But these within the ice are not so numerous nor obvious as those beneath. I sometimes used to cast on stones to try the strength of the ice, and those which broke through carried in air with them, which formed very large and conspicuous white bubbles beneath. One day when I came to the same place forty-eight hours afterward, I found that those large bubbles were still perfect, though an inch more of ice had formed, as I could see distinctly by the seam in the edge of a cake. But as the last two days had been very warm, like an Indian summer, the ice was not now transparent, showing the dark green color of the water, and the bottom, but opaque and whitish or gray, and though twice as thick was hardly stronger than before, for the air bubbles had greatly expanded under this heat and run together, and lost their regularity; they were no longer one directly over another, but often like silvery coins poured from a bag, one overlapping another, or in thin flakes, as if occupying slight cleavages. The beauty of the ice was gone, and it was too late to study the bottom. Being curious to know what position my great bubbles occupied with regard to the new ice, I broke out a cake containing a middling sized one, and turned it bottom upward. The new ice had formed around and under the bubble, so that it was included between the two ices. It was wholly in the lower ice, but close against the upper, and was flattish, or perhaps slightly lenticular, with a rounded edge, a quarter of an inch deep by four inches in diameter; and I was surprised to find that directly under the bubble the ice was melted with great regularity in the form of a saucer reversed, to the height of five eighths of an inch in the middle, leaving a thin partition there between the water and the bubble, hardly an eighth of an inch thick; and in many places the small bubbles in this partition had burst out downward, and probably there was no ice at all under the largest bubbles, which were a foot in diameter. I inferred that the infinite number of minute bubbles which I had first seen against the under surface of the ice were now frozen in likewise, and that each, in its degree, had operated like a burning-glass on the ice beneath to melt and rot it. These are the little air-guns which contribute to make the ice crack and whoop.

At length the winter set in in good earnest, just as I had finished plastering, and the wind began to howl around the house as if it had not had permission to do so till then. Night after night the geese came lumbering in in the dark with a clangor and a whistling of wings, even after the ground was covered with snow, some to alight in Walden, and some flying low over the woods toward Fair Haven, bound for Mexico. Several times, when returning from the village at ten or eleven o'clock at night, I heard the tread of a flock of geese, or else ducks, on

the dry leaves in the woods by a pond-hole behind my
dwelling, where they had come up to feed, and the faint
honk or quack of their leader as they hurried off. In
1845 Walden froze entirely over for the first time on the
night of the 22d of December, Flint's and other shallower
ponds and the river having been frozen ten days or
more; in '46, the 16th; in '49, about the 31st; and in
'50, about the 27th of December; in '52, the 5th of January; in '53, the 31st of December. The snow had already covered the ground since the 25th of November,
and surrounded me suddenly with the scenery of winter.
I withdrew yet farther into my shell, and endeavored to
keep a bright fire both within my house and within my
breast. My employment out of doors now was to collect
the dead wood in the forest, bringing it in my hands or
on my shoulders, or sometimes trailing a dead pine tree
under each arm to my shed. An old forest fence which
had seen its best days was a great haul for me. I sacrificed it to Vulcan, for it was past serving the god Terminus. How much more interesting an event is that
man's supper who has just been forth in the snow to
hunt, nay, you might say, steal, the fuel to cook it with!
His bread and meat are sweet. There are enough fagots
and waste wood of all kinds in the forests of most of our
towns to support many fires, but which at present warm
none, and, some think, hinder the growth of the young
wood. There was also the driftwood of the pond. In the
course of the summer I had discovered a raft of pitch
pine logs with the bark on, pinned together by the Irish
when the railroad was built. This I hauled up partly
on the shore. After soaking two years and then lying

high six months it was perfectly sound, though water-logged past drying. I amused myself one winter day with sliding this piecemeal across the pond, nearly half a mile, skating behind with one end of a log fifteen feet long on my shoulder, and the other on the ice; or I tied several logs together with a birch withe, and then, with a longer birch or alder which had a hook at the end, dragged them across. Though completely waterlogged and almost as heavy as lead, they not only burned long, but made a very hot fire; nay, I thought that they burned better for the soaking, as if the pitch, being confined by the water, burned longer, as in a lamp.

Gilpin, in his account of the forest borderers of England, says that "the encroachments of trespassers, and the houses and fences thus raised on the borders of the forest," were "considered as great nuisances by the old forest law, and were severely punished under the name of *purprestures*, as tending *ad terrorem ferarum — ad nocumentum forestae*, etc.," to the frightening of the game and the detriment of the forest. But I was interested in the preservation of the venison and the vert more than the hunters or woodchoppers, and as much as though I had been the Lord Warden himself; and if any part was burned, though I burned it myself by accident, I grieved with a grief that lasted longer and was more inconsolable than that of the proprietors; nay, I grieved when it was cut down by the proprietors themselves. I would that our farmers when they cut down a forest felt some of that awe which the old Romans did when they came to thin, or let in the light to, a consecrated grove (*lucum conlucare*), that is, would believe that it is sacred to some god. The Roman made an expiatory offering, and prayed, Whatever god or goddess thou art to whom this grove is sacred, be propitious to me, my family, and children, etc.

It is remarkable what a value is still put upon wood even in this age and in this new country, a value more permanent and universal than that of gold. After all our discoveries and inventions no man will go by a pile of wood. It is as precious to us as it was to our Saxon and Norman ancestors. If they made their bows of it, we make our gun-stocks of it. Michaux, more than thirty years ago, says that the price of wood for fuel in New York and Philadelphia "nearly equals, and sometimes exceeds, that of the best wood in Paris, though this immense capital annually requires more than three hundred thousand cords, and is surrounded to the distance of three hundred miles by cultivated plains." In this town the price of wood rises almost steadily, and the only question is, how much higher it is to be this year than it was the last. Mechanics and tradesmen who come in person to the forest on no other errand, are sure to attend the wood auction, and even pay a high price for the privilege of gleaning after the woodchopper. It is now many years that men have resorted to the forest for fuel and the materials of the arts: the New Englander and the New Hollander, the Parisian and the Celt, the farmer and Robin Hood, Goody Blake and Harry Gill; in most parts of the world the prince and the peasant, the scholar and the savage, equally require still a few sticks from the forest to warm them and cook their food. Neither could I do without them.

Every man looks at his wood-pile with a kind of affection. I loved to have mine before my window, and the more chips the better to remind me of my pleasing work. I had an old axe which nobody claimed, with which by spells in winter days, on the sunny side of the house, I played about the stumps which I had got out of my bean-field. As my driver prophesied when I was plowing, they warmed me twice, — once while I was splitting them, and again when they were on the fire, so that no fuel could give out more heat. As for the axe, I was advised to get the village blacksmith to " jump " it; but I jumped him, and, putting a hickory helve from the woods into it, made it do. If it was dull, it was at least hung true.

A few pieces of fat pine were a great treasure. It is interesting to remember how much of this food for fire is still concealed in the bowels of the earth. In previous years I had often gone "prospecting" over some bare hillside, where a pitch pine wood had formerly stood, and got out the fat pine roots. They are almost indestructible. Stumps thirty or forty years old, at least, will still be sound at the core, though the sapwood has all become vegetable mould, as appears by the scales of the thick bark forming a ring level with the earth four or five inches distant from the heart. With axe and shovel you explore this mine, and follow the marrowy store, yellow as beef tallow, or as if you had struck on a vein of gold, deep into the earth. But commonly I kindled my fire with the dry leaves of the forest, which I had stored up in my shed before the snow came. Green hickory finely split makes the woodchopper's kindlings, when he has a camp in the woods. Once in a while I got a little of this. When the villagers were lighting their fires beyond the horizon, I too gave notice to the various wild inhabitants of Walden vale, by a smoky streamer from my chimney, that I was awake. —

> Light-winged Smoke, Icarian bird,
> Melting thy pinions in thy upward flight,
> Lark without song, and messenger of dawn,
> Circling above the hamlets as thy nest;
> Or else, departing dream, and shadowy form
> Of midnight vision, gathering up thy skirts;
> By night star-veiling, and by day
> Darkening the light and blotting out the sun;
> Go thou my incense upward from this hearth,
> And ask the gods to pardon this clear flame.

Hard green wood just cut, though I used but little of that, answered my purpose better than any other. I sometimes left a good fire when I went to take a walk in a winter afternoon; and when I returned, three or four hours afterward, it would be still alive and glowing. My house was not empty though I was gone. It was as if I had left a cheerful housekeeper behind. It was I and Fire that lived there; and commonly my housekeeper proved trustworthy. One day, however, as I was splitting wood, I thought that I would just look in at the window and see if the house was not on fire; it was the only time I remember to have been particularly anxious on this score; so I looked and saw that a spark had caught my bed, and I went in and extinguished it when it had burned a place as big as my hand. But my house occupied so sunny and sheltered a position, and its roof was so low, that I could afford to let the fire go out in the middle of almost any winter day.

The moles nested in my cellar, nibbling every third potato, and making a snug bed even there of some hair left after plastering and of brown paper; for even the wildest animals love comfort and warmth as well as man, and they survive the winter only because they are so careful to secure them. Some of my friends spoke as if I was coming to the woods on purpose to freeze myself. The animal merely makes a bed, which he warms with his body, in a sheltered place; but man, having discovered fire, boxes up some air in a spacious apartment, and warms that, instead of robbing himself, makes that his bed, in which he can move about divested of more cumbrous clothing, maintain a kind of summer in the midst of winter, and by means of windows even admit the light, and with a lamp lengthen out the day. Thus he goes a step or two beyond instinct, and saves a little time for the fine arts. Though, when I had been exposed to the rudest blasts a long time, my whole body began to grow torpid, when I reached the genial atmosphere of my house I soon recovered my faculties and prolonged my life. But the most luxuriously housed has little to boast of in this respect, nor need we trouble ourselves to speculate how the human race may be at last destroyed. It would be easy to cut their threads any time with a little sharper blast from the north. We go on dating from Cold Fridays and Great Snows; but a little colder Friday, or greater snow would put a period to man's existence on the globe.

The next winter I used a small cooking-stove for economy, since I did not own the forest; but it did not keep fire so well as the open fireplace. Cooking was then, for the most part, no longer a poetic, but merely a chemic process. It will soon be forgotten, in these days of stoves, that we used to roast potatoes in the ashes, after the Indian fashion. The stove not only took up room and scented the house, but it concealed the fire, and I felt as if I had lost a companion. You can always see a face in the fire. The laborer, looking into it at evening, purifies his thoughts of the dross and earthiness which they have accumulated during the day. But I could no longer sit and look into the fire, and the pertinent words of a poet recurred to me with new force. —

> " Never, bright flame, may be denied to me
> Thy dear, life imaging, close sympathy.
> What but my hopes shot upward e'er so bright?
> What but my fortunes sunk so low in night?
> Why art thou banished from our hearth and hall,
> Thou who art welcomed and beloved by all?
> Was thy existence then too fanciful
> For our life's common light, who are so dull?
> Did thy bright gleam mysterious converse hold
> With our congenial souls? secrets too bold?
>
> Well, we are safe and strong, for now we sit
> Beside a hearth where no dim shadows flit,
> Where nothing cheers nor saddens, but a fire
> Warms feet and hands — nor does to more aspire;
> By whose compact utilitarian heap
> The present may sit down and go to sleep,
> Nor fear the ghosts who from the dim past walked,
> And with us by the unequal light of the old wood fire talked."

XIV

FORMER INHABITANTS; AND WINTER VISITORS

I WEATHERED some merry snow-storms, and spent some cheerful winter evenings by my fireside, while the snow whirled wildly without, and even the hooting of the owl was hushed. For many weeks I met no one in my walks but those who came occasionally to cut wood and sled it to the village. The elements, however, abetted me in making a path through the deepest snow in the woods, for when I had once gone through the wind blew the oak leaves into my tracks, where they lodged, and by absorbing the rays of the sun melted the snow, and so not only made a dry bed for my feet, but in the night their dark line was my guide. For human society I was obliged to conjure up the former occupants of these woods. Within the memory of many of my townsmen the road near which my house stands resounded with the laugh and gossip of inhabitants, and the woods which border it were notched and dotted here and there with their little gardens and dwellings, though it was then much more shut in by the forest than now. In some places, within my own remembrance, the pines would scrape both sides of a chaise at once, and women and children who were compelled to go this way to Lincoln alone and on foot did it with fear, and often ran a good part of the distance. Though mainly but a humble route to neighboring villages, or for the woodman's team, it once amused the traveller more than now by its variety, and lingered longer in his memory. Where now firm open fields stretch from the village to the woods, it then ran through a maple swamp on a foundation of logs, the remnants of which, doubtless, still underlie the present dusty highway, from the Stratton, now the Alms-House, Farm, to Brister's Hill.

East of my bean-field, across the road, lived Cato Ingraham, slave of Duncan Ingraham, Esquire, gentleman, of Concord village, who built his slave a house, and gave him permission to live in Walden Woods; — Cato, not Uticensis, but Concordiensis. Some say that he was a Guinea Negro. There are a few who remember his little patch among the walnuts, which he let grow up till he should be old and need them; but a younger and whiter speculator got them at last. He too, however, occupies an equally narrow house at present. Cato's half-obliterated cellar-hole still remains, though known to few, being concealed from the traveller by a fringe of pines. It is now filled with the smooth sumach (*Rhus glabra*), and one of the earliest species of goldenrod (*Solidago stricta*) grows there luxuriantly.

Here, by the very corner of my field, still nearer to town, Zilpha, a colored woman, had her little house, where she spun linen for the townsfolk, making the Walden Woods ring with her shrill singing, for she had a loud and notable voice. At length, in the war of 1812, her dwelling was set on fire by English soldiers, prisoners on parole, when she was away, and her cat and dog and hens were all burned up together. She led a hard life, and somewhat inhumane. One old frequenter of these woods remembers, that as he passed her house one noon he heard her muttering to herself over her gurgling pot, — "Ye are all bones, bones!" I have seen bricks amid the oak copse there.

Down the road, on the right hand, on Brister's Hill, lived Brister Freeman, "a handy Negro," slave of Squire Cummings once, — there where grow still the apple trees which Brister planted and tended; large old trees now, but their fruit still wild and ciderish to my taste. Not long since I read his epitaph in the old Lincoln burying-ground, a little on one side, near the unmarked graves of some British grenadiers who fell in the retreat from Concord, — where he is styled "Sippio Brister," — Scipio Africanus he had some title to be called, — "a man of color," as if he were discolored. It also told me, with staring emphasis, when he died; which was but an indirect way of informing me that he ever lived. With him dwelt Fenda, his hospitable wife, who told fortunes, yet pleasantly, — large, round, and black, blacker than any of the children of night, such a dusky orb as never rose on Concord before or since.

Farther down the hill, on the left, on the old road in the woods, are marks of some homestead of the Stratton family; whose orchard once covered all the slope of Brister's Hill, but was long since killed out by pitch pines, excepting a few stumps, whose old roots furnish still the wild stocks of many a thrifty village tree.

Nearer yet to town, you come to Breed's location, on

the other side of the way, just on the edge of the wood; ground famous for the pranks of a demon not distinctly named in old mythology, who has acted a prominent and astounding part in our New England life, and deserves, as much as any mythological character, to have his biography written one day; who first comes in the guise of a friend or hired man, and then robs and murders the whole family, — New-England Rum. But history must not yet tell the tragedies enacted here; let time intervene in some measure to assuage and lend an azure tint to them. Here the most indistinct and dubious tradition says that once a tavern stood; the well the same, which tempered the traveller's beverage and refreshed his steed. Here then men saluted one another, and heard and told the news, and went their ways again.

Breed's hut was standing only a dozen years ago, though it had long been unoccupied. It was about the size of mine. It was set on fire by mischievous boys, one Election night, if I do not mistake. I lived on the edge of the village then, and had just lost myself over Davenant's " Gondibert," that winter that I labored with a lethargy, — which, by the way, I never knew whether to regard as a family complaint, having an uncle who goes to sleep shaving himself, and is obliged to sprout potatoes in a cellar Sundays, in order to keep awake and keep the Sabbath, or as the consequence of my attempt to read Chalmers' collection of English poetry without skipping. It fairly overcame my Nervii. I had just sunk my head on this when the bells rung fire, and in hot haste the engines rolled that way, led by a strag-

gling troop of men and boys, and I among the foremost, for I had leaped the brook. We thought it was
far south over the woods, — we who had run to fires
before, — barn, shop, or dwelling-house, or all together. "It's Baker's barn," cried one. "It is the Cod-
man place," affirmed another. And then fresh sparks
went up above the wood, as if the roof fell in, and
we all shouted "Concord to the rescue!" Wagons
shot past with furious speed and crushing loads, bearing, perchance, among the rest, the agent of the Insurance Company, who was bound to go however far;
and ever and anon the engine bell tinkled behind, more
slow and sure; and rearmost of all, as it was afterward
whispered, came they who set the fire and gave the
alarm. Thus we kept on like true idealists, rejecting
the evidence of our senses, until at a turn in the road
we heard the crackling and actually felt the heat of the
fire from over the wall, and realized, alas! that we
were there. The very nearness of the fire but cooled
our ardor. At first we thought to throw a frog-pond on
to it; but concluded to let it burn, it was so far gone
and so worthless. So we stood round our engine, jostled
one another, expressed our sentiments through speak-
ing-trumpets, or in lower tone referred to the great
conflagrations which the world has witnessed, including
Bascom's shop, and, between ourselves, we thought
that, were we there in season with our "tub," and a
full frog-pond by, we could turn that threatened last
and universal one into another flood. We finally retreated without doing any mischief, — returned to sleep
and "Gondibert." But as for "Gondibert," I would

except that passage in the preface about wit being the soul's powder, — "but most of mankind are strangers to wit, as Indians are to powder."

It chanced that I walked that way across the fields the following night, about the same hour, and hearing a low moaning at this spot, I drew near in the dark, and discovered the only survivor of the family that I know, the heir of both its virtues and its vices, who alone was interested in this burning, lying on his stomach and looking over the cellar wall at the still smouldering cinders beneath, muttering to himself, as is his wont. He had been working far off in the river meadows all day, and had improved the first moments that he could call his own to visit the home of his fathers and his youth. He gazed into the cellar from all sides and points of view by turns, always lying down to it, as if there was some treasure, which he remembered, concealed between the stones, where there was absolutely nothing but a heap of bricks and ashes. The house being gone, he looked at what there was left. He was soothed by the sympathy which my mere presence implied, and showed me, as well as the darkness permitted, where the well was covered up; which, thank Heaven, could never be burned; and he groped long about the wall to find the well-sweep which his father had cut and mounted, feeling for the iron hook or staple by which a burden had been fastened to the heavy end, — all that he could now cling to, — to convince me that it was no common "rider." I felt it, and still remark it almost daily in my walks, for by it hangs the history of a family.

Once more, on the left, where are seen the well and

lilac bushes by the wall, in the now open field, lived Nutting and Le Grosse. But to return toward Lincoln.

Farther in the woods than any of these, where the road approaches nearest to the pond, Wyman the potter squatted, and furnished his townsmen with earthenware, and left descendants to succeed him. Neither were they rich in worldly goods, holding the land by sufferance while they lived; and there often the sheriff came in vain to collect the taxes, and "attached a chip," for form's sake, as I have read in his accounts, there being nothing else that he could lay his hands on. One day in midsummer, when I was hoeing, a man who was carrying a load of pottery to market stopped his horse against my field and inquired concerning Wyman the younger. He had long ago bought a potter's wheel of him, and wished to know what had become of him. I had read of the potter's clay and wheel in Scripture, but it had never occurred to me that the pots we use were not such as had come down unbroken from those days, or grown on trees like gourds somewhere, and I was pleased to hear that so fictile an art was ever practiced in my neighborhood.

The last inhabitant of these woods before me was an Irishman, Hugh Quoil (if I have spelt his name with coil enough), who occupied Wyman's tenement, — Col. Quoil, he was called. Rumor said that he had been a soldier at Waterloo. If he had lived I should have made him fight his battles over again. His trade here was that of a ditcher. Napoleon went to St. Helena; Quoil came to Walden Woods. All I know of him is tragic. He was a man of manners, like one who had seen the world, and was capable of more civil speech than you could well attend to. He wore a greatcoat in midsummer, being affected with the trembling delirium, and his face was the color of carmine. He died in the road at the foot of Brister's Hill shortly after I came to the woods, so that I have not remembered him as a neighbor. Before his house was pulled down, when his comrades avoided it as "an unlucky castle," I visited it. There lay his old clothes curled up by use, as if they were himself, upon his raised plank bed. His pipe lay broken on the hearth, instead of a bowl broken at the fountain. The last could never have been the symbol of his death, for he confessed to me that, though he had heard of Brister's Spring, he had never seen it; and soiled cards, kings of diamonds, spades, and hearts, were scattered over the floor. One black chicken which the administrator could not catch, black as night and as silent, not even croaking, awaiting Reynard, still went to roost in the next apartment. In the rear there was the dim outline of a garden, which had been planted but had never received its first hoeing, owing to those terrible shaking fits, though it was now harvest time. It was overrun with Roman wormwood and beggar-ticks, which last stuck to my clothes for all fruit. The skin of a woodchuck was freshly stretched upon the back of the house, a trophy of his last Waterloo; but no warm cap or mittens would he want more.

Now only a dent in the earth marks the site of these dwellings, with buried cellar stones, and straw-berries, raspberries, thimble-berries, hazel-bushes, and sumachs growing in the sunny sward there; some pitch

pine or gnarled oak occupies what was the chimney
nook, and a sweet-scented black birch, perhaps, waves
where the door-stone was. Sometimes the well dent
is visible, where once a spring oozed; now dry and
tearless grass; or it was covered deep, — not to be
discovered till some late day, — with a flat stone under
the sod, when the last of the race departed. What a
sorrowful act must that be, — the covering up of wells!
coincident with the opening of wells of tears. These
cellar dents, like deserted fox burrows, old holes, are all
that is left where once were the stir and bustle of human life, and "fate, free will, foreknowledge absolute,"
in some form and dialect or other were by turns dis-
cussed. But all I can learn of their conclusions amounts
to just this, that "Cato and Brister pulled wool;" which
is about as edifying as the history of more famous
schools of philosophy.

Still grows the vivacious lilac a generation after the
door and lintel and the sill are gone, unfolding its sweet-
scented flowers each spring, to be plucked by the mus-
ing traveller; planted and tended once by children's
hands, in front-yard plots, — now standing by wall-
sides in retired pastures, and giving place to new-rising
forests; — the last of that stirp, sole survivor of that
family. Little did the dusky children think that the
puny slip with its two eyes only, which they stuck in
the ground in the shadow of the house and daily watered,
would root itself so, and outlive them, and house itself
in the rear that shaded it, and grown man's garden and
orchard, and tell their story faintly to the lone wanderer
a half-century after they had grown up and died, —

blossoming as fair, and smelling as sweet, as in that first spring. I mark its still tender, civil, cheerful, lilac colors.

But this small village, germ of something more, why did it fail while Concord keeps its ground? Were there no natural advantages, — no water privileges, forsooth? Ay, the deep Walden Pond and cool Brister's Spring, — privilege to drink long and healthy draughts at these, all unimproved by these men but to dilute their glass. They were universally a thirsty race. Might not the basket, stable-broom, mat-making, corn-parching, linen-spinning, and pottery business have thrived here, making the wilderness to blossom like the rose, and a numerous posterity have inherited the land of their fathers? The sterile soil would at least have been proof against a lowland degeneracy. Alas! how little does the memory of these human inhabitants enhance the beauty of the landscape! Again, perhaps, Nature will try, with me for a first settler, and my house raised last spring to be the oldest in the hamlet.

I am not aware that any man has ever built on the spot which I occupy. Deliver me from a city built on the site of a more ancient city, whose materials are ruins, whose gardens cemeteries. The soil is blanched and accursed there, and before that becomes necessary the earth itself will be destroyed. With such reminiscences I repeopled the woods and lulled myself asleep.

At this season I seldom had a visitor. When the snow lay deepest no wanderer ventured near my house for a week or fortnight at a time, but there I lived as snug as a meadow mouse, or as cattle and poultry which are said to have survived for a long time buried in drifts, even without food; or like that early settler's family in the town of Sutton, in this State, whose cottage was completely covered by the great snow of 1717 when he was absent, and an Indian found it only by the hole which the chimney's breath made in the drift, and so relieved the family. But no friendly Indian concerned himself about me; nor needed he, for the master of the house was at home. The Great Snow! How cheerful it is to hear of! When the farmers could not get to the woods and swamps with their teams, and were obliged to cut down the shade trees before their houses, and, when the crust was harder, cut off the trees in the swamps, ten feet from the ground, as it appeared the next spring.

In the deepest snows, the path which I used from the highway to my house, about half a mile long, might have been represented by a meandering dotted line, with wide intervals between the dots. For a week of even weather I took exactly the same number of steps, and of the same length, coming and going, stepping deliberately and with the precision of a pair of dividers in my own deep tracks, — to such routine the winter reduces us, — yet often they were filled with heaven's own blue. But no weather interfered fatally with my walks, or rather my going abroad, for I frequently tramped eight or ten miles through the deepest snow to keep an appointment with a beech tree, or a yellow birch, or an old acquaintance among the pines; when the ice and snow causing their limbs to droop, and so sharpening their tops, had changed the pines into fir trees; wading to the tops of the highest hills when the snow was nearly two feet deep on a level, and shaking down another snow-storm on my head at every step; or sometimes creeping and floundering thither on my hands and knees, when the hunters had gone into winter quarters. One afternoon I amused myself by watching a barred owl (*Strix nebulosa*) sitting on one of the lower dead limbs of a white pine, close to the trunk, in broad daylight, I standing within a rod of him. He could hear me when I moved and cronched the snow with my feet, but could not plainly see me. When I made most noise he would stretch out his neck, and erect his neck feathers, and open his eyes wide; but their lids soon fell again, and he began to nod. I too felt a slumberous influence after watching him half an hour, as he sat thus with his eyes half open, like a cat, winged brother of the cat. There was only a narrow slit left between their lids, by which he preserved a peninsular relation to me; thus, with half-shut eyes, looking out from the land of dreams, and endeavoring to realize me, vague object or mote that interrupted his visions. At length, on some louder noise or my nearer approach, he would grow uneasy and sluggishly turn about on his perch, as if impatient at having his dreams disturbed; and when he launched himself off and flapped through the pines, spreading his wings to unexpected breadth, I could not hear the slightest sound from them. Thus, guided amid the pine boughs rather by a delicate sense of their neighborhood than by sight, feeling his twilight way, as it were, with his sensitive pinions, he found a new perch, where he might in peace await the dawning of his day.

As I walked over the long causeway made for the railroad through the meadows, I encountered many a blustering and nipping wind, for nowhere has it freer play; and when the frost had smitten me on one cheek, heathen as I was, I turned to it the other also. Nor was it much better by the carriage road from Brister's Hill. For I came to town still, like a friendly Indian, when the contents of the broad open fields were all piled up between the walls of the Walden road, and half an hour sufficed to obliterate the tracks of the last traveller. And when I returned new drifts would have formed, through which I floundered, where the busy northwest wind had been depositing the powdery snow round a sharp angle in the road, and not a rabbit's track, nor even the fine print, the small type, of a meadow mouse was to be seen. Yet I rarely failed to find, even in midwinter, some warm and springy swamp where the grass and the skunk-cabbage still put forth with perennial verdure, and some hardier bird occasionally awaited the return of spring.

Sometimes, notwithstanding the snow, when I returned from my walk at evening I crossed the deep tracks of a woodchopper leading from my door, and found his pile of whittlings on the hearth, and my house filled with the odor of his pipe. Or on a Sunday afternoon, if I chanced to be at home, I heard the cronching of the snow made by the step of a long-headed farmer, who from far through the woods sought my house, to have a social "crack;" one of the few of his vocation

who are "men on their farms;" who donned a frock
instead of a professor's gown, and is as ready to ex-
tract the moral out of church or state as to haul a load
of manure from his barn-yard. We talked of rude and
simple times, when men sat about large fires in cold,
bracing weather, with clear heads; and when other
dessert failed, we tried our teeth on many a nut which
wise squirrels have long since abandoned, for those
which have the thickest shells are commonly empty.

The one who came from farthest to my lodge, through
deepest snows and most dismal tempests, was a poet.
A farmer, a hunter, a soldier, a reporter, even a philosopher, may be daunted; but nothing can deter a
poet, for he is actuated by pure love. Who can pre-
dict his comings and goings? His business calls him
out at all hours, even when doctors sleep. We made
that small house ring with boisterous mirth and resound with the murmur of much sober talk, making
amends then to Walden vale for the long silences.
Broadway was still and deserted in comparison. At
suitable intervals there were regular salutes of laughter,
which might have been referred indifferently to the
last-uttered or the forth-coming jest. We made many
a "bran new" theory of life over a thin dish of gruel,
which combined the advantages of conviviality with
the clear-headedness which philosophy requires.

I should not forget that during my last winter at the
pond there was another welcome visitor, who at one
time came through the village, through snow and rain
and darkness, till he saw my lamp through the trees, and
shared with me some long winter evenings. One of the

last of the philosophers, — Connecticut gave him to the world, — he peddled first her wares, afterwards, as he declares, his brains. These he peddles still, prompting God and disgracing man, bearing for fruit his brain only, like the nut its kernel. I think that he must be the man of the most faith of any alive. His words and attitude always suppose a better state of things than other men are acquainted with, and he will be the last man to be disappointed as the ages revolve. He has no venture in the present. But though comparatively disregarded now, when his day comes, laws unsuspected by most will take effect, and masters of families and rulers will come to him for advice. —

"How blind that cannot see serenity !"

A true friend of man; almost the only friend of human progress. An Old Mortality, say rather an Immortality, with unwearied patience and faith making plain the image engraven in men's bodies, the God of whom they are but defaced and leaning monuments. With his hospitable intellect he embraces children, beggars, insane, and scholars, and entertains the thought of all, adding to it commonly some breadth and elegance. I think that he should keep a caravansary on the world's highway, where philosophers of all nations might put up, and on his sign should be printed, "Entertainment for man, but not for his beast. Enter ye that have leisure and a quiet mind, who earnestly seek the right road." He is perhaps the sanest man and has the fewest crotchets of any I chance to know; the same yesterday and to-morrow. Of yore we had sauntered and talked, and effect-

ually put the world behind us; for he was pledged to
no institution in it, freeborn, *ingenuus*. Whichever way
we turned, it seemed that the heavens and the earth
had met together, since he enhanced the beauty of the
landscape. A blue-robed man, whose fittest roof is the
overarching sky which reflects his serenity. I do not
see how he can ever die; Nature cannot spare him.

Having each some shingles of thought well dried, we
sat and whittled them, trying our knives, and admiring
the clear yellowish grain of the pumpkin pine. We
waded so gently and reverently, or we pulled together
so smoothly, that the fishes of thought were not scared
from the stream, nor feared any angler on the bank, but
came and went grandly, like the clouds which float
through the western sky, and the mother-o'-pearl flocks
which sometimes form and dissolve there. There we
worked, revising mythology, rounding a fable here and
there, and building castles in the air for which earth
offered no worthy foundation. Great Looker! Great
Expecter! to converse with whom was a New England
Night's Entertainment. Ah! such discourse we had,
hermit and philosopher, and the old settler I have
spoken of, — we three, — it expanded and racked my
little house; I should not dare to say how many pounds'
weight there was above the atmospheric pressure on
every circular inch; it opened its seams so that they had
to be calked with much dulness thereafter to stop the
consequent leak; — but I had enough of that kind of
oakum already picked.

There was one other with whom I had "solid sea
sons," long to be remembered, at his house in the vil

lage, and who looked in upon me from time to time; but I had no more for society there.

There too, as everywhere, I sometimes expected the Visitor who never comes. The Vishnu Purana says, "The house-holder is to remain at eventide in his court-yard as long as it takes to milk a cow, or longer if he pleases, to await the arrival of a guest." I often performed this duty of hospitality, waited long enough to milk a whole herd of cows, but did not see the man approaching from the town.

WINTER ANIMALS

When the ponds were firmly frozen, they afforded not only new and shorter routes to many points, but new views from their surfaces of the familiar landscape around them. When I crossed Flint's Pond, after it was covered with snow, though I had often paddled about and skated over it, it was so unexpectedly wide and so strange that I could think of nothing but Baffin's Bay. The Lincoln hills rose up around me at the extremity of a snowy plain, in which I did not remember to have stood before; and the fishermen, at an indeterminable distance over the ice, moving slowly about with their wolfish dogs, passed for sealers or Esquimaux, or in misty weather loomed like fabulous creatures, and I did not know whether they were giants or pygmies. I took this course when I went to lecture in Lincoln in the evening, travelling in no road and passing no house between my own hut and the lecture room. In Goose Pond, which lay in my way, a colony of muskrats dwelt, and raised their cabins high above the ice, though none could be seen abroad when I crossed it. Walden, being like the rest usually bare of snow, or with only shallow and interrupted drifts on it, was my yard where I could walk freely when the snow was nearly two feet deep on a level elsewhere and the villagers were confined to their streets. There, far from the village street, and except at very long intervals, from the jingle of sleigh-bells, I slid and skated, as in a vast moose-yard well trodden, overhung by oak woods and solemn pines bent down with snow or bristling with icicles.

For sounds in winter nights, and often in winter days, I heard the forlorn but melodious note of a hooting owl indefinitely far; such a sound as the frozen earth would yield if struck with a suitable plectrum, the very *lingua vernacula* of Walden Wood, and quite familiar to me at last, though I never saw the bird while it was making it. I seldom opened my door in a winter evening without hearing it; *Hoo hoo hoo, hoorer hoo*, sounded sonorously, and the first three syllables accented somewhat like *how der do;* or sometimes *hoo hoo* only. One night in the beginning of winter, before the pond froze over, about nine o'clock, I was startled by the loud honking of a goose, and, stepping to the door, heard the sound of their wings like a tempest in the woods as they flew low over my house. They passed over the pond toward Fair Haven, seemingly deterred from settling by my light, their commodore honking all the while with a regular beat. Suddenly an unmistakable cat owl from very near me, with the most harsh and tremendous voice I ever heard from any inhabitant of the woods, responded at regular intervals to the goose, as if determined to expose and disgrace this intruder from Hudson's Bay by exhibiting a greater compass and volume of voice in a native, and *boo-hoo* him out of Concord horizon. What do you mean by alarming the citadel at this time of night consecrated to me? Do you think I am ever caught napping at such an hour, and that I have not got lungs and a larynx as well as yourself? *Boo-hoo, boo-hoo, boo-hoo!* It was one of the most thrilling discords I ever heard. And yet, if you had a discriminating ear, there were in it the elements of a concord such as these plains never saw nor heard.

I also heard the whooping of the ice in the pond, my great bed-fellow in that part of Concord, as if it were restless in its bed and would fain turn over, were troubled with flatulency and bad dreams; or I was waked by the cracking of the ground by the frost, as if some one had driven a team against my door, and in the morning would find a crack in the earth a quarter of a mile long and a third of an inch wide.

Sometimes I heard the foxes as they ranged over the snow-crust, in moonlight nights, in search of a partridge or other game, barking raggedly and demoniacally like forest dogs, as if laboring with some anxiety, or seeking expression, struggling for light and to be dogs outright and run freely in the streets; for if we take the ages into our account, may there not be a civilization going on among brutes as well as men? They seemed to me to be rudimental, burrowing men, still standing on their defence, awaiting their transformation. Sometimes one came near to my window, attracted by my light, barked a vulpine curse at me, and then retreated.

Usually the red squirrel (*Sciurus Hudsonius*) waked me in the dawn, coursing over the roof and up and down the sides of the house, as if sent out of the woods for this purpose. In the course of the winter I threw out half a bushel of ears of sweet corn, which had not got ripe, on to the snow-crust by my door, and was amused by watching the motions of the various animals which were baited by it. In the twilight and the night the rabbits came regularly and made a hearty meal. All day long the red squirrels came and went, and afforded me much entertainment by their manœuvres. One would approach at first warily through the shrub oaks, running over the snow-crust by fits and starts like a leaf blown by the wind, now a few paces this way, with wonderful speed and waste of energy, making inconceivable haste with his "trotters," as if it were for a wager, and now as many paces that way, but never getting on more than half a rod at a time; and then suddenly pausing with a ludicrous expression and a gratuitous somerset, as if all the eyes in the universe were fixed on him, — for all the motions of a squirrel, even in the most solitary recesses of the forest, imply spectators as much as those of a dancing girl, — wasting more time in delay and circumspection than would have sufficed to walk the whole distance, — I never saw one walk, — and then suddenly, before you could say Jack Robinson, he would be in the top of a young pitch pine, winding up his clock and chiding all imaginary spectators, soliloquizing and talking to all the universe at the same time, — for no reason that I could ever detect, or he himself was aware of, I suspect. At length he would reach the corn, and selecting a suitable ear, frisk about in the same uncertain trigonometrical way to the topmost stick of my wood-pile, before my window, where he looked me in the face, and there sit for hours, supplying himself with a new ear from time

to time, nibbling at first voraciously and throwing the
half-naked cobs about; till at length he grew more
dainty still and played with his food, tasting only the
inside of the kernel, and the ear, which was held bal-
anced over the stick by one paw, slipped from his care-
less grasp and fell to the ground, when he would look
over at it with a ludicrous expression of uncertainty, as
if suspecting that it had life, with a mind not made up
whether to get it again, or a new one, or be off; now
thinking of corn, then listening to hear what was in
the wind. So the little impudent fellow would waste
many an ear in a forenoon; till at last, seizing some
longer and plumper one, considerably bigger than himself, and skilfully balancing it, he would set out with it
to the woods, like a tiger with a buffalo, by the same
zigzag course and frequent pauses, scratching along
with it as if it were too heavy for him and falling all the
while, making its fall a diagonal between a perpendicular and horizontal, being determined to put it through
at any rate; — a singularly frivolous and whimsical
fellow; — and so he would get off with it to where he
lived, perhaps carry it to the top of a pine tree forty or
fifty rods distant, and I would afterwards find the cobs
strewn about the woods in various directions.

At length the jays arrive, whose discordant screams
were heard long before, as they were warily making
their approach an eighth of a mile off, and in a stealthy
and sneaking manner they flit from tree to tree, nearer
and nearer, and pick up the kernels which the squirrels
have dropped. Then, sitting on a pitch pine bough, they
attempt to swallow in their haste a kernel which is too

big for their throats and chokes them; and after great labor they disgorge it, and spend an hour in the endeavor to crack it by repeated blows with their bills. They were manifestly thieves, and I had not much respect for them; but the squirrels, though at first shy, went to work as if they were taking what was their own.

Meanwhile also came the chickadees in flocks, which, picking up the crumbs the squirrels had dropped, flew to the nearest twig, and, placing them under their claws, hammered away at them with their little bills, as if it were an insect in the bark, till they were sufficiently reduced for their slender throats. A little flock of these titmice came daily to pick a dinner out of my wood-pile, or the crumbs at my door, with faint flitting lisping notes, like the tinkling of icicles in the grass, or else with sprightly *day day day*, or more rarely, in springlike days, a wiry summery *phe-be* from the woodside. They were so familiar that at length one alighted on an armful of wood which I was carrying in, and pecked at the sticks without fear. I once had a sparrow alight upon my shoulder for a moment while I was hoeing in a village garden, and I felt that I was more distinguished by that circumstance than I should have been by any epaulet I could have worn. The squirrels also grew at last to be quite familiar, and occasionally stepped upon my shoe, when that was the nearest way.

When the ground was not yet quite covered, and again near the end of winter, when the snow was melted on my south hillside and about my wood-pile, the partridges came out of the woods morning and evening to feed

there. Whichever side you walk in the woods the partridge bursts away on whirring wings, jarring the snow
from the dry leaves and twigs on high, which comes sift-
ing down in the sunbeams like golden dust, for this brave
bird is not to be scared by winter. It is frequently covered up by drifts, and, it is said, "sometimes plunges
from on wing into the soft snow, where it remains concealed for a day or two." I used to start them in the
open land also, where they had come out of the woods
at sunset to "bud" the wild apple trees. They will
come regularly every evening to particular trees, where
the cunning sportsman lies in wait for them, and the
distant orchards next the woods suffer thus not a little.
I am glad that the partridge gets fed, at any rate.
It is Nature's own bird which lives on buds and diet-
drink.

In dark winter mornings, or in short winter afternoons,
I sometimes heard a pack of hounds threading all the
woods with hounding cry and yelp, unable to resist the
instinct of the chase, and the note of the hunting-horn at
intervals, proving that man was in the rear. The woods
ring again, and yet no fox bursts forth on to the open
level of the pond, nor following pack pursuing their
Actæon. And perhaps at evening I see the hunters returning with a single brush trailing from their sleigh for
a trophy, seeking their inn. They tell me that if the fox
would remain in the bosom of the frozen earth he would
be safe, or if he would run in a straight line away no
foxhound could overtake him; but, having left his pursuers far behind, he stops to rest and listen till they come
up, and when he runs he circles round to his old haunts,

where the hunters await him. Sometimes, however, he will run upon a wall many rods, and then leap off far to one side, and he appears to know that water will not retain his scent. A hunter told me that he once saw a fox pursued by hounds burst out on to Walden when the ice was covered with shallow puddles, run part way across, and then return to the same shore. Ere long the hounds arrived, but here they lost the scent. Sometimes a pack hunting by themselves would pass my door, and circle round my house, and yelp and hound without regarding me, as if afflicted by a species of madness, so that nothing could divert them from the pursuit. Thus they circle until they fall upon the recent trail of a fox, for a wise hound will forsake everything else for this. One day a man came to my hut from Lexington to inquire after his hound that made a large track, and had been hunting for a week by himself. But I fear that he was not the wiser for all I told him, for every time I attempted to answer his questions he interrupted me by asking, "What do you do here?" He had lost a dog, but found a man.

One old hunter who has a dry tongue, who used to come to bathe in Walden once every year when the water was warmest, and at such times looked in upon me, told me that many years ago he took his gun one afternoon and went out for a cruise in Walden Wood; and as he walked the Wayland road he heard the cry of hounds approaching, and ere long a fox leaped the wall into the road, and as quick as thought leaped the other wall out of the road, and his swift bullet had not touched him. Some way behind came an old hound and her three pups in full pursuit, hunting on their own account, and disappeared again in the woods. Late in the afternoon, as he was resting in the thick woods south of Walden, he heard the voice of the hounds far over toward Fair Haven still pursuing the fox; and on they came, their hounding cry which made all the woods ring sounding nearer and nearer, now from Well Meadow, now from the Baker Farm. For a long time he stood still and listened to their music, so sweet to a hunter's ear, when suddenly the fox appeared, threading the solemn aisles with an easy coursing pace, whose sound was concealed by a sympathetic rustle of the leaves, swift and still, keeping the ground, leaving his pursuers far behind; and, leaping upon a rock amid the woods, he sat erect and listening, with his back to the hunter. For a moment compassion restrained the latter's arm; but that was a short-lived mood, and as quick as thought can follow thought his piece was levelled, and *whang !* — the fox, rolling over the rock, lay dead on the ground. The hunter still kept his place and listened to the hounds. Still on they came, and now the near woods resounded through all their aisles with their demoniac cry. At length the old hound burst into view with muzzle to the ground, and snapping the air as if possessed, and ran directly to the rock; but, spying the dead fox, she suddenly ceased her hounding, as if struck dumb with amazement and walked round and round him in silence ; and one by one her pups arrived, and, like their mother, were sobered into silence by the mystery. Then the hunter came forward and stood in their midst, and the mystery was solved. They waited in silence while he skinned the fox, then followed the brush a while, and at length turned off into the woods again. That evening a Weston squire came to the Concord hunter's cottage to inquire for his hounds, and told how for a week they had been hunting on their own account from Weston woods. The Concord hunter told him what he knew and offered him the skin; but the other declined it and departed. He did not find his hounds that night, but the next day learned that they had crossed the river and put up at a farm-house for the night, whence, having been well fed, they took their departure early in the morning.

The hunter who told me this could remember one Sam Nutting, who used to hunt bears on Fair Haven Ledges, and exchange their skins for rum in Concord village; who told him, even, that he had seen a moose there. Nutting had a famous foxhound named Burgoyne, — he pronounced it Bugine, — which my inform-ant used to borrow. In the "Wast Book" of an old trader of this town, who was also a captain, town-clerk, and representative, I find the following entry. Jan. 18th, 1742–3, "John Melven Cr. by 1 Grey Fox 0 — 2 — 3;" they are not now found here; and in his ledger, Feb. 7th, 1743, Hezekiah Stratton has credit "by ½ a Catt skin 0 — 1 — 4½;" of course, a wild-cat, for Stratton was a sergeant in the old French war, and would not have got credit for hunting less noble game. Credit is given for deerskins also, and they were daily sold. One man still preserves the horns of the last deer that was killed in this vicinity, and another has told me the particulars of the hunt in which his uncle was engaged. The hunters were formerly a numerous and merry crew here. I remember

well one gaunt Nimrod who would catch up a leaf by
the roadside and play a strain on it wilder and more
melodious, if my memory serves me, than any hunting-
horn.

At midnight, when there was a moon, I sometimes
met with hounds in my path prowling about the woods,
which would skulk out of my way, as if afraid, and stand
silent amid the bushes till I had passed.

Squirrels and wild mice disputed for my store of nuts.
There were scores of pitch pines around my house, from
one to four inches in diameter, which had been gnawed
by mice the previous winter, — a Norwegian winter for
them, for the snow lay long and deep, and they were
obliged to mix a large proportion of pine bark with their
other diet. These trees were alive and apparently flourishing at midsummer, and many of them had grown a
foot, though completely girdled; but after another winter such were without exception dead. It is remarkable
that a single mouse should thus be allowed a whole pine
tree for its dinner, gnawing round instead of up and
down it; but perhaps it is necessary in order to thin these
trees, which are wont to grow up densely.

The hares (*Lepus Americanus*) were very familiar.
One had her form under my house all winter, separated
from me only by the flooring, and she startled me each
morning by her hasty departure when I began to stir, —
thump, thump, thump, striking her head against the
floor timbers in her hurry. They used to come round my
door at dusk to nibble the potato parings which I had
thrown out, and were so nearly the color of the ground
that they could hardly be distinguished when still. Some-

times in the twilight I alternately lost and recovered
sight of one sitting motionless under my window. When
I opened my door in the evening, off they would go with
a squeak and a bounce. Near at hand they only excited
my pity. One evening one sat by my door two paces
from me, at first trembling with fear, yet unwilling to
move; a poor wee thing, lean and bony, with ragged
ears and sharp nose, scant tail and slender paws. It
looked as if Nature no longer contained the breed of
nobler bloods, but stood on her last toes. Its large eyes
appeared young and unhealthy, almost dropsical. I took
a step, and lo, away it scud with an elastic spring over
the snow-crust, straightening its body and its limbs into
graceful length, and soon put the forest between me and
itself, — the wild free venison, asserting its vigor and
the dignity of Nature. Not without reason was its slen-
derness. Such then was its nature. (*Lepus, levipes*, light-
foot, some think.)

What is a country without rabbits and partridges?
They are among the most simple and indigenous animal
products; ancient and venerable families known to antiquity as to modern times; of the very hue and substance
of Nature, nearest allied to leaves and to the ground, —
and to one another; it is either winged or it is legged.
It is hardly as if you had seen a wild creature when a
rabbit or a partridge bursts away, only a natural one, as
much to be expected as rustling leaves. The partridge
and the rabbit are still sure to thrive, like true natives
of the soil, whatever revolutions occur. If the forest is
cut off, the sprouts and bushes which spring up afford
them concealment, and they become more numerous

than ever. That must be a poor country indeed that does
not support a hare. Our woods teem with them both,
and around every swamp may be seen the partridge or
rabbit walk, beset with twiggy fences and horse-hair
snares, which some cow-boy tends.

THE POND IN WINTER

AFTER a still winter night I awoke with the impression that some question had been put to me, which I had been endeavoring in vain to answer in my sleep, as what — how — when — where? But there was dawning Nature, in whom all creatures live, looking in at my broad windows with serene and satisfied face, and no question on *her* lips. I awoke to an answered question, to Nature and daylight. The snow lying deep on the earth dotted with young pines, and the very slope of the hill on which my house is placed, seemed to say, Forward! Nature puts no question and answers none which we mortals ask. She has long ago taken her resolution. " O Prince, our eyes contemplate with admiration and transmit to the soul the wonderful and varied spectacle of this universe. The night veils without doubt a part of this glorious creation; but day comes to reveal to us this great work, which extends from earth even into the plains of the ether."

Then to my morning work. First I take an axe and pail and go in search of water, if that be not a dream. After a cold and snowy night it needed a divining-rod to find it. Every winter the liquid and trembling surface of the pond, which was so sensitive to every breath, and reflected every light and shadow, becomes solid to the depth

of a foot or a foot and a half, so that it will support the
heaviest teams, and perchance the snow covers it to an
equal depth, and it is not to be distinguished from any
level field. Like the marmots in the surrounding hills,
it closes its eyelids and becomes dormant for three months
or more. Standing on the snow-covered plain, as if in a
pasture amid the hills, I cut my way first through a foot
of snow, and then a foot of ice, and open a window under my feet, where, kneeling to drink, I look down into
the quiet parlor of the fishes, pervaded by a softened
light as through a window of ground glass, with its bright
sanded floor the same as in summer; there a perennial
waveless serenity reigns as in the amber twilight sky,
corresponding to the cool and even temperament of the
inhabitants. Heaven is under our feet as well as over
our heads.

Early in the morning, while all things are crisp with
frost, men come with fishing-reels and slender lunch,
and let down their fine lines through the snowy field to
take pickerel and perch; wild men, who instinctively follow other fashions and trust other authorities than their
townsmen, and by their goings and comings stitch towns
together in parts where else they would be ripped. They
sit and eat their luncheon in stout fear-naughts on the
dry oak leaves on the shore, as wise in natural lore as the
citizen is in artificial. They never consulted with books,
and know and can tell much less than they have done.
The things which they practice are said not yet to be
known. Here is one fishing for pickerel with grown perch
for bait. You look into his pail with wonder as into a
summer pond, as if he kept summer locked up at home,

or knew where she had retreated. How, pray, did he get these in midwinter? Oh, he got worms out of rotten logs since the ground froze, and so he caught them. His life itself passes deeper in nature than the studies of the naturalist penetrate; himself a subject for the naturalist. The latter raises the moss and bark gently with his knife in search of insects; the former lays open logs to their core with his axe, and moss and bark fly far and wide. He gets his living by barking trees. Such a man has some right to fish, and I love to see nature carried out in him. The perch swallows the grub-worm, the pickerel swallows the perch, and the fisherman swallows the pickerel; and so all the chinks in the scale of being are filled.

When I strolled around the pond in misty weather I was sometimes amused by the primitive mode which some ruder fisherman had adopted. He would perhaps have placed alder branches over the narrow holes in the ice, which were four or five rods apart and an equal distance from the shore, and having fastened the end of the line to a stick to prevent its being pulled through, have passed the slack line over a twig of the alder, a foot or more above the ice, and tied a dry oak leaf to it, which, being pulled down, would show when he had a bite. These alders loomed through the mist at regular intervals as you walked half way round the pond.

Ah, the pickerel of Walden! when I see them lying on the ice, or in the well which the fisherman cuts in the ice, making a little hole to admit the water, I am always surprised by their rare beauty, as if they were fabulous fishes, they are so foreign to the streets, even to the

woods, foreign as Arabia to our Concord life. They
possess a quite dazzling and transcendent beauty which
separates them by a wide interval from the cadaverous
cod and haddock whose fame is trumpeted in our streets.
They are not green like the pines, nor gray like the
stones, nor blue like the sky; but they have, to my eyes,
if possible, yet rarer colors, like flowers and precious
stones, as if they were the pearls, the animalized *nuclei*
or crystals of the Walden water. They, of course, are
Walden all over and all through; are themselves small
Waldens in the animal kingdom, Waldenses. It is surprising that they are caught here, — that in this deep
and capacious spring, far beneath the rattling teams and
chaises and tinkling sleighs that travel the Walden road,
this great gold and emerald fish swims. I never chanced
to see its kind in any market; it would be the cynosure
of all eyes there. Easily, with a few convulsive quirks,
they give up their watery ghosts, like a mortal translated before his time to the thin air of heaven.

As I was desirous to recover the long lost bottom of
Walden Pond, I surveyed it carefully, before the ice
broke up, early in '46, with compass and chain and
sounding line. There have been many stories told about
the bottom, or rather no bottom, of this pond, which
certainly had no foundation for themselves. It is remarkable how long men will believe in the bottomless-
ness of a pond without taking the trouble to sound it. I
have visited two such Bottomless Ponds in one walk in
this neighborhood. Many have believed that Walden
reached quite through to the other side of the globe.

Some who have lain flat on the ice for a long time, looking down through the illusive medium, perchance with watery eyes into the bargain, and driven to hasty conclusions by the fear of catching cold in their breasts, have seen vast holes "into which a load of hay might be driven," if there were anybody to drive it, the undoubted source of the Styx and entrance to the Infernal Regions from these parts. Others have gone down from the village with a "fifty-six" and a wagon load of inch rope, but yet have failed to find any bottom; for while the "fifty-six" was resting by the way, they were paying out the rope in the vain attempt to fathom their truly immeasurable capacity for marvellousness. But I can assure my readers that Walden has a reasonably tight bottom at a not unreasonable, though at an unusual, depth. I fathomed it easily with a cod-line and a stone weighing about a pound and a half, and could tell accurately when the stone left the bottom, by having to pull so much harder before the water got underneath to help me. The greatest depth was exactly one hundred and two feet; to which may be added the five feet which it has risen since, making one hundred and seven. This is a remarkable depth for so small an area; yet not an inch of it can be spared by the imagination. What if all ponds were shallow ? Would it not react on the minds of men ? I am thankful that this pond was made deep and pure for a symbol. While men believe in the infinite some ponds will be thought to be bottomless.

A factory-owner, hearing what depth I had found, thought that it could not be true, for, judging from his acquaintance with dams, sand would not lie at so steep an

angle. But the deepest ponds are not so deep in proportion to their area as most suppose, and, if drained, would
not leave very remarkable valleys. They are not like
cups between the hills; for this one, which is so unusually
deep for its area, appears in a vertical section through its
centre not deeper than a shallow plate. Most ponds,
emptied, would leave a meadow no more hollow than
we frequently see. William Gilpin, who is so admirable
in all that relates to landscapes, and usually so correct,
standing at the head of Loch Fyne, in Scotland, which
he describes as "a bay of salt water, sixty or seventy
fathoms deep, four miles in breadth," and about fifty
miles long, surrounded by mountains, observes, "If we
could have seen it immediately after the diluvian crash,
or whatever convulsion of nature occasioned it, before
the waters gushed in, what a horrid chasm must it have
appeared!

> "So high as heaved the tumid hills, so low
> Down sunk a hollow bottom broad and deep,
> Capacious bed of waters."

But if, using the shortest diameter of Loch Fyne, we
apply these proportions to Walden, which, as we have
seen, appears already in a vertical section only like a
shallow plate, it will appear four times as shallow. So
much for the *increased* horrors of the chasm of Loch
Fyne when emptied. No doubt many a smiling valley
with its stretching cornfields occupies exactly such a
"horrid chasm," from which the waters have receded,
though it requires the insight and the far sight of the
geologist to convince the unsuspecting inhabitants of
this fact. Often an inquisitive eye may detect the shores

of a primitive lake in the low horizon hills, and no subsequent elevation of the plain have been necessary to conceal their history. But it is easiest, as they who work on the highways know, to find the hollows by the puddles after a shower. The amount of it is, the imagination, give it the least license, dives deeper and soars higher than Nature goes. So, probably, the depth of the ocean will be found to be very inconsiderable compared with its breadth.

As I sounded through the ice I could determine the shape of the bottom with greater accuracy than is possible in surveying harbors which do not freeze over, and I was surprised at its general regularity. In the deepest part there are several acres more level than almost any field which is exposed to the sun, wind, and plow. In one instance, on a line arbitrarily chosen, the depth did not vary more than one foot in thirty rods; and generally, near the middle, I could calculate the variation for each one hundred feet in any direction beforehand within three or four inches. Some are accustomed to speak of deep and dangerous holes even in quiet sandy ponds like this, but the effect of water under these circumstances is to level all inequalities. The regularity of the bottom and its conformity to the shores and the range of the neighboring hills were so perfect that a distant promontory betrayed itself in the soundings quite across the pond, and its direction could be determined by observing the opposite shore. Cape becomes bar, and plain shoal, and valley and gorge deep water and channel.

When I had mapped the pond by the scale of ten

rods to an inch, and put down the soundings, more than a hundred in all, I observed this remarkable coincidence. Having noticed that the number indicating the greatest depth was apparently in the centre of the map, I laid a rule on the map lengthwise, and then breadthwise, and found, to my surprise, that the line of greatest length intersected the line of greatest breadth *exactly* at the point of greatest depth, notwithstanding that the middle is so nearly level, the outline of the pond far from regular, and the extreme length and breadth were got by measuring into the coves; and I said to myself, Who knows but this hint would conduct to the deepest part of the ocean as well as of a pond or puddle? Is not this the rule also for the height of mountains, regarded as the opposite of valleys? We know that a hill is not highest at its narrowest part.

Of five coves, three, or all which had been sounded, were observed to have a bar quite across their mouths and deeper water within, so that the bay tended to be an expansion of water within the land not only horizontally but vertically, and to form a basin or independent pond, the direction of the two capes showing the course of the bar. Every harbor on the sea-coast, also, has its bar at its entrance. In proportion as the mouth of the cove was wider compared with its length, the water over the bar was deeper compared with that in the basin. Given, then, the length and breadth of the cove, and the character of the surrounding shore, and you have almost elements enough to make out a formula for all cases.

In order to see how nearly I could guess, with this

experience, at the deepest point in a pond, by observing the outlines of its surface and the character of its shores alone, I made a plan of White Pond, which contains about forty-one acres, and, like this, has no island in it, nor any visible inlet or outlet; and as the line of greatest breadth fell very near the line of least breadth, where two opposite capes approached each other and two opposite bays receded, I ventured to mark a point a short distance from the latter line, but still on the line of greatest length, as the deepest. The deepest part was found to be within one hundred feet of this, still farther in the direction to which I had inclined, and was only one foot deeper, namely, sixty feet. Of course, a stream running through, or an island in the pond, would make the problem much more complicated.

If we knew all the laws of Nature, we should need only one fact, or the description of one actual phenomenon, to infer all the particular results at that point. Now we know only a few laws, and our result is vitiated, not, of course, by any confusion or irregularity in Nature, but by our ignorance of essential elements in the calculation. Our notions of law and harmony are commonly confined to those instances which we detect; but the harmony which results from a far greater number of seemingly conflicting, but really concurring, laws, which we have not detected, is still more wonderful. The particular laws are as our points of view, as, to the traveller, a mountain outline varies with every step, and it has an infinite number of profiles, though absolutely but one form. Even when cleft or bored through it is not comprehended in its entirety.

What I have observed of the pond is no less true in ethics. It is the law of average. Such a rule of the two diameters not only guides us toward the sun in the system and the heart in man, but draw lines through the length and breadth of the aggregate of a man's particular daily behaviors and waves of life into his coves and inlets, and where they intersect will be the height or depth of his character. Perhaps we need only to know how his shores trend and his adjacent country or circumstances, to infer his depth and concealed bottom. If he is surrounded by mountainous circumstances, an Achillean shore, whose peaks overshadow and are reflected in his bosom, they suggest a corresponding depth in him. But a low and smooth shore proves him shallow on that side. In our bodies, a bold projecting brow falls off to and indicates a corresponding depth of thought. Also there is a bar across the entrance of our every cove, or particular inclination ; each is our harbor for a season, in which we are detained and partially land-locked. These inclinations are not whimsical usually, but their form, size, and direction are determined by the promontories of the shore, the ancient axes of elevation. When this bar is gradually increased by storms, tides, or currents, or there is a subsidence of the waters, so that it reaches to the surface, that which was at first but an inclination in the shore in which a thought was harbored becomes an individual lake, cut off from the ocean, wherein the thought secures its own conditions, — changes, perhaps, from salt to fresh, becomes a sweet sea, dead sea, or a marsh. At the advent of each individual into this life, may we not suppose that such a bar has risen to the surface somewhere? It is true, we are such poor navigators that our thoughts, for the most part, stand off and on upon a harborless coast, are conversant only with the bights of the bays of poesy, or steer for the public ports of entry, and go into the dry docks of science, where they merely refit for this world, and no natural currents concur to individualize them.

As for the inlet or outlet of Walden, I have not discovered any but rain and snow and evaporation, though perhaps, with a thermometer and a line, such places may be found, for where the water flows into the pond it will probably be coldest in summer and warmest in winter. When the ice-men were at work here in '46-7, the cakes sent to the shore were one day rejected by those who were stacking them up there, not being thick enough to lie side by side with the rest; and the cutters thus discovered that the ice over a small space was two or three inches thinner than elsewhere, which made them think that there was an inlet there. They also showed me in another place what they thought was a "leach-hole," through which the pond leaked out under a hill into a neighboring meadow, pushing me out on a cake of ice to see it. It was a small cavity under ten feet of water; but I think that I can warrant the pond not to need soldering till they find a worse leak than that. One has suggested, that if such a "leach-hole" should be found, its connection with the meadow, if any existed, might be proved by conveying some colored powder or sawdust to the mouth of the hole, and then putting a strainer over the spring in the meadow, which would catch some of the particles carried through by the current.

While I was surveying, the ice, which was sixteen inches thick, undulated under a slight wind like water. It is well known that a level cannot be used on ice. At one rod from the shore its greatest fluctuation, when observed by means of a level on land directed toward a graduated staff on the ice, was three quarters of an inch, though the ice appeared firmly attached to the shore. It was probably greater in the middle. Who knows but if our instruments were delicate enough we might detect an undulation in the crust of the earth? When two legs of my level were on the shore and the third on the ice, and the sights were directed over the latter, a rise or fall of the ice of an almost infinitesimal amount made a difference of several feet on a tree across the pond. When I began to cut holes for sounding there were three or four inches of water on the ice under a deep snow which had sunk it thus far; but the water began immediately to run into these holes, and continued to run for two days in deep streams, which wore away the ice on every side, and contributed essentially, if not mainly, to dry the surface of the pond; for, as the water ran in, it raised and floated the ice. This was somewhat like cutting a hole in the bottom of a ship to let the water out. When such holes freeze, and a rain succeeds, and finally a new freezing forms a fresh smooth ice over all, it is beautifully mottled internally by dark figures, shaped somewhat like a spider's web, what you may call ice rosettes, produced by the channels worn by the water flowing from all sides to a centre. Sometimes, also, when the ice was covered with shallow puddles, I saw a double shadow of myself, one standing on the head of the other, one on the ice, the other on the trees or hillside.

While yet it is cold January, and snow and ice are thick and solid, the prudent landlord comes from the village to get ice to cool his summer drink; impressively, even pathetically, wise, to foresee the heat and thirst of July now in January, — wearing a thick coat and mittens ! when so many things are not provided for. It may be that he lays up no treasures in this world which will cool his summer drink in the next. He cuts and saws the solid pond, unroofs the house of fishes, and carts off their very element and air, held fast by chains and stakes like corded wood, through the favoring winter air, to wintry cellars, to underlie the summer there. It looks like solidified azure, as, far off, it is drawn through the streets. These ice-cutters are a merry race, full of jest and sport, and when I went among them they were wont to invite me to saw pit-fashion with them, I standing underneath.

In the winter of '46-7 there came a hundred men of Hyperborean extraction swoop down on to our pond one morning, with many carloads of ungainly-looking farming tools, — sleds, plows, drill-barrows, turf-knives, spades, saws, rakes, and each man was armed with a double-pointed pike-staff, such as is not described in the New-England Farmer or the Cultivator. I did not know whether they had come to sow a crop of winter rye, or some other kind of grain recently introduced from Iceland. As I saw no manure, I judged that they meant to skim the land, as I had done, thinking the soil was deep and had lain fallow long enough. They said that a gentleman farmer, who was behind the scenes, wanted to double his money, which, as I understood, amounted to half a million already; but in order to cover each one of his dollars with another, he took off the only coat, ay, the skin itself, of Walden Pond in the midst of a hard winter. They went to work at once, plowing, harrowing, rolling, furrowing, in admirable order, as if they were bent on making this a model farm; but when I was looking sharp to see what kind of seed they dropped into the furrow, a gang of fellows by my side suddenly began to hook up the virgin mould itself, with a peculiar jerk, clean down to the sand, or rather the water, — for it was a very springy soil, — indeed all the *terra firma* there was, — and haul it away on sleds, and then I guessed that they must be cutting peat in a bog. So they came and went every day, with a peculiar shriek from the locomotive, from and to some point of the polar regions, as it seemed to me, like a flock of arctic snowbirds. But sometimes Squaw Walden had her revenge, and a hired man, walking behind his team, slipped through a crack in the ground down toward Tartarus, and he who was so brave before suddenly became but the ninth part of a man, almost gave up his animal heat, and was glad to take refuge in my house, and acknowledged that there was some virtue in a stove; or sometimes the frozen soil took a piece of steel out of a plowshare, or a plow got set in the furrow and had to be cut out.

To speak literally, a hundred Irishmen, with Yankee overseers, came from Cambridge every day to get out the ice. They divided it into cakes by methods too well known to require description, and these, being sledded to the shore, were rapidly hauled off on to an ice platform, and raised by grappling irons and block and tackle, worked by horses, on to a stack, as surely as so many barrels of flour, and there placed evenly side by side, and row upon row, as if they formed the solid base of an obelisk designed to pierce the clouds. They told me that in a good day they could get out a thousand tons, which was the yield of about one acre. Deep ruts and "cradle-holes" were worn in the ice, as on *terra firma*, by the passage of the sleds over the same track, and the horses invariably ate their oats out of cakes of ice hollowed out like buckets. They stacked up the cakes thus in the open air in a pile thirty-five feet high on one side and six or seven rods square, putting hay between the outside layers to exclude the air; for when the wind, though never so cold, finds a passage through, it will wear large cavities, leaving slight supports or studs only here and there, and finally topple it down. At first it looked like a vast blue fort or Valhalla; but when they began to tuck the coarse meadow hay into the crevices, and this became covered with rime and icicles, it looked like a venerable moss-grown and hoary ruin, built of azure-tinted marble, the abode of Winter, that old man we see in the almanac, — his shanty, as if he had a design to estivate with us. They calculated that not twenty-five per cent. of this would reach its destination, and that two or three per cent. would be wasted in the cars. However, a still greater part of this heap had a different destiny from what was intended; for, either because the ice was found not to keep so well as was expected, containing more air than usual, or for some other reason, it never got to market. This heap, made in the winter of '46-7 and estimated to contain ten thousand tons, was finally covered with hay and boards; and though it was unroofed the following July, and a part of it carried off, the rest remaining exposed to the sun, it stood over that summer and the next winter, and was not quite melted till September, 1848. Thus the pond recovered the greater part.

Like the water, the Walden ice, seen near at hand, has a green tint, but at a distance is beautifully blue, and you can easily tell it from the white ice of the river, or the merely greenish ice of some ponds, a quarter of a mile off. Sometimes one of those great cakes slips from the ice-man's sled into the village street, and lies there for a week like a great emerald, an object of interest to all passers. I have noticed that a portion of Walden which in the state of water was green will often, when frozen, appear from the same point of view blue. So the hollows about this pond will, sometimes, in the winter, be filled with a greenish water somewhat like its own, but the next day will have frozen blue. Perhaps the blue color of water and ice is due to the light and air they contain, and the most transparent is the bluest. Ice is an interesting subject for contemplation. They told me that they had some in the ice-houses at Fresh Pond five years old which was as good as ever. Why is it that a bucket of water soon becomes putrid, but frozen remains sweet forever? It is commonly said that this is the difference between the affections and the intellect.

Thus for sixteen days I saw from my window a hundred men at work like busy husbandmen, with teams and horses and apparently all the implements of farming, such a picture as we see on the first page of the almanac; and as often as I looked out I was reminded of the fable of the lark and the reapers, or the parable of the sower, and the like; and now they are all gone, and in thirty days more, probably, I shall look from the same window on the pure sea-green Walden water there, reflecting the clouds and the trees, and sending up its evaporations in solitude, and no traces will appear that a man has ever stood there. Perhaps I shall hear a solitary loon laugh as he dives and plumes himself, or shall see a lonely fisher in his boat, like a floating leaf, beholding his form reflected in the waves, where lately a hundred men securely labored.

Thus it appears that the sweltering inhabitants of Charleston and New Orleans, of Madras and Bombay and Calcutta, drink at my well. In the morning I bathe my intellect in the stupendous and cosmogonal philosophy of the Bhagvat-Geeta, since whose composition years of the gods have elapsed, and in comparison with which our modern world and its literature seem puny and trivial; and I doubt if that philosophy is not to be referred to a previous state of existence, so remote is its sublimity from our conceptions. I lay down the book and go to my well for water, and lo! there I meet the servant of the Bramin, priest of Brahma and Vishnu and

Indra, who still sits in his temple on the Ganges reading the Vedas, or dwells at the root of a tree with his crust and water jug. I meet his servant come to draw water for his master, and our buckets as it were grate together in the same well. The pure Walden water is mingled with the sacred water of the Ganges. With favoring winds it is wafted past the site of the fabulous islands of Atlantis and the Hesperides, makes the periplus of Hanno, and, floating by Ternate and Tidore and the mouth of the Persian Gulf, melts in the tropic gales of the Indian seas, and is landed in ports of which Alexander only heard the names.

SPRING

THE opening of large tracts by the ice-cutters commonly causes a pond to break up earlier; for the water, agitated by the wind, even in cold weather, wears away the surrounding ice. But such was not the effect on Walden that year, for she had soon got a thick new garment to take the place of the old. This pond never breaks up so soon as the others in this neighborhood, on account both of its greater depth and its having no stream passing through it to melt or wear away the ice. I never knew it to open in the course of a winter, not excepting that of '52–3, which gave the ponds so severe a trial. It commonly opens about the first of April, a week or ten days later than Flint's Pond and Fair Haven, beginning to melt on the north side and in the shallower parts where it began to freeze. It indicates better than any water hereabouts the absolute progress of the season, being least affected by transient changes of temperature. A severe cold of a few days' duration in March may very much retard the opening of the former ponds, while the temperature of Walden increases almost uninterruptedly. A thermometer thrust into the middle of Walden on the 6th of March, 1847, stood at 32°, or freezing point; near the shore at 33°; in the middle of Flint's Pond, the same day, at $32\frac{1}{2}°$;

at a dozen rods from the shore, in shallow water, under
ice a foot thick, at 36°. This difference of three and a
half degrees between the temperature of the deep water
and the shallow in the latter pond, and the fact that a
great proportion of it is comparatively shallow, show
why it should break up so much sooner than Walden.
The ice in the shallowest part was at this time several
inches thinner than in the middle. In midwinter the
middle had been the warmest and the ice thinnest there.
So, also, every one who has waded about the shores
of a pond in summer must have perceived how much
warmer the water is close to the shore, where only three
or four inches deep, than a little distance out, and on
the surface where it is deep, than near the bottom. In
spring the sun not only exerts an influence through
the increased temperature of the air and earth, but its
heat passes through ice a foot or more thick, and is reflected from the bottom in shallow water, and so also
warms the water and melts the under side of the ice, at
the same time that it is melting it more directly above,
making it uneven, and causing the air bubbles which
it contains to extend themselves upward and downward until it is completely honeycombed, and at last
disappears suddenly in a single spring rain. Ice has its
grain as well as wood, and when a cake begins to rot or
"comb," that is, assume the appearance of honeycomb,
whatever may be its position, the air cells are at right
angles with what was the water surface. Where there
is a rock or a log rising near to the surface the ice over
it is much thinner, and is frequently quite dissolved by
this reflected heat; and I have been told that in the

experiment at Cambridge to freeze water in a shallow
wooden pond, though the cold air circulated underneath, and so had access to both sides, the reflection of
the sun from the bottom more than counterbalanced
this advantage. When a warm rain in the middle of the
winter melts off the snow ice from Walden, and leaves a
hard dark or transparent ice on the middle, there will be
a strip of rotten though thicker white ice, a rod or more
wide, about the shores, created by this reflected heat.
Also, as I have said, the bubbles themselves within the
ice operate as burning-glasses to melt the ice beneath.

The phenomena of the year take place every day in
a pond on a small scale. Every morning, generally speaking, the shallow water is being warmed more rapidly
than the deep, though it may not be made so warm after
all, and every evening it is being cooled more rapidly
until the morning. The day is an epitome of the year.
The night is the winter, the morning and evening are
the spring and fall, and the noon is the summer. The
cracking and booming of the ice indicate a change of
temperature. One pleasant morning after a cold night,
February 24th, 1850, having gone to Flint's Pond to
spend the day, I noticed with surprise, that when I
struck the ice with the head of my axe, it resounded like
a gong for many rods around, or as if I had struck on a
tight drum-head. The pond began to boom about an
hour after sunrise, when it felt the influence of the sun's
rays slanted upon it from over the hills; it stretched
itself and yawned like a waking man with a gradually
increasing tumult, which was kept up three or four
hours. It took a short siesta at noon, and boomed once

more toward night, as the sun was withdrawing his influence. In the right stage of the weather a pond fires its evening gun with great regularity. But in the middle of the day, being full of cracks, and the air also being less elastic, it had completely lost its resonance, and probably fishes and muskrats could not then have been stunned by a blow on it. The fishermen say that the "thundering of the pond" scares the fishes and prevents their biting. The pond does not thunder every evening, and I cannot tell surely when to expect its thundering; but though I may perceive no difference in the weather, it does. Who would have suspected so large and cold and thick-skinned a thing to be so sensitive? Yet it has its law to which it thunders obedience when it should as surely as the buds expand in the spring. The earth is all alive and covered with papillæ. The largest pond is as sensitive to atmospheric changes as the globule of mercury in its tube.

One attraction in coming to the woods to live was that I should have leisure and opportunity to see the Spring come in. The ice in the pond at length begins to be honeycombed, and I can set my heel in it as I walk. Fogs and rains and warmer suns are gradually melting the snow; the days have grown sensibly longer; and I see how I shall get through the winter without adding to my wood-pile, for large fires are no longer necessary. I am on the alert for the first signs of spring, to hear the chance note of some arriving bird, or the striped squirrel's chirp, for his stores must be now nearly exhausted, or see the woodchuck venture out of his winter quarters. On the 13th of March, after I had heard the bluebird, song sparrow, and red-wing, the ice was still nearly a foot thick. As the weather grew warmer it was not sensibly worn away by the water, nor broken up and floated off as in rivers, but, though it was completely melted for half a rod in width about the shore, the middle was merely honeycombed and saturated with water, so that you could put your foot through it when six inches thick; but by the next day evening, perhaps, after a warm rain followed by fog, it would have wholly disappeared, all gone off with the fog, spirited away. One year I went across the middle only five days before it disappeared entirely. In 1845 Walden was first completely open on the 1st of April; in '46, the 25th of March; in '47, the 8th of April; in '51, the 28th of March; in '52, the 18th of April; in '53, the 23d of March; in '54, about the 7th of April.

Every incident connected with the breaking up of the rivers and ponds and the settling of the weather is particularly interesting to us who live in a climate of so great extremes. When the warmer days come, they who dwell near the river hear the ice crack at night with a startling whoop as loud as artillery, as if its icy fetters were rent from end to end, and within a few days see it rapidly going out. So the alligator comes out of the mud with quakings of the earth. One old man, who has been a close observer of Nature, and seems as thoroughly wise in regard to all her operations as if she had been put upon the stocks when he was a boy, and he had helped to lay her keel, — who has come to his growth, and can hardly acquire more of natural lore if he should live to the age of Methuselah, — told me —

and I was surprised to hear him express wonder at any
of Nature's operations, for I thought that there were
no secrets between them — that one spring day he took
his gun and boat, and thought that he would have a
little sport with the ducks. There was ice still on the
meadows, but it was all gone out of the river, and he
dropped down without obstruction from Sudbury,
where he lived, to Fair Haven Pond, which he found,
unexpectedly, covered for the most part with a firm
field of ice. It was a warm day, and he was surprised to
see so great a body of ice remaining. Not seeing any
ducks, he hid his boat on the north or back side of an
island in the pond, and then concealed himself in the
bushes on the south side, to await them. The ice was
melted for three or four rods from the shore, and there
was a smooth and warm sheet of water, with a muddy
bottom, such as the ducks love, within, and he thought
it likely that some would be along pretty soon. After
he had lain still there about an hour he heard a low
and seemingly very distant sound, but singularly grand
and impressive, unlike anything he had ever heard,
gradually swelling and increasing as if it would have a
universal and memorable ending, a sullen rush and
roar, which seemed to him all at once like the sound of
a vast body of fowl coming in to settle there, and, seizing his gun, he started up in haste and excited; but he
found, to his surprise, that the whole body of the ice
had started while he lay there, and drifted in to the
shore, and the sound he had heard was made by its
edge grating on the shore, — at first gently nibbled and
crumbled off, but at length heaving up and scattering

its wrecks along the island to a considerable height before it came to a standstill.

At length the sun's rays have attained the right angle, and warm winds blow up mist and rain and melt the snowbanks, and the sun, dispersing the mist, smiles on a checkered landscape of russet and white smoking with incense, through which the traveller picks his way from islet to islet, cheered by the music of a thousand tinkling rills and rivulets whose veins are filled with the blood of winter which they are bearing off.

Few phenomena gave me more delight than to observe the forms which thawing sand and clay assume in flowing down the sides of a deep cut on the railroad through which I passed on my way to the village, a phenomenon not very common on so large a scale, though the number of freshly exposed banks of the right material must have been greatly multiplied since railroads were invented. The material was sand of every degree of fineness and of various rich colors, commonly mixed with a little clay. When the frost comes out in the spring, and even in a thawing day in the winter, the sand begins to flow down the slopes like lava, sometimes bursting out through the snow and overflowing it where no sand was to be seen before. Innumerable little streams overlap and interlace one with another, exhibiting a sort of hybrid product, which obeys half way the law of currents, and half way that of vegetation. As it flows it takes the forms of sappy leaves or vines, making heaps of pulpy sprays a foot or more in depth, and resembling, as you look down on them, the laciniated, lobed, and imbricated thalluses of some lichens; or you are reminded of coral, of leopards' paws or birds' feet, of brains or lungs or bowels, and excrements of all kinds. It is a truly *grotesque* vegetation, whose forms and color we see imitated in bronze, a sort of architectural foliage more ancient and typical than acanthus, chiccory, ivy, vine, or any vegetable leaves; destined perhaps, under some circumstances, to become a puzzle to future geologists. The whole cut impressed me as if it were a cave with its stalactites laid open to the light. The various shades of the sand are singularly rich and agreeable, embracing the different iron colors, brown, gray, yellowish, and reddish. When the flowing mass reaches the drain at the foot of the bank it spreads out flatter into *strands*, the separate streams losing their semicylindrical form and gradually becoming more flat and broad, running together as they are more moist, till they form an almost flat *sand*, still variously and beautifully shaded, but in which you can trace the original forms of vegetation; till at length, in the water itself, they are converted into *banks*, like those formed off the mouths of rivers, and the forms of vegetation are lost in the ripple-marks on the bottom.

The whole bank, which is from twenty to forty feet high, is sometimes overlaid with a mass of this kind of foliage, or sandy rupture, for a quarter of a mile on one or both sides, the produce of one spring day. What makes this sand foliage remarkable is its springing into existence thus suddenly. When I see on the one side the inert bank, — for the sun acts on one side first, — and on the other this luxuriant foliage, the creation of an hour, I am affected as if in a peculiar sense I stood

in the laboratory of the Artist who made the world and
me, — had come to where he was still at work, sporting
on this bank, and with excess of energy strewing his
fresh designs about. I feel as if I were nearer to the
vitals of the globe, for this sandy overflow is something
such a foliaceous mass as the vitals of the animal body.
You find thus in the very sands an anticipation of the
vegetable leaf. No wonder that the earth expresses
itself outwardly in leaves, it so labors with the idea in-
wardly. The atoms have already learned this law, and
are pregnant by it. The overhanging leaf sees here its
prototype. *Internally*, whether in the globe or animal
body, it is a moist thick *lobe*, a word especially applicable
to the liver and lungs and the *leaves* of fat (λείβω, *labor*,
lapsus, to flow or slip downward, a lapsing; λοβός, *globus*,
lobe, globe; also lap, flap, and many other words); *externally*, a dry thin *leaf*, even as the *f* and *v* are a pressed
and dried *b*. The radicals of *lobe* are *lb*, the soft mass of
the *b* (single-lobed, or B, double-lobed), with the liquid *l*
behind it pressing it forward. In globe, *glb*, the guttural
g adds to the meaning the capacity of the throat. The
feathers and wings of birds are still drier and thinner
leaves. Thus, also, you pass from the lumpish grub in
the earth to the airy and fluttering butterfly. The very
globe continually transcends and translates itself, and
becomes winged in its orbit. Even ice begins with delicate crystal leaves, as if it had flowed into moulds which
the fronds of water-plants have impressed on the watery
mirror. The whole tree itself is but one leaf, and rivers
are still vaster leaves whose pulp is intervening earth,
and towns and cities are the ova of insects in their axils.

When the sun withdraws the sand ceases to flow, but in the morning the streams will start once more and branch and branch again into a myriad of others. You here see perchance how blood-vessels are formed. If you look closely you observe that first there pushes forward from the thawing mass a stream of softened sand with a drop-like point, like the ball of the finger, feeling its way slowly and blindly downward, until at last with more heat and moisture, as the sun gets higher, the most fluid portion, in its effort to obey the law to which the most inert also yields, separates from the latter and forms for itself a meandering channel or artery within that, in which is seen a little silvery stream glancing like lightning from one stage of pulpy leaves or branches to another, and ever and anon swallowed up in the sand. It is wonderful how rapidly yet perfectly the sand organizes itself as it flows, using the best material its mass affords to form the sharp edges of its channel. Such are the sources of rivers. In the silicious matter which the water deposits is perhaps the bony system, and in the still finer soil and organic matter the fleshy fibre or cellular tissue. What is man but a mass of thawing clay? The ball of the human finger is but a drop congealed. The fingers and toes flow to their extent from the thawing mass of the body. Who knows what the human body would expand and flow out to under a more genial heaven? Is not the hand a spreading *palm* leaf with its lobes and veins? The ear may be regarded, fancifully, as a lichen, *Umbilicaria*, on the side of the head, with its lobe or drop. The lip — *labium*, from *labor* (?) — laps or lapses from the sides

of the cavernous mouth. The nose is a manifest congealed drop or stalactite. The chin is a still larger drop,
the confluent dripping of the face. The cheeks are a
slide from the brows into the valley of the face, opposed
and diffused by the cheek bones. Each rounded lobe
of the vegetable leaf, too, is a thick and now loitering
drop, larger or smaller; the lobes are the fingers of the
leaf; and as many lobes as it has, in so many directions
it tends to flow, and more heat or other genial influences
would have caused it to flow yet farther.

Thus it seemed that this one hillside illustrated the
principle of all the operations of Nature. The Maker
of this earth but patented a leaf. What Champollion
will decipher this hieroglyphic for us, that we may turn
over a new leaf at last? This phenomenon is more
exhilarating to me than the luxuriance and fertility of
vineyards. True, it is somewhat excrementitious in its
character, and there is no end to the heaps of liver,
lights, and bowels, as if the globe were turned wrong
side outward; but this suggests at least that Nature has
some bowels, and there again is mother of humanity.
This is the frost coming out of the ground; this is
Spring. It precedes the green and flowery spring, as
mythology precedes regular poetry. I know of nothing
more purgative of winter fumes and indigestions. It
convinces me that Earth is still in her swaddling-
clothes, and stretches forth baby fingers on every side.
Fresh curls spring from the baldest brow. There is nothing inorganic. These foliaceous heaps lie along the
bank like the slag of a furnace, showing that Nature
is "in full blast" within. The earth is not a mere frag-

ment of dead history, stratum upon stratum like the
leaves of a book, to be studied by geologists and anti-
quaries chiefly, but living poetry like the leaves of a
tree, which precede flowers and fruit, — not a fossil
earth, but a living earth; compared with whose great
central life all animal and vegetable life is merely parasitic. Its throes will heave our exuviæ from their graves.
You may melt your metals and cast them into the most
beautiful moulds you can; they will never excite me
like the forms which this molten earth flows out into.
And not only it, but the institutions upon it are plastic
like clay in the hands of the potter.

Ere long, not only on these banks, but on every hill
and plain and in every hollow, the frost comes out of the
ground like a dormant quadruped from its burrow,
and seeks the sea with music, or migrates to other
climes in clouds. Thaw with his gentle persuasion is
more powerful than Thor with his hammer. The one
melts, the other but breaks in pieces.

When the ground was partially bare of snow, and a
few warm days had dried its surface somewhat, it was
pleasant to compare the first tender signs of the infant
year just peeping forth with the stately beauty of the
withered vegetation which had withstood the winter, —
life-everlasting, goldenrods, pinweeds, and graceful wild
grasses, more obvious and interesting frequently than
in summer even, as if their beauty was not ripe till
then ; even cotton-grass, cat-tails, mulleins, johnswort,
hardhack, meadow-sweet, and other strong-stemmed
plants, those unexhausted granaries which entertain
the earliest birds, — decent weeds, at least, which

widowed Nature wears. I am particularly attracted by the arching and sheaf-like top of the wool-grass; it brings back the summer to our winter memories, and is among the forms which art loves to copy, and which, in the vegetable kingdom, have the same relation to types already in the mind of man that astronomy has. It is an antique style, older than Greek or Egyptian. Many of the phenomena of Winter are suggestive of an inexpressible tenderness and fragile delicacy. We are accustomed to hear this king described as a rude and boisterous tyrant ; but with the gentleness of a lover he adorns the tresses of Summer.

At the approach of spring the red squirrels got under my house, two at a time, directly under my feet as I sat reading or writing, and kept up the queerest chuckling and chirruping and vocal pirouetting and gurgling sounds that ever were heard; and when I stamped they only chirruped the louder, as if past all fear and respect in their mad pranks, defying humanity to stop them. No, you don't — chickaree — chickaree. They were wholly deaf to my arguments, or failed to perceive their force, and fell into a strain of invective that was irresistible.

The first sparrow of spring! The year beginning with younger hope than ever! The faint silvery warblings heard over the partially bare and moist fields from the bluebird, the song sparrow, and the red-wing, as if the last flakes of winter tinkled as they fell! What at such a time are histories, chronologies, traditions, and all written revelations? The brooks sing carols and glees to the spring. The marsh hawk, sailing low over the

meadow, is already seeking the first slimy life that
awakes. The sinking sound of melting snow is heard in
all dells, and the ice dissolves apace in the ponds. The
grass flames up on the hillsides like a spring fire, — " et
primitus oritur herba imbribus primoribus evocata,"
— as if the earth sent forth an inward heat to greet the
returning sun; not yellow but green is the color of its
flame; — the symbol of perpetual youth, the grass-blade,
like a long green ribbon, streams from the sod into the
summer, checked indeed by the frost, but anon pushing
on again, lifting its spear of last year's hay with the
fresh life below. It grows as steadily as the rill oozes
out of the ground. It is almost identical with that, for
in the growing days of June, when the rills are dry, the
grass-blades are their channels, and from year to year
the herds drink at this perennial green stream, and the
mower draws from it betimes their winter supply. So
our human life but dies down to its root, and still puts
forth its green blade to eternity.

Walden is melting apace. There is a canal two rods
wide along the northerly and westerly sides, and wider
still at the east end. A great field of ice has cracked off
from the main body. I hear a song sparrow singing
from the bushes on the shore, — *olit, olit, olit,* — *chip,
chip, chip, che char,* — *che wiss, wiss, wiss.* He too is
helping to crack it. How handsome the great sweeping
curves in the edge of the ice, answering somewhat to
those of the shore, but more regular ! It is unusually
hard, owing to the recent severe but transient cold, and
all watered or waved like a palace floor. But the wind
slides eastward over its opaque surface in vain, till it

reaches the living surface beyond. It is glorious to behold this ribbon of water sparkling in the sun, the bare
face of the pond full of glee and youth, as if it spoke the
joy of the fishes within it, and of the sands on its shore,
— a silvery sheen as from the scales of a leuciscus, as it
were all one active fish. Such is the contrast between
winter and spring. Walden was dead and is alive again.
But this spring it broke up more steadily, as I have said.

The change from storm and winter to serene and mild
weather, from dark and sluggish hours to bright and
elastic ones, is a memorable crisis which all things pro-
claim. It is seemingly instantaneous at last. Suddenly an
influx of light filled my house, though the evening was at
hand, and the clouds of winter still overhung it, and the
eaves were dripping with sleety rain. I looked out the
window, and lo! where yesterday was cold gray ice there
lay the transparent pond already calm and full of hope
as in a summer evening, reflecting a summer evening
sky in its bosom, though none was visible overhead, as if
it had intelligence with some remote horizon. I heard a
robin in the distance, the first I had heard for many a
thousand years, methought, whose note I shall not forget for many a thousand more, — the same sweet and
powerful song as of yore. O the evening robin, at the
end of a New England summer day! If I could ever find
the twig he sits upon! I mean *he;* I mean *the twig.* This
at least is not the *Turdus migratorius.* The pitch pines
and shrub oaks about my house, which had so long
drooped, suddenly resumed their several characters,
looked brighter, greener, and more erect and alive, as if
effectually cleansed and restored by the rain. I knew

that it would not rain any more. You may tell by looking at any twig of the forest, ay, at your very wood-pile,
whether its winter is past or not. As it grew darker, I was
startled by the honking of geese flying low over the woods,
like weary travellers getting in late from Southern lakes,
and indulging at last in unrestrained complaint and
mutual consolation. Standing at my door, I could hear
the rush of their wings; when, driving toward my house,
they suddenly spied my light, and with hushed clamor
wheeled and settled in the pond. So I came in, and shut
the door, and passed my first spring night in the woods.

In the morning I watched the geese from the door
through the mist, sailing in the middle of the pond, fifty
rods off, so large and tumultuous that Walden appeared
like an artificial pond for their amusement. But when
I stood on the shore they at once rose up with a great
flapping of wings at the signal of their commander, and
when they had got into rank circled about over my
head, twenty-nine of them, and then steered straight
to Canada, with a regular *honk* from the leader at intervals, trusting to break their fast in muddier pools. A
"plump" of ducks rose at the same time and took the
route to the north in the wake of their noisier cousins.

For a week I heard the circling, groping clangor of
some solitary goose in the foggy mornings, seeking its
companion, and still peopling the woods with the sound
of a larger life than they could sustain. In April the
pigeons were seen again flying express in small flocks,
and in due time I heard the martins twittering over my
clearing, though it had not seemed that the township
contained so many that it could afford me any, and I

fancied that they were peculiarly of the ancient race that dwelt in hollow trees ere white men came. In almost all climes the tortoise and the frog are among the precursors and heralds of this season, and birds fly with song and glancing plumage, and plants spring and bloom, and winds blow, to correct this slight oscillation of the poles and preserve the equilibrium of nature.

As every season seems best to us in its turn, so the coming in of spring is like the creation of Cosmos out of Chaos and the realization of the Golden Age. —

"Eurus ad Auroram Nabathaeaque regna recessit,
  Persidaque, et radiis juga subdita matutinis."

"The East-Wind withdrew to Aurora and the Nabathæan kingdom,
  And the Persian, and the ridges placed under the morning rays.
  . . . .
  Man was born. Whether that Artificer of things,
  The origin of a better world, made him from the divine seed;
  Or the earth, being recent and lately sundered from the high
  Ether, retained some seeds of cognate heaven."

A single gentle rain makes the grass many shades greener. So our prospects brighten on the influx of better thoughts. We should be blessed if we lived in the present always, and took advantage of every accident that befell us, like the grass which confesses the influence of the slightest dew that falls on it; and did not spend our time in atoning for the neglect of past opportunities, which we call doing our duty. We loiter in winter while it is already spring. In a pleasant spring morning all men's sins are forgiven. Such a day is a truce to vice. While such a sun holds out to burn, the vilest inner may return. Through our own recovered innocence

we discern the innocence of our neighbors. You may
have known your neighbor yesterday for a thief, a drunkard, or a sensualist, and merely pitied or despised him,
and despaired of the world; but the sun shines bright and
warm this first spring morning, re-creating the world, and
you meet him at some serene work, and see how his
exhausted and debauched veins expand with still joy
and bless the new day, feel the spring influence with the
innocence of infancy, and all his faults are forgotten.
There is not only an atmosphere of good will about him,
but even a savor of holiness groping for expression,
blindly and ineffectually perhaps, like a new-born instinct, and for a short hour the south hillside echoes to
no vulgar jest. You see some innocent fair shoots preparing to burst from his gnarled rind and try another
year's life, tender and fresh as the youngest plant.
Even he has entered into the joy of his Lord. Why the
jailer does not leave open his prison doors, — why the
judge does not dismiss his case, — why the preacher
does not dismiss his congregation! It is because they do
not obey the hint which God gives them, nor accept the
pardon which he freely offers to all.

"A return to goodness produced each day in the tranquil and beneficent breath of the morning, causes that in
respect to the love of virtue and the hatred of vice, one
approaches a little the primitive nature of man, as the
sprouts of the forest which has been felled. In like manner the evil which one does in the interval of a day prevents the germs of virtues which began to spring up again
from developing themselves and destroys them.

"After the germs of virtue have thus been prevented

many times from developing themselves, then the beneficent breath of evening does not suffice to preserve them.
As soon as the breath of evening does not suffice longer
to preserve them, then the nature of man does not differ
much from that of the brute. Men seeing the nature
of this man like that of the brute, think that he has
never possessed the innate faculty of reason. Are those
the true and natural sentiments of man?"

" The Golden Age was first created, which without any avenger
    Spontaneously without law cherished fidelity and rectitude.
    Punishment and fear were not; nor were threatening words read
  On suspended brass; nor did the suppliant crowd fear
    The words of their judge; but were safe without an avenger.
    Not yet the pine felled on its mountains had descended
    To the liquid waves that it might see a foreign world,
    And mortals knew no shores but their own.

.   .   .   .

    There was eternal spring, and placid zephyrs with warm
    Blasts soothed the flowers born without seed."

On the 29th of April, as I was fishing from the bank
of the river near the Nine-Acre-Corner bridge, standing
on the quaking grass and willow roots, where the muskrats lurk, I heard a singular rattling sound, somewhat
like that of the sticks which boys play with their fingers,
when, looking up, I observed a very slight and graceful
hawk, like a nighthawk, alternately soaring like a ripple
and tumbling a rod or two over and over, showing
the under side of its wings, which gleamed like a satin
ribbon in the sun, or like the pearly inside of a shell.
This sight reminded me of falconry and what nobleness
and poetry are associated with that sport. The merlin
it seemed to me it might be called: but I care not for its

name. It was the most ethereal flight I had ever witnessed. It did not simply flutter like a butterfly, nor soar like the larger hawks, but it sported with proud reliance in the fields of air; mounting again and again with its strange chuckle, it repeated its free and beautiful fall, turning over and over like a kite, and then recovering from its lofty tumbling, as if it had never set its foot on *terra firma*. It appeared to have no companion in the universe, — sporting there alone, — and to need none but the morning and the ether with which it played. It was not lonely, but made all the earth lonely beneath it. Where was the parent which hatched it, its kindred, and its father in the heavens? The tenant of the air, it seemed related to the earth but by an egg hatched some time in the crevice of a crag; — or was its native nest made in the angle of a cloud, woven of the rainbow's trimmings and the sunset sky, and lined with some soft midsummer haze caught up from earth? Its eyry now some cliffy cloud.

Beside this I got a rare mess of golden and silver and bright cupreous fishes, which looked like a string of jewels. Ah! I have penetrated to those meadows on the morning of many a first spring day, jumping from hummock to hummock, from willow root to willow root, when the wild river valley and the woods were bathed in so pure and bright a light as would have waked the dead, if they had been slumbering in their graves, as some suppose. There needs no stronger proof of immortality. All things must live in such a light. O Death, where was thy sting? O Grave, where was thy victory, then?

Our village life would stagnate if it were not for the un-

explored forests and meadows which surround it. We
need the tonic of wildness, — to wade sometimes in
marshes where the bittern and the meadow-hen lurk,
and hear the booming of the snipe; to smell the whisper-
ing sedge where only some wilder and more solitary fowl
builds her nest, and the mink crawls with its belly close
to the ground. At the same time that we are earnest to
explore and learn all things, we require that all things be
mysterious and unexplorable, that land and sea be infinitely wild, unsurveyed and unfathomed by us because
unfathomable. We can never have enough of nature.
We must be refreshed by the sight of inexhaustible vigor,
vast and titanic features, the sea-coast with its wrecks,
the wilderness with its living and its decaying trees, the
thunder-cloud, and the rain which lasts three weeks and
produces freshets. We need to witness our own limits
transgressed, and some life pasturing freely where we
never wander. We are cheered when we observe the vul-
ture feeding on the carrion which disgusts and disheart-
ens us, and deriving health and strength from the repast.
There was a dead horse in the hollow by the path to my
house, which compelled me sometimes to go out of my
way, especially in the night when the air was heavy, but
the assurance it gave me of the strong appetite and in-
violable health of Nature was my compensation for this.
I love to see that Nature is so rife with life that myriads
can be afforded to be sacrificed and suffered to prey on
one another; that tender organizations can be so serenely
squashed out of existence like pulp, — tadpoles which
herons gobble up, and tortoises and toads run over in the
road; and that sometimes it has rained flesh and blood!

With the liability to accident, we must see how little account is to be made of it. The impression made on a wise man is that of universal innocence. Poison is not poisonous after all, nor are any wounds fatal. Compassion is a very untenable ground. It must be expeditious. Its pleadings will not bear to be stereotyped.

Early in May, the oaks, hickories, maples, and other trees, just putting out amidst the pine woods around the pond, imparted a brightness like sunshine to the landscape, especially in cloudy days, as if the sun were breaking through mists and shining faintly on the hillsides here and there. On the third or fourth of May I saw a loon in the pond, and during the first week of the month I heard the whip-poor-will, the brown thrasher, the veery, the wood pewee, the chewink, and other birds. I had heard the wood thrush long before. The phoebe had already come once more and looked in at my door and window, to see if my house was cavern-like enough for her, sustaining herself on humming wings with clinched talons, as if she held by the air, while she surveyed the premises. The sulphur-like pollen of the pitch pine soon covered the pond and the stones and rotten wood along the shore, so that you could have collected a barrelful. This is the "sulphur showers" we hear of. Even in Calidas' drama of Sacontala, we read of "rills dyed yellow with the golden dust of the lotus." And so the seasons went rolling on into summer, as one rambles into higher and higher grass.

Thus was my first year's life in the woods completed; and the second year was similar to it. I finally left Walden September 6th, 1847.

XVIII

CONCLUSION

To the sick the doctors wisely recommend a change of air and scenery. Thank Heaven, here is not all the world. The buckeye does not grow in New England, and the mockingbird is rarely heard here. The wild goose is more of a cosmopolite than we; he breaks his fast in Canada, takes a luncheon in the Ohio, and plumes himself for the night in a southern bayou. Even the bison, to some extent, keeps pace with the seasons, cropping the pastures of the Colorado only till a greener and sweeter grass awaits him by the Yellowstone. Yet we think that if rail fences are pulled down, and stone walls piled up on our farms, bounds are henceforth set to our lives and our fates decided. If you are chosen town clerk, forsooth, you cannot go to Tierra del Fuego this summer: but you may go to the land of infernal fire nevertheless. The universe is wider than our views of it.

Yet we should oftener look over the tafferel of our craft, like curious passengers, and not make the voyage like stupid sailors picking oakum. The other side of the globe is but the home of our correspondent. Our voyaging is only great-circle sailing, and the doctors prescribe for diseases of the skin merely. One hastens to southern Africa to chase the giraffe; but surely that is not the game he would be after. How long, pray, would a man hunt giraffes if he could? Snipes and woodcocks also may afford rare sport; but I trust it would be nobler game to shoot one's self. —

> Direct your eye right inward, and you'll find
> A thousand regions in your mind
> Yet undiscovered. Travel them, and be
> Expert in home-cosmography.

What does Africa, — what does the West stand for? Is not our own interior white on the chart? black though it may prove, like the coast, when discovered. Is it the source of the Nile, or the Niger, or the Mississippi, or a Northwest Passage around this continent, that we would find? Are these the problems which most concern mankind? Is Franklin the only man who is lost, that his wife should be so earnest to find him? Does Mr. Grinnell know where he himself is? Be rather the Mungo Park, the Lewis and Clark and Frobisher, of your own streams and oceans; explore your own higher latitudes, — with shiploads of preserved meats to support you, if they be necessary; and pile the empty cans sky-high for a sign. Were preserved meats invented to preserve meat merely? Nay, be a Columbus to whole new continents and worlds within you, opening new channels, not of trade, but of thought. Every man is the lord of a realm beside which the earthly empire of the Czar is but a petty state, a hummock left by the ice. Yet some can be patriotic who have no *self*-respect, and sacrifice the greater to the less. They love the soil which makes their graves, but have no sympathy with the spirit which may still animate their clay. Patriotism is a maggot in their heads.

What was the meaning of that South-Sea Exploring Expedition, with all its parade and expense, but an indirect recognition of the fact that there are continents and seas in the moral world to which every man is an isthmus or an inlet, yet unexplored by him, but that it is easier to sail many thousand miles through cold and storm and cannibals, in a government ship, with five hundred men and boys to assist one, than it is to explore the private sea, the Atlantic and Pacific Ocean of one's being alone. —

> "Erret, et extremos alter scrutetur Iberos.
> Plus habet hic vitae, plus habet ille viae."

Let them wander and scrutinize the outlandish Australians. I have more of God, they more of the road.

It is not worth the while to go round the world to count the cats in Zanzibar. Yet do this even till you can do better, and you may perhaps find some "Symmes' Hole" by which to get at the inside at last. England and France, Spain and Portugal, Gold Coast and Slave Coast, all front on this private sea; but no bark from them has ventured out of sight of land, though it is without doubt the direct way to India. If you would learn to speak all tongues and conform to the customs of all nations, if you would travel farther than all travellers, be naturalized in all climes, and cause the Sphinx to dash her head against a stone, even obey the precept of the old philosopher, and Explore thyself. Herein are demanded the eye and the nerve. Only the defeated and deserters go to the wars, cowards that run away and enlist. Start now on that farthest western way, which does not pause at the

Mississippi or the Pacific, nor conduct toward a worn-out China or Japan, but leads on direct, a tangent to this sphere, summer and winter, day and night, sun down, moon down, and at last earth down too.

It is said that Mirabeau took to highway robbery "to ascertain what degree of resolution was necessary in order to place one's self in formal opposition to the most sacred laws of society." He declared that "a soldier who fights in the ranks does not require half so much courage as a foot-pad," — "that honor and religion have never stood in the way of a well-considered and a firm resolve." This was manly, as the world goes; and yet it was idle, if not desperate. A saner man would have found himself often enough "in formal opposition" to what are deemed "the most sacred laws of society," through obedience to yet more sacred laws, and so have tested his resolution without going out of his way. It is not for a man to put himself in such an attitude to society, but to maintain himself in whatever attitude he find himself through obedience to the laws of his being, which will never be one of opposition to a just government, if he should chance to meet with such.

I left the woods for as good a reason as I went there. Perhaps it seemed to me that I had several more lives to live, and could not spare any more time for that one. It is remarkable how easily and insensibly we fall into a particular route, and make a beaten track for ourselves. I had not lived there a week before my feet wore a path from my door to the pond-side; and though it is five or six years since I trod it, it is still quite distinct. It is true, I fear, that others may have fallen into it, and so helped to keep it open. The surface of the earth is soft and impressible by the feet of men; and so with the paths which the mind travels. How worn and dusty, then, must be the highways of the world, how deep the ruts of tradition and conformity! I did not wish to take a cabin passage, but rather to go before the mast and on the deck of the world, for there I could best see the moonlight amid the mountains. I do not wish to go below now.

I learned this, at least, by my experiment: that if one advances confidently in the direction of his dreams, and endeavors to live the life which he has imagined, he will meet with a success unexpected in common hours. He will put some things behind, will pass an invisible boundary; new, universal, and more liberal laws will begin to establish themselves around and within him; or the old laws be expanded, and interpreted in his favor in a more liberal sense, and he will live with the license of a higher order of beings. In proportion as he simplifies his life, the laws of the universe will appear less complex, and solitude will not be solitude, nor poverty poverty, nor weakness weakness. If you have built castles in the air, your work need not be lost; that is where they should be. Now put the foundations under them.

It is a ridiculous demand which England and America make, that you shall speak so that they can understand you. Neither men nor toadstools grow so. As if that were important, and there were not enough to understand you without them. As if Nature could support but one order of understandings, could not sustain birds as well as quadrupeds, flying as well as creeping things, and *hush* and *whoa*, which Bright can understand, were

THOREAU'S COVE, WALDEN POND

The cairn in the foreground, raised by visitors to the spot, marks the site of Thoreau's cabin

the best English. As if there were safety in stupidity alone. I fear chiefly lest my expression may not be *extra-vagant* enough, may not wander far enough beyond the narrow limits of my daily experience, so as to be adequate to the truth of which I have been convinced. *Extra vagance!* it depends on how you are yarded. The migrating buffalo, which seeks new pastures in another latitude, is not extravagant like the cow which kicks over the pail, leaps the cowyard fence, and runs after her calf, in milking time. I desire to speak somewhere *without* bounds; like a man in a waking moment, to men in their waking moments; for I am convinced that I cannot exaggerate enough even to lay the foundation of a true expression. Who that has heard a strain of music feared then lest he should speak extravagantly any more forever? In view of the future or possible, we should live quite laxly and undefined in front, our outlines dim and misty on that side; as our shadows reveal an insensible perspiration toward the sun. The volatile truth of our words should continually betray the inadequacy of the residual statement. Their truth is instantly *translated;* its literal monument alone remains. The words which express our faith and piety are not definite; yet they are significant and fragrant like frankincense to superior natures.

Why level downward to our dullest perception always, and praise that as common sense? The commonest sense is the sense of men asleep, which they express by snoring. Sometimes we are inclined to class those who are once-and-a-half-witted with the half-witted, because we appreciate only a third part of their wit. Some would find fault with the morning red, if they ever got up early enough. "They pretend," as I hear, "that the verses of Kabir have four different senses; illusion, spirit, intellect, and the exoteric doctrine of the Vedas;" but in this part of the world it is considered a ground for complaint if a man's writings admit of more than one interpretation. While England endeavors to cure the potato-rot, will not any endeavor to cure the brain-rot, which prevails so much more widely and fatally?

I do not suppose that I have attained to obscurity, but I should be proud if no more fatal fault were found with my pages on this score than was found with the Walden ice. Southern customers objected to its blue color, which is the evidence of its purity, as if it were muddy, and preferred the Cambridge ice, which is white, but tastes of weeds. The purity men love is like the mists which envelop the earth, and not like the azure ether beyond.

Some are dinning in our ears that we Americans, and moderns generally, are intellectual dwarfs compared with the ancients, or even the Elizabethan men. But what is that to the purpose? A living dog is better than a dead lion. Shall a man go and hang himself because he belongs to the race of pygmies, and not be the biggest pygmy that he can? Let every one mind his own business, and endeavor to be what he was made.

Why should we be in such desperate haste to succeed and in such desperate enterprises? If a man does not keep pace with his companions, perhaps it is because he hears a different drummer. Let him step to the

music which he hears, however measured or far away.
It is not important that he should mature as soon as an
apple tree or an oak. Shall he turn his spring into summer? If the condition of things which we were made
for is not yet, what were any reality which we can substitute? We will not be shipwrecked on a vain reality.
Shall we with pains erect a heaven of blue glass over
ourselves, though when it is done we shall be sure to
gaze still at the true ethereal heaven far above, as if
the former were not?

There was an artist in the city of Kouroo who was
disposed to strive after perfection. One day it came into
his mind to make a staff. Having considered that in an
imperfect work time is an ingredient, but into a perfect work time does not enter, he said to himself, It
shall be perfect in all respects, though I should do nothing else in my life. He proceeded instantly to the
forest for wood, being resolved that it should not be
made of unsuitable material; and as he searched for
and rejected stick after stick, his friends gradually deserted him, for they grew old in their works and died,
but he grew not older by a moment. His singleness
of purpose and resolution, and his elevated piety,
endowed him, without his knowledge, with perennial
youth. As he made no compromise with Time, Time
kept out of his way, and only sighed at a distance because he could not overcome him. Before he had found
a stock in all respects suitable the city of Kouroo was
a hoary ruin, and he sat on one of its mounds to peel
the stick. Before he had given it the proper shape the
dynasty of the Candahars was at an end, and with the

point of the stick he wrote the name of the last of that
race in the sand, and then resumed his work. By the
time he had smoothed and polished the staff Kalpa
was no longer the pole-star; and ere he had put on the
ferule and the head adorned with precious stones,
Brahma had awoke and slumbered many times. But
why do I stay to mention these things? When the
finishing stroke was put to his work, it suddenly expanded before the eyes of the astonished artist into the
fairest of all the creations of Brahma. He had made a
new system in making a staff, a world with full and fair
proportions; in which, though the old cities and dynas-
ties had passed away, fairer and more glorious ones had
taken their places. And now he saw by the heap of
shavings still fresh at his feet, that, for him and his
work, the former lapse of time had been an illusion,
and that no more time had elapsed than is required for
a single scintillation from the brain of Brahma to fall on
and inflame the tinder of a mortal brain. The material
was pure, and his art was pure; how could the result
be other than wonderful?

No face which we can give to a matter will stead us
so well at last as the truth. This alone wears well. For
the most part, we are not where we are, but in a false
position. Through an infirmity of our natures, we suppose a case, and put ourselves into it, and hence are in
two cases at the same time, and it is doubly difficult
to get out. In sane moments we regard only the facts,
the case that is. Say what you have to say, not what
you ought. Any truth is better than make-believe. Tom
Hyde, the tinker, standing on the gallows, was asked if

he had anything to say. "Tell the tailors," said he, "to remember to make a knot in their thread before they take the first stitch." His companion's prayer is forgotten.

However mean your life is, meet it and live it; do not shun it and call it hard names. It is not so bad as you are. It looks poorest when you are richest. The fault-finder will find faults even in paradise. Love your life, poor as it is. You may perhaps have some pleasant, thrilling, glorious hours, even in a poor-house. The setting sun is reflected from the windows of the alms-house as brightly as from the rich man's abode; the snow melts before its door as early in the spring. I do not see but a quiet mind may live as contentedly there, and have as cheering thoughts, as in a palace. The town's poor seem to me often to live the most independent lives of any. Maybe they are simply great enough to receive without misgiving. Most think that they are above being supported by the town; but it oftener happens that they are not above supporting themselves by dishonest means, which should be more disreputable. Cultivate poverty like a garden herb, like sage. Do not trouble yourself much to get new things, whether clothes or friends. Turn the old; return to them. Things do not change; we change. Sell your clothes and keep your thoughts. God will see that you do not want society. If I were confined to a corner of a garret all my days, like a spider, the world would be just as large to me while I had my thoughts about me. The philosopher said: "From an army of three divisions one can take away its general, and put it in disorder;

from the man the most abject and vulgar one cannot take away his thought." Do not seek so anxiously to be developed, to subject yourself to many influences to be played on; it is all dissipation. Humility like darkness reveals the heavenly lights. The shadows of poverty and meanness gather around us, "and lo! creation widens to our view." We are often reminded that if there were bestowed on us the wealth of Crœsus, our aims must still be the same, and our means essentially the same. Moreover, if you are restricted in your range by poverty, if you cannot buy books and newspapers, for instance, you are but confined to the most significant and vital experiences; you are compelled to deal with the material which yields the most sugar and the most starch. It is life near the bone where it is sweetest. You are defended from being a trifler. No man loses ever on a lower level by magnanimity on a higher. Superfluous wealth can buy superfluities only. Money is not required to buy one necessary of the soul.

I live in the angle of a leaden wall, into whose composition was poured a little alloy of bell-metal. Often, in the repose of my mid-day, there reaches my ears a confused *tintinnabulum* from without. It is the noise of my contemporaries. My neighbors tell me of their adventures with famous gentlemen and ladies, what notabilities they met at the dinner-table; but I am no more interested in such things than in the contents of the Daily Times. The interest and the conversation are about costume and manners chiefly; but a goose is a goose still, dress it as you will. They tell me of California and Texas, of England and the Indies, of the

Hon. Mr. —— of Georgia or of Massachusetts, all transient and fleeting phenomena, till I am ready to leap from their court-yard like the Mameluke bey. I delight to come to my bearings, — not walk in procession with pomp and parade, in a conspicuous place, but to walk even with the Builder of the universe, if I may, — not to live in this restless, nervous, bustling, trivial Nineteenth Century, but stand or sit thoughtfully while it goes by. What are men celebrating? They are all on a committee of arrangements, and hourly expect a speech from somebody. God is only the president of the day, and Webster is his orator. I love to weigh, to settle, to gravitate toward that which most strongly and rightfully attracts me; — not hang by the beam of the scale and try to weigh less, — not suppose a case, but take the case that is; to travel the only path I can, and that on which no power can resist me. It affords me no satisfaction to commence to spring an arch before I have got a solid foundation. Let us not play at kittly-benders. There is a solid bottom everywhere. We read that the traveller asked the boy if the swamp before him had a hard bottom. The boy replied that it had. But presently the traveller's horse sank in up to the girths, and he observed to the boy, "I thought you said that this bog had a hard bottom." "So it has," answered the latter, "but you have not got half way to it yet." So it is with the bogs and quicksands of society; but he is an old boy that knows it. Only what is thought, said, or done at a certain rare coincidence is good. I would not be one of those who will foolishly drive a nail into mere lath and plastering; such a deed would keep me awake nights. Give me a hammer, and let me feel for the furring. Do not depend on the putty. Drive a nail home and clinch it so faithfully that you can wake up in the night and think of your work with satisfaction, — a work at which you would not be ashamed to invoke the Muse. So will help you God, and so only. Every nail driven should be as another rivet in the machine of the universe, you carrying on the work.

Rather than love, than money, than fame, give me truth. I sat at a table where were rich food and wine in abundance, and obsequious attendance, but sincerity and truth were not; and I went away hungry from the inhospitable board. The hospitality was as cold as the ices. I thought that there was no need of ice to freeze them. They talked to me of the age of the wine and the fame of the vintage; but I thought of an older, a newer, and purer wine, of a more glorious vintage, which they had not got, and could not buy. The style, the house and grounds and "entertainment" pass for nothing with me. I called on the king, but he made me wait in his hall, and conducted like a man incapacitated for hospitality. There was a man in my neighborhood who lived in a hollow tree. His manners were truly regal. I should have done better had I called on him.

How long shall we sit in our porticoes practising idle and musty virtues, which any work would make impertinent? As if one were to begin the day with long-suffering, and hire a man to hoe his potatoes; and in the afternoon go forth to practise Christian meekness and charity with goodness aforethought! Consider the

China pride and stagnant self-complacency of mankind. This generation inclines a little to congratulate itself on being the last of an illustrious line; and in Boston and London and Paris and Rome, thinking of its long descent, it speaks of its progress in art and science and literature with satisfaction. There are the Records of the Philosophical Societies, and the public Eulogies of *Great Men!* It is the good Adam contemplating his own virtue. "Yes, we have done great deeds, and sung divine songs, which shall never die," — that is, as long as *we* can remember them. The learned societies and great men of Assyria, — where are they? What youthful philosophers and experimentalists we are! There is not one of my readers who has yet lived a whole human life. These may be but the spring months in the life of the race. If we have had the seven-years' itch, we have not seen the seventeen-year locust yet in Concord. We are acquainted with a mere pellicle of the globe on which we live. Most have not delved six feet beneath the surface, nor leaped as many above it. We know not where we are. Beside, we are sound asleep nearly half our time. Yet we esteem ourselves wise, and have an established order on the surface. Truly, we are deep thinkers, we are ambitious spirits! As I stand over the insect crawling amid the pine needles on the forest floor, and endeavoring to conceal itself from my sight, and ask myself why it will cherish those humble thoughts, and hide its head from me who might, perhaps, be its benefactor, and impart to its race some cheering information, I am reminded of the greater Benefactor and Intelligence that stands over me the human insect.

There is an incessant influx of novelty into the world, and yet we tolerate incredible dulness. I need only suggest what kind of sermons are still listened to in the most enlightened countries. There are such words as joy and sorrow, but they are only the burden of a psalm, sung with a nasal twang, while we believe in the ordinary and mean. We think that we can change our clothes only. It is said that the British Empire is very large and respectable, and that the United States are a first-rate power. We do not believe that a tide rises and falls behind every man which can float the British Empire like a chip, if he should ever harbor it in his mind. Who knows what sort of seventeen-year locust will next come out of the ground? The government of the world I live in was not framed, like that of Britain, in after-dinner conversations over the wine.

The life in us is like the water in the river. It may rise this year higher than man has ever known it, and flood the parched uplands; even this may be the eventful year, which will drown out all our muskrats. It was not always dry land where we dwell. I see far inland the banks which the stream anciently washed, before science began to record its freshets. Every one has heard the story which has gone the rounds of New England, of a strong and beautiful bug which came out of the dry leaf of an old table of apple-tree wood, which had stood in a farmer's kitchen for sixty years, first in Connecticut, and afterward in Massachusetts, — from an egg deposited in the living tree many years earlier still, as appeared by counting the annual layers beyond it; which was heard gnawing out for several weeks, hatched perchance by the heat of an urn. Who does not feel his faith in a resurrection and immortality strengthened by hearing of this? Who knows what beautiful and winged life, whose egg has been buried for ages under many concentric layers of woodenness in the dead dry life of society, deposited at first in the alburnum of the green and living tree, which has been gradually converted into the semblance of its well-seasoned tomb, — heard perchance gnawing out now for years by the astonished family of man, as they sat round the festive board, — may unexpectedly come forth from amidst society's most trivial and handselled furniture, to enjoy its perfect summer life at last!

I do not say that John or Jonathan will realize all this; but such is the character of that morrow which mere lapse of time can never make to dawn. The light which puts out our eyes is darkness to us. Only that day dawns to which we are awake. There is more day to dawn. The sun is but a morning star.

NOTES

Page 4, lines 16, 17. **You who read these pages, who are said to live in New England.** Note the limited audience which Thoreau had in mind. It may have been from modesty, as if he expected only his friends and neighbors to take an interest in his book; or it may be that he depended chiefly on the interest in the Transcendental movement, which was largely confined to New England, to attract readers. His experience with his first book, *A Week on the Concord and Merrimack Rivers*, of which only a little over two hundred copies were sold in the first four years, was such as to prepare him for a small sale.

Line 17. **Are said to live.** Implies some doubt as to whether they really *live* in the best sense of the word.

Lines 21, 22. **I have travelled a good deal in Concord.** Thoreau regarded Concord — or indeed any man's home — as an epitome of the world. It was not necessary, in his opinion, to go far in order to see all that was really worth seeing. This opinion did not prevent his refreshing himself by occasional somewhat more extended journeys into the country, however.

Line 7 from bottom. **Bramins.** More often spelled Brahmins or Brahmans. The religious upper caste of the Hindoos. Some of the more rigorous devotees tortured themselves in many ways and lived by begging. Thoreau was an earnest student of the Hindoo philosophy and mythology, reading translations of the sacred books.

Page 5, line 11. **Iolaus.** One of the twelve labors imposed upon Hercules by King Eurystheus was the fight with a monstrous water-snake called the Hydra, which had nine heads, one of which was immortal. Whenever a head was cut off, two grew in its place, until Hercules' charioteer Iolaus (I-o-lā'us) seared the stumps with a red-hot iron. The immortal head was buried under a mass of rock.

Line 18. **Suckled by a wolf.** Like Romulus and Remus.

Line 22. **Peck of dirt.** The allusion is to the old saying that every person must eat a peck of dirt before he dies, quoted to children who are thought over-particular about the cleanliness of their food.

Line 4 from bottom. **Augean stables.** The cleansing of the Augean stable was one of Hercules' labors.

Page 6, line 6. **An old book.** The Bible.

Line 12. **Inde genus**, etc. From Ovid's story of Deucalion and Pyrrha in the *Metamorphoses*.

Line 14. **Raleigh.** Sir Walter Raleigh was the subject of an early essay by Thoreau, who greatly admired his literary style (see *A Week on the Concord and Merrimack Rivers*, "Sunday "). The lines are Raleigh's translation of the Latin of Ovid, which he quotes in his *History of the World*.

Page 7, line 16. **On the limits.** Mr. Sanborn, in the Bibliophile edition of *Walden*, suggests that this has reference to the jail-limits for imprisoned debtors.

Page 8, lines 11, 12. **Divinity stir within him.**

> " It must be so, — Plato, thou reasonest well!
> Else whence this pleasing hope, this fond desire,
> This longing after immortality ?
> Or whence this secret dread and inward horror
> Of falling into naught ? Why shrinks the soul
> Back on herself, and startles at destruction ?
> 'T is the divinity that stirs within us ;
> 'T is Heaven itself that points out an hereafter,
> And intimates eternity to man."
>
> JOSEPH ADDISON, *Cato*, Act V, Sc. i.

Line 9 from bottom. **Wilberforce.** William Wilberforce (1759–1833), an English philanthropist and anti-slavery leader.

Last line, page 9, line 1. **Bravery of minks and muskrats.** See p. 73, line 15, and note.

Page 9, line 9 from bottom. **Whirled round the globe.** That is in railroad trains and steamships.

Page 10, line 7 from bottom. **Evelyn.** John Evelyn (1620–1706), a famous English diarist and writer, an authority on gardening. His book on trees, entitled *Sylva*, was a favorite with Thoreau.

Line 2 from bottom. **Hippocrates.** An ancient Greek physician, called the " father of medicine."

Page 13, line 4 from bottom. **Second nature.** Habit is second nature. — Cicero, Plutarch, Montaigne, and others.

Page 14, line 1. **Darwin.** Charles Darwin, the great English naturalist. His famous book on the *Origin of Species* was not published at the time *Walden* was written, but Thoreau had read his *Voyage of a Naturalist round the World*, and he quotes and comments upon it extensively in his *Journal*.

Line 7. **New Hollander.** New Holland is an old name for Australia.

Line 11. **Liebig.** Baron Justus von Liebig, a famous German chemist (1803–1873).

Page 18, lines 16, 17. **Notch it on my stick.** As Robinson Crusoe kept his calendar.

Lines 17, 18. **The meeting of two eternities, the past and future.**

> " This narrow isthmus 'twixt two boundless seas,
> The past, the future, — two eternities ! "
>
> THOMAS MOORE, *Lalla Rookh.*

" One life, — a little gleam of time between two eternities." — Thomas Carlyle's *Heroes and Hero-Worship*, " The Hero as Man of Letters."

Line 6 from bottom. **I long ago lost a hound, a bay horse, and a turtle-dove.** These may be taken to represent the vague desires and aspirations of man's spiritual nature, things that we seek for as belonging of right to us, but existing somewhere out of our reach.

Page 19, line 19. **Gazette.** Any daily paper.

Line 7 from bottom. **Reporter to a journal.** Probably his own " journal " is meant. When this journal passed into the hands of another " editor," the contributions referred to were printed in full. They occupy fourteen volumes of the Walden Edition of Thoreau, and were published in 1906.

Page 20, lines 11-13. **The red huckleberry . . . the yellow violet.** These were all rarities in Concord, and as such especially cherished by Thoreau. The *Journal* gives account of them from time to time. The red huckleberry is not a separate species, but was probably what is known as a " sport."

Page 21, lines 24, 25. **My purpose in going to Walden Pond.** This statement is explicit. It controverts the popular idea that Thoreau was posing as a hermit in living alone at Walden. A part of this " private business " was the writing of his first book, *A Week on the Concord and Merrimack Rivers.* But see also pp. 100, 101.

Page 22, line 2. **Celestial Empire.** There is, of course, a play upon the words here. The early American trade with China — often called the Celestial Empire — was largely from the port of Salem, Mass., but it is an intercourse with the spiritual world of which Thoreau is thinking.

Lines 5, 6. **Ice and pine timber and a little granite.** The chief raw products exported from New England in Thoreau's time.

Line 3 from bottom. **La Pérouse.** Jean-François de Galaup, Comte de La Pérouse (1741-1788), a famous French navigator, who made discoveries in the Far East. His fate did not remain entirely untold, for, some forty years after his death, it was learned that he was shipwrecked in the New Hebrides and perished with all his crew.

Page 23, line 1. **Hanno.** A Carthaginian navigator who explored the west coast of Africa.

Page 24, line 6 from bottom. **The owner of the farm.** That is, his clothes on the scarecrow. " Clothes make the man."

Page 25, line 4. **Madam Pfeiffer.** Ida Reyer Pfeiffer (1797–1858), a Viennese traveller, whose *A Woman's Journey round the World* was published in 1850.

Page 26, line 12. **New wine in old bottles.** "Neither do men put new wine into old bottles." — *Matthew*, ix, 17.

Page 27, line 3. **The old philosopher.** Bias, one of the Seven Wise Men of Greece, who lived at Priene in Ionia, where he was born about B. C. 570. Under date of July 12, 1840, Thoreau notes this anecdote about him in his Journal : " In the sack of Priene, when the inhabitants with much hurry and bustle were carrying their effects to a place of safety, some one asked Bias, who remained tranquil amid the confusion, why he was not thinking how he should save something, as the others were. 'I do so,' said Bias, ' for I carry all my effects with me.' "

Page 28, line 2. **The Parcæ.** The Fates who, according to the Greek mythology, controlled the lives of men as if spinning and cutting a thread.

Line 15. **Egyptian wheat.** This old story of the longevity of the wheat germ is now denied. Thoreau corrected his own copy of the book to read " is said to have been handed down."

Line 6 from bottom. **All costume off a man,** etc. Thoreau originally said this apropos of the costumes of a party of Tyrolese singers who visited Concord in February, 1841. (See the *Journal*, vol. i, pp. 196, 197.) This is a good instance of the way he made the entries in his Journal serve his purposes, or rather of the way particular observations led to generalizations which later proved of use to him in his writing.

Page 29, line 3 from bottom. **Samuel Laing.** A Scotch traveller who published several books on Norway and Sweden.

Page 30, line 6. **Domestic.** From the Latin *domesticus*, from *domus*, house.

Page 31, lines 24, 25. **Penobscot Indians.** Indians of this tribe came down from Maine to Massachusetts in Thoreau's time to sell baskets, etc. See pp. 20, 21.

Page 32, lines 7, 8. **Have freedom in his love, and in his soul be free.**

" Stone walls do not a prison make,
    Nor iron bars a cage ;

> Minds innocent and quiet take
> That for an hermitage ;
> If I have freedom in my love,
> And in my soul am free,
> Angels alone that soar above
> Enjoy such liberty."
>
> RICHARD LOVELACE, " To Althea from Prison."

Line 20. Gookin. Daniel Gookin, who was born in England about 1612, and died at Cambridge, Mass., in 1687. His book on the Indians was written in 1674, but remained unpublished until the Massachusetts Historical Society printed it in 1792.

Page 33, lines, 13, 14. The birds of the air have their nests, and the foxes their holes. " And Jesus saith unto him, The foxes have holes, and the birds of the air have nests ; but the Son of man hath not where to lay his head." — *Matthew*, viii, 20.

Page 34, line 3. Rumford fireplace. Benjamin Thompson, Count Rumford, discovered the principles upon which fireplaces and chimneys are properly constructed.

Lines 12–14. The cost of a thing is the amount of what I will call life which is required to be exchanged for it. Is this a good definition ?

Page 35, lines 9, 10. The poor ye have always with you, etc. " For the poor always ye have with you." — *John*, xii, 8. "What mean ye, that ye use this proverb concerning the land of Israel, saying, The fathers," etc. This and the two verses following are from *Ezekiel*, xviii (2–4).

Page 36, line 9 from bottom. Suent. Working smoothly. On February 3, 1852, Thoreau wrote in his Journal : " ' Suent ' is an expressive word, applied to machinery whose joints are worn, which has got into working order, — apparently from *sueo*, to be accustomed. So of the writer's faculties." For Thoreau's definition of the word one looks in vain in the regular dictionaries (Murray's *New English Dictionary* has not yet reached the letter S). One learns from them that it is a dialectic word, used in some provinces in England and locally in the United States, that " suant " is the usual spelling, and that the ordinary meaning is " evenly spread," " smooth " in that sense, as of the sowing of grain. Most of the dialect dictionaries make a similar report, but the large *English Dialect Dictionary* by Joseph Wright (1904) gives, as an adverbial usage, " Smoothly, easily, without friction ; evenly, regularly," and quotes J. Drummond Robinson writing of Gloucestershire, " A carpenter, if the wood planes easily, would say it works suent," and F. T. Elworthy, who heard in West Somerset, " A drap o' oil 'll make the wheel turn suanter by half." This usage of the word is Thoreau's precisely, except that he makes it an adjective instead of an adverb.

He probably got the word in conversation with some workman, as it does not appear to have found its way into literature until Thoreau himself made use of it. As the word is not a literary one, it seems doubtful if the etymology that he suggests is correct, and the dictionary derivation from the Old French *suant*, "following," is more likely to be the right one.

Line 4 from bottom. **A hair springe.** Perhaps "springe" is a misprint for "spring," though all the editions have it so. It is difficult to conceive of any serious harm coming to a man from his catching his foot in a horsehair noose, but if it were in a steel bear-trap set so delicately that a hair would spring it, that would be quite another matter.

Page 37, line 1. **Chapman.** George Chapman (1559 ?–1634), an English poet of the Elizabethan age.

Line 9. **Momus.** In Greek mythology the spirit of mockery and fault-finding.

Page 38, line 5. **Silent poor.** The poor who do not let the world know of their poverty and are not inmates of almshouses or recipients of public charity.

Line 7. **Garlic.** Herodotus names garlic as one of the principal foods of the pyramid-builders.

Page 39, line 6 from bottom. **Glow-shoes.** A corruption of the word "galoshes," the rubber overshoes now commonly called "rubbers" in New England.

Page 40, lines 9, 10. **Memnon.** In Greek mythology the son of Aurora, goddess of the dawn. The Greeks gave his name to a colossal statue at Thebes, Egypt, which was supposed to send forth music when struck by the rays of the rising sun.

Line 21. **Sardanapalus** was a rich and luxurious king of Assyria, in the seventh century B. C.

Last line. **Jonathan.** Brother Jonathan is the American people, Uncle Sam is the nation. Now that the American people is a less homogeneous entity than formerly, we hear less of Brother Jonathan.

Page 41, line 5. **Breathe a malaria.** The word "malaria" means in itself "bad air," being taken directly from the Italian *mal' aria* or *mala aria.* Modern scientific research has shown us, however, that the disease cannot be breathed in, but is communicated by the bites of the anopheles mosquito.

Line 19. **Agri-culture.** The division calls attention to the derivation of the word from the Latin *agri cultura*, the culture, or tilling, of a field.

Page 42, line 6 from bottom. **Johnson.** Edward Johnson (1600–1682) author of *The Wonder-Working Providence of Zion's Saviour in*

New England, an account of the founding and early history of Massachusetts.

Page 43, lines 5, 6. **The secretary of the Province of New Netherland.** This was Cornelis van Tienhoven. The document referred to will be found in translation in E. B. O'Callaghan's *Documents relative to the Colonial History of the State of New York*, vol. i, p. 365.

Page 45, line 1. **I borrowed an axe.** He borrowed it of his friend A. Bronson Alcott, who was a prominent member of the Concord literary group.

Line 21. **Lark and pewee.** The meadowlark and the phœbe.

Line 8 from bottom. **Winter of man's discontent.**

> " Now is the winter of our discontent
> Made glorious summer by this sun of York."
> SHAKESPEARE, *Richard III*, Act I, Sc. i, lines 1, 2.

Page 46, line 12. **Stray goose.** A wild goose, at that time on its way to its breeding-grounds in the north. The geese migrate in flocks, and this bird must have become separated from its companions by some accident.

Verse. **Men say they know many things**, etc. Thoreau, though a genuine poet in some ways, was not an accomplished writer of verse. He seems to have lacked a delicate ear for rhyme and rhythm, and the study of meters and verse-forms did not interest him. He wrote a good deal of verse, however, especially in his younger years, and much of it in more or less fragmentary form. His first book, *A Week on the Concord and Merrimack Rivers*, is plentifully sprinkled with it, and *Walden* contains four pieces, of which one, a ten-line stanza on " Smoke," is a true poem. The others would, perhaps, be called doggerel by undiscerning critics, but, though rude and unbeautiful in form, they embody poetic thoughts.

Page 49, line 6. **The removal of the gods of Troy.** See book ii of the *Æneid*.

Line 8 from bottom. **Acquaintances.** These " raisers " were A. Bronson Alcott, Ralph Waldo Emerson, William Ellery Channing (the poet), George William Curtis and his brother Burrill, and Edmund Hosmer of Concord with his sons John, Edmund, and Andrew. (George Willis Cooke's Introduction to George William Curtis's *Early Letters to John S. Dwight*.)

Page 50, line 2 from bottom. **Cowbirds and cuckoos.** The American cowbird and the European cuckoo have this parasitic habit.

Page 51, lines 7, 8. **The tailor . . . the ninth part of a man.** The allusion, of course, is to the familiar saying, " It takes nine tailors to make a man."

Lines 15, 16. **One . . . possessed with the idea of making architectural ornaments have a core of truth.** Horatio Greenough, the sculptor, in a letter which Emerson showed to Thoreau. See *Journal*, vol. iii, pp. 181–183 (Jan. 11, 1852).

Page 52, line 1. **Trinity Church.** The particular Trinity Church referred to is that on Broadway, opposite the head of Wall St., New York.

Line 3 from bottom. **No olives nor wines.** That is, no luxuries.

Page 53, line 12 from bottom. **I built a chimney.** See pp. 266, 267.

Line 7 from bottom. **Plastered house.** He plastered the house in November. (See p. 271.) To give the plastering time to dry, as we learn from the *Journal*, he left the house from November 12 to December 6.

Page 55, line 11. **The devil's attorney.** A "devil's advocate" is "one given to bringing forward accusations against personal character" (*Century Dictionary*). The term was originally applied in its Latin form of *Advocatus Diaboli* to the advocate in the Papal court whose duty it was to bring in all possible evidence and urge all possible objections against any person who was proposed for canonization.

Line 12. **Cambridge College.** Harvard College, of which Thoreau was a graduate, is referred to, of course.

Page 57, line 6. **Motes in his eyes.** The words, though not the thought, are Biblical. See *Matthew*, vii, 3–5.

Line 15. **Rodgers penknife.** Joseph Rodgers and Sons were, and are, famous cutlers of Sheffield, England. The house was founded in 1682 and is still doing business.

Line 8 from bottom. **Adam Smith, Ricardo, and Say.** Adam Smith (1723–1790, Scotch), David Ricardo (1772–1823, English Jew), Jean Baptiste Say (1767–1832, French), three noted political economists.

Page 58, line 16. **Princess Adelaide** appears to have been an imaginary princess.

Line 19. **Eating locusts and wild honey.** Like John the Baptist.

Line 20. **Flying Childers.** A celebrated English race-horse of the early eighteenth century. He is said never to have been beaten.

Line 24. **Fitchburg.** In Massachusetts; the nearest large town to the west of Concord, and then the terminus of the Fitchburg Railroad.

Page 61, line 9 from bottom. **Arthur Young.** An English agriculturist (1741–1820), author of many books on farming.

Page 63, line 20. **Bhagvat-Geeta.** Or Bhagavad-Gîtâ, one of the sacred books of the Hindoos.

Line 27. **When I was there**. Arcadia was a pastoral country of ancient Greece. The name has long been used figuratively for any ideally simple and poetic place or state of existence. The particular allusion here is to the expression, found in the literature of several languages, " I too have lived in Arcadia." This seems to have originated with the Italian painter Bartolommeo Schedone (1560–1616), who placed at the bottom of one of his pictures, formerly in the Sciarra collection (now dispersed) in Rome, the words " Et ego in Arcadia."

Page 64, line 3. **Thebes**. It is the Egyptian, not the Greek, Thebes that is referred to. Homer calls it " hundred-gated " (*Iliad*, book ix, line 383).

Lines 21, 22. **It costs more than it comes to**. A familiar saying in New England when a thing costs more in time or labor or worry than it does in money.

Line 24. **Vitruvius**. Marcus Vitruvius Pollio, a Roman architect of the time of Julius Cæsar and Augustus, author of an important work on architecture.

Line 26. **Thirty centuries**. Thoreau probably meant to say " forty centuries." Napoleon, in a short address to his soldiers in Egypt, said of the Pyramids, " From the summit of those monuments forty centuries look down upon you."

Page 65, line 9. **As many trades as fingers**. Thoreau's regular occupations — besides his main vocation of literature, which brought him in but little money — were teaching, surveying, manufacturing lead-pencils, and lecturing, but in his young manhood, as he indicates here, he earned an occasional dollar by manual labor of various kinds. In connection with his lead-pencil business, which descended to him from his father, he dealt in plumbago, as is shown by numerous scraps of correspondence preserved among his papers.

Last line. **Salt**. Note that this is not included among the " experiments that failed." In most editions of *Walden* after the first, the brace, through a printer's error, is made to include this necessary of life.

Page 66, line 21. **Their bills have not yet been received**. Naturally, since the washing and mending were done at home. Thoreau's writings are full of such touches of dry humor as this. Note that the syntax of this sentence is a little weak.

Page 67, line 2 from bottom. **A comparative statement**. Is Thoreau quite logical here ? Is it a comparative or a positive statement that he has been making ?

Page 68, line 6. **Purslane**. This familiar weed is sometimes used for greens.

Line 9. **Trivial name**. A technical term, signifying the second part of the scientific name, the " specific " name, or that applied to the species, the first part being the "generic," as applied to the genus. *Oleracea* means "partaking of the nature of herbs or vegetables."

Page 69, line 1. **Egyptian his hatching eggs.** From ancient times the Egyptians have hatched eggs artificially. Sir Gardner Wilkinson, in his important work on *The Manners and Customs of the Ancient Egyptians* (edition of 1847), describes at length the method in use in modern Egypt, which he believes to have been handed down from the ancients, and quotes the historian Diodorus (i, 74) : "Dispensing with the incubation of the hens, they with their own hands bring the eggs to maturity ; and the young chickens thus produced are not inferior in any respect to those hatched by natural means."

Line 15. **Spiritus.** Latin for "breath" and also for "spirit." Since it means *both* breath and spirit, it serves Thoreau's purpose better than either of the English words. Why ?

Page 70, lines 8, 9. **Marcus Porcius Cato.** Cato the Censor (B. C. 234–149), a Roman statesman and soldier, author of *De Re Rustica* (Concerning Rural Matters), a book which Thoreau quotes freely in the *Journal*.

Page 71, lines 10–12. **For we can make liquor**, etc. These lines are from a song or piece of verse entitled "New England's Annoyances," written by one of the early settlers and said to be "the oldest known composition in English verse by an American Colonist." "Notes and Queries" in the *Boston Transcript* quotes it in full from *Fugitive Poetry* in the Chandos Classics, and cites a slightly different version in Lewis's *History of Lynn*, quoted by Barber in his *Historical Collections of Massachusetts*. Thoreau probably saw it in Barber and was attracted by the quaint and humorous lines.

Last line. **Squatting.** It was on his friend Emerson's land that he squatted.

Page 72, line 13. **Their thirds.** Their widows' thirds in inheritance.

Page 73, line 9. **Exuviæ.** Things cast off (Latin).

Line 15. **The muskrat will gnaw his third leg off to be free.** In the *Journal*, vol. i, p. 481 (undated), Thoreau quotes from a conversation with a Concord trapper, one George Melvin, the astonishing statement: " 'Oh, the muskrats are the greatest fellows to gnaw their legs off. Why, I caught one once that had just gnawed his third leg off, this being the third time he had been trapped ; and he lay dead by the trap, for he could n't run on one leg.' " Neither Melvin nor Thoreau seems to have offered any explanation of how a muskrat could run on *two* legs, and the story as it stands can hardly be credited. It seems to be an undisputed fact that many animals when caught in steel traps will gnaw off the leg to free themselves, and it is not incredible that one caught a second time might gnaw off the second leg, but beyond that the thing appears to be impossible. The *Journal* goes on to say: "Such tragedies are enacted even in this sphere and along our peaceful streams, and dignify at least the hunter's trade. Only courage does anywhere prolong life, whether of man or beast."

Page 74, line 10 from bottom. **The moon will not sour milk nor taint meat of mine.** Alluding to a current popular superstition.

Page 75, line 3. **" The evil that men do lives after them."** — Shakespeare, *Julius Cæsar*, Act III, Sc. ii, line 80.

Line 8. **Bonfire.** The word was formerly applied to fires for the burning of heretics, proscribed books, etc.

Line 9. **Auction.** The emphasis is on the derivation of the word, from the Latin *auctio*, meaning an increasing, that is of the price by bidding.

Line 21. **Bartram.** William Bartram (1739–1823), an American botanist, son of the botanist John Bartram. The book quoted from is his *Travels through North and South Carolina, Georgia*, etc.

Page 76, lines 15–17. **The Mexicans**, etc. See the account in Prescott's *Conquest of Mexico*, Book i, Chapter iv.

Page 77, line 9. **A good business.** See *Journal*, vol. i, p. 251, April 20, 1841 : " There are certain current expressions and blasphemous moods of viewing things, as when we say ' he is doing a good business,' more profane than cursing and swearing. There is death and sin in such words. Let not the children hear them." This passage was printed with two or three verbal alterations in the first edition of *A Week on the Concord and Merrimack Rivers*, but was omitted from the second edition. The blasphemy, of course, consists in calling a lucrative business a *good* one.

Line 22. **To keep the flocks of Admetus.** Apollo, god of poetry and song, was compelled for nine years to tend the flocks of Admetus, king of Pheræ.

Page 80, line 3 after break. **Philanthropic enterprises.** In spite of a certain impatience with formal charities, Thoreau was by no means uncharitable towards the poor people of Concord with whom he came in contact.

Page 81, line 3 from bottom. **Robin Goodfellow.** The well-disposed but mischievous elf also known as Puck.

Page 82, line 3 from bottom. **Howard.** The famous English philanthropist John Howard (1726?–1790).

Page 84, line 2. **Intra.** Inside (Latin), as *extra* means literally outside.

Page 85, line 5. **Mrs. Fry.** Elizabeth Fry (1780–1845), an Englishwoman who accomplished much in the field of prison-reform.

Lines 20, 21. **Charity that hides a multitude of sins.** See 1 *Peter*, iv, 8.

Page 86, lines 3 and 2 from bottom. **Do not let your left hand**

know what your right hand does. "But when thou doest alms, let not thy left hand know what thy right hand doeth." — *Matthew*, vi, 3.

Page 87, lines 3, 4. **Our manners have been corrupted by communication with the saints.** "Evil communications corrupt good manners." — *1 Corinthians*, xv, 33.

Line 5. **Cursing of God and enduring Him forever.** According to the Westminster Catechism, the chief end of man is "to glorify God and to enjoy him forever."

Line 15. **Indian, botanic, magnetic.** So quacks have been wont to characterize their methods.

Line 22. **Sadi.** A famous Persian poet of the thirteenth century.

Page 89, last line. **T. Carew.** Thomas Carew, an English poet of the early seventeenth century.

Page 91, line 15. **The Hollowell place.** On the Sudbury River, between the Corner road and Nut Meadow Brook.

Page 92, line 3. **Survey.** Thoreau was a surveyor by occupation and a punster on occasion. The lines are quoted from Cowper's "Verses supposed to be written by Alexander Selkirk."

Lines 9–12. **Put his farm in rhyme . . . skimmed milk.** Note the changes in the figures, — from a farm to a cow, from the cow to her milk. Mixed metaphors are usually undesirable, but in this case the things are naturally related together and the effect is rather pleasing than otherwise.

Page 93, line 1. **Atlas.** According to the Greek myth, the Titan who bore the sky upon his shoulders. In art he is sometimes represented as supporting the spherical world.

Page 94, line 2. **As I have said.** See page 2.

Lines 2, 3. **Ode to dejection.** Doubtless alluding to Coleridge's poem so entitled.

Line 19. **A certain house on a mountain.** A saw-miller's house in the Catskills, where he lodged in the summer of 1844. It is described in the *Journal*, vol. i, pp. 361, 362.

Page 95, lines 1, 2. **From hand to hand.** Thoreau sold the boat in which he made his Concord and Merrimack voyage to Nathaniel Hawthorne, who wrote of it in his Journal (published as *American Note-Books*), and later it passed into the hands of William Ellery Channing, poet and friend of Thoreau.

Line 11. **The Harivansa.** A Sanskrit poem, one of the sacred books of the Hindoos. Also spelled Harivansha.

Page 97, line 6. **Keep butter cool.** The well is the old-fashioned country refrigerator.

Line 10 from bottom. **Damodara.** A name given to the divine hero Krishna of the Hindoo mythology. His exploits are related in the Mahabharata.

Page 98, line 4. **Pleiades, Hyades, Aldebaran, Altair.** The first two are constellations, and the last two stars of the first magnitude, Aldebaran being in the constellation of the Hyades.

Lines 21–24. **Characters were engraven,** etc. Commentary of the philosopher Tsang on Confucius' *The Great Learning*, Chapter ii.

Last line, and page 99, line 1. **Singing its own wrath and wandering.** The *Iliad* begins, "Sing, goddess, of the wrath of Achilles, the son of Peleus"; and the *Odyssey*, "Tell me, muse, of the much-travelled man who wandered far."

Page 99, line 2. **Till forbidden.** This phrase, abbreviated "t f," is the printer's sign for a standing advertisement.

Line 8 from bottom. **Transpire.** Is this a good word here?

Line 7 from bottom. **The Vedas.** The early sacred books of India.

Line 4 from bottom. **Memnon.** See note on p. 40.

Page 100, last two lines. **I went to the woods because I wished to live deliberately,** etc. See p. 21. The two statements are not conflicting. There is more than one motive for many human actions.

Page 101, line 6. **Spartan-like.** The ancient Spartans lived a brave, hardy, simple life, to fit themselves for war and the service of the state.

Line 16. **The chief end of man.** From the Westminster Catechism.

Lines 18, 19. **The fable tells us that we were long ago changed into men.** "According to fable, when the island of Ægina was depopulated by sickness, at the instance of Æacus, Jupiter turned the ants into men, that is, as some think, he made men of the inhabitants who lived meanly like ants." — *A Week on the Concord and Merrimack Rivers*, Riverside Edition, p. 72.

Lines 19, 20. **Like pygmies we fight with cranes.** Homer in book iii of the *Iliad* tells of the pygmies and their battles with the cranes.

Line 21. **Clout upon clout.** Patch upon patch. The expression may have been suggested to Thoreau by its use in the song "New England's Annoyances," quoted on p. 71. Speaking of the difficulty of getting new clothing in the Colony, the writer says, —

> "If we get a garment to cover without,
> Our other in-garments are clout upon clout."

Page 102, line 3. **Dead reckoning.** A nautical term which is defined in the dictionaries.

Line 7. **German Confederacy.** The German Confederation, which included Austria, existed from 1815 to 1866, when it was succeeded by the North German Confederation, Austria withdrawing. The present Empire was established in 1871.

Page 103, lines 5, 6. **Riding on a rail**. Note the play upon words.

Lines 22, 23. **Setting the bell**. Turning it till it rests mouth upward just beyond the balancing-point, kept from going farther by the " stop-stay's " coming into contact with the " slider." The next pull of the bell-rope brings it back down again, carries it up the other side, and sets it again there. Each pull of the rope gives the bell a complete revolution beginning and ending mouth upward. This method of ringing is called ringing " high," and it is the one used in calling the congregation to church. The blows of the clapper come more slowly than when the bell is rung " low," that is without setting it, which was the old-fashioned way of giving the fire-alarm. For the above information the editor is indebted to the kindness of Dr. Arthur H. Nichols of Boston, one of the few Americans who are thoroughly conversant with the old English art of bell-ringing.

Page 104, line 12. **Wachito River**. The Washita River, as it is now commonly called, rises in Arkansas and empties into the Red River in Louisiana. " Gouging " is, or was, a barbarous practice of the inhabitants of that region in connection with fighting. It was done by a peculiar turn of the thumb. It has also been practiced in some parts of Europe, as in Norway.

Line 14. **Rudiment of an eye**. Alluding to the blind fishes of the Mammoth Cave of Kentucky.

Page 105, line 7 from bottom. **French Revolution**. " This was written before the last (1848) Revolution broke out ; but a revolution in France might be expected any day ; and it would be as easy to tell where it would end, before it was born, as after it was five years old." — Thoreau's footnote in an early draft of *Walden*, printed by Mr. Sanborn as a note in the Bibliophile edition of the book.

Page 106, line 3. **Come to the end of them**. In his personal copy of *Walden*, now in the possession of Mr. Paul Lemperly of Cleveland, Ohio, Thoreau altered this to " accomplish it."

Page 107, line 18. **Mill-dam**. This was the spot in the centre of the village of Concord where the inhabitants congregated to gossip.

Page 108, line 12 from bottom. **Tied to the mast like Ulysses**. Ulysses, it will be remembered, had his sailors tie him to the mast in passing the Sirens, while their ears were stopped to prevent their hearing the fatal song.

Line 2 from bottom. **In place**. In their original positions ; a geological term.

Page 112, line 11. **Delphi and Dodona**. The two principal oracles of the Greeks were at the temple of Apollo at Delphi in Phocis and at the temple of Zeus at Dodona in Epirus.

Line 16. **The athletes.** That is, the athletes of ancient Greece, who underwent very severe training.

Line 2 from bottom. **Born again.** See *John*, iii, 3.

Page 114, line 1. **Alexander carried the Iliad with him.** He is also said to have slept nightly with the *Iliad* and his sword under his pillow.

Page 115, line 11. **Homer has never yet been printed in English.** That is, the true spirit of the old Greek poet cannot be adequately expressed in English or in any other modern language.

Line 8 from bottom. **The Vaticans.** The Vatican, the Papal palace in Rome, contains a large library. Thoreau is looking forward to the time when all such libraries shall be filled full with the great religious and poetical works of the world and of all ages.

Line 7 from bottom. **Zendavestas.** The Zend-Avesta is the bible of Zoroastrianism, a religion of Persia and India.

Page 116, line 9. **What we have to stand on tip-toe to read.** That which cannot be read without making an effort, and reaching up to it.

Line 14. **The lowest and foremost form.** In the old district schools the youngest children sat on a low form, or bench, in front.

Line 3 from bottom. **The course of their true love.** "The course of true love never did run smooth." — *A Midsummer-Night's Dream*, Act I, Sc. i, line 134.

Page 117, line 14. **To appear in monthly parts.** This method of publication obtained to some extent in the middle of the last century, and was particularly adapted to the long novels in vogue in those days. The novels were issued thus separately, not as serials in magazines.

Line 17. **Corrugations.** The gizzards, or principal stomachs, of fowls and all seed-eating birds are provided with muscular, corrugated walls.

Page 118, line 8. **Woodchopper.** This man's characteristics are described at some length on pp. 159–166. His name was Alek Therien, and he appears again and again in the *Journal*.

Page 119, line 7 from bottom. **Tit-men.** Little men, pygmies. The word seems to have been original with Thoreau. He used it also in *A Week on the Concord and Merrimack Rivers*, Riverside Edition, p. 503, and in the *Journal*, vol. i, p. 373. The word "tit" apparently meant originally something small. It is now chiefly used in such compounds as "titmouse" and "titlark."

Page 121, line 1. **Lyceum.** The Lyceum in Concord was an organization which provided lectures and lecture-courses by various persons in a central hall. Thoreau was actively interested in it. Lectures were very popular in New England in the middle of the last century, and were an important element in the culture of communities. Every considerable town had its lyceum. The original Lyceum in Athens was a gymnasium near the temple of Apollo Lycius, where Aristotle walked, and taught his philosophy.

Line 14. **Abélard.** Pierre Abélard (1079–1142), a celebrated French theologian and philosopher.

Line 22. **Utopian.** Sir Thomas More's (1478–1535) *Utopia* is a book describing an imaginary island and the ideal social state existing upon it. Hence "Utopian" means ideal but impracticable.

Page 122, line 6. **Olive-Branches.** The *Olive Branch* was a Methodist weekly published in Boston for a number of years beginning with 1836.

Line 9. **Harper & Brothers and Redding & Co.** The old New York publishing house of Harper & Bros. is still in active business. George W. Redding & Co. were booksellers at No. 8 State St., Boston.

Page 123, last line but one. **Bath.** That is, in the pond. That is why Thoreau makes a point of mentioning it. The daily bath was not in those days the universal custom that it has since become.

Page 124, line 6. **Corn in the night.** On warm summer nights the Indian corn is said to grow so rapidly that the process can be heard.

Line 22. **The Puri Indians.** A Brazilian tribe, of a very low order of social development.

Page 127, line 7. **Tantivy.** A hunting-cry indicating that the chase is at full speed, supposed to be imitative of the sound of the hunting-horn. The accent is on the second syllable, — tan-tiv′y. The word is here used figuratively, of course, but it is not necessary to assume that its meaning is otherwise different from the original one. See also p. 177, last line.

Line 14. **Reed-birds.** Thoreau probably used the word indefinitely to indicate any small birds among the sedges and reeds. The reed-bird of the Middle States is the bobolink of New England, and Thoreau knew it only by the latter name.

Lines 16, 17. **The beat of a partridge.** The drum of the ruffed grouse, almost invariably called partridge in New England.

Verse. **"In truth, our village has become a butt,"** etc. From a poem entitled "Walden Spring," by Thoreau's friend William Ellery Channing, second of the name. It was printed in *The Woodman, and other Poems* (1848).

Page 128, lines 9 and 8 from bottom. **Indian huckleberry hills.** The hills where the Indians formerly gathered huckleberries. Thoreau sometimes used the word huckleberries to include blueberries.

Page 129, lines 6, 7. **Cloud-compeller.** A name for the god Zeus, or Jupiter.

Page 130, lines 23, 24. **Dismal Swamp.** The name is used generically; no particular swamp is referred to.

Page 131, line 11. **Atropos.** One of the Parcæ. The Fate who cut the thread of man's life. See note on p. 28.

Lines 17, 18. **Sons of Tell.** The allusion, of course, is to the legend of William Tell shooting the apple from his son's head.

Line 4 from bottom. **Buena Vista.** In the Battle of Buena Vista, fought Feb. 22 and 23, 1847, the Americans won a victory over the Mexicans in the face of great odds.

Last line. **Three-o'clock-in-the-morning courage.** Thoreau's memory was at fault as to the precise hour in the morning named by Napoleon. " As to moral courage, he had found very rare, he said, that of two hours after midnight, that is to say the courage of the unprepared . . . he had found that he himself possessed the courage of two hours after midnight in the greatest degree." — *Mémorial de Ste.-Hélène,* by Las Cases.

Page 132, line 4. **Great Snow.** Probably no particular storm is referred to. There was a " Great Snow " in 1717 and another in 1780, and very likely still other snowstorms have been so called.

Line 12. **Daisies and the nests of field mice.** Thoreau is alluding to Robert Burns's ploughshare and his poems " To a Mountain Daisy " and " To a Mouse."

Line 11 from bottom. **Long Wharf.** In Boston.

Line 7 from bottom. **Palm-leaf.** The making of hats from palmleaves was formerly a Massachusetts industry. These hats, such as the Panama hat, are now made in the countries where the palms grow, and where labor is much cheaper than in this country.

Line 5 from bottom. **Cocoanut husks.** The fibre of the husk is called coir, and is used in making door-mats and matting.

Page 133, line 6. **Cedar.** The "cedar" of the Maine woods is the arbor-vitæ (*Thuya occidentalis*). Its wood is used for fence-posts, railroad-ties, etc., and it is grown largely for hedges and ornamental purposes.

Line 8. **Thomaston lime.** Lime from Thomaston, Maine.

Line 13. **Milwaukee.** At the time when Thoreau was writing, Milwaukee was a young and rapidly growing city, fast filling up with immigrants from Germany.

Page 135, lines 3, 4. " **To be the mast,**" etc. — Milton, *Paradise Lost,* book i, lines 293, 294.

Lines 5, 6. **Cattle of a thousand hills.** " The cattle upon a thousand hills." — *Psalm* l, 10.

Lines 13, 14. **The mountains . . . skip like rams and the little hills like lambs.** See *Psalm* cxiv, 4.

Line 20. **The Peterboro' Hills**. In southern New Hampshire. They form Concord's northwest horizon.

Page 136, line 5. **I cross it like a cart-path**. He finally came to realize its possibilities as a *footpath*, however ! " The railroad is perhaps our pleasantest and wildest road." — *Journal*, vol. iii, p. 342.

Page 137, lines 5, 6. **In the horizon**. Thoreau habitually used this somewhat antiquated form instead of the more common " *on* the horizon."

Page 138, line 4. **U-lu-lu**. The word seems to have been adapted by Thoreau from the Latin *ululo*, to howl, to utter a mournful cry. *Ulula* was the Latin name for a species of owl. The word is translated "screech owl," but the bird was not nearly related to our American screech owl, unhappily so named.

Line 5. **Ben Jonsonian**. In thus alluding to Ben Jonson it seems probable that Thoreau had in mind the witches' scene in Jonson's " Masque of Queens," in which the hags inform their dame of the various grewsome things they have gathered to go into their cauldron.

Line 11 from bottom. **Bor-r-r-n**. This is intended to suggest a quaver on the vowel, not a trill of the *r*. The *Journal* (vol. i, p. 379) with " bor-or-or-or-orn " perhaps indicates the sound more nearly, the *r*, of course, after the New England fashion, not being pronounced itself, but simply governing the sound of the *o*.

Line 5 from bottom. **A hooting owl**. See note on " cat owl," p. 300.

Page 139, line 12 from bottom. **Single spruce**. In his own copy of *Walden*, Thoreau corrected this to " double spruce," which is an old name for the black spruce, the common spruce of the New England *swamps*, and the only species found in the neighborhood of Concord. The " single," or white, spruce is more northerly in its range, but is found on the Maine coast and in the forests of northern New England. The common spruce of northern New England, however, and ranging much farther south than the white, is the red spruce, a tree which in Thoreau's time was not distinguished from the black spruce. The significance of the words " single " and " double " as applied to the white and black spruces is not at all clear.

Page 140, line 2. **Stygian**. The river Styx in Grecian mythology flowed around Hades, the world of the dead. Hence Stygian means "of Hades," " of the lower world."

Line 11. **Aldermanic**. The traditional alderman is a corpulent person, especially as to the paunch. Green turtle and other rich and expensive foods are said to be responsible for this.

Line 12. **Heart-leaf.** The floating-heart (*Nymphoides lacunosum*).

Line 19. **Down to his mark.** In drinking-bouts it was customary to pass round a large cup with marks on the inside to indicate how much each man was expected to drink.

Line 6 from bottom. **Under the pond.** As one would say " under the table."

Page 141, line 16. **Healthy, wealthy, and wise.**

> " Early to bed and early to rise
> Makes a man healthy, wealthy, and wise."
> BENJAMIN FRANKLIN, *Poor Richard's Almanack.*

Page 142, line 4. **Cat owl.** A name for the great horned owl (*Bubo virginianus*), the face of which, with its large " horns," or " ears," bears some resemblance to that of a cat.

Line 5. **Laughing loon.** A common note of the loon resembles wild, demoniac laughter.

Line 6. **Lark.** That is, a meadowlark.

Page 145, line 8. **"The world to darkness and to me."** From Gray's " Elegy in a Country Churchyard."

Line 11. **Hung.** "Hanged" is the form preferred in this sense, but Thoreau, like most good writers, did not always bind himself by the rules which lesser men have to follow.

Line 17. **Black melancholy.** The word " melancholy " is from two Greek words signifying " black bile," an imaginary secretion which the ancient and mediæval physiologists supposed to be the cause of melancholy.

Line 19. **Æolian music.** Æolus was the Greek god of the winds. An æolian harp is an instrument provided with strings for the wind to play upon.

Page 146, verse. **"Mourning untimely consumes the sad,"** etc. From a metrical version of James Macpherson's prose " translation " of the Gaelic poem " Croma," by Ossian. It is now generally believed that Ossian was only a legendary character, and that the poems which Macpherson pretended to have translated were inventions of his own.

Page 147, line 13 from bottom. **Men frequently say to me.** In transcribing this and the following sentence from his Journal, where doubtless he first wrote them, Thoreau seems to have neglected to change the tense.

Page 148, line 4. **Beacon Hill.** The Massachusetts State House, where the legislature meets, occupies the summit of Beacon Hill in Boston. In Thoreau's day the most aristocratic residential section of Boston was also on Beacon Hill, and perhaps Thoreau coupled it with the Five Points for the sake of the contrast.

The Five Points. A down-town section of New York, formerly famed as the most evil part of the city, but now invaded by business. It was so named on account of an intersection of streets forming five points, the name becoming extended to cover a considerable district.

Line 12. **A fair view**. The man's property, accumulated and kept by sordid labor, did not appear fair, or beautiful, to Thoreau.

Line 18. **Brighton**. A town near Boston and now a part of that city. It was the seat of the cattle-market and abattoir.

Line 19. **Bright-town**. " Bright " is a favorite name for oxen.

Page 149, line 8 from bottom. **Indra**. One of the chief gods of the Hindoo mythology. He was the head of the gods of the air.

Page 152, line 7. **Mock sun**. A parhelion, or sun-dog.

Line 9. **Legion**. Alluding, of course, to the devils which Jesus cast out from the man with an unclean spirit in the country of the Gadarenes. " And he asked him, What is thy name ? And he answered, saying, My name is Legion : for we are many." — *Mark*, v, 9.

Line 12. **The Mill Brook**. A brook flowing through the village of Concord.

Lines 24, 25. **Goffe** and **Whalley** were two of the " regicides " under indictment for the killing of King Charles I. They lay in hiding in the neighborhood of New Haven, Conn., and later near Hadley, Mass.

Line 25. **He is thought to be dead**. The " old settler and original proprietor " was probably Pan, the Greek god of flocks and shepherds, pastures and forests, whose dominion has been extended by some later writers to include all nature, on account of the identity of his name in the nominative case with πάν, *pan*, the neuter gender of the Greek adjective πάς, *pas*, meaning all. The familiar words " The great god Pan is dead " come from Plutarch's essay on " Why the Oracles cease to give Answers," wherein a story is told of a great voice having been heard out of the sea addressing a sailor on board ship and saying, " When you are arrived at Palodes, take care to make it known that the great god Pan is dead " (Dr. Robert Midgley's translation). " Pan is dead " forms the refrain to Mrs. Browning's poem " The Dead Pan."

Line 26. **An elderly dame**. Doubtless Dame Nature.

Page 153, line 11 from bottom. **Old Parrs**. Thomas Parr, who died in London in 1635, was called " Old Parr." He was said to have been born in 1483, which would make his age 152 years at the time of his death.

Line 8 from bottom. **Acheron**. A river in Hades.

Page 154, line 4. **Hygeia**. The Greek goddess of health.

Line 5. **Æsculapius**. The Greek god of physicians and healing.

Line 9. **Daughter of Juno and wild lettuce**. Homer calls

Hebe the daughter of Jupiter and Juno, that is of Zeus and Hera, but, according to other accounts, her birth was the result of her mother, Juno, having eaten heartily of wild lettuce at a banquet given by Jupiter. (*Bell's New Pantheon*, J. Bell, London, 1790.)

Page 155, line 2 from bottom. **Tremont or Astor or Middlesex House.** The Tremont House was in Boston, the Astor House in New York, and the Middlesex House in Concord.

Page 156, line 1. **Ridiculous mouse.** The allusion is to the Latin fable of the mountain in labor and the birth of the *ridiculus mus.*

Line 13. **Form their columns.** As in military operations.

Page 157, lines 8, 9. **On whose carpet the sun rarely fell.** It was the custom in the country to keep the " best " room, or parlor, closed most of the time, with the shades drawn to prevent the carpet from fading. The room was reserved for the most important occasions, such as funerals and weddings.

Page 158, line 3. **Cerberus.** The three-headed dog guarding the entrance to Hades.

Lines 7, 8. **Lines of Spenser.** The lines quoted are from Edmund Spenser's *The Faerie Queene*, book i, Canto i, stanza 35.

Line 1 after verse. **Winslow.** Edward Winslow (1595–1655). The narrative from which Thoreau quotes is given in full in Alexander Young's *Chronicles of the Pilgrim Fathers of the Colony of Plymouth* (Boston, 1841).

Page 159, line 3 from bottom. **Homeric or Paphlagonian man.** This man, Therien, has been referred to before. See note to p. 118. In the Trojan War the Paphlagonians came to the assistance of the Trojans from their country on the shores of the Black Sea. The Bibliophile Society's edition of *Walden* prints a note of Thoreau's from his manuscript: " Aleck Therien, he calls himself — (Terrien, — Alexander the Farmer)." This explains the characterization of the name as " suitable and poetic," *terrien* being French for " landowner." In the man's native French, " Therien " would be practically equivalent in pronunciation to " Terrien "; but, in Concord, as the editor learns from Dr. E. W. Emerson, the name was pronounced as if it were English, — Thē′rĭ-ĕn.

Page 160, lines 10–15. **" Why are you in tears,"** etc. *Iliad*, beginning of book xvi.

Lines 16, 17. **White oak bark . . . for a sick man.** White oak bark is a powerful astringent, and is used in medicine both externally and internally to a limited extent.

Page 161, lines 9–11. **He wasn't a-going . . . earned his board.** An indirect quotation.

Line 18. **How thick the pigeons are!** The wild pigeons,

which are now suspected to be extinct, were common in Concord in Thoreau's time.

Page 163, line 12. **He had got to.** "He" evidently refers to the neighbor. In the next sentence "he" is the woodchopper.

Page 165, line 8. **Pecunia.** Whence "pecuniary"; the Latin word for money, from *pecus*, cattle.

Page 167, lines 4, 5. **Offering to lend them a dipper.** One Sunday, as we learn from his *Journal* (vol. iii, p. 198), he lent his dipper to two young women who came asking for water, but they failed to return it, and he indulges in some playful anathemas upon them. "They will never know peace till they have returned the dipper. In all the worlds this is decreed."

Line 7 from bottom. **Inferior.** One of Thoreau's plays upon words. The point is that, humility being lowliness, anything exceeding it must be lower still.

Page 169, lines 11, 12. **I have too good a memory to make that necessary.** "As if it were of any use, when a man failed to make any memorable impression on you, for him to leave his name. . . . No! I kept a book to put their fames in." — *Journal*, vol. iii, pp. 215, 216.

Page 170, line 8. **Com-munity, a league for mutual defence.** Thoreau is supposing a derivation of the word "community" from the Latin *munio*, to defend, with the prefix *com-*, signifying together, rather than from *communitas*, the real original of the word. *Communitas* comes from *communis*, common, general, from *com-* and the root *mu*, to bind.

Line 17. **This is the home that I built.** The allusion here is apparent to any one familiar with nursery rhymes.

Line 22. **Hen-harriers.** Hen-harrier is an old name for the marsh hawk. It comes from England, where it is applied to a similar species of hawk. The name is inappropriate, as applied to our bird at least, for the marsh hawk seldom disturbs poultry.

Line 2 from bottom. "**Welcome, Englishmen!**" The words with which the Indian Samoset greeted the Pilgrims at Plymouth.

Page 171, line 10. **Antæus.** A giant, son of Earth. Whenever he fell to the ground, he arose again with renewed strength. Hercules killed him by holding him up away from contact with the earth, his mother.

Line 13. **Johnswort.** St. John's-wort, one species of which, *Hypericum perforatum*, is a familiar yellow flower of the summer fields.

Page 172, line 4. **Brought from Boston.** Thoreau's father removed his family from Concord to Chelmsford in October, 1818, and thence, in March, 1821, to Boston, where they lived about two years, returning to Concord in 1823.

Line 7. **My flute.** The flute was Thoreau's only musical instrument, — except a music-box, which he prized highly. Miss Louisa M. Alcott, the story-writer, who knew Thoreau, wrote a poem on " Thoreau's Flute " after his death.

Line 11 from bottom. **Arrowheads.** Thoreau had a remarkable faculty for finding these. His friend the poet Channing says that a companion on a walk once remarked to him, " I do not see where you find your Indian arrowheads," whereupon, " stooping to the ground, Henry picked one up, and presented it to him, crying, 'Here is one.' " His collection of Indian implements was deposited in the Peabody Museum, Cambridge, Mass.

Page 173, line 14. **Wormwood.** Doubtless the Roman wormwood, so called, or ragweed (*Ambrosia artemisiæfolia*), is referred to.

Lines 14, 15. **Piper and millet grass.** " Piper-grass " is a name for the couch-grass, quitch-grass, or witch-grass (*Agropyron repens*), a very troublesome weed. The name is commonly used in Concord, and perhaps elsewhere, but appears not to have found its way into the books. Miss Jane Hosmer, of Concord, has kindly identified this plant for the editor. As to the millet grass, we learn from Thoreau's *Journal* (Aug. 25, 1858) that he had given that name to two species of grass, *Setaria glauca* and *Setaria viridis*.

Page 174, line 4. **The ministerial husbandman.** He is probably alluding to some passing minister who made the exclamation.

Line 5. " **Corn, my boy, for fodder.**" The reply of the minister's companion.

Line 8. **Grateful dobbin.** Dobbin is, or was, a favorite name for a farm horse. Dobbin was grateful for any stop that gave him a brief rest.

Line 17. **Mr. Colman.** Rev. Henry Colman (1785–1849), who devoted himself for many years to the study of agriculture and rural economy. He was State Commissioner for the Agricultural Survey of Massachusetts.

Line 20. **English hay.** The various species of grass grown for the fodder hay crop in New England and elsewhere in the United States are not native, but introduced from Europe. The hay is called English hay to distinguish it from the meadow hay harvested for bedding.

Last two lines. **Ranz des Vaches.** The air played or sung by the Swiss herdsmen to call their cattle. It varies in the different cantons of Switzerland.

Page 175, line 9. **Paganini.** Niccolò Paganini (1784–1840) was a celebrated Italian violinist, who could play astonishingly upon a single string.

Line 10 from bottom, **Music.** Thoreau had a deep feeling for music, which to him was perhaps another name for poetry. He heard it in many natural sounds, as we have seen in a previous chapter, and the wind over the telegraph-wire excited him almost to rhapsody and " reminded him of Anacreon." He heard it, too, in a hand-organ, but he knew nothing of the more elaborate expressions of musical art, and such things as oratorios had no particular attractions for him.

Page 176, line 1. **A sound as if the heavens were rent.** The sudden swoops or dives in which the nighthawk indulges during the breeding-season are accompanied by a loud booming sound probably made by the wings.

Line 8. **The hawk.** The nighthawk, however, as Thoreau well knew, is not a hawk at all, but a species of goatsucker.

Page 177, line 4. " **Trainers.**" Concord had a drill-ground, or " training "-ground, for the militia.

Line 7. **Tintinnabulum.** Virgil's word in the passage alluded to, which is to be found in the Fourth Book of the *Georgics*, is *tinnitus*, jingling. *Tintinnabulum* is the word for a bell.

Line 7 from bottom. **Spit a Mexican.** This was the time of the Mexican War.

Last line. **Tantivy.** See note on p. 127, l. 7.

Page 178, line 10. **Know beans.** A familiar phrase in New England, most commonly used in the negative. Of an ignorant person, or one comparatively ignorant, it is said, " He does n't know beans."

Line 3 from bottom. **Hector.** The Trojan hero in the *Iliad*. He wore a plumed helmet.

Page 179, line 6. **A Pythagorean.** A follower of Pythagoras, the famous Greek philosopher of the sixth century B. C. He is said to have prohibited the eating of beans, as well as of meat and fish, by his disciples, but there is some doubt as to the universality of these prohibitions.

Line 8. **Voting.** Beans were used in voting by the ancient Greeks and Romans.

Line 16. **Lætation.** Manuring or manure. The word occurs frequently in Evelyn and is perhaps confined to him.

Line 17. **Repastination.** Digging over again.

Lines 26, 27. **Sir Kenelm Digby.** An English diplomatist, philosopher, and author, who was born in 1603 and died in 1665. He dabbled extensively in the occult sciences, and was also in some measure a serious student of natural phenomena. Among his books is *A Discourse concerning the Vegetation of Plants.*

Page 180, line 7. **Crow fence**. A white string surrounding a field, for use as a scarecrow.

Lines 11, 12. **Patremfamilias . . . oportet.** "A householder must be a seller, not a buyer." From Cato's *De Re Rustica*.

Line 8 from bottom. **Plant the common small white bush bean**, etc. Thoreau here writes half in fun, half in earnest, after the style of the agricultural journals.

Page 182, line 7. **Our ambassadors**, etc. It is one of the duties of our consuls to send home to Washington such seeds as may be expected to be of value to our farmers. Formerly Congress distributed seeds, but this work is now done by the Agricultural Department.

Page 183, line 7. **Ceres.** The Roman goddess of agriculture.

The Terrestrial Jove. So called to distinguish him from Pluto, the Infernal Jove.

Line 8. **Plutus.** The god of wealth. He is not to be confused with Pluto, and he had no connection in mythology with the infernal regions. The adjective "infernal" which Thoreau joins to him is perhaps a slip in his usually accurate classical lore.

Line 15. **Varro.** Marcus Terentius Varro Reatinus (B. C. 116–28), author of a *De Re Rustica* and many other books.

Page 184, lines 3–6. **The ear of wheat**, etc. Thoreau got his etymology from Varro. See the Journal entry for Jan. 29, 1854.

Page 185, line 2 from bottom. **Redding & Company's**. George W. Redding & Co. kept a "newspaper depot" at No. 8 State St., Boston, in the thirties and a "periodical depot" there in the forties, and when Thoreau published *Walden* they were booksellers on State St. and tea-dealers on Washington St.

Page 186, line 5. **Etesian winds.** The name given by Greek and Latin writers to the northerly winds that blow regularly in the summer season over the Ægean Sea and the eastern Mediterranean. The regularity of these winds is doubtless the quality that Thoreau had in mind in using the figure.

Line 6 from bottom. **Lick**. A colloquial word which has the sanction of old and good usage.

Page 187, line 2. **Window tax.** A tax was formerly levied in England on the windows of houses. The words as applied to Concord are not to be taken literally.

Line 14. **Orpheus.** According to legend, the earliest Greek poet and a son of Apollo. He sailed as one of the Argonauts in search of the Golden Fleece, and in passing the Sirens saved himself and his companions in the manner described.

Page 188, line 4. **"As I sailed."** This is the refrain of the grim old ballad of Captain Kidd, which is really not at all suggestive of "genial thoughts."

Page 190, lines 7, 8. **As I have elsewhere related.** In an essay entitled " Resistance to Civil Government," printed in a volume entitled *Æsthetic Papers*, edited by Elizabeth P. Peabody and published by her at Boston in 1849. The essay, which was probably originally delivered as a lecture, is included among Thoreau's *Miscellanies* under the title of " Civil Disobedience." The incident is characteristic of his independence of spirit.

Line 16. **Amok.** Usually spelled "amuck."

Lines 26, 27. **A fortnight in the woods of Maine.** " Ktaadn " in *The Maine Woods* is the narrative of this excursion.

Page 191, line 6. **A soldier of our camp.** That is, one of our friends, some one who would appreciate the book.

Verse. **Nec bella fuerunt**, etc. From the Elegies of Tibullus, book i, Elegy 10, lines 7, 8.

Last five lines, "**You . . . bends.**" — Analects of Confucius, Book xii, Chapter xix.

Page 192, lines 4, 5. **"To fresh woods and pastures new."** From Milton's *Lycidas*.

Line 7. **Fair Haven Hill.** A hill overlooking Fair Haven Pond on the Sudbury River about half a mile from Walden Pond.

Line 12. **Cow-boy.** The farm boy who drives the cows to and from pasture; not the " cow-puncher " of the West.

Line 17. **The bloom.** It is evident that Thoreau is using the term huckleberry here to include the marketable blueberries. The true huckleberry, which is seldom sent to market, has no bloom in its common black form.

Page 193, line 3. **Cœnobites.** A cœnobite is a member of any religious community; a monk living in a monastery as opposed to a hermit or anchorite. This is another of Thoreau's puns: the unsuccessful fisherman could *see no bites*.

Page 195, lines 6–4 from bottom. **The sea, however, is said to be blue one day and green another without any perceptible change in the atmosphere.** The reader will find the color of the sea treated rather exhaustively from the æsthetic point of view in Mr. John C. Van Dyke's *The Opal Sea* (New York, 1906).

Page 197, line 18. **Studies of a Michael Angelo.** Michael Angelo's figures often show an overdevelopment of muscle.

Page 198, lines 6–12. **Making another hole . . . axe out again.** An instance of Thoreau's practical ingenuity.

Line 19. **Some think it is bottomless.** See p. 315.

Line 25. **Heart-leaves.** See note on p. 140, l. 12.

Line 26. **Water-target.** The water-shield (*Brasenia peltata*), an aquatic plant with floating peltate leaves and jelly-covered stems.

Page 199, line 5. **Nine Acre Corner.** A small village in the southern part of Concord.

Line 17. **The fall**. That is, the fall of man.

Line 22. **Who knows**, etc. A mere fancy of Thoreau's. It is hardly to be believed that he expected to be taken literally.

Lines 23, 24. **Castalian Fountain**. A spring on the slopes of Mt. Parnassus in Greece, sacred to Apollo and the Muses.

Page 201, line 13. **Flint's Pond**. Also called Sandy Pond; in the town of Lincoln. See p. 216.

Page 202, line 16. **Tradition**. Thoreau made a note to this passage in his own copy of *Walden* as follows: "This is told of Alexander's Lake, Killingly, Ct., by Barber. Vide his *Connecticut Historical Collections*."

Line 2 from bottom. **Settler whom I have mentioned**. On p. 152.

Last line. **Divining-rod**. A forked stick of witch-hazel or other tree or shrub, with which certain persons were supposed to discover the presence of water underground. The branch was grasped by the two forks and carried about in a horizontal position until the end turned down and pointed towards the ground. The spot where this happened was the place where the well must be dug.

Page 203, line 11. **The paver**. The glacier which during the glacial period brought the boulders and drift from a distance and deposited them here.

Line 12. **Saffron Walden**. A borough in the County of Essex, about forty miles from London. Thoreau got the name from Evelyn's Diary, as we learn from a note in his private copy of *Walden*.

Line 5 from bottom. **Boiling Spring**. A spring about half a mile from Thoreau's hut. A "boiling spring" in New England is one in which the water can be seen coming up through the sandy bottom, giving the sand a boiling appearance. The term has no reference to the temperature of the water.

Page 204, line 16. **Chivins or roach**. The fish which Thoreau called chivin is the common American chub, now known to science as *Semotilus bullaris*.

Line 17. **A very few breams**. "Bream" is a name for the fresh-water sunfish, or "pumpkin-seed." The true bream is a European fish not found in this country. Thoreau had a note here in his personal copy of the book, reading, "*Pomotis obesus* (Nov. 26, 1858); one trout weighing a little over 5 lbs. (*vide* Nov. 14, 1857)." The references are to his Journal, where we find that he discovered some small "breams" in Walden on the date first mentioned, which were pronounced by Mr. F. W. Putnam at a meeting of the Boston Society of Natural History to be *Pomotis* (or *Bryttus*) *obesus*,[1] also that the trout was speared early in November, 1857, by a man who

[1] Now called *Enneacanthus obesus*.

also "saw another not quite so large." Thoreau frequently sent specimens of one kind or another to the Boston Society of Natural History, which still exhibits in its museum some very well preserved birds'-nests contributed by him.

Line 20. **The only eels I have heard of here.** The presence of eels in a pond without visible outlet is particularly interesting because eels spawn only in the sea, and are dependent upon a free passage up and down the rivers and brooks.

Page 205, line 4. **Reticulatus.** Marked like a net. *Esox reticulatus* is the scientific name of the pond pickerel.

Line 5. **Guttatus.** Spotted.

Lines 13, 14. **Mussels.** Freshwater clams (*Unio*).

Line 15. **Mud-turtle.** Thoreau's name for the snapping turtle (*Chelonura serpentina*).

Line 20. **Hirundo bicolor.** Now called *Iridoprocne bicolor*, and commonly known as the tree swallow in the vernacular.

Line 21. **Totanus macularius.** The name now in use is *Actitis macularia*. The bird is the spotted sandpiper, the common tip-up or teeter-tail of our shores and inland streams. In his own copy of the book Thoreau inserted "kingfishers dart away from its coves," before "and the peetweets."

Line 8 from bottom. **Fair Haven.** Fairhaven Pond, or Fairhaven Bay, is a widening of the Sudbury River in Concord, about three quarters of a mile from Walden Pond.

Page 206, line 8. **Perhaps they are the nests of the chivin.** Thoreau was right in this conjecture, though he apparently never satisfied himself fully in regard to the origin of these stone-heaps. They are built by the chivin, or chub (*Semotilus bullaris*). An account of this fish and its nest-building habits will be found in a paper on *The Fishes of the Connecticut Lakes and Neighboring Waters*, by W. C. Kendall and E. L. Goldsborough, published as Document No. 633 of the United States Bureau of Fisheries.

Page 207, line 9. **When you invert your head.** This method of viewing the landscape was a favorite recreation of Thoreau's. Every one who has tried it knows how much more beautiful and picturesque the landscape appears when so seen than when viewed in the ordinary way. Several theories to account for this have been advanced, and Thoreau, as his Journal shows, puzzled over the phenomenon a good deal, but never settled the matter satisfactorily.

Page 208, line 5. **Boom.** Like a logger's boom.

Line 14. **Water-bug.** Of the kind commonly called lucky-bugs, or whirligig beetles.

Page 210, line 4. **We shall, perhaps, look down,** etc. That is, after death.

Page 211, line 13. **One.** This use of the word, for "some one," is common with Thoreau, one of the somewhat antiquated forms of speech which are so characteristic of his dignified style. Note that this is not the impersonal " one."

Page 212, line 8. **He did not know whose it was ; it belonged to the pond.** One of those concealed indirect quotations of which Thoreau was fond. The old man said, " I don't know whose it was," and then added, humorously, " It belonged to the pond."

Page 213, last six lines. **The villagers,** etc. This plan of taking water from Walden for the use of the town of Concord was abandoned, and Sandy Pond was drawn upon for the purpose, though not till some years after Thoreau's death.

Page 214, line 4. **Trojan horse.** The Trojan horse was a huge wooden horse filled with soldiers, by means of which the Greeks finally captured Troy.

Line 6. **Moore of Moore Hall.** The knight who, according to a satirical old ballad, slew the Dragon of Wantley.

Line 3 from bottom. **In whom there was no guile.** " Jesus saw Nathanael coming to him, and saith of him, Behold an Israelite indeed, in whom is no guile ! " — *John*, i, 47.

Page 215, line 3, 4. **It is no dream of mine,**
         To ornament a line.

That is, the Walden he is telling about is not a mere dream, used for literary purposes only. In the draft of *Walden* printed by the Bibliophile Society, these lines are preceded by —

     " It is a real place, —
       (Boston, I tell it to your face.")

The whole poem — if such it may be called — is a somewhat mystical identification of himself with the place which he had made so peculiarly his own.

Lines 7, 8 after verse. **State Street.** Then as now the " Wall Street " of Boston, the street of the bankers and stock-brokers.

Page 216, lines 3, 4. **Waste its sweetness in the ocean wave.**

     " Full many a flower is born to blush unseen,
       And waste its sweetness on the desert air."
               GRAY's " Elegy in a Country Churchyard."

Line 10 from bottom. **Pad.** A lily-pad, the leaf of the water-lily.

Page 217, line 2. **Curious balls.** The reader who is interested to learn more of these balls, which are not so very uncommon on sea-beaches and the shores of ponds, is referred to two papers " On Balls of Vegetable Matter from Sandy Shores," by W. F. Ganong, in the botanical journal *Rhodora* (Boston), for March, 1905, and August, 1909.

Line 17. **The unclean and stupid farmer.** No particular farmer is referred to, of course. It is improbable that Thoreau knew what particular Flint had given his name to the pond. He is simply venting his indignation against a cheap and easy way of naming the features of the landscape which is too common in America, though now less so than formerly. In so characterizing a stranger who doubtless lived and died many years before, he takes perhaps a rather dangerous liberty.

Line 25. **So it is not named for me.** That is, so far as I am concerned, it shall not bear the name of such a man.

Page 218, lines 11, 12. **Privilege.** The allusion is to the "mill privilege" or "water privilege," granted to an individual by the community, whereby he is at liberty to use the water of a stream to run his mill or for other private purposes.

Page 219, line 3. **Icarian Sea.** A part of the Ægean, where Icarus was fabled to have fallen to his death on flying too near the sun.

Line 5 after blank. **Lake country.** The Lake Country of England, in Cumberland and Westmoreland, is famous for its literary associations.

Line 6 after blank. **Water privileges.** The term here refers, not to the right to use water, but to the water itself. It is very commonly so used in this country.

Page 220, line 1. **Pitch pine.** Mr. Charles Sprague Sargent, the leading authority on North American trees, recognizes only one form of this species.

Page 221, line 14. **White lily.** The white water-lily.

Lines 27, 28. **The diamond of Kohinoor.** One of the largest and most valuable diamonds in the world, the property of the British Crown. It is supposed to have been found in India before the Christian era, and it has had an eventful history, passing through the hands of many Indian princes before it was acquired for Queen Victoria in 1850. Koh-i-nur, as it is more properly written, is the name of the stone itself, and means "mountain of light." It is, therefore, not entirely accurate to speak of the diamond *of* Kohinoor.

Page 223, line 7. **Valhalla.** The abode of the Norse gods.

Line 8. **Creeping juniper.** It is not the true creeping juniper (*Juniperus horizontalis*) that Thoreau refers to, but what is known as the common juniper (*Juniperus communis*, var. *depressa*), which grows in spreading circular patches in pasture-lands.

Line 10. **White spruce.** For "white" read "black" See note on p. 139. Thoreau changed it to "black" in his own personal copy.

Line 13. **Swamp-pink.** White azalea.

Line 14. **Dogwood.** The flowering dogwood (*Cornus florida*) is doubtless referred to.

Red alder berry. The red berry of the so-called black alder, or winterberry, which is not an alder at all, but a species of holly, *Ilex verticillata.*

Line 15. **Waxwork.** The Roxbury waxwork, or bittersweet.

Line 16. **Wild holly.** *Nemopanthus mucronata.*

Page 224, line 7. **Pigeons.** The wild pigeons were caught by means of nets in Concord in Thoreau's day. He describes a "pigeon-place" in his Journal under date of Sept. 12, 1851.

Line 12. **Shingle tree.** It seems probable that this is in apposition with the word "pine," meaning a particularly good tree to make shingles of. There seems to be no current usage that applies the term "shingle tree" to any particular species of tree growing naturally in Concord. A correspondent informs the editor that shingles were formerly made of red pine (*Pinus resinosa*) extensively, and it is possible that Thoreau referred to that tree, which he found growing in one or two places in Concord, and to which he would have made a point of "paying a visit." The "taller mast of a pine" he speaks of here, however, must have been a white pine, for no other species grew tall in Concord.

Lines 16, 17. **I stood in the very abutment of a rainbow's arch.** Under date of Aug. 9, 1851, Thoreau wrote in his Journal, "It was a splendid sunset . . . . , a celestial light on all the land, so that all people went to their doors and windows to look on the grass and leaves and buildings and the sky, and it was equally glorious in whatever quarter you looked; a sort of fulgor as of stereotyped lightning filled the air. Of which this is my solution. We were in the westernmost edge of the shower at the moment the sun was setting, and its rays shone through the cloud and the falling rain. We were, in fact, in a rainbow, and it was here its arch rested on the earth. At a little distance we should have seen all the colors." This is doubtless the occasion referred to here. Whatever may have been the cause of the atmospheric effect described, it can hardly have been literally as Thoreau suggests, for the rainbow is always centred directly opposite the spectator standing with his back to the sun, and it is, of course, impossible for one to stand in the abutment of the arch. The rainbow is a reflection from the raindrops, not a palpable arch that one can approach and enter. No two persons see precisely the same bow. With all his minute and painstaking study of natural phenomena, Thoreau sometimes jumped at conclusions without careful consideration. It was poetic, not scientific, truth that was his main pursuit, and since he combined science with his poetry more successfully than most, we can pardon an occasional slip of this kind.

Line 21. **Like a dolphin.** The dolphin which in dying assumes beautiful colors and has hence acquired a poetic celebrity is not the true dolphin, but a fish more properly called a coryphene, any species of the genus *Coryphœna*.

Line 28. **Benvenuto Cellini.** A famous Italian goldsmith and sculptor of the Renaissance period, whose autobiography is one of the most celebrated books of the kind.

Page 225, line 4 after blank. **Baker Farm.** Now included in the estate of Mr. Charles Francis Adams.

A poet. William Ellery Channing, the second of the name, Thoreau's friend before referred to. The poem is entitled "Baker Farm."

Page 226, verse. "**And here a poet builded,**" etc. These lines also are from Channing's "Baker Farm."

Page 228, line 16. **Irishman.** Thoreau is writing, of course, about the poor class of Irish immigrant of his day, a time when the Irish were practically the only foreigners coming to Massachusetts.

Page 229, lines 12, 13. "**I catch shiners with fishworms, and bait the perch with them.**" See Thoreau's comment on p. 231. Perch — yellow perch, that is, the kind referred to — can generally be caught with worms, so that it is not necessary to catch the worthless shiners first.

"**You'd better go now.**" That is, go fishing. The emphasis is on the "now."

Line 23. **Was seemingly distilled.** It took so long to prepare it.

Page 230, lines 11, 12. **Remember thy Creator in the days of thy youth.** Is this original with Thoreau? If not, is it quoted exactly? and why does it not appear in quotation marks?

Verse. "**Landscape where the richest element,**" etc. Thoreau is still quoting Channing's "Baker Farm."

Page 231, line 2 from bottom. **Webbed.** People living on wet ground or leading a more or less aquatic life are often humorously styled "web-footed."

Page 232, line 10. **Venison.** Though now restricted to deer-meat, except in poetic usage, the term formerly signified the flesh of any beast of the chase.

Lines 13-15. **An instinct toward a higher, or, as it is named, spiritual life, and another toward a primitive rank and savage one.** Each of these instincts was stronger in Thoreau than in most men, and the combined presence of the two made itself more manifest in him, perhaps, than in any other writer of equal eminence.

Line 16. **I love the wild.** "Thoreau's Wildness" is the subject of a short essay by John Burroughs in his *Literary Values.*

Page 233, lines 15-20. **They mistake who assert,** etc. This is, of course, no longer true of American sports. Many more outdoor games are now played in this country than in Thoreau's day.

Page 234, lines 19, 20. **I am compelled to doubt if equally valuable sports are ever substituted for these.** He might have written differently if he had lived to learn the modern sport of animal photography.

Line 25. **Mighty hunters.** See note on Nimrod, p. 309, line 1.

Line 28. **Fishers of men.** See *Mark*, i, 17.

Line 29. **Chaucer's nun.** It was really the monk, not the nun, of Chaucer's *Canterbury Tales* that gave not a plucked hen for the text that says that hunters are not holy men.

Page 235, lines 12, 13. **Phil-anthropic.** The word comes from the Greek φιλέω (*phileo*), to love, and ἄνθρωπος (*anthropos*), man. Thoreau italicizes the latter part so as to suggest that his love for living things is not confined to man.

Page 236, lines 5, 6. **The Governor and his Council . . . went a-fishing there.** This doubtless does not refer to any actual event. The Governor and his Council are used figuratively.

Page 237, line 5 from bottom. **Kirby and Spence.** *An Introduction to Entomology*, by William Kirby and William Spence, 4 vols., London, 1815–1826.

Page 239, line 2 from bottom. **Star-dust.** Star-dust is literally cosmic dust, which is supposed to fall on the earth from outside space like the meteorites. It has been found on the snow in high latitudes, but it is probable that much that is so called is in reality volcanic dust from terrestrial sources.

Page 240, line 10. **A dish of tea.** A cup of tea. The former phrase, once common, is now seldom heard.

Line 5 from bottom. **Ved.** Veda. See note on p. 99, line 7 from bottom.

Page 241, line 1. **Vedant.** The Vedic philosophy.

Lines 9, 10. **Says Thseng-tseu.** In the commentary on Confucius' book, *The Great Learning*, Chapter vii.

Line 16. **An alderman to his turtle.** See note on " aldermanic," p. 140, line 11.

Lines 16, 17. **Not that food which entereth into the mouth defileth a man.** Quoted (inexactly) from *Matthew*, xv, 11.

Page 242, line 1. **The harp which trembles round the world.** The music of nature, perhaps; or it may be that the music of the spheres is referred to.

Line 6 from bottom. **Mencius.** A Chinese philosopher of the third and fourth centuries B. C., one of the leading teachers of Confucianism. The name is Latinized from Meng-Tse.

Page 243, verse. **" How happy 's he who hath due place as-**

signed," etc. From Dr. John Donne's Epistle "To Sir Edward Herbert, since Lord Herbert of Cherbury."

Page 245, line 8. **Every man is the builder of a temple, called his body.** "Know ye not that ye are the temple of God, and that the Spirit of God dwelleth in you?" — *1 Corinthians*, iii, 16.

Page 247, line 1. **A companion.** This was Thoreau's intimate friend William Ellery Channing, the poet.

Line 5. **Hermit.** The hermit is Thoreau, of course. This fashion of writing in dialogue form, as in Izaak Walton's *Compleat Angler*, was once common. As used here it gives an antiquated flavor to the text in keeping with Thoreau's style.

Line 14. **Bose.** A sort of generic name for the farm dog.

Lines 15–21. **And oh, the housekeeping,** etc. Put into more colloquial form this would probably read somewhat as follows: "Who wants to live out in the world, where housekeeping with its endless routine of drudgery is necessary? Better not keep house at all, but live in a hollow tree, where there are no such things as calls and dinner-parties and only a woodpecker taps at the door. Out there in the world people swarm like flies in the sun. They are born into too complex an existence for me. I do very well with my spring-water and my loaf of brown bread."

Page 249, line 11. **Confut-see.** The Chinese form of Confucius.

Line 13. **Mem.** Abbreviation for "memorandum."

Line 3 from bottom. **Pilpay & Co.** Pilpay and the other fable-makers. Pilpay, or Bidpai, as the Arabic word is more correctly rendered, was formerly supposed to be a Hindoo philosopher and the author of the fables translated into Arabic as the Fables of Bidpai, but it is now known that the word is not a proper name, but comes from a Sanskrit word meaning "master of knowledge," and that the fables are collected from very ancient sources, — Indian, Persian, and Arabic.

Page 250, line 3. **A wild native kind.** In his own copy Thoreau inserts as a note here, "*Mus leucopus.*" This is the white-footed mouse, or deer mouse, now called by the mammalogists *Peromyscus leucopus noveboracensis.*

Line 8 from bottom. **Tetrao umbellus.** Now called *Bonasa umbellus,* the ruffed grouse.

Page 251, line 2 from bottom. **Sportsman.** No "true sportsman," as the phrase is used nowadays, would shoot grouse in the breeding-season.

Page 253, line 6. **Turtle doves.** Mourning doves. The true turtle dove is not an American bird.

Line 11 from bottom. **Duellum.** Latin for "duel."

Line 10 from bottom. **Bellum.** Latin for "war."

Page 254, lines 20, 21. **Whose mother had charged him to return with his shield or upon it.** This is the well-known charge of a Spartan woman to her son upon his departure to war. It comes down to us through Plutarch, in whose " Apothegms of the Laconian Women," the story appears thus : " Another [Spartan mother] on handing her boy his shield, exhorting him, said, ' My son, either this or upon this.' " This truly Laconic exhortation is generally extended to read as Thoreau gives it.

Lines 22, 23. **Achilles . . . Patroclus.** Achilles, the Greek hero of the Trojan War, sulked in his tent on account of a quarrel with Agamemnon, until his friend Patroclus was killed by the Trojans, when he sallied out to avenge him.

Page 255, line 13. **Austerlitz.** At the Battle of Austerlitz in Moravia, Dec. 2, 1805, Napoleon defeated the combined forces of Russia and Austria.

Dresden. This was another of Napoleon's victories. The battle was fought Aug. 26–27, 1813, and resulted in a signal defeat for the Allies, — Russia, Austria, and Prussia.

Two killed, etc. The allusions are to the Concord Fight of April 19, 1775.

Page 256, line 15. **Hôtel des Invalides.** A great home for disabled soldiers in Paris. It contains the tomb of Napoleon.

Line 22. **Kirby and Spence.** See note on page 237, line 5 from bottom.

Line 24. **Huber.** François Huber (1750–1831), a Swiss naturalist, noted especially for his researches in connection with bees.

Line 25. **Æneas Sylvius.** Enea Silvio Piccolomini (1405–1464), a learned Italian ecclesiastic and writer, who occupied the Papal throne as Pius II from 1458 until his death. He is best known as a writer under the Latinized form of his name.

Page 257, lines 2, 3. **Olaus Magnus.** A Swedish ecclesiastic and historian, author of a History of the Northern Nations which was published in Latin in 1555.

Lines 9, 10. **Webster's Fugitive-Slave Bill.** Daniel Webster was an influential supporter of this bill, but Senator James M. Mason of Virginia was its author.

Line 11 from bottom. **Jerbilla.** Another, and probably an incorrect, form of *Gerbillus*, the name of a genus of Old-World jumping mice, jerboas.

Page 258, line 8 from bottom. **His horse.** The allusion is to Pegasus, the winged horse of Greek mythology, who, with a kick of his hoof, caused the fountain Hippocrene to spring forth on Mt. Helicon in Bœotia. Hippocrene was the inspiring well of the Muses, and hence in modern poetry Pegasus is called the horse of the Muses and the poet's steed. Note that Thoreau here calls himself a poet; and such he really was, though most of his poetry was written in prose.

Line 7 from bottom. **Colymbus glacialis.** The loon is now called by ornithologists *Gavia immer.*

Page 260, last line. **Swam much faster there.** It is a fact that the loon and probably all other diving birds progress more rapidly under water than on the surface. Many birds fly under water, but the loon uses its feet alone under ordinary circumstances, according to the latest writer on the subject, Dr. Charles W. Townsend, in *The Auk*, July, 1909.

Page 261, line 8 from bottom. **Looning.** Thoreau may have heard this word somewhere, but it is very probable that he coined it himself from a fancy that the loon was named from this howling note. The word "loon," however, as applied to a bird, appears to come from an Old Norse word through the Shetland dialect, which gives the name "loom" to several diving birds. "Looning" has now found its way into some of the dictionaries, apparently solely on the strength of Thoreau's using it. He used it again in *The Maine Woods*

Page 262, lines 13–19. **They would sometimes circle . . . to a distant part which was left free.** Of what service to the ducks is this well-known habit of circling and doubling?

Line 19. **What beside safety they got.** The black duck, the species which Thoreau would have seen most commonly at Walden, feeds at night and often rests by day in wide and deep ponds where it can get no food, but where it is safe from its enemies.

Page 263, line 3–11. **There, too, I admired . . . lovers of Nature there.** Is this a correctly constructed sentence?

Line 11. **Butchers rake the tongues of bison,** etc. The "butchers" since Thoreau's time have killed the last of the bison, except for a few small herds which are being protected and fostered in the Yellowstone Park and elsewhere.

Line 6 from bottom. **They now sleep.** Note the play upon the word "sleep."

Page 264, line 4. **When in flower.** When does the chestnut tree bloom?

Lines 10, 11. **A good substitute for bread.** Chestnuts contain a large percentage of starch, the element that gives bread its food value.

Line 25. **The totem of an Indian tribe.** In E. B. O'Callaghan's *Documents relative to the Colonial History of the State of New York*, a French document of 1666 is quoted which names the "*pomme-de-terre*," or potato, as the totem of one of the Iroquois tribes. The figures, taken from Indian drawings, might equally well represent the ground-nut, which we learn from Lewis Henry Morgan's *League of the Iroquois* was one of their principal foods. It seems probable that this Iroquois tribe is the one Thoreau refers to, though just where he obtained his information it is not easy to ascertain. He accumulated a large amount of material for a book about the Indians which his early death prevented him from writing.

Page 265, line 5. **Ceres or Minerva.** Ceres was the Roman goddess of agriculture. Minerva, or her Greek counterpart Athene, according to the myth, gave the Greeks the olive tree and the plough.

Lines 12, 13. **Ah, many a tale their color told.** Thoreau evidently had in mind the lines by Thomas Moore, —

"Those evening bells! those evening bells!
How many a tale their music tells," etc.

Lines 4 and 3 from bottom. **Avoiding winter and unspeakable cold.** Probably an echo of the line in the *Iliad* (book iii, line 4), where the cranes are spoken of as avoiding winter and unspeakable *rain*.

Page 266, line 6 from bottom. **Nebuchadnezzar.** King of Babylonia, B. C. 604–561.

Page 267, line 6. **A poet.** Channing again.

Page 268, lines 15, 16. **Keeping-room.** Sitting-room. The term is, or was, used locally in England and in New England.

Page 269, line 5. **Saturn.** An Italian god, identified by the Romans with the Greek Cronos, who was the chief of the gods till his son Zeus deposed him. It is, of course, the sill of the house that is so designated here.

Line 5 from bottom. **Put out.** Note the play on the words.

Page 270, line 10. **Keeping.** Why is the word italicized?

Line 18. **Backing out.** The proper method of leaving the presence of royalty.

Page 272, line 2. **Unio fluviatilis.** A species of freshwater clam. Many species of *Unio* are found in our ponds and streams.

Page 275, line 3. **Honk or quack.** *Honk* is the note of the wild goose; the black duck quacks, much like the domestic duck.

Line 19. **Vulcan.** The god of fire in the classical mythology.

Lines 19, 20. **Terminus.** The Roman god of boundaries.

Line 22. **Steal.** It is the harmless "stealing" of dead wood for which the owner of the land has no use that Thoreau is talking of.

Line 3 from bottom. **The Irish.** The Fitchburg Railroad was built largely by the labor of Irish immigrants.

Page 276, line 13. **Gilpin.** William Gilpin (1724–1804), an English clergyman, author of theological works and of many volumes on the picturesque in landscape scenery and gardening, including a two-volume book on "Forest Scenery."

Line 9 from bottom. **Lord Warden.** Under date of April 12, 1852, Thoreau, who had evidently just been reading Gilpin, writes in his Journal : " In the New Forest in Hampshire they had a chief officer called the Lord Warden and under him two distinct officers, one to preserve the *venison* of the forest, another to preserve its *vert, i. e.* woods, lawns, etc. Does not our Walden need such ? The Lord Warden was a person of distinction, as the Duke of Gloucester."

Last two lines. **Lucum conlucare.** See Cato, *De Re Rustica*, 139.

Page 277, line 11. **Michaux.** François André Michaux, son of André Michaux, and like his father a French botanist who travelled in America. His *Histoire des Arbres forestiers de l'Amérique septentrionale* was published 1810–13.

Line 6 from bottom. **New Hollander.** See note, p. 370.

Line 5 from bottom. **Goody Blake and Harry Gill.** See Wordsworth's poem of this title.

Page 278, line 11. "**Jump**" it. That is, shape it on his anvil. The word is perhaps not quite correctly used here. See the dictionaries.

Line 14. **Fat pine.** Pine that is full of pitch. This seems to be an Americanism.

Page 279, line 9 of verse. **Go thou my incense.** Go thou as my incense.

Page 280, line 8 from bottom. **Cut their threads.** See note on *Atropos*, p. 385.

Line 6 from bottom. **Cold Fridays.** The cold day alluded to, which Thoreau mentions several times in his Journal, occurred Jan. 19, 1810. Under date of Jan. 11, 1857, he wrote : " Mother remembers the Cold Friday very well. She lived in the house where I was born. The people in the kitchen . . . drew up close to the fire, but the dishes which the Hardy girl was washing froze as fast as she washed them, close to the fire." In the entry for the 22d of the same month, he wrote : " I asked M. [Mr. George Minott of Concord] about the Cold Friday. He said, 'It was plaguy cold ; it stung like a wasp.' He remembers seeing them toss up water in a shoemaker's shop, usually a very warm place, and when it struck the floor it was frozen and rattled like so many shot." The Great Snow alluded to was probably that of 1780. See note, p. 385.

Page 281, verse. "**Never, bright flame, may be denied to me,**" etc. These lines are from a poem entitled " The Wood-Fire," by Ellen H. Hooper, which appeared in the second number of *The Dial*, in 1840. Mrs. Hooper was a daughter of William Sturgis and wife of Dr. Robert W. Hooper, a Boston physician.

Page 283, line 6. **On a foundation of logs.** The corduroy road, as it is called, made of logs laid side by side across the roadway, is much used for crossing swampy places on cart-paths and backwoods roads.

Lines 13, 14. **Cato Uticensis.** Marcus Porcius Cato, great-grandson of Cato the Censor of the same name, called Uticensis from the fact of his having died at Utica. He was a celebrated Roman philosopher and patriot of the first century B. C.

Line 8 from bottom. **Solidago stricta.** Thoreau afterwards found himself in some doubt as to the identification of the particular species of goldenrod, and he substituted *arguta* (with a question-mark) for *stricta* on his personal copy of the book. It could hardly have been *stricta*, which does not grow in New England, and *arguta*, though common in the Massachusetts woodland, is not an early species.

Page 284, lines 8, 9. **Squire Cummings.** A Concord physician of Scotch parentage, who died in 1788. (Sanborn in the Bibliophile edition of *Walden.*)

Line 16. **Scipio Africanus.** Publius Cornelius Scipio Africanus, a celebrated Roman general, who was born probably in B. C. 237 and died about B. C. 183.

Last line. **Breed's location.** Breed was a barber who kept a shop in Concord together with a tailor named Newell. Their sign read, —

> " Tailoring and barbering done with speed
> By John C. Newell & John C. Breed."

Journal, vol. ii, p. 20.

Page 285, line 10 from bottom. **Davenant's " Gondibert."** Sir William D'Avenant, or Davenant, was an English poet and dramatist of the Seventeenth Century, whose best-known work is his epic poem " Gondibert." He was at one time poet laureate, but like many another occupant of that position, he is now but little read.

Line 8 from bottom. **An uncle.** Charles Dunbar, a brother of Thoreau's mother and a very eccentric man, about whom many amusing anecdotes are related in the *Journal.*

Line 4 from bottom. **Chalmers' collection of English poetry.** *Works of the English Poets from Chaucer to Cowper,* with Johnson's Lives, and additional Lives, by Alexander Chalmers, a Scottish editor and biographer living in London, published in 1810 in twenty-one volumes.

Line 3 from bottom. **Nervii.** A powerful and warlike people of Belgic Gaul who were conquered by Cæsar.

Page 286, line 12. **The engine bell tinkled behind.** This was before the days of steam fire-engines, of course, and the engine was drawn by hand.

Line 5 from bottom. **Tub.** This is still the humorous name for the hand fire-engines, which are now, except in a few small towns, used only in athletic contests by firemen's associations.

Page 287, line 3 from bottom. **Rider.** A rail of a stake-and-rider fence.

Page 288, line 8 from bottom. **Hugh Quoil.** This story of a poor drunkard, an admirable bit of human nature and pathos, is told at greater length in the *Journal*, vol. i, pp. 414–418. Aside from its intrinsic interest, it will also serve to show something of Thoreau's method in adapting his journal entries for use in more permanent form.

" I had one neighbor within half a mile for a short time when I first went to the woods, Hugh Quoil, an Irishman who had been a soldier at Waterloo, Colonel Quoil, as he was called, — I believe that he had killed a colonel and ridden off his horse, — who lived from hand — sometimes to mouth, — though it was commonly a glass of rum that the hand carried. He and his wife awaited their fate together in an old ruin in Walden woods. What life he got — or what means of death — he got by ditching.

" I never was much acquainted with Hugh Quoil, though sometimes I met him in the path, and now do believe that a solid shank-bone, and skull which no longer aches, lie somewhere, and can still be produced, which once with garment of flesh and broadcloth were called and hired to do work as Hugh Quoil. He was a man of manners and gentlemanlike, as one who had seen the world, and was capable of more civil speech than you could well attend to. At a distance he had seemingly a ruddy face as of biting January, but nearer at hand it was bright carmine. It would have burnt your finger to touch his cheek. He wore a straight-bodied snuff-colored coat which had long been familiar with him, and carried a turf-knife in his hand — instead of a sword. He had fought on the English side before, but he fought on the Napoleon side now. Napoleon went to St. Helena ; Hugh Quoil came to Walden Pond. I heard that he used to tell travellers who inquired about myself that ——— and Thoreau owned the *farm* together, but Thoreau lived on the *place* and carried it on.

" He was thirstier than I, and drank more, probably, but not out of the pond. That was never the lower for him. Perhaps I ate more than he. The last time I met him, the only time I spoke with him, was at the foot of the hill on the highway, as I was crossing to the spring one summer afternoon, the pond water being too warm for me. I was crossing the road with a pail in my hand, when Quoil came down the hill, wearing his snuff-colored coat, as if it were winter, and shaking with delirium tremens. I hailed him and told him that my errand was to get water at a spring close by, only at the foot of the hill over the fence. He answered, with stuttering and parched lips, bloodshot eye, and staggering gesture, he 'd like to see it. ' Follow me there, then.' But I had got my pail full and back before he scaled the fence. And he, drawing his coat about him, to warm him, or to cool him, answered in delirium-tremens hydrophobia dialect, which is not easy to be written here, he 'd heard of it, but had never seen it ; and so shivered his way along to town, — to liquor and to oblivion.

" On Sundays, brother Irishmen and others, who had gone far astray from steady habits and the village, crossed my bean-field with empty jugs toward Quoil's. But what for ? Did they sell rum there ? I asked. ' Respectable people they,' ' Know no harm of them,' ' Never heard that they drank too much,' was the answer of all wayfarers. They went by sober, stealthy, silent, skulking (no harm to get elm bark Sundays) ; returned loquacious, sociable, having long intended to call on you.

" At length one afternoon Hugh Quoil, feeling better, perchance, with snuff-colored coat, as usual, paced solitary and soldier-like, thinking of Waterloo, along the woodland road to the foot of the hill by the spring ; and there the Fates met him, and threw him down in his snuff-colored coat on the gravel, and got ready to cut his thread ; but not till travellers passed, who would raise him up, get him perpendicular, then settle, settle quick ; but legs, what are they ? ' Lay me down,' says Hugh hoarsely. ' House locked up — key — in pocket — wife in town.' And the Fates cut, and there he lay by the wayside, five feet ten, and looking taller than in life.

" He has gone away ; his house here ' all tore to pieces.' What kind of fighting or ditching work he finds to do now, how it fares with him, whether his thirst is quenched, whether there is still some semblance of that carmine cheek, struggles still with some liquid demon — perchance on more equal terms — till he swallow him completely, I cannot by any means learn. What his salutation is now, what his January-morning face, what he thinks of Waterloo, what start he has gained or lost, what work still for the ditcher and forester and soldier now, there is no evidence. He was here, the likes of him, for a season, standing light in his shoes like a faded gentleman, with gesture almost learned in drawing-rooms ; wore clothes, hat, shoes, cut ditches, felled wood, did farm work for various people, kindled fires, worked enough, ate enough, drank too much. He was one of those unnamed, countless sects of philosophers who founded no school.

" Now that he was gone, and his wife was gone too, — for she could not support the solitude, — before it was too late and the house was torn down, I went over to make a call. Now that Irishmen with jugs avoided the old house, I visited it, — an ' unlucky castle now,' said they. There lay his old clothes curled up by habit, as if it were himself, upon his raised plank bed. His pipe lay broken on the hearth; and scattered about were soiled cards — king of diamonds, hearts, spades — on the floor. One black chicken, which they could not catch, still went to roost in the next apartment, stepping silent over the floor, frightened by the sound of its own wings, black as night and as silent, too, not even croaking; awaiting Reynard, its god actually dead. There was the dim outline of a garden which had been planted, but had never received its first hoeing, now overrun with weeds, with burs and cockles, which stick to your clothes; as if in the spring he had contemplated a harvest of corn and beans before that strange trembling of the limbs overtook him. Skin of woodchuck fresh-stretched, never to be cured, met once in bean-field by the Waterloo man with uplifted hoe; no cap, no mittens wanted. Pipe on hearth no more to be lighted, best buried with him."

Page 289, lines 11, 12. **A bowl broken at the fountain.** "Or ever the silver cord be loosed, or the golden bowl be broken, or the pitcher be broken at the fountain, or the wheel broken at the cistern." — *Ecclesiastes*, xii, 6.

Page 290, line 12. "**Fate, free will, foreknowledge absolute.**" "Fixed fate, free will, foreknowledge absolute." — Milton's *Paradise Lost*, book ii, line 560.

Line 15. "**Cato and Brister pulled wool.**" There is, perhaps, a double, or even a triple, meaning here in Thoreau's mind.

Page 291, line 13. **Blossom like the rose.** See *Isaiah* xxxv, 1.

Page 292, lines 7 and 6 from bottom. **Filled with heaven's own blue.** The reflection of the blue sky from the snow where it lies in shadow, as in the deep footprints. This reflection of the blue sky on shadowed ground is universal in summer and winter, but is seldom noticed, except by persons who have trained themselves to see it. It is more observable on the white snow than elsewhere, but it is to be seen everywhere out of doors in fair weather. — But we must not lose sight of the poetry of Thoreau's thought in considering the natural phenomenon.

Page 293, line 8. **Strix nebulosa.** Now known as *Strix varia*.

Line 20. **Peninsular relation.** If he had closed his eyes entirely, he would, to follow up the metaphor, have islanded himself.

Line 4 from bottom. **I could not hear the slightest sound.** What makes an owl's flight noiseless; and of what service is such a flight to the bird?

Page 294, line 2. **The dawning of his day.** That is, the coming on of night.

Line 7. Heathen as I was. Thoreau did not profess to be a Christian in religion, though he was an intensely religious man. The allusion here is, of course, to a well-known saying of Christ's.

Line 17. Meadow mouse. Thoreau corrected this to "deer mouse" in his personal copy.

Line 7 from bottom. A woodchopper. Doubtless the French-Canadian, Therien, of whom we have heard before.

Line 3 from bottom. A long-headed farmer. Mr. Sanborn in the Bibliophile *Walden* tells us that this was Thoreau's friend Edmund Hosmer of Concord.

Page 295, lines 7, 8. **We tried our teeth on many a nut which wise squirrels have long since abandoned.** That is, they tried to solve some of the world's unsolvable problems.

Line 11. A poet. Channing.

Line 17. Boisterous mirth. Thoreau was no such stiff and unbending Stoic philosopher as he is sometimes imagined.

Line 4 from bottom. Another welcome visitor. Amos Bronson Alcott (1799–1888). His early efforts as a peddler of Yankee goods in the South were unsuccessful commercially, but he afterwards became widely known as a philosopher and lecturer. His daughter, Louisa M. Alcott, is better known to young people. She went to school to Thoreau.

Page 296, line 4. **Disgracing man.** Putting man to shame. An obsolete usage of the word.

Line 2 after verse. Old Mortality. The character who gives the name to one of Scott's novels. He was an old man who travelled over Scotland cleaning and making plain the inscriptions on old gravestones.

Lines 6 and 5 from bottom. Entertainment for man, etc. On the signs of inns were formerly placed the words "Entertainment for man and beast."

Page 297, line 2. **Ingenuus.** Freeborn; hence, worthy of a freeman, noble, upright, candid, ingenuous.

Line 10. Pumpkin pine. "When growing densely in deep and damp old forests, with only a few branches near the top, the slowly-grown wood [of the white pine] is perfectly clear and soft, destitute of resin, and almost without sap-wood, and has a yellowish color, like the flesh of the pumpkin. It is then called pumpkin pine. . . . [The name is] little used except in Maine, and by persons who import wood from that State." — George B. Emerson, 1846.

Line 15. Flocks. In the sense of flocks of wool, not of flocks of sheep.

Lines 20, 21. A New England Night's Entertainment. Alluding, of course, to *The Arabian Nights' Entertainments*.

Line 22. **The old settler.** See p. 152.

Line 2 from bottom. **One other.** Ralph Waldo Emerson.

Page 298, line 4. **Visitor who never comes.** The angel of God, perhaps. Or, perhaps, rather, the ideal man, the Friend for whom Thoreau was always looking, but never found because there never was, nor could be, such a friend. This is one of those vague and mystical thoughts which we find frequently in Thoreau's writings, which we can understand in some measure without being able to explain.

The Vishnu Purana. The best-known of the Puranas, or later religious writings of the Hindoos, manuals of sectarian Brahmanism.

Page 300, line 3. **Moose-yard.** Moose and deer are well-known to "yard" in winter when the snow is deep. They congregate in some secluded and remote place in the woods and by trampling the snow keep a yard clear where they can get about comfortably and feed.

Line 10. **Lingua vernacula.** Language of the common people.

Line 8 from bottom. **Cat owl.** The great horned owl. A careful study of all Thoreau's references to owls in his *Journal* leads to the conviction that the hooting owl spoken of above and on pages 138 and 139 was also of this species.

Last two lines. **Alarming the citadel.** When the Gauls took Rome in B. C. 390, the citadel, which still held out, was saved by the cackling of the sacred geese in the temple of Juno, which warned the garrison of an assault.

Page 301, line 7. **The whooping of the ice.** See pp. 332, 333.

Line 5 from bottom. **Sciurus Hudsonius.** Now called *Sciurus hudsonicus*.

Page 302, line 9 from bottom. **Winding up his clock.** A familiar note of the red squirrel resembles the sound made by the winding of a clock.

Page 305, line 8 from bottom. **Actæon.** A hunter who, according to the Greek myth, surprised Artemis (Diana) at her bath, and was changed by her into a stag and then attacked and killed by his own dogs.

Page 306, line 10. **Hound.** Thoreau, here and on page 307, apparently uses the word as synonymous with "bay," just as we have found him coining the word "looning" to signify the note of the loon, and probably for the same reason; but he is not warranted in doing so by the etymology of the word, which originally meant any kind of dog and was spelled "hund."

Line 15. **A man came to my hut from Lexington.** The conversation is given in detail in the *Journal*, vol. i, pp. 398, 399. "'Have you seen my hound, sir? I want to know — what! a lawyer's office ? law books ? — if you've seen anything of a hound about here. Why, what do you do here ?' 'I live here. No, I haven't.' 'Haven't you heard one in the woods anywhere ?' 'Oh, yes, I heard one in this evening.' 'What do you do here ?' 'But he was some way off.' 'Which side did he seem to be ?' 'Well, I should think he was the other side of the pond.' 'This is a large dog ; makes a large track. He's been out hunting from Lexington for a week. How long have you lived here ?' 'Oh, about a year.' 'Somebody said there was a man up here had a camp in the woods somewhere, and he'd got him.' 'Well, I don't know of anybody. There's Britton's camp over on the other road. It may be there.' 'Isn't there anybody in these woods ?' 'Yes, they are chopping right up here behind me.' 'How far is it ?' 'Only a few steps. Hark a moment. There, don't you hear the sound of their axes ?'"

Line 6 from bottom. **A cruise.** The word is habitually used by hunters, apparently without thought of any nautical associations.

Page 308, line 14 from bottom. **Wast Book.** Waste-book, or day-book. The cover of this old account-book which Thoreau examined was inscribed : —

> "Mr. Ephraim Jones
> His Wast Book
> Anno Domini
> 1742."

In the *Journal*, vol. vi, pp. 77–80, 88, 94–96, 101, Thoreau tells of some of the interesting and amusing things he found in this book and two ledgers which he afterwards looked over.

Line 12 from bottom. **Representative.** In the General Court, the legislature of Massachusetts.

Line 11 from bottom. **0—2—3.** These figures and those a few lines down stand for pounds, shillings, and pence, of course.

Line 9 from bottom. **Catt.** Thoreau had misgivings as to this after printing it, and he wrote in the margin of his own copy, "Can it be calf ? *Vide* small ledger, near beginning." There seems to be no inherent reason for doubting that it might have been a wild-cat's skin, however. Wildcats have been killed in eastern Massachusetts, even in recent years.

Line 4 from bottom. **The last deer.** Under the protection that has been afforded them deer have recently increased very considerably all over New England, and they are now not very rare in the neighborhood of Concord.

Page 309, line 1. **Nimrod.** According to Genesis, Nimrod was "a mighty hunter before the Lord," and this seems to be all that is known of him. Few men are so celebrated on so slight a foundation of known fact.

Line 9 from bottom. **The hares.** The common gray rabbit, now known to naturalists as *Lepus floridanus transitionalis*, but called by Dr. Ebenezer Emmons, with whose Report on the Quadrupeds of Massachusetts, published in 1840, Thoreau was familiar, *Lepus Americanus*. The true *L. americanus*[1] is the larger varying hare, which turns white in winter. The subspecies *L. americanus virginianus* is, or was, found in Concord, and Thoreau knew it by hearsay under the name of the white rabbit. He saw its tracks occasionally in the snow, but it is not certain that he ever saw the animal itself alive.

Page 310, lines 9, 10. **The breed of nobler bloods.** "Rome, thou hast lost the breed of noble bloods!"—Shakespeare's *Julius Cæsar*, Act I, Sc. ii, line 151.

Line 15. **Venison.** See note on p. 232.

Line 18. **Some think.** Lucius Ælius, according to Varro, thought the word *lepus* was so derived, on account of the hare's swiftness. Varro himself thought it came from the Greek. (*De Re Rustica*, 3, 12.)

Page 313, line 4. **Marmots.** That is, the woodchucks, a species of marmot.

Page 315, line 4. **Whose fame is trumpeted.** This is to be taken literally. Formerly the travelling vender of fish in New England villages blew a horn from time to time as he drove through the streets. The "fish-horn" still survives, though it is no longer used by the fish-man.

Line 11. **Waldenses.** The Waldenses, or Waldensians, upon whose name Thoreau is playing here, are a small religious sect chiefly located in the north of Italy, which was started by Peter Waldo of Lyons, France, in 1170, as a reform movement in the Roman Catholic Church. Thoreau is also thinking of the Latin termination *-enses* signifying "inhabitants of."

Line 3 from bottom. **Two such Bottomless Ponds.** "Yesterday, September 14, [1850,] walked to White Pond in Stow, on the Marlborough road, having passed one pond called sometimes Pratt's Pond, sometimes Bottomless Pond, in Sudbury. Saw afterward another pond beyond Willis's also called Bottomless Pond, in a thick swamp. To name two ponds bottomless when both have a bottom! Verily men choose darkness rather than light."—*Journal*, vol. ii, p. 68.

[1] In modern usage the specific names of animals are never capitalized, even when they are proper nouns in the genitive case or proper adjectives.

Page 316, line 9. **A "fifty-six."** A fifty-six pound weight, half the old-fashioned hundredweight of one hundred and twelve pounds.

Page 317, line 8. **William Gilpin.** See note on p. 276. The quotation is from his *Observations on the Highlands of Scotland.* The verse he quotes from *Paradise Lost,* book vii, lines 288–290.

Page 323, line 12. **An undulation in the crust of the earth.** This reminds one of the modern seismographs. The instrument in the museum of Harvard University detects vibrations which are supposed to be caused by the beat of the surf upon the shore about seven miles away.

Page 324, lines 16, 17 after blank. **To saw pit-fashion.** Logs are sometimes sawed in this way, one sawyer standing in a pit below the log and another above.

Last line. **Winter rye.** As Thoreau very well knew, this crop is sown in the autumn. It is called winter rye because it lives through the winter to grow and ripen in the following spring and summer.

Page 325, line 7 from bottom. **Tartarus.** The lowest of the lower worlds, according to the mythology of the *Iliad.* Later it was used as synonymous with Hades.

Page 328, line 12 from bottom. **Thus it appears,** etc. This paragraph tells what *might* have happened to the Walden ice.

Last line, page 329, line 1. **Brahma and Vishnu and Indra.** Three great gods of the Hindoo mythology.

Page 329, lines 7, 8. **Atlantis.** A mythical island in the Atlantic Ocean, an account of which is given in Plato's dialogue " Timæus."

Line 8. **The Hesperides.** The Hesperides, according to Greek mythology, were three sisters (or four, or seven, for the accounts vary), whose parentage is variously given. The islands of their abode were generally located in the extreme west.

The periplus of Hanno. See note on Hanno, p. 372. Periplus, or *periplous,* is a Greek word meaning sailing round. Hanno's periplus was his voyage along the west coast of Africa. His account of it is still extant in a Greek translation, which has been translated into English.

Line 9. **Ternate and Tidore.** Two of the Spice Islands of the Melanesian Archipelago. Thoreau's ship takes a somewhat irregular course, — makes a genuine periplus, in fact.

Page 333, lines 6, 7. **Fishes and muskrats . . . stunned by a blow on it.** Fishes, such as pickerel, seen through the ice in shallow water may be stunned by a sharp blow on the ice above them and so captured.

Page 335, line 10. **Field of ice.** This is the technical term in the Arctic regions for a large sheet of ice.

Page 337, line 5. **Acanthus.** A European plant, the conventionalized leaf of which was much used in classical architecture, as on the capital of the Corinthian column.

Chiccory. The leaf of this well-known and beautiful plant of the roadsides and waste places was imitated in the Gothic ornamentation of the Fifteenth Century.

Ivy. The conventionalized ivy leaf is an ancient architectural ornament, being found in Etruscan and Græco-Roman design.

Line 6. **Vine.** The vine came into use as an architectural ornament in the early Christian and Byzantine period.

Page 338, lines 13–21. **Lobe,** etc. These lines illustrate Thoreau's fondness for etymological speculations.

Line 14. **Labor.** The verb *lăbor,* not to be confused with the noun *lăbor* (English " labor "), which seems to come from a different root.

Page 339, line 4 from bottom. **Palm.** Our word "palm" in both its senses comes from the Latin *palma,* which also was used for the palm tree as well as for the palm of the hand. The original meaning was the latter, however, the word coming from the Greek παλάμη (*palame*), which was used only in this original sense, the Greeks employing a different word for the tree.

Line 3 from bottom. **Umbilicaria.** A genus of lichens.

Page 340, line 13. **Champollion.** Jean François Champollion, a famous French archæologist, who by means of the celebrated Rosetta Stone discovered the key to the Egyptian hieroglyphics, announcing his discovery in 1822.

Page 341, line 5. **A living earth.** The geologists teach us that the earth is constantly undergoing change and growth, that geological processes are not things of the past, but are still going on.

Lines 16, 17. **Seeks the sea with music or migrates to other climes in clouds.** Note the alliteration.

Page 342, line 1. **Widowed Nature.** Why is nature so characterized ?

Page 343, line 2. **The sinking sound of melting snow.** We have all heard this sound in the spring woods, but how many of us have ever even thought of it ? and who else has ever written about it ? The reader of *Walden* and of Thoreau's other books and Journals must be impressed with the universality of his observation of nature. He saw and heard so many various things that it is not to be wondered at that he failed to attain the specialist's knowledge of any one branch of natural history. Note the alliteration in this sentence.

Line 4, 5. **Et primitus oritur herba imbribus primoribus evocata.** "And for the first time the grass springs up, called forth by the early rains."— Varro, *De Re Rustica,* 2, 2, 14.

Lines 8 and 7 from bottom. **Olit, olit, olit**, etc. Is this a good rendering of the song sparrow's song?

Page 344, line 5. **Leuciscus.** *Leuciscus* is a genus of freshwater fishes which in Thoreau's time was considered to include those commonly known as the roach, the dace, the shiner, and the minnow. No fishes belonging to this genus as at present constituted are known to occur in Massachusetts.

Line 7. **Was dead and is alive again.** In what connection do these words occur in the Bible?

Lines 15, 16. **Out the window.** "Out" is thus used prepositionally instead of "out of" in Chaucer and Shakespeare as well as in some more recent writers, but it is more common colloquially than in literature.

Line 6 from bottom. **I mean he; I mean the twig.** Give your idea of what Thoreau *does* mean here.

Line 5 from bottom. **Turdus migratorius.** Long the accepted scientific name of the American robin, which is now known to ornithologists as *Planesticus migratorius.*

Page 345, line 11. **My first spring night in the woods.** We must not miss the beauty of this description of the first spring evening, — the sudden outshoot of sunset light from under the storm-clouds, the song of the first robin singing as gloriously after his winter absence as if it were still the summer before, the freshness and life of the pines and oaks wet with the rain and gleaming in the western light, the arrival of the honking geese from their long Southern journey, their hushed clamor as they settle in the pond near by, and finally silence and the closed door and the thinker alone with his thoughts. The date of this evening, as we learn from the *Journal,* was March 26, 1846.

Page 346, verse. **Eurus ad Auroram**, etc. From Ovid's *Metamorphoses,* book i, lines 61, 62, 78-81.

Last two lines. **While such a sun,** etc. "And while the lamp holds out to burn, The vilest sinner may return." — Isaac Watts's *Hymns and Spiritual Songs,* book i, Hymn 88.

Page 347, line 17. **Entered into the joy of his Lord.** "Enter thou into the joy of thy lord." — *Matthew,* xxv, 21 and 23.

Page 348, verse. **The Golden Age,** etc. Translated (doubtless by Thoreau himself) from Ovid's *Metamorphoses,* book i, lines 89-96, 107, 108.

Line 5 after verse. **The sticks which boys play with their fingers.** Evidently clappers, or "bones," are referred to.

Lines 6-10 after verse. **I observed a very slight and graceful hawk,** etc. The tumbling described is a well-known habit of the marsh hawk during the mating-season.

Page 349, lines 3 and 2 from bottom. **O Death, where was thy sting?** etc. "O death, where is thy sting? O grave, where is thy victory." — *1 Corinthians*, xv, 55.

Page 350, line 3. **The meadow-hen.** The term is said to be applied to the American coot, but Thoreau used it for the Virginia rail and perhaps the sora, or Carolina rail. See the *Journal* (Index).

Line 4. **The booming of the snipe.** The sound made by the snipe's wings as he performs his strange courtship flight. The performance is observed in Massachusetts only during the spring migration and most commonly in the evening. Thoreau writes in his Journal under date of April 9, 1858: "I hear the booming of snipe this evening, and Sophia [his sister] says she heard them on the 6th. The meadows having been bare so long, they may have begun yet earlier. Persons walking up or down our village street in still evenings at this season hear this singular *winnowing* sound in the sky over the meadows and know not what it is. This 'booming' of the snipe is our regular village serenade. I heard it this evening for the first time, as I sat in the house, through the window. Yet common and annual and remarkable as it is, not one in a hundred of the villagers hears it, and hardly so many know what it is. . . . Mr. Hoar was almost the only inhabitant of this street whom I had heard speak of this note, which he used annually to hear and listen for in his sundown or evening walks."

Last six lines. **I love to see that Nature is so rife,** etc. We must not infer any cruelty from all this. Thoreau could be tender and sympathetic when the concrete occasion arose, but just now he is glorying in one aspect of Nature, — her inexhaustible vigor and prodigality. His outlook was broad enough to see the health of the whole in the disease and death and corruption of a part.

Page 351, line 16. **The wood thrush.** It must have been the hermit thrush that he had heard "long before" the first week in May. The wood thrush does not usually arrive in the latitude of Concord till the second week of that month, but the hermit comes about the middle of April or even earlier. Thoreau did not distinguish between the songs of these two birds, both of which are found in the Concord woods. In the White Mountains and in Maine he mistook the olive-backed thrushes also as well as the hermits for the species with which he was more familiar, and called them all wood thrushes. Some of the most beautiful passages in his Journal are devoted to the song of the " wood thrush."

Line 7 from bottom. **Calidas.** Kalidasa, a poet and dramatist of India and accounted one of the great poets of the world. The *Sacontala* is his best-known drama.

Page 352, lines 5-7. **He breaks his fast,** etc. For poetic purposes

Thoreau condenses into a single day a migration flight that in reality occupies weeks of time undoubtedly. The flight is not performed all at one time, but the birds linger to rest and feed on the way, moving along as circumstances impel.

Line 14. **Tierra del Fuego**. The Spanish signifies "land of fire."

Line 5 from bottom. **Picking oakum**. Picking old rope-ends for calking the seams of ships. An occupation for sailors when they are not required for more active work.

Line 3 from bottom. **Great-circle sailing**. A great circle is a circle on the surface of a sphere the plane of which passes through the centre of the sphere. It is the largest possible circle that can be drawn on a sphere, but the number of possible great circles to a sphere is, of course, infinite. Great-circle sailing is navigation along the arc of a great circle of the earth. It traverses the shortest distances between any two points. Thoreau's figure, therefore, means that we sail stupidly straight ahead without going out of our course to see the interesting things that are happening elsewhere in the world.

Lines 3 and 2 from bottom. **The doctors prescribe for diseases of the skin merely**. That is, they do not go below the surface of things.

Page 353, line 10. **White on the chart**. The coast charts leave the interior of the country white and unmarked.

    Black. That is, with evil.

Line 15. **Franklin**. Sir John Franklin, the explorer, who perished in the Arctic Ocean in 1847. His fate remained unknown until 1859, and many expeditions went in search of him in the mean time, among them two fitted out by Henry Grinnell, a New York merchant.

Lines 17, 18. **Mungo Park**. A Scottish explorer who was drowned in 1806 during a fight with the natives while exploring the course of the river Niger.

Line 18. **Lewis and Clark**. Meriwether Lewis and William Clark, who conducted an important exploration of our Northwest in 1803–1806.

    Frobisher. Sir Martin Frobisher, an English navigator who tried to discover the Northwest Passage in 1576.

Line 5 from bottom. **A hummock left by the ice**. Thoreau's *Journal* contains many observations on the transportation of meadow hummocks by the ice, and especially of the transplanting of the buttonbush by that means. The ice on overflowed meadows often freezes solid to the ground, and then, being raised and broken up by a rise of the river, drifts down-stream, carrying here and there the hummocks which have adhered to its under surface, to deposit them in a new place and raise the level there.

Lines 4 and 3 from bottom. **Sacrifice the greater to the less.** Perhaps most of us would not put it this way. Thoreau had little or none of what we commonly call patriotism, — none, at least, of the kind that says, "Our country, right or wrong"; but he was not lacking in public spirit, and his aims were noble, not selfish.

Page 354, lines 1, 2. **South-Sea Exploring Expedition.** The United States Exploring Expedition of 1838–1842, commanded by Lieut. Charles Wilkes, U. S. N. It explored the Pacific Ocean and its islands, and particularly that part of the Antarctic continent which was afterwards called Wilkes Land.

Lines 11, 12. "**Erret, et extremos alter scrutetur Iberos,**" etc. These are the closing lines of the poem "On an Old Man of Verona who has never been out of the Suburbs" (*De Sene Veronensi qui Suburbium nunquam egressus est*), by Claudian, a Latin poet of the fourth and fifth centuries A. D. In his journal entry for May 10, 1841, Thoreau says, "A good warning to the restless tourists of these days is contained in the last verses of Claudian's 'Old Man of Verona,'" which he proceeds to quote.

Lines 13, 14. **Let them wander,** etc. The literal translation is, "Let another wander and scrutinize the farthest Iberians (Spaniards). This one has more of life, that one has more of the road." Thoreau substitutes "Australians" for "Iberians," as better suiting the conditions of modern geography.

Lines 3, 4 after verse. **Symmes' Hole.** Capt. John Cleves Symmes of St. Louis in 1818 advanced the theory that the earth was hollow within and open at the poles, and that the interior was habitable if not actually inhabited. An amusing account of Symmes and the methods he took to promulgate his ideas will be found in John Fiske's *A Century of Science.*

Line 5 after verse. **Gold Coast and Slave Coast.** Two sections of the African coast on the north shore of the Gulf of Guinea.

Lines 11, 12 after verse. **Cause the Sphinx to dash her head against a stone.** That is, guess all riddles, solve all problems. According to Hesiod, the Sphinx propounded a riddle to all comers, and when they could not guess it, flung them from the rock near the city of Thebes where she had taken her station. Finally Œdipus guessed her riddle, and she destroyed herself in the same way that she had killed her victims.

Line 4 from bottom. **Explore thyself.** Γνῶθι σεαυτόν (*gnothi seauton*), "Know thyself," an old Greek maxim, the origin of which is unknown, though it has been enumerated among the sayings of the Seven Wise Men of Greece, some attributing it to Thales, others to Chilon, and still others to Solon. It has also been attributed to Plato, Socrates, Pythagoras, and other philosophers.

Lines 3 and 2 from bottom **Only the defeated and deserters go to the wars.** Paradox was a favorite figure of Thoreau's. He means that men who have not the courage to study themselves and live their own life allow themselves to be swept away by outside influences.

Last line **That farthest western way.** The road to the ultimate good. Thoreau says "*western* way" because that is the direction that exploration has taken, — exploration and the "star of empire." The western way had always an attraction for him. See his essay on "Walking" in *Excursions.*

Page 355, line 5. **Mirabeau.** The Count de Mirabeau (1749–1791) was a celebrated·orator and statesman of the French Revolution.

Line 12. **Firm resolve.** The Journal entry for July 21, 1851, goes on to quote here from *Chambers' Edinburgh Journal* (through *Harper's Magazine*, vol. i, p. 648) Mirabeau's further conversation : "Tell me, Du Saillant, when you lead your regiment into the heat of battle, to conquer a province to which he whom you call your master has no right whatever, do you consider that you are performing a better action than mine, in stopping your friend on the king's highway, and demanding his purse ? ' 'I obey without reasoning,' replied the count. 'And I reason without obeying, when obedience appears to me to be contrary to reason,' rejoined Mirabeau."

Page 356, last line. **Hush and whoa.** Words of command to oxen.
Bright. A favorite name for an ox.

Page 357, line 3. **Extra-vagant.** The division is to call attention to the literal meaning of the Latin from which the word is derived, — wandering beyond.

Line 10 from bottom. **Translated.** Carried across, the literal meaning of the word.

Page 358, line 3. **Kabir.** A Hindoo religious reformer of the late Fifteenth and early Sixteenth centuries.

Lines 9 and 8 from bottom. **A living dog is better than a dead lion.** From *Ecclesiastes,* ix, 4.

Page 359, last paragraph. **There was an artist.** Mr. Sanborn considers this story to have been either adapted or invented by Thoreau. It seems probable that it is entirely original, though modelled after the Hindoo fables with which Thoreau was familiar.

Page 360, line 3. **Kalpa.** This is the Sanskrit word for a day of Brahma, a period of 4,320,000,000 of our years.

Line 6. Brahma had awoke and slumbered many times.
That is, many "Kalpas" had passed by.

Page 362, lines 6, 7. **And lo! creation widens to our view.**
Adapted from the line "And lo! creation widened in man's view" in the famous sonnet on "Night and Death" by Blanco White. Joseph Blanco White (1775–1841) was a Spaniard of Irish descent who lived in England from 1810. He was a theologian, but is best known as the author of this sonnet, which Coleridge declared to be "the finest and most grandly conceived sonnet in our language." The thought in the preceding sentence, as to darkness revealing the heavenly lights, is also taken from this sonnet.

Line 8. **Crœsus.** A king of Lydia in the sixth century B. C. His immense wealth became proverbial.

Line 15. **Near the bone where it is sweetest.** Alluding to the old proverb, "The nearer the bone the sweeter the meat."

Line 9 from bottom. **Tintinnabulum.** Here again Thoreau uses the Latin word for "bell" when he means the sound produced by a bell, a tintinnabulation.

Page 363, line 3. **The Mameluke bey.** When Mohammed Ali, viceroy of Egypt, in 1811 massacred the members of the historic body of cavalry known as the Mamelukes, after feasting them in the citadel at Cairo, a single man, Emin Bey, was said to have escaped by leaping his horse from the ramparts to the ground. The story is denied on good authority, the actual fact being that the sole survivor of the massacre had been prevented by illness from attending the banquet at all, and had afterwards been spared by Mohammed Ali. (*The Spectator*, Nov. 9 and 16, 1907.)

Lines 11, 12. **God is only the president of the day, and Webster is his orator.** That is, in these days of parades and celebrations God is looked upon only as a master of ceremonies, a presiding officer to introduce the speakers.

Lines 19, 20. **Kittly-benders.** It is hardly necessary to define this word, though it is not found in all the dictionaries. Other forms which occur in the juvenile vernacular are "tittlety-benders," "teetlety-benders," and the shorter "tittleties" and "teetleties." Thoreau's word may very well be the original one, the first part, "kittly" being the old Scotch word for ticklish. The sport of "running tittleties" on thin ice is always ticklish business.

Page 364, line 8 from bottom. **Hollow tree.** See p. 247.

Page 365, line 1. **China pride.** All mankind, in Thoreau's thought, were in the same state of unprogressive self-sufficiency as the Chinese.

Line 16. **The seven-years' itch.** "As bad as the seven-years' itch" was formerly, and perhaps is still, a current expression, but the editor is informed by a well-known specialist on skin diseases that it is a purely mythical complaint.

Line 17. **The seventeen-year locust.** A species of cicada which makes its appearance in the mature form every seventeen years, living the intervening time in the larval state under ground. The brood which occurred in 1852 in Franklin, Hampshire, and Bristol Counties, Massachusetts, is probably the particular one referred to.

Page 366, lines 8 and 7 from bottom. **The story which has gone the rounds of New England.** Doubtless a newspaper story, which, like many such tales, may or may not have been true; but it served Thoreau's purpose for an analogy. He was always looking for analogies between the physical world and the spiritual.

Page 367, line 6 from bottom. **John or Jonathan.** John Bull and Brother Jonathan are referred to. For the latter personage see note, p. 374.

SUGGESTIVE QUESTIONS AND COMMENTS

CHAPTER I. ECONOMY

Page 1. Is the beginning a good one? Why?

Was Thoreau right in using the first person singular so frankly? Was he right in explaining his use of it?

Do you see in this a similarity to the Sir Roger de Coverley papers?

Page 5. **Why should they eat their sixty acres?** Is there a peculiar value in a startling figure like this?

Is the use of questions in writing of this kind a good way to emphasize the points made?

Do Thoreau's allusions to mythological subjects add or detract from your interest? Do you find in current writing so many references to classical stories? Why, or why not?

Page 6. Why did Thoreau use Raleigh's translation of Ovid's lines instead of making one of his own?

Is the metrical translation of poetry more forcible and appropriate than a (perhaps more literal) prose one?

Page 8. What is your opinion of the *divinity* in teamsters, or men of that class? Is Burns's picture of the Cotter, for instance, too highly idealized, or are there many homes of just such an atmosphere?

How would you characterize Thoreau's attitude — wholesome? cynical? sympathetic? kindly? humorous?

Page 9. Do you agree with Thoreau in viewing the advice of your elders as useless? Do we learn wisdom solely through experience?

How do you account for Thoreau's radical view?

Page 11. What makes it difficult for us to view things from the standpoint of some one else?

Page 12. Does this plea for a more trusting spirit mean that we need no more care than we bestow upon others, or that we may neglect ourselves in order to help others, and be provided for, as a reward? Do we habitually overvalue our own work and fail to appreciate that of others? Cite examples.

Page 13. Think of the things which are *absolutely necessary* to your existence.

Page 16. In reverting to primitive life and methods, Thoreau's ideas are similar to those of Tolstoi. Can you explain this more particularly?

Do people nowadays make as many sacrifices for the sake of

their principles and ideals as they did years ago ? Are we not more prone to entertain mere theories without putting them to practical account ? But is there not a growing tendency toward "getting back to nature," just at the present time ? What can you assign as causes for this ?

Page 17. Are the tallest plants usually the most deeply rooted in the ground ? Cite examples.

Page 18. Why the blank line on this page ?

Page 26. What do you think of the idea of having only such clothing as is absolutely necessary, regardless of style or appearance ?

Page 27. Why do we always say "they," in a case like the one referred to ? What other word or phrase could be used ?

Page 28. How many things are done simply and honestly ? How simply and honestly do you yourself act ? Would not the world be very different if all of us always acted simply and honestly ? Call to mind some things that are usually done with regard to convention and formality, and try to realize how it would be if they were performed only in accordance with common sense and in a perfectly natural manner. What can you say in support of convention ?

Page 29. Compare "though they should fail immediately, they had better aim at something high" with Browning's lines in *The Inn Album* : —

> "Better have failed in the high aim, as I
> Than vulgarly in the low aim succeed."

Page 30. Why did not Thoreau himself revert completely to the primitive manner of living ? Why did he have a house to live in ? What do you think he would reply to this question, could you ask him ? Would it be desirable for the world in general to go back to a strictly *natural* mode of life ? Why ? Could it be done suddenly, and in one generation, without being fatal to the lives of most persons ?

Page 31. Can you think of other ways in which a child seems to "hark back" to his primitive ancestors ?

Page 32. Thoreau's idea of living in the box reminds you of what ancient Greek philosopher ?

Page 33. If people as a rule lived more simply, could not more persons own their homes ? Or is it better that some should live on a grander scale and thus establish standards for those on a lower scale ?

Page 35. If we were content to have external things more simple, should we not have more time and more money for the things that are really worth while — the things of the spirit, which are lasting ?

Antecedent of "they" in second line ? What do you think of the absorption of the *individual* for the *collective good* ?

Page 39. Is not this the tendency of the present day ? — "gradually leaving off palm-leaf hat or cap of woodchuck skin, complain of hard times because he could not buy him a crown ! "

Page 40. How much do you think mental and spiritual progress is *hindered* and how much *helped* by material prosperity ? Do you think the help or hindrance is the same to all persons ?

Page 44. When he speaks of the beauty inside of the house — the beautiful *lining* of the house — does he speak literally, or are we to put a spiritual interpretation on the words ?

Page 45. What do you think of Thoreau's description of the woods ?

Page 46. What do you think of his description of the manner of building his hut ?

Pages 46–47. What are the little touches which make the account of his days in the woods so vivid ?

Page 48. Do you see any reason for the cat's being introduced into this paragraph, or, at least, for any further information about the cat after it was first mentioned ? Does it make this account any more interesting ?

Page 50. Do you think manual labor is conducive to poetical or any other intellectual attainment ? Might this not differ with different individuals ? Find out all you can about the Brook Farm Experiment.

Page 53. Why did Thoreau shingle the sides of his house, if they were "already impervious to rain" ? Was it to make it warmer ? Was it to make it *look* better ? If so, was he *consistent* in shingling it ?

Page 56. What do you think of this idea ?

Page 60. Would it not have been better to tell this while he was describing the building of his house ?

Page 64. What of the fine churches that are built nowadays ?

Page 67. How does Thoreau's experiment appeal to you by this time ? Would you like to try it ? Do the details he mentions make you more or less curious to try it ? Why ?

Page 68. What do you think of eating only what is necessary to maintain strength and health, from " a dietetic point of view " ?

Page 71. Why does Thoreau call salt " that grossest of groceries " ?

Page 72. Can *you* understand Thoreau's answer ?

Page 79. Here, Thoreau seems to say that if you *will* to do a thing, you *can do it*. Keep your ideal clear before you, and follow it.

Page 80. Depend on yourself alone. That is the only way to attain your object. Can you cite some striking example of such a will ? Read Matthew Arnold's " Self-Dependence."

Page 81. Is being good better than doing good ? Comment. Cf. Polonius's advice to Laertes in *Hamlet :* " To thine own self be true, and it must follow, as the night the day, thou canst not then be false to any man."

Page 84. Do the wealthy and well-to-do help the poor more by giving
them employment, or would the truer way be to do their work
themselves, thus living more simply, and so making living easier
for the poor ? Does the elegant and complicated manner of living
of the wealthy class have any influence in making prices high ?
Or is it better economically that the wealthy should spend lavishly ?

Page 85. Are all philanthropists necessarily Christians ? Does Thoreau
make out a good case against the popular idea of philanthropy ?

Page 86. **I believe that what so saddens the reformer is not
his sympathy with his fellows in distress, but, though
he be the holiest son of God, is his private ail. Let this
be righted, let the spring come to him, the morning rise
over his couch, and he will forsake his generous companions without apology.** Do you believe this is the rule ?
Do you think Thoreau is quite fair to humanity in this belief ?

Page 88. Comment on the effectiveness or the ineffectiveness of ending
the chapter with these quotations.

CHAPTER II. WHERE I LIVED, AND WHAT I LIVED FOR

Page 92. The sentence commencing " The real attractions " is long.
What prevents it from being obscure ?

Page 93. Note the *dash constructions* on this page. What effect do they
produce ?

Page 94. Look up Coleridge's *Ode to Dejection* and Shelley's *Lines
written in Dejection near Naples.*

Page 95. **I was seated,** etc. Analyze the effectiveness of this description. Do you feel strongly the presence of Thoreau ? To what
senses is the appeal strongest ? What comment can you make on
the effectiveness of the figures of speech ?

Page 98. In what sense was Thoreau near the Pleiades ?

Comment on the skill with which Thoreau creates his atmosphere of the morning.

Page 100. Can you cite some striking example of particular men who
have elevated themselves by conscious endeavor ? Do you think it
lies within the power of each of us ?

I went to the woods, etc. Study this statement of Thoreau's carefully. What advantage did the woods offer ? Do they
offer this advantage to each of us, regardless of our temperament ?
Can the man who lives in the woods best interpret life ? Or do we
need the experience of the crowded city as well ?

Page 102. Since Thoreau wrote this, life has steadily grown more complicated. Does this mean, then, that civilization is on the wrong track; or is Thoreau himself wrong?

What do you think of the kind of simplicity preached by Charles Wagner in *The Simple Life*? Is it better suited to modern conditions than Thoreau's? Is it the " real thing " ?

What does Thoreau mean when he says the railroad rides upon us?

Pages 103, 104. Do you agree with Thoreau when he says *we have no work of any consequence*? Are we too curious about trifles? What distinction can you draw between productive and non-productive curiosity?

Page 104. What is your opinion about the value of newspapers and the post-office? Comment on the value of letters. Within the past decade, how many events have happened in the United States that have been of great import?

Page 106. **Shams and delusions**, etc. Compare this with Tennyson's phrasing in *Geraint and Enid* : —

> " O purblind race of miserable men,
> How many among us at this very hour
> Do forge a lifelong trouble for ourselves,
> By taking true for false, or false for true ;
> Here, thro' the feeble twilight of this world
> Groping, how many, until we pass and reach
> That other where we see as we are seen ! "

Is it always possible for us to observe realities only?

Children, who play life, discern, etc. Wordsworth, addressing the child, says : —

> " Thou best philosopher ! thou eye among the blind ! "

Do you think there is any real truth in the opinion of Thoreau and Wordsworth?

Page 107. **God himself culminates in the present moment.** What, exactly, is Thoreau's meaning? Would the statement apply to men as well? Why, or why not?

Page 108. **Let us spend**, etc. Just how easy is it to follow this advice of Thoreau? What are the things which make it difficult? Are we hindered more by lack of intellect or by lack of will?

As you review this chapter in your own mind, try to decide which ideas of Thoreau's are most significant. Which seem to you personally the most novel? Do his utterances impress you as being settled convictions — the result of long and deep and conservative thinking — or do you sometimes feel that Thoreau is being a bit bold for effect — or possibly to arouse controversy? Or would you say that he is undoubtedly sincere?

Does his style reveal any affectation ? Are his illustrations at all far-fetched ; or are they simply the natural and appropriate items which make the abstract notion clear ?

CHAPTER III. READING

Page 118. What nations other than the Hebrew have had a scripture ? What are the titles ?

Page 119. Is it not true that the majority of *educated* people, even, read only the *lighter* literature ? Are the highest forms of art very popular ? Cite examples. In this respect, were not people very much the same in that day as now ?

Page 122. What do you think of the thought in this chapter ? What of the *style* as compared to the first chapter ? What of the practicability of the ideas ?

CHAPTER IV. SOUNDS

Page 123. **I did not read books the first summer; I hoed beans.** Marian Evans, who afterwards became famous as the novelist George Eliot, reviewing *Walden* in 1856, quoted the passage beginning here and spoke of it as having great beauty. Do you agree with her as to its beauty ? If so, in what does its beauty consist ? What makes the peculiar quality of this first sentence ?

Page 124. Does this impress you as idleness, or as being really advantageous to spiritual and intellectual development ?

Pages 127–130. Note the imagination in this passage (describing the train).

Page 128. **Here's your pay.** Why this colloquial form ?

Page 131. Here he seems partially resigned to the railroad. He concedes that it at least makes men punctual.

What does he mean by saying that " every path but your own is the path of fate " ?

Page 132. If he truly cared nothing for travelling and seeing foreign countries, would the freight train with its odors of " foreign parts " really have any attraction for him ? Would he feel "refreshed and expanded" when he saw it ?

Page 136. Note the transition from the noise and bustle of the railway and commerce to the peaceful quietude of the wood. How does Thoreau make you feel this sense of relief and calm ?

Page 137. Whence does the whip-poor-will get its name ? Have you often heard the cluck in its song ? Or the buzzing sound that Thoreau speaks of ?

Page 138. Why do so many people fail to hear any music in the screech
owl's song ? Is it because of the bird's name ? Have you heard
any other notes from the screech owl than the wail Thoreau describes ?

What do you think of his conceit about the screech owls, the
"suicide lovers " ? What do you think of his manner of expressing this idea ?

Page 141. Why does Thoreau use the name Chanticleer ? Does he
gain anything in effectiveness by it ?

Notice the poetry and the imagination in this chapter. What do
you think of Thoreau's humor ?

Comment upon his love of nature, and his description of things
in nature.

What of his power to make the reader see and hear what he
describes ? Can you not see and hear and smell all these things that
he sees and hears and smells, and do you not feel yourself to be in
the little cabin ?

What of the vividness of the last bit of description in this chapter
— the cabin in the snow — with *no gate, no yard, no path ?* What
particular impression or feeling does it convey ?

CHAPTER V. SOLITUDE

Page 143. Have you ever felt this sensation of delight through your
whole body, or the feeling of being a part of nature ?

Why is the first paragraph, and the first part of the second, in the
present tense ? Does it give greater vividness to the idea ?

In the beginning of this chapter, he seems to be describing some
particular evening, but in the second paragraph he returns to gener-
alities. What do you think of this ? How would you improve it ?
Or, does he mean that all of these visitors called on this particular evening ? Why should Thoreau's visitors write their names on
a leaf or a chip rather than leave a calling-card ? Can you think of
several reasons ?

Page 144. Why should " they who come *rarely* to the woods take some
little piece of the forest into their hands to play with " more than
those who go often ?

Do you think it can ever be judged *accurately* as to the sex, age,
or quality of a person by such a trace as " a flower dropped, or
a bunch of grass plucked and thrown away " ? Why ?

Comment on Thoreau's use of " Nay." Is it effective ?

Page 145. Why this sudden change of tense ? Is there any reason
for it ?

Interpret " They plainly fished much more in the Walden Pond of their own natures, and baited their hooks with darkness."

Why does Thoreau use " profaned," here ?

Why do most people have a fear of the dark, and why do many dread solitude ?

Do you believe that if persons were perfectly normal they would not be afraid of storms, but would enjoy the Æolian music of which Thoreau speaks ?

Do you believe that " nothing can rightly compel a simple and brave man to a vulgar sadness " ? What does Thoreau mean by " a *vulgar* sadness " ? Does he mean that *all* sadness is *vulgar* ?

He could *trust* that while he enjoyed the friendship of the seasons, nothing could make life a burden to him, but he could not *be sure* of this. You cannot be certain of the effect of anything upon you, until you have the actual experience.

The gentle rain, etc. Is not this a beautiful and happy spirit, and would it not be much better if every one could sincerely possess it ?

Page 146. Do you think the proximity of man is an " essential to a serene and healthy life " ?

Do you think this feeling in Thoreau was " a slight insanity "; or, since most people have the feeling, is it not rather a sign of insanity or an abnormal condition of mind not to have it ? Is this one of Thoreau's touches of humor, or is he wholly serious ?

Pages 147, 148. Which is the greater lonesomeness — that of merely physical environment, or the lack of sympathetic or congenial minds ? Have you not sometimes felt most lonesome in a crowd ?

Here, the contrast which Thoreau draws between his own condition, that night, and that of the man driving cattle to Brighton, renders his argument stronger than all his philosophical theories could do. Do you agree ?

Page 148. **Any prospect of awakening or coming to life to a dead man.** What do you think Thoreau means by this ? Could it possibly be taken literally, or is it necessary to interpret it as meaning that the coming to life means a spiritual awakening ? Dwell upon Thoreau's words until they seem quite clear.

Page 151. Do you believe that friends think more of each other if they meet infrequently ; or do they as a rule grow apart and learn to do without each other's company ?

Page 152. How did Thoreau know that a spider could not be lonely ? Do you think it would be impossible ? How much is known of animal psychology ?

How does Thoreau receive these visits from the old man ? Do you think he is a real man and actually visits Thoreau ? Are we to

put a spiritual interpretation on this ? Or does Thoreau merely
spend these pleasant evenings with him by reading something the
old settler may have written ? Who is the old dame ? Do you
agree with the editor in considering these two persons to be the
god Pan and Dame Nature ?

CHAPTER VI. VISITORS

What is the significance of having this chapter on *Visitors* follow immediately after that on *Solitude* ?

Page 156. Does this mean *literally* a *mouse?*

Do you agree with Thoreau that it is easier to utter " big
thoughts " in a large space ?

Page 159. Does the truest hospitality demand that we give our guests
better than we have ourselves, or give them just what we have
when alone.?

Pages 159–166. What do you think of the character of this Canadian ?

Page 170. What kind of people did Thoreau evidently like best ?

CHAPTER VII. THE BEAN–FIELD

Page 171. In endowing the beans with human feeling and saying they
were impatient to be hoed, Thoreau has given us an example of
what Ruskin calls the Pathetic Fallacy. Ruskin strongly objects to
such a device. Do you agree with Ruskin ?

Page 172. Was this place more interesting to Thoreau because of this
early association ?

Do you suppose the discovery of the arrowheads added to the
interest of Thoreau's task ? Would it add to yours ?

Page 173. Close the book after you have read this page, and make
a list of the sensory images. What two or three are most vivid to
you ? Do these appeal to your eye, or to some other organ ?

Page 174. **Asks the black bonnet of the gray coat.** Comment
on the effectiveness of this. Is it better than merely saying " asked
one of another " ?

Page 175, line 2. Can you justify Thoreau's use of " love " here ? Is it
better than " like " ?

What suggests *top-dressing* to Thoreau ?

What primitive implements do you imagine Thoreau to have
brought to light ?

Do you think it an exaggeration for Thoreau to compare the
music about his field to that heard by those persons in the city
who attend the oratorios ?

Pages 175, 176. Try to reproduce in your imagination the various sounds Thoreau heard.

Pages 176, 177. Comment on the satiric strain in the paragraphs descriptive of the *gala days.*

Does Thoreau succeed in giving you a clear conception of the slight sounds which reached him — sounds just on the threshold of his perceptions ? Comment.

Page 178. What passage on this page impresses you with its colloquial style ? Do you like it ?

Page 179. Do you think the erudition which Thoreau displays in the midst of these details on agriculture mars or improves ?

Page 181. Comment on the ethical turn which Thoreau gives to his agricultural theme. Is it clever or far-fetched ? Is Thoreau more interested in agriculture or in ethics ?

Page 182. What does Thoreau mean when he says most men are busy about their beans ?

In looking back over this chapter, which ideas would you mention as having particularly impressed you ? Do you think the general dissemination of these ideas would produce any appreciable effect upon the world ? Or would they be viewed by many as the musings of an unpractical philosopher ?

CHAPTER VIII. THE VILLAGE

Page 185. Are you surprised to learn that Thoreau went to the village to hear some of the gossip ? Does it follow that because a naturalist is deeply interested in animals he is less interested in men ? What can you say in defence of *curiosity ?*

Pages 187–189. As you read this portion of the book, are you impressed with the enjoyment which Thoreau derived from his experiences ? Does he succeed in making you share his feelings ? Do these feelings last after the reading ? What specific thing have you done in the past day or two which you can trace to Thoreau's influence ?

Page 189. Does Thoreau make you feel more the vastness or the minute perfection of nature ? Cite specific passages in *Walden.*

Page 190. Do you sympathize with Thoreau in his imprisonment ? Or do you think he simply received his just punishment ? If every one adopted the attitude toward the government which Thoreau adopted, what would result ? Think of the probable defence which the officials would make for placing Thoreau in jail. Do you imagine Thoreau entertained any personal feeling against them ?

CHAPTER IX. THE PONDS

Page 192. Do you know of other fruits that taste best and sweetest when just picked ? Is Thoreau thinking only of the actual physical flavor ?

Page 194. **But now I had made my home by the shore.** Does this make a strong or a weak ending to the paragraph ?

Page 199. After reading the description, do you not feel that you have been in a boat upon the pond, looking down into its clear depths, or that you have stood on the water's edge and watched the changing hues, or upon a distant hill and seen the blue of the sky reflected in the waves ? Can you analyze the method by which Thoreau secures these results ?

Page 200. Does the path, and the idea that it was trodden by the feet of the aboriginal tribes, make the description of the pond more interesting to you ? What can you, in fancy, see upon the path when you think of this ?

Page 202. **It licks its chaps from time to time.** Is this a *pleasing* metaphor ? Is it vivid ? Is it necessary that a figure of speech or a piece of art be beautiful in order to be effective ?

Why should the blueberry bushes bear more abundantly at this time ?

Page 203. What do you think of the derivation of the name of the pond ?

Pages 206, 207. How can one measure the depths of one's own nature by looking into the waters of a lake ?

Page 215. " Resort — thought." This rhyme, although natural to a New Englander, is *not* a true rhyme. What prevents its being true ?

Do you think that every nature is bettered at least a little, even though unconsciously, by each good or beautiful thing with which it comes in contact ?

Pages 215, 216. Does Thoreau imply that he, like the pond, might gain such purity by living alone in the woods ? that he would be contaminated by mingling again with the people of the neighboring village or with the world in general ?

Page 217. Do you sympathize with Thoreau's idea of naming a pond ?

Page 218. Do you agree entirely with him in his estimate of " a model farm," or do you consider his view radical ? With which, if any, of his ideas of the farmer do you agree ?

Page 219. What do you think of *Goose Pond* as a name in comparison with *Flint's* ? What of *White* ? Are they better ? If so, why ? If not, why not ?

Page 220. Have you a theory as to the presence of the tree in White Pond ? Can you imagine a story about it ?

What is your opinion of this chapter in point of *beauty* of thought and expression ? In point of interest ? What of its ideals ? Its philosophy ? Its instruction in scientific facts or theories ?

How does this chapter affect you ? Does it leave you with a feeling of calm and serenity, and a sense of having looked upon a beautiful scene, or does it bring to you sensations different from these ?

CHAPTER X. BAKER FARM

Page 223. Do you think pine groves look like "fleets at sea" ? Or is this a far-fetched fantasy ?

Pages 223, 224. Do you know the trees mentioned ?

Pages 224, 225. Have you ever noticed the phenomenon recounted by Cellini and Thoreau ?

Pages 223–225. Notice the poetry and imagination in this passage, and the *dazzling* effect of the description.

Page 225. Do you like the introduction of the slang expression "hooked" ? Does it or does it not seem to fit in here ?

Notice the rhythm to the sentence beginning, " I ' hooked' the apples." It reads like poetry. Is this good style in prose writing ?

Can you recall one of these seemingly long afternoons in your own experience ?

Pages 225, 226. How does the introduction of the storm help the narrative ?

Page 227. In the case of John Field, would it not have been better if he had given up tea, coffee, butter, milk, and fresh meat, and so have been able to live in a comfortable and decent house ? Comment on the wisdom of Thoreau's philosophy.

Page 229. Have you not seen and felt the gloom and squalor of the Irishman's hut so keenly that you are glad to get out again into the pure air, and shake off the feeling of repulsion and contamination, and try to forget the pitiful faces of the wife and babe ? Do you consider the effect artistic ?

Page 231. Cf. these lines from Whittier's " Snow-Bound," —

> " Alas for him who never sees
> The stars shine through his cypress-trees ! "

We can go far away in spirit, if not in body, and gain something, each day, to strengthen and enrich our character. Does Thoreau help you to do this ?

Why did not Thoreau persevere in his attempt to improve the condition of John Field ? In your opinion, would he have met with success ? Why ?

CHAPTER XI. HIGHER LAWS

Page 232. Do you think that living constantly in the woods might have the effect of causing one to revert completely to the primitive, developing the animal nature rather than the spiritual?

Page 233. To know Nature, is it necessary that you live with her? Really to *know* a person, must you live under the same roof for a time? Does an occasional visit reveal but little?

Do you believe that a man who hunts merely for the pleasure of it is a *friend* to the animals? How do you suppose the *animals* would look upon this? What does Thoreau mean? Who is the more active in preventing the extermination of game, the hunter or the person who never hunts? In considering these things, should we think only of the individual animal, or only of the race, or of both?

Page 237. Have you felt this repugnance to animal food?

Page 238. To what notions does Thoreau refer?

Page 239. Do you believe that as the human race becomes more civilized, we shall stop eating animal food, as the savages have left off eating one another? What are the chief arguments for and against vegetarianism?

Should we always follow the dictates of what Thoreau calls our genius? Is it our duty to ourselves and to mankind in general that we strive to prevail against opinions and customs which something within us tells us should not exist?

Perhaps the facts most astounding and most real are never communicated by man to man. The true harvest of my daily life is somewhat as intangible and indescribable as the tints of morning or evening. Is it true that the *real* things, the things most valuable, are intangible and invisible? Comment and cite examples.

Page 242. In the chapter on "Sounds," you will recall that he speaks of the music in the distant lowing of a cow.

CHAPTER XII. BRUTE NEIGHBORS

Page 247. Thoreau teaches the converse of the old law of Captain John Smith, and of St. Paul before him: "He that will not work shall not eat."

Page 248. Did you find the hermit's first speech misleading? Did you think his companion was already there, and this was the beginning of the conversation?

What is the effect upon you when the *poet* appears immediately after Thoreau has mentioned the possibility of his expected visitor's being a *pig*? Do you think it was done with any intention of humor?

Note the informality of the meeting. Is it just what we should expect of a philosopher and a poet — no preliminaries, no conventional greetings?

Why should the account of the poet's visits have been put in this chapter, the subject of which is "Brute Neighbors"? Why, for instance, were we not told of the poet in the chapter on "Visitors"?

Pages 253–256. Do you think Thoreau was sincere in attributing so much importance to the battle of the ants? Do you agree with him in this? Would you have been as deeply interested in it as he? If not, why not? Do you suppose the ants were fighting for a principle? Would you have been more inclined to watch them to the end, or to help the side which seemed to be getting the worst of it? In this case, would it be your duty, humanely speaking, to interfere, or would it be simply meddling? What do you suppose became of the crippled ant, granting that he could live in that condition? Do you think he would find his way to home and friends? What do you know of friends and enemies among ants? What is the effect upon you of Thoreau's account of the battle? What, do you think, would be the effect upon you of witnessing such a scene yourself? Would you feel merely a cold and purely scientific interest, or as Thoreau felt, that you had witnessed a human battle?

Page 260. What do you think of the reasoning powers of animals and birds? Cite examples to prove your opinion.

Page 262. Would the cry of the loon have impressed you as being a prayer for help, and would the arrival of the wind and rain have seemed to you to be the answer to that prayer? Is it not at least a pretty and poetical conceit? Whether or not you consider the cry a prayer, may not the wind and rain have been sent by God to the relief of the bird? Or was it merely a fortunate coincidence for the loon? Do you believe that anything ever "just happens," or do you think that even the slightest circumstance is a part of a great and wise plan?

Do you think this chapter is well-named? Why?

CHAPTER XIII.   HOUSE-WARMING

Page 263. Here, again, the æsthetic side of the writer's nature is uppermost. Compare the sentiments expressed on this page with his desire to seize and eat *raw* a woodchuck which crossed his path, p. 232.

Does the robbing of the squirrels and jays of their nuts seem consistent with the mood in the first part of the paragraph ?

Page 268. Did you ever notice the feeling of satisfaction in something you have done yourself ?

Pages 268–270. Would you like to live in such a house ? Would it be practical, or convenient ? Do you think Thoreau is really serious about this ? Is he not merely exaggerating his ideal of a house in which simplicity might reign ? Do you agree with his idea in a modified form ?

Page 279. What do you make of Thoreau's having the feeling that his house might be on fire, and then finding that it was ? Have you had similar experiences ? Do you know of persons who have ?

Page 281. Did you ever feel the companionship of a fire ?

What are the virtues of a fire aside from its heat ?

CHAPTER XIV. FORMER INHABITANTS AND WINTER VISITORS

Page 284. Old Zilpha, bending over " her gurgling pot," with her muttered words, recalls the witches in *Macbeth*.

Page 285. How does the story of the fire impress you as to naturalness ?

Page 287. Do you feel the pathos of the story of this last member of the family returning to visit his childhood home and finding it in ruins ; of his searching in the dark for the well-sweep and showing the staple to Thoreau in order to convince him that he had actually found it ?

Page 291. **But this small village. . . . They were universally a thirsty race.** Is there a temperance lecture in these few lines ?

Do you sympathize with Thoreau's idea about building a new city upon the site of a more ancient one ?

Page 297. Do you like the metaphors of the shingles of thought, and of the wading and the fishes ?

Page 298. Which of the " former inhabitants " is most interesting to you ? Why ? Which seems most pathetic ? Which most amusing ? Which of Thoreau's winter visitors interests you most ? Why ? Why did Thoreau not mention their names ?

CHAPTER XV. WINTER ANIMALS

Page 299. Is your interest enhanced by the reading of Thoreau's leaving his lonely cabin in the woods and walking across the snow-covered fields and frozen ponds to deliver a lecture in a town ? Does it make him and his life seem more real to you ? Is the picture of the winter night with the one solitary figure of a man moving along through the whiteness clear and real in your mind ? Do you wish you might have heard Thoreau lecture ?

Page 311. Are you more, or less, interested in Thoreau's animal friends, neighbors, and visitors, than in his human ones ? Why ?

CHAPTER XVI. THE POND IN WINTER

Page 312. Did you ever think of Nature's indifference to man ? No matter what man's mood, Nature goes on in her own way, not changing in sympathy. Man must adjust himself to her, if he would be in harmony.

Page 313. Would you enjoy getting your winter-morning draught of water as Thoreau did ?

Interpret " by their goings and comings stitch towns together in parts where else they would be ripped."

Page 315. Is it commonly true that people, especially in a small locality, will simply accept a statement, a general opinion, such as that a pond is bottomless, and never try to find a proof ?

Page 319. Are you struck by the justice of this equalizing in Nature ?

Page 321. Do you feel the truth of the comparison between the pond and the human being ? May we not draw a lesson from almost everything in Nature ?

Page 328. Do you feel like heaving a sigh of relief with Thoreau when the last ice-cutter has taken his departure ?

Pages 328, 329. Do you enjoy such flights of the imagination as that in which Thoreau indulges in the last paragraph of this chapter ?

CHAPTER XVII. SPRING

Pages 330–332. These purely scientific observations are in the manner of Darwin and Huxley. Do you enjoy Thoreau's discussion here, or do you find those portions more interesting which have either a more literary or a more ethical tone ?

Page 334. Comment on the *dash constructions* at the bottom of this page.

Pages 334, 335. Do you imagine the old man's account as given to Thoreau was more, or less, interesting than this written description ? Would it have been better for Thoreau to have given the old man's exact words ?

Study in this passage the words which suggest motion and sound.

Page 336. Do you think it effective for Thoreau to use such technical words as those found at the bottom of this page ? Was it perfectly natural that he should use them ? Do they smack at all of pedantry ?

Pages 336–340. Does Thoreau's playing with this leaf-theme impress you as mere fantasy, or does it possess scientific value ?

Page 338. Has Thoreau impressed you as a deeply religious man ?

Page 340–343. This portion is particularly rich in its mention of observed detail. Would you say that it is so full that it is confusing ? or is the abundance pleasant to contemplate ?

Page 342. **The first sparrow of spring**, etc. Study the paragraph and try to explain its peculiar charm. If you find the analysis of the charm difficult, simply try to absorb its beauty.

Page 346. Does every season seem to you best in its turn ? Just now would you prefer this to be a different season ?

A single gentle rain, etc. Comment on this ethical simile.

As you review this chapter, try to decide upon the things which give it peculiar distinction. How would you characterize the feelings created ? Do you think Thoreau could have infused so much interest in it if he himself had not been thoroughly aroused ? Could this interest of his have come from reading, or was direct intercourse with nature necessary ? Do you think his treatment of any season — autumn, let us say — would have been just as interesting to him and to us ? Why ? Would your enjoyment of the chapter be more complete if you possessed a more detailed knowledge of nature ? Where, for example, do you feel your limitations ? Does Thoreau's treatment stimulate your desire to know more of these details ?

CHAPTER XVIII. CONCLUSION

Page 353. **But I trust**, etc. Explain. Comment on the way Thoreau elaborates this metaphor ? Is he a bit garrulous with his figure ? Are the short sentences of this page effective ? Select those which are especially so.

Page 355. **I left the woods**, etc. Does this strike you as abrupt ? Is it effective ?

Page 356. **How deep the ruts of tradition**. Cite examples.

I learned this, etc. After a careful reading of this paragraph, what comment can you make ? Do you agree with Thoreau ? Are we in danger of making our lives too complex ? How could we be practical and simplify them ?

Page 357. **Why level**, etc. Do most people do this ? Does Thoreau refrain from doing so ?

Is it better to be beyond your time, or to serve your own generation?

Page 358. Have we, since Thoreau's day, made any great advance in curing the *brain-rot* ?

Page 359. What lesson has the story of the artist of Kouroo for you personally ? Or does it fail to make any special appeal ?

Page 361. Do you like the didacticism of this page.

As you think back over this last chapter, what idea do you note standing out above all others ? Is it what he says about *truth* ? Gather up in a phrase of your own Thoreau's attitude toward truth.

INDEX